BLEEDING BLUE AND GRAY

*Civil War Surgery and the
Evolution of American Medicine*

IRA RUTKOW

STACKPOLE
BOOKS

Copyright © 2005 by Ira Rutkow

Published in paperback in the U.S. in 2015 by
STACKPOLE BOOKS
5067 Ritter Road
Mechanicsburg, PA 17055
www.stackpolebooks.com

Printed in the United States of America

10 9 8 7 6 5 4 3 2 1

Cover design by Caroline M. Stover

Library of Congress Cataloging-in-Publication Data

Names: Rutkow, Ira M., author.
Title: Bleeding blue and gray : Civil War surgery and the evolution of
  American medicine / Ira M. Rutkow.
Description: [First paperback edition]. | Mechanicsburg, PA : Stackpole
  Books, 2015. | Includes bibliographical references and index.
Identifiers: LCCN 2015029686 | ISBN 9780811716727
Subjects: LCSH: United States—History—Civil War, 1861-1865—Medical care. |
  Medicine, Military—United States—History—19th century. | Medicine,
  Military—Confederate States of America—History. | United
  States—History—Civil War, 1861-1865—Health aspects.
Classification: LCC E621 .R88 2015 | DDC 973.7/75—dc23 LC record available at
  http://lccn.loc.gov/2015029686

CONTENTS

We had served faithfully as great a cause as earth has known; we had built novel hospitals, organized such an ambulance service as had never before been seen, contributed numberless essays on disease and wounds, and passed again into private life. . . .

What has been our reward? The great leaders in war have been promoted and universally honored. Countless statues commemorate in Washington and elsewhere the popular heroes. Statues of generals are in every town, some of them memorials of men it were wiser to forget, some of whom history will judge severely. Every village has its statue to the private soldier.

There is not a state or national monument to a surgeon. At Gettysburg, every battery site is marked with a recording tablet; every general who fell, Union or Confederate, is remembered in bronze or marble; but what of the surgeon who died? Nothing!

—S. Weir Mitchell, M.D., Philadelphia,
"The Medical Department in the Civil War,"
Journal of the American Medical Association, 1914

PREFACE

BURIED IN THE STACKS of Philadelphia's venerable College of Physicians is a sheaf of newspaper clippings dated December 1859. These yellowed scraps of paper tell of a little-known incident in the annals of American medicine: the dramatic secession of some 250 pro-slavery Southern students from Philadelphia's acclaimed Jefferson and University of Pennsylvania medical schools to more politically sympathetic teaching environments below the Mason-Dixon line.

The mass withdrawal was not unexpected. Philadelphians were from the first strongly antislavery in sentiment, and it was in that city that the American Anti-Slavery Society was organized. Although Southern students had long studied in Philadelphia's schools, there existed an undercurrent of anti-Southern feeling centered around the city fathers' commitment to the abolishment of slavery. Disagreements between Southern sympathizers and antislavery Philadelphians were not uncommon, and when John Brown's body was paraded through the streets of Philadelphia in early December 1859 as an abolitionist martyr (Brown, an antislavery zealot, had been convicted by the state of Virginia of treason, murder, and fomenting insurrection following his unsuccessful October raid on an army arsenal at Harpers Ferry and was hanged), many of the city's Southern medical students engaged in a verbal protest, which devolved into a riot.

A few days later, a contingent of Southern students threw stones at abolitionists outside a meeting of the American Anti-Slavery Society. Within minutes of this incident, it was rumored that twenty-five Georgians had been put in a calaboose and "otherwise insulted" for their violent outburst. Over the next forty-eight hours, police intervention failed to quell additional student disturbances. A whispering campaign soon arose advocating the swift transfer of all Southern medical students from Philadelphia.

Two weeks later, in the brisk early morning hours of December 20, a small group of Southern medical students gathered outside Philadelphia's Assembly Building. Soon the hall was filled with hundreds of angry young men who were informed by a student leader that a cordial homecoming awaited them at medical colleges in Augusta, Charleston, Nashville, New Orleans, Richmond, and Savannah. Virginia's governor even offered funds to defray the students' traveling expenses. The students, mostly teenagers or young men in their early twenties, unanimously deemed themselves secessionists and agreed to depart for points south the following day.

In the late hours of December 21, the students marched by torchlight to Philadelphia's train depot. Twelve hours later, several hundred arrived, exhausted and hungry, in Richmond. They paraded triumphantly to Capitol Square, accompanied by the elite Governor's Guard, while a local band struck up "Carry Me Back to Old Virginny." The students assembled on the steps of the Governor's Mansion as cheers greeted them from the crowd. The governor welcomed the students with a rousing speech, decreeing, "If those people of the North . . . will not learn to let us alone . . . you doctors know that a little phlebotomy—a little blood-letting will reduce a fever."

Meanwhile, the Northern press accused Southern doctors of bribing the students, and Southern politicians were portrayed as secession-mongers who heightened animosities. Bitter charges and recriminations were leveled in the medical journals of the day. Suddenly, a vitriolic division split the whole of American medicine as the country's physicians were confronted with their own civil dispute. In the South, with flags waving and bands playing, the young secessionists marched toward a perilous future. The Virginia governor's voice proved the most darkly prescient of the day when he further declared, "May you, young gentlemen, prove a blessing to your State. May you cure her diseases in peace, or apply the lint and tourniquet in war." In the North, the era's commentators haughtily pointed out that "there is a connection between medicine and politics. Both are often hard to take. Both frequently nauseate the stomach."

IT WAS TWO decades ago that I first read accounts of this little-known but momentous event in our country's medical past. That America's physicians engaged in their own internecine confrontation, almost eighteen months prior to the beginning of the national discord, was a revelation to me. My interest in the medical side of the Civil War piqued. I studied the classic histories about this era and came to the conclusion that the story of medicine during the Civil War was largely unknown.

I found that traditional Civil War–related works, both fiction and non-fiction, typically dealt with men in the heat of battle and their personal anguish. Wartime exploits were brought to life by writers who visited battlefields, studied military strategies, understood political machinations, and read the correspondence, diaries, and memoirs of everyday soldiers, generals, and politicians. To a certain extent, combat, suffering, and death became glorified. One only has to read Michael Shaara's *The Killer Angels* or his son Jeff's *Gods and Generals* to understand this viewpoint. Pomp and circumstance masks the deadly ferociousness of the battlefield. Such classic tomes as Allan Nevins's four-volume *The War for the Union*, Bruce Catton's works on the Army of the Potomac, or Shelby Foote's massive *The Civil War: A Narrative* are awe inspiring, in both content and form. But for me, as a surgeon and historian, despite the brilliance of the writing something was always missing—an understanding of the slaughter and medical realities inherent to war.

Surely if a description of armed conflict is ever to be considered faithful, then the brutality of combat as well as the painful physical and mental restoration of maimed bodies should be spoken of. The reader must gain a surgeon's perspective of the aggression of war. The specifics of a soldier's ghastly wound or the vivid description of a combatant's torturous death following a surgical procedure allow the quotidian and sobering truths of warfare to surface. As medical historian Richard Shryock noted, the authentic impact of the Civil War cannot be fully grasped without comprehending its medical aspects; "the story is not only incomplete but unrealistic as a total picture."

It is not that books on Civil War medicine have not been written. George Adams's *Doctors in Blue*, Alfred Bollet's *Civil War Medicine*, Stewart Brooks's *Civil War Medicine*, Horace Cunningham's *Doctors in Gray*, Robert Denney's *Civil War Medicine*, and Frank Freemon's *Gangrene and Glory* are all outstanding contributions. However, they are close in spirit to textbooks and fail to explain the complex cause-and-effect relationships that marked 1860s American medicine. But for my second chapter, which details colonial and antebellum medicine, I have preferred a narrative framework that, hopefully, integrates various story lines into a more seamless and accessible account. Only in this way can it be shown how military, political, and socioeconomic events affected medical and scientific developments and created the dynamics of medicine during the Civil War. For example, the on-again, off-again relationship between the United States Sanitary Commission and its military surrogate, Surgeon General William Alexander Hammond, and their antagonist, Secretary of War Edwin McMasters Stanton, influenced a wide variety of medical issues. As well, the complex connections between the formation of an ambulance corps, the evolving status of nurses, and the construction of military hospitals are all crucial to understanding that era's medical care.

Certainly, the drama that was Civil War medicine can be told in countless ways. For a number of reasons, I have chosen to focus on medical care in the North. First, my research revealed no great differences in the practice of medicine between the North and the South. The manner of delivering health care, the indications for surgery, and the rationale for giving drugs were much the same. Clearly, the Union was superior to the Confederacy in the general organization of the Medical Department of its army. And the North was more successful than the South in developing a system for rapid evacuation of the wounded. But whether a soldier had meningitis in the North or the South or suffered from blood poisoning following an amputation in the South or the North, he was just as likely to die. Medicine, at that time, was decidedly unscientific and riddled with the misguided notions of past thinking. Northern and Southern politics, military strategy, and socioeconomics were all secondary to the primitive state of health care.

This meant that the book could be written from either a Northern or a Southern viewpoint. I settled on the former for two main reasons. First, the preponderance of existing military medical information relates to the Union army, since virtually all of the Confederate Medical Department's records were lost in the fire that consumed much of Richmond in April 1865. The remaining records of individual Southern doctors and hospitals are incomplete and unable to provide the breadth of information available about Northern physicians, medical facilities, and combatants. Second, and more important, the institutions that most affected the maturation of American medicine following the Civil War were largely outgrowths of Northern military medicine. From the United States Sanitary Commission and its emphasis on hygiene and public health to the Northern military's massive program of hospital construction to the urging that surgical operations be performed by only a select few military physicians, these initiatives most directly spurred on the eventual professionalization of American medicine.

This does not diminish the medical contributions made by Southern physicians and the Confederate Medical Department. Their accomplishments were many and praiseworthy. Chimborazo Hospital in Richmond was a model of organizational efficiency and, with a capacity for more than eight thousand patients, was the war's largest military medical facility. The Army of Tennessee's and the Army of Northern Virginia's mobile field infirmaries were precursors of the highly successful MASH (mobile army surgical hospital) units found in World War II and the Korean War. Female nurses staffed many of the Confederate hospitals, and their courage and sacrifice is a story unto itself. Several physicians who held leadership positions in the Confederate Medical Department assumed important roles in the postwar development of American medicine. For example, Henry Campbell, Alexander Garnett, Hunter McGuire, Tobias Richardson, and David Yandell were all elected presidents of the American Medical Association. The *Confederate States Medical and Surgical Journal,* under the guidance of Samuel Preston Moore, the Confederate surgeon general, was the only major medical journal started by either side during the war. And Francis Porcher's efforts to supply the Confederate army's drug needs with medicines made from plants indigenous to the Southern states helped to maintain the war effort. Despite these achievements, my own convictions about how best to tell the story of medicine during the Civil War remain planted in Northern soil; the uniqueness of the Northern experience forever changed medical care for all Americans.

INTRODUCTION

IT IS ESPECIALLY TIMELY that the editors of Stackpole Books have chosen to publish a paperback version of *Bleeding Blue and Gray* soon following the sesquicentennial of the Civil War. The Civil War was both the greatest health tragedy this country ever experienced and the starting point from which American medicine began its triumphant march out of ignorance. In April 1861, it mattered little that medical care stood on the cusp of a transformation in science, to be heralded within a short two decades by the likes of Louis Pasteur, Robert Koch, and Joseph Lister. Nor did it make a difference that advances in technology would shortly change the way physicians diagnosed and treated diseases. Civil War–era doctors and combatants remained in the grip of old-school and error-filled medical thinking. The physical horrors that made up military medicine during the Civil War—the dreadfulness of camps teeming with cholera and dysentery, or surgical operations performed in dirt-laden settings, complicated by devastating infections—embodied the cruel fate of mistiming for a conflict that occurred barely twenty years ahead of the revolution in the medical sciences.

Unlike more modern warfare that saw astonishing medical and technological innovations, America's doctors made no astounding clinical breakthroughs during the Civil War. Communicable diseases ran rampant in unsanitary field encampments as soldiers recovered from illness more by chance than by a healer's skill. No surgeon introduced ingenious procedures to treat battlefield injuries. Even as shrapnel injuries and broken bones piled up, surgical techniques remained crude and postoperative infections deadly.

Nonetheless, America's physicians obtained unprecedented insight into clinical conditions, along with much-needed organizational skills in treating millions of sick and injured. Doctors faced illnesses and their clinical manifestations on a scale never before seen. Physicians with little background in treating complex problems such as heart failure, kidney disorders, or lung ailments experienced a lifetime of practice in several months of marching, camping, and fighting. The war created surgeons out of physicians who had no familiarity with surgical techniques. This broad, hands-on experience hastened the movement toward specialization in American medicine. Most importantly, the country's doctors acquired managerial skills not attainable in antebellum America. Physicians organized ambulance corps, designed and administered general hospitals, served on draft boards, and resolved complicated issues of medical manpower. Doctors began to recognize that a patient's wellbeing depended on simple measures such as cleanliness, nutrition, and ventilation. Similarly, physicians acknowledged mental health as a vital component of overall health. Finally, with over twelve thousand doctors providing military medical care, the war imposed much-needed comradeship and discipline on what was a fractious craft. The result was the beginning of medical uniformity on a national basis and more unified points of view on the part of the nation's physicians.

The Civil War may not have represented a turning point in American health care in the sense that remarkable clinical successes did not occur. There were shortcomings and soldiers suffered, but what the nation's doctors did during the conflict was as up-to-date to them as anything physicians do today. What is key to remember is that the war functioned as medicine's "Big Bang" in its progress toward social acceptability as a true science and the surgical operation as a bona fide therapeutic necessity.

Ira Rutkow
New York, New York
July 4, 2015

CHAPTER ONE

"It was like the days when there was no King in Israel"

WHEN WILLIAM WILLIAMS KEEN, an assistant surgeon for the Fifth Massachusetts Infantry, walked into Sudley Church, he was startled by what he saw. The small house of worship, located on the northern fringe of the Bull Run battlefield, had been transformed into a field hospital for Union troops. This makeshift treatment facility, along with its outbuildings, was overflowing with the wounded and dying. The church's pews were piled outside, and the building's floor was covered with hay and blankets for emergency bedding. Buckets of dirty water, wooden boxes with surgical instruments, and paper packages containing beeswax-coated sutures and dressings were strewn about. The operating table, little more than a few boards laid on crates, stood in front of the pulpit. A bloodied communion stand served as a resting spot for the weary.

Both inside and outside the hospital, medical activity was frenetic and groans filled the air. From their perch in a small upstairs gallery, those with minor injuries craned their necks to observe the physicians, aided by a number of local women, go about the messy work of cutting. Amputations were performed in full view of the assembled, with blood splattering those too near, including the next victim of the surgeon's scalpel. Keen, assisting at an amputation of a shoulder, quickly realized that the operating surgeon had little knowledge of the anatomy of the upper arm. To keep the soldier from bleeding to death, Keen had to tell the surgeon where to cut and sew.

In his memoirs, Keen explains that his clinical discomfort was compounded by the unnerving realization that "up to that time, and, in fact, during the entire [Bull Run] engagement, I never received a single order from either Colonel or other officer, Medical Inspector, the surgeon of my regiment, or any one else." Keen acknowledged, "It was like the days when there was no King in Israel, and every man did that which was right in his own eyes." Indeed, just two weeks earlier, twenty-four-year-old Keen had been a first-year medical student at Philadelphia's Jefferson Medical College. Keen, who later became professor of surgery at his alma mater and eventually fifty-second president of the American Medical Association (AMA), had begun the study of medicine only in September 1860 and was hastily recruited to join the army's medical corps several months later. "My preceptor, Dr. John H. Brinton, had received a telegram from a former student (let us call him Smith) who had graduated in March 1861, and was Assistant Surgeon of the Fifth Massachusetts, saying that he was going to leave the regiment." Under orders to replace this assistant surgeon, Brinton "very kindly offered the place to me." Immediately, Keen confided his concerns about his clinical capabilities to Brinton. The preceptor replied, "It is perfectly true that you know very little, but, on the other hand, you know a good deal more than Smith." With just fourteen days of military service to guide him, Keen considered himself to be "as green as the grass around me as to my duties on the field."

The battle at Bull Run had not gone well for the Union troops. With defeat imminent, the North's evacuating columns moved rapidly by Sudley Church as Keen applied a splint and eight yards of bandage to a man who had been shot in the upper arm. The passing soldiers yelled, "The rebs are after us," and Keen's charge, despite a potentially mortal wound, "broke away from me," Keen noted, "rushing for the more distant woods. As he ran, four or five yards of the bandage unwound, and I last saw him disappearing in the distance with this fluttering bobtail bandage flying all abroad."[1] With Keen ordered to retreat to Washington, it became obvious to all concerned that no exiting strategy or armed protection had been arranged for the field hospital's wounded. By early evening, with Confederate forces swarming over the church grounds, the three hundred or so Union injured, along with several medical personnel, faced a very uncertain fate.

IF EVER AN event served as a harbinger of medical misery, it was this July 21, 1861, First Battle of Bull Run (Manassas, in Southern parlance). Evidence of much that was wrong with mid-nineteenth-century American medicine, Bull Run, with its 750 killed, 2,494 wounded, and more than 1,500 missing, was essentially a savage military engagement fought by poorly trained troops who received treatment from inadequately prepared physicians in a chaotic setting. According to one contemporary account, "The conception was unwise; the plan faulty; the execution imperfect."[2] From the wretched state of the wounded to the disorganized scattering of surgeons over the rolling battlefield, Bull Run became a tragic lesson in military medical hubris. With few available surgical supplies and no plans in place to evacuate casualties, the injured lay for days on the ground where they fell, suffocating on their own vomit and delirious from infection. Many received neither medical attention nor so much as a mouthful of water.

"The profession, as the conservator of life, asks in the name of the Republic why the wounded were not brought off the field, and why the hospital was not guarded?" editorialized one physician. "It asks why the surgeons were not sustained and protected in the discharge of their duty?"[3] By proclaiming his indignation, this doctor drew attention to a concern that was developing among America's physicians over the part they would play in the nation's civil conflict. But medical doctors were not the only ones anxious about the government's role in the rapid expansion of military medicine. Every day, ordinary citizens attempted to reckon with the growing number of battlefield and illness-related deaths, as well as the attendant suffering that soldiers endured. One New York woman wrote, "We ought to remember that for every one that falls on the battlefield or suffers a languishing death in the hospitals, some friends mourn and weep their lives away."[4]

After Bull Run, America's physicians called for organizational reforms and urged President Lincoln, the United States Congress, and state legislatures to respond to the medical tragedies of the internecine struggle. "The lives of thousands of citizens, the strength of the State, and the efficiency of the armies of the Republic, demand new, enlightened, and liberal legislation," wrote one physician activist.[5] The doctor's concerns were well-founded. What would happen to sick and wounded soldiers if politics controlled camp and battlefield medical care? Who would be held accountable: politicians, physicians, or society as a whole?

In 1860, many Americans had a romantic idea of war that ignored the day-to-day medical horrors of armed conflict. This was revealed when, following the fall of Fort Sumter in April 1861, Abraham Lincoln issued a proclamation calling for seventy-five thousand state militiamen to provide ninety days of voluntary national service to put down the secessionists. Patriotic fervor swept the land as citizens rallied to the cause and all manner of physicians enthusiastically offered their services. According to an article in *The New York Times*, even renowned medical professors forsook "their luxurious chairs to join the hardships of a soldier's life," leaving "a practice worth tens of thousands, that they may go to alleviate the sufferings of the camp."[6] From the most humble hamlets to the largest cities, state military regiments were organized, funds raised, flags unfurled, food stocked, and equipment supplied, but little consideration seemed to be given to the medical realities of military life.

These early volunteer troops followed the well-established militia tradition whereby a prominent businessman or a politically influential individual would, under a governor's authority, recruit a fighting force and, in return, be named the unit's commander, usually with a rank of "colonel." This often meant that an individual of wealth or celebrity became a wartime leader simply by purchasing uniforms and providing supplies to a ragtag collection of men and sometimes boys. As one young Pennsylvanian recruit wrote home to his mother in the summer of 1861, "Col. Roberts has showed himself to be ignorant of the most simple company movements. There is a total lack of system about our regiment. . . . Nothing is attended to at the proper time, nobody looks ahead to the morrow, and business heads to direct are wanting. . . . We can only be justly called a mob & not one fit to face the enemy."[7]

President Lincoln directed state governors to also appoint a surgeon and an assistant surgeon for each of the new volunteer regiments, "after having passed an examination by a competent Medical Board . . . the appointments to be subject to the approval of the Secretary of War."[8] Despite the law's intent, when companies of one hundred men and even whole regiments of one thousand individuals consisted entirely of enlistees from a single village, township, county, or city, it frequently came down to little more than asking the amiable local doctor to accompany the troops. "He may have been a good family medical attendant in the town where he resided and perhaps has given some attention to domestic hygiene, but he knows nothing of the habits of soldiers; of their diet; of the sites, choice, and ventilation of tents," groused one physician. Furthermore, the same doctor added, even if he enjoyed an enviable reputation as a surgeon, he may "never have met an accident peculiar to the field of action."[9]

Eventually, the (Northern) United States Army would maintain on its payroll more than eleven thousand physicians. However, during the opening weeks of what was by all accounts to be a limited military affair, there was little more than a handful of "experienced" army surgeons and a multitude of "inexperienced" physician volunteers. Disorder and frustration ruled the day, as revealed in Charles Tripler's official report to the surgeon general. Tripler, who was named medical director of the North's Army of the Potomac immediately following Bull Run, told of how "the Secretary of War had accepted what were termed independent regiments, the colonels of which asserted a right to appoint their own medical officers." The result of this decidedly arbitrary recruitment process was often total confusion: "Colonels of state regiments refused to receive the medical officers appointed in conformity with the law and went so far as to put these gentlemen out of their camps by force," wrote Tripler. Furthermore, Tripler complained that these "irregularities created great embarrassment and confusion in organizing my department, and many regiments were thus left with surgeons as to whose competency nothing was known. In other instances, regiments, or parts of regiments, were sent on without their medical officers, the colonels assuming authority to leave them at home under various pretexts."[10]

Often serving as mere rubber stamps for the political whims of governors, their political backers, and the well-to-do, the boards' physician appointees also demonstrated gross variations in their levels of competency. "The State Boards of Medical Examiners have proved, in many instances, either negligent, or culpably ignorant of their duties," complained an editorial in the widely circulated *American Medical Times*. "We may estimate by hundreds the number of unqualified persons who have received the endorsement of these bodies as capable Surgeons and Assistant-Surgeons of regiments. Indeed, these examinations have in some cases been so conducted to prove the merest farce."[11]

Professional concern mounted as the government's ability to organize an efficient medical corps was called into question. "It is no holiday service that is expected now, and no qualifications short of the highest should authorize the government to entrust the care of the health of our troops to any man. There should be no favoritism here," exclaimed a physician in the *Boston Medical and Surgical Journal*. "Shall it be said that our friends and brothers, whose patriotism calls them to the field at this trying hour, shall be subjected to the dangers of surgical inexperience as well?"[12] Even on the front page of prominent newspapers, pleas were made that only "skillful men" be allowed to retain commissions as volunteer surgeons.

To compound difficulties, a natural antagonism existed between physician volunteers and their full-time army counterparts. With few knowledgeable personnel to instruct medical recruits as to the military code of behavior, difficulties soon arose due to a fundamental failure to grasp the difference between civilian practice and a military way of life. According to one participant, "In the vast majority of volunteer organizations, the surgeon has no one to instruct him in his duties; and not apprehending, as was very natural to a civilian, the importance of a rigid adherence to prescribed forms, he was very apt to deem them a species of red-tapeism, to be discarded by men of energy."[13]

This failure to appoint appropriately qualified medical men was partly responsible for one of the earliest health-related scandals of the war: the tragicomic physical examination of those recruits serving for ninety days. According to the War Department's General Order No. 51, all regimental surgeons were expected to examine the men in the following manner:

> In passing a recruit the medical officer is to examine him stripped; to see that he has free use of all his limbs; that his chest is ample; that his hearing, vision, and speech are perfect; that he has no tumors, or ulcerated or extensively cicatrized [scarred] legs; no rupture or chronic cutaneous affection; that he has not received any contusion, or wound of the head, that may impair his faculties; that he is not a drunkard; is not subject to convulsions; and has no infectious disorder, nor any other that may unfit him for military service.[14]

However, during the organizational morass of late spring and early summer 1861, this proviso was sometimes, perhaps for political purposes, ignored. "So notorious was the neglect of its behests, or the incompetency of those who pretended to obey it," noted medical director Tripler, "that another general order from the same authority was demanded and issued . . . which threatened to make the derelict officers pecuniarily responsible for disregarding it."[15]

Haste was the operative word, and endless abuses of Order No. 51 led to ridiculously unbalanced ratios of sick to healthy. According to Tripler, the physician of the Sixty-first New York Infantry (also known as the Clinton Guard) reported that "he had a large number of broken-down men: many sixty to seventy years old," most of whom had "hernia, old ulcers, epilepsy, and the like."[16] Tripler told of one brigade surgeon who found that in many of the regiments under his purview, there had been absolutely no medical examination prior to the soldiers' enrollment. The Fifth New York Cavalry (also known as the First Ira

Harris's Guard) had as many as eighty men with ruptures and neurologic conditions out of its total force of a few hundred. One private wrote home to his parents about how his examining doctor palpated his collarbone and said, "You have pretty good health, don't you?" The soldier-to-be replied that he felt fine, and the examiner remarked, "You look as though you did." Such was the sum and substance of his physical examination, and upon further inquiry regarding "fits or piles," the new recruit was pronounced ready for service.[17] It seemed, according to Tripler's evaluation, "as if the army called out to defend the life of the nation had been made use of as a grand eleemosynary [charitable] institution for the reception of the aged and infirm, the blind, the lame, and the deaf, where they might be housed, fed, paid, clothed, and pensioned, and their townships relieved of the burden of their support."[18]

SUNDAY, JULY 21, 1861, a sweltering day by anyone's reckoning, was an exciting time for the elite of Washington society. The potential of an armed conflict twenty-seven miles south of the city, near the northeastern Virginia city of Manassas, with its small dividing stream called Bull Run, had been publicly announced twenty-four hours earlier. Dressed in their holiday finest, toting picnic baskets, transported by horse and buggy, a large segment of the city's populace left the capital to observe the battle. Although there was little to see but smoke from their viewing site, which was several miles from the epicenter of fighting, concerned citizens, congressmen, hangers-on, and reporters talked excitedly about morning reports of a Union victory.

Initially, the thirty-five-thousand-strong Army of the Potomac, led by Brigadier General Irvin McDowell, appeared to be defeating the outnumbered rebels under the command of General Pierre G. T. Beauregard. For the noncombatant spectators, it remained a festive occasion until midafternoon, when several thousand screaming Shenandoah Valley–based troops, controlled by Joseph E. Johnston, suddenly reinforced the collapsing Confederate line. With Thomas (soon-to-be- "Stonewall") Jackson's First Brigade plus the Rockbridge Artillery and James Ewell Brown ("Jeb") Stuart's First Virginia Cavalry leading the stand, the battle, which had started so well for the Union troops, suddenly took a menacing turn.

Poised at the foot of Henry House Hill, the Eleventh New York Infantry, best known as the First Fire Zouaves, may never have seen Johnston's troops as they gathered at the ridge's crest, but Johnston's men could not miss the Yankees. Advancing up the slope, the 950 or so Northerners were a colorful lot. Sporting dark blue waistcoats accented in red and gold trim, bright red blouses, flowing crimson bloomers with blue piping and white spats, all capped off by a red fez, these warriors were the height of mid-nineteenth-century military haute couture. Modeling themselves after well-known French troops who had adopted the name and uniforms of fierce Algerian tribesmen famed for their precise, acrobatic military drills, the Zouaves, with their street talk and swagger, seemed perfectly prepared for battle; indeed, there was little to suggest otherwise.

They had a typical volunteer's story, from recruitment in mid-April among the firemen of New York City to a tumultuous departure a few weeks later down Canal Street to a waiting steamer. Accompanied by the likes of socialite Mrs. John Jacob Astor, five thousand fellow firefighters, and a six-by-ten-foot crimson satin flag embroidered in white silk with the words *U.S. National Guards, First Regiment Zouaves, New York*, the Manhattanites marched to one of that era's most patriotic tunes, "The Red, White and Blue." Their commanding officer, with admittedly scant knowledge of his charges, casually remarked to a friend, "I want the New York firemen, for there are no more effective men in the country, and none with whom I can do so much. Our friends at Washington are sleeping on a volcano, and I want men who are ready at a moment to plunge into the thickest of the fight."[19]

Arriving in Washington on May 3, the Fire Zouaves, like some other volunteer regiments, were initially sheltered in the Capitol building itself. There, according to one contemporary source, they "lounged in the cushioned seats of members of Congress."[20] Commenting on the Zouaves' accommodations, a *New York Times* reporter noted dryly, "The opportunity for building up the discipline of the regiment has not been much, such as would have been offered by placing them in camp." With few organized activities to participate in, the Zouaves enjoyed a taste of their former life when three hundred of them helped control a fire on May 9, at a clothing store adjoining the Capitol's renowned Willard's Hotel. According to the same journalist, "The boys astonished the natives when they rushed up the avenue to the scene of the fire, by the celerity of their movements and the confident manner in which measures were adopted for putting out the flames!"[21]

Having spent May and June in the area around Arlington and Alexandria, the Fire Zouaves were given orders in mid-July, as part of McDowell's overall contingent, to march on Centreville, Virginia. Abandoning training camp was not an altogether unpleasant or unwelcomed proposition. With tens of thousands of men milling about, these vast acreages were essentially giant cesspools and garbage dumps. Water was scarce, cleanliness was by no means apparent; "the walls of the tents are seldom, if ever raised to admit fresh air," asserted one surgeon. "The straw is saturated with emanations from the bodies and breaths of men."[22] "It was a common subject of remark," wrote another, "that men who, but a few weeks before, occupied positions in society demanding cleanliness and care for personal appearance, now disregarded it, and either from apathy or laziness neither washed their persons nor the clothing they carried upon them."[23] This lack of hygiene and poor sanitation led to medical director Tripler's notation that "thirty-three per centum of the troops encamped on the flats near Arlington were reported sick with diarrhoea and malarial fevers."[24]

During the early years of the war, camp sanitation was so poor that diseases quickly outnumbered injuries and wounds as a cause of disability and death. For instance, loose stools, euphemistically called "the quickstep" or "flux," became a soldier's constant companion, with Union physicians reporting almost five hundred thousand cases of diarrhea and dysentery a year. In the hastily erected and vastly overcrowded camps, latrines, commonly situated adjacent to ponds, streams, and other water sources, were dug too shallowly and chronically overflowed. The inevitable result was that water contaminated with human waste was also used for bathing, cooking, and drinking.

Medical scientists of the day never associated fecal contamination of food and water with outbreaks of the "flux." Rather, contemporary experts blamed the situation on eating unripe fruit or uncooked vegetables or enjoying fresh meat after having been fed only salt provisions for weeks. Also topping the list of offenses was sleeping on the damp ground, or in wet clothes, and picket duty or marching in rainy weather. The end result was what the Third Wisconsin Infantry experienced after traveling east in July 1861 and establishing camp near Harpers Ferry, West Virginia. According to the regiment's historian, "The worst foe with which the soldiers had to contend, was the camp diarrhoea. Under its debilitating effects the vigor and strength soon vanished; men wasted to skeletons; and while most of its victims still clung to duty, did their drilling and guard duty, it was in weakness and languor. When it became chronic, as in many instances it did, the poor victim, with a face like shriveled parchment, lips bloodless, and nearly paralyzed with sheer muscular weakness, was an object pitiful to see."[25]

Long endemic and epidemic in Washington and points south, malaria, with its accompanying paroxysms of chills, was the second most common camp-related disease. Northern medical records detail almost 1.4 million cases with more than 15,000 deaths during the forty-eight months of conflict. Incomplete Confederate records for 1861 and 1862 total 165,000 cases and more than 1,300 deaths. And since a bout of malaria did not confer lasting immunologic protection, its incidence and mortality rates increased steadily throughout the four years.

Much like diarrhea with its debilitating dehydration, an epidemic of malaria, or so-called remittent fever, could seriously weaken the effectiveness of any combat unit. Stationed near Sharpsburg, Maryland, physician Charles Nordquist told of how his men in the Eighty-third New York Infantry were "exposed to a drenching rain-storm for eighteen hours. They were without shelter of any description, and remained in their wet clothing for forty-eight hours; this, in connection with the unsanitary conditions of their camp, decaying vegetable matter, a clayey, moist soil and muddy brackish water, caused a marked change in their health." Nordquist goes on to relate that "remittent, intermittent, bilious and typhoid fevers prevailed to an alarming extent, and fully one-third of the regiment succumbed to the evil influence exerted on their systems."[26]

In 1861, the existence of pathogenic microorganisms was unknown. However, most of the day's common infectious diseases, including cholera, gonorrhea, measles, mumps, tuberculosis, and yellow fever to name but a few, were clinically recognized. What was not understood was their causation, transmission, and treatment. The exception to this list was smallpox, for which rudimentary inoculations had been given since the mid-eighteenth century. The vaccine, consisting of unadulterated pus from an active smallpox scab, was introduced into another individual's system by scratching the skin with a needle dipped in the putrid mix. Intended to induce a mild case of the disease that would confer lifelong resistance without pockmarking or other serious side effects, these inoculations were not completely effective. Still, they were administered to large enough numbers of Civil War soldiers so as to lessen the presence of smallpox and prevent the virus from gaining epidemic proportions.

While physicians might not have understood the pathogenic role of bacteria and viruses or specific causal relationships such as malaria and mosquitoes, the supposed perils of bad air and odoriferous gases given off by rotting vegetables or flesh, so-called miasmas and effluvia, were well documented. Malaria, for example, was also known as "marsh miasm," and according to Joseph Woodward, an army surgeon and author of *Chief Camp Diseases of the United States Armies*, outbreaks normally occurred in warm, wet areas such as swamps. Suggesting vegetable decomposition as one possible cause, Woodward tells of how a "subtle gas or gaseous compound" is released during the decaying process that acts on the respiratory tract. "Crowd poisoning," from men sleeping packed into unventilated tents, was considered a primary source of deadly effluvia. According to Woodward, "When great numbers of individuals are crowded together within very narrow limits, the consumption of atmospheric oxygen and the substitution of carbonic acid in the ordinary process of respiration may take place to such an extent as even to induce fatal results."[27]

It was during the 1850s, in response to the evils of poor personal hygiene and effluvia and miasmas, that an informal sanitarian movement evolved. The initiative, championed by reform-minded physicians and supported by a nationwide cadre of civic leaders, lobbied for the creation of a more structured organization. At the start of the Civil War, the United States Sanitary Commission was formally established, with improvement of military sanitary conditions as one of its prime objectives. "Every Army surgeon should make it his religious duty to comprehend and control such diseases and causes of disease as are prone to hover about encampments, and secretly break down the strength of armies," intoned Stephen Smith, a thirty-eight-year-old physician and editor of New York City's newly established *American Medical Times.* Destined to live another sixty-one years, Smith would serve at various times as commissioner of health of New York City, commissioner of lunacy of New York State, and president of the American Public Health Association— and these only hint at the breadth of his medical interests. For now, he was an amalgamation of surgeon, social activist, and chief propagandist for the fledgling Sanitary Commission. "Let this matter be thoroughly appreciated by our Federal and State bureau of Medicine, and our nation is secure from any assaults of its foes,"[28] proclaimed Smith.

Declaring battle on filth and odors and maintaining faith in fresh air and sunlight, the Sanitary Commission played a leading role in attending to the overall health needs of Union troops. While also regarding themselves as defenders of the public's health and welfare, commission members promulgated exacting principles for both camp sanitation and public hygiene. Through its involvement in the political maneuverings to restructure the U.S. Army's Medical Department, this civilian relief agency would have a decided influence on the daily work experience and professional thinking of tens of thousands of physicians. And as a result, it would shape American medicine for decades to come.

⟝⟝►●◄⟞

ON THE MORNING OF July 18, 1861, Union Brigadier General McDowell's ragtag Army of the Potomac abandoned their camps around Arlington and Alexandria and moved cautiously into position near Centreville, Virginia. Around noontime, a sharp clash occurred between Northern and Southern reconnaissance units at Blackburn's Ford. Although New York's Fire Zouaves were not directly involved in the action, according to an eyewitness account, two of them "contrived" to lose their regiment and plunge into the middle of the assault "on their own hook, with all imaginable gusto." "Whenever a rebel soldier appeared anywhere near them in this straggling, skulking fight," wrote the eyewitness, "they hunted him down like hounds and killed him, regardless of the numbers by whom they were surrounded."[29] In later years, the three-hour affair at Blackburn's Ford, with its nineteen Union dead and thirty-eight wounded and sixty or so Confederate casualties, would be relegated to little more than a minor skirmish. But in the late afternoon of July 18, it was considered a major battle. As described by a Union surgeon, most of the "wounds were chiefly from small arms loaded with round balls. I saw no [surgical] operations performed on the field." This surgeon noted that supplies for the wounded were generally sufficient; "there was, however, difficulty in obtaining water."[30] Initially, those shot were taken to a ravine near the Union battery, but soon an accompanying physician and his assistants moved the wounded two hundred yards away from the action. After the application of dressings, the injured were conveyed two miles to Centreville.

Describing a scene that would augur the surreal qualities of Bull Run military medicine, Brigadier General McDowell's aged and ineffectual medical director, William S. King, tells of being in Centreville and going out to meet the returning ambulances with their dead and wounded. Only then did the war's medical realities become evident to physician King, who decided there was an urgency to "select suitable buildings for hospital purposes." King watched helplessly as two rickety ambulances approached an area where twelve thousand troops were marching and the vehicles' drivers were told to sit and wait. For two hours, as their fellow Union troops tramped by with indifference, some of the Blackburn's Ford wounded lay without medical attention less than fifty yards from Centreville's Stone Church, now extemporized as an army hospital. Adding to these injured soldiers' misery was a continued lack of water, as thirsty marchers, oblivious to the medical needs of the wounded, drank dry all the surgical basins placed in front of the church. The medical absurdities continued when an unnamed volunteer surgeon refused to treat several of the seriously injured soldiers because, according to King, "he considered his obligation to extend no further than to his own regiment." Exhausted and disheartened by the inadequacy of his organization, King retired near midnight, "sensible of the want of additional medical supplies which would be needed in the event of the expected battle."[31]

King, a twenty-four-year veteran of the Medical Department, had reason to worry. Not only were medical provisions in short supply, but any semblance of plans and strategies was nonexistent. Two nights later, on Saturday, July 20, despite knowing that a confrontation faced them, King and his immediate subordinate, David Magruder, had provided no coordination of assignments for the mass of volunteer physicians, no definitive guidelines for wound treatment, no plans for evacuating the injured, and no detailed postbattle hospital arrangements. Within twenty-four hours, the North's medical preparedness, like that of its politically dominated army, would find itself inadequate to the task at hand.

At approximately two A.M. on July 21, the mass of McDowell's thirty-five thousand Union troops began their final march to battle. The Fire Zouaves, however, brigaded with the First Michigan Infantry, the Thirty-eighth New York Infantry (also known as the Second Scott's Life Guard), and Captain Richard Arnold's battery of the Fifth U.S. Artillery, remained in camp until later that morning, at which time they started forward. It was a difficult ten miles or so to traverse in what would become the most extreme of physical conditions. Under a broiling sun and through choking dust, they marched and halted and marched until they arrived at Sudley Ford, with its picturesque country church, around midday. With little to sustain them besides watery coffee and hardtack, the firemen were doubtless hungry and fatigued. Then, pushing forward another mile or two, they converged on the smoky maelstrom of combat.

Things seemed to be going well for the Northern troops. Their secessionist foes had been driven back from one position after another, and a final and hopefully decisive Union assault against Confederate positions on Henry House Hill was imminent. To further soften the enemy line, two artillery batteries with eleven large guns were ordered to position themselves on the northwest slope of the ridge, with promised infantry support to be provided by the Fire Zouaves. Around three in the afternoon, advancing at double-quick pace, the New Yorkers began their ascent. "Up, up, not a single enemy in sight, not a shot from his side. Up, up, till we gained the top and then...," wrote one Zouave.[32]

Jackson's men held their fire until the Eleventh New York had gone slightly beyond the two cannon units. Then, like lambs led to the slaughter, the Zouaves were cut down by several volleys of rifle fire. Bewildered, weary, and about to be broken, the surviving firemen returned perhaps one hundred shots. Two companies of the regiment withdrew to the foot of the hill, only to encounter a new danger: Jeb Stuart's menacing Black Horse Cavalry. As the cavalry charged, the Zouaves, according to James Fry, McDowell's chief of staff, began "fleeing to the rear in their gaudy uniforms."[33] As the desperate firemen abandoned their positions, the now defenseless artillery units were left exposed to Jackson's withering fusillade.

The Fire Zouaves' commander, Colonel Noah Farnham, exhorted his troops, but according to one eyewitness, "soon the slopes behind were swarming with retreating and disorganized forces, whilst riderless horses and artillery teams ran furiously through the flying crowd." With most of his cannoneers dead or dying and more than fifty battery horses slain, the captain of one of the Union artillery units ran back to the Zouaves and begged for support. The unnerved firemen declined to return, and all further efforts at encouragement were futile. According to the same observer, "The words, gestures, and threats of the officers were thrown away upon men who had lost all presence of mind and only longed for absence of body. Some of our noblest and best officers lost their lives in trying to rally them."[34]

Like a row of falling dominoes, a slow-moving panic spread across the Union lines. The inexperienced Northern troops, exhausted from more than a half day's worth of quickstep maneuvering, little nourishment, and sustained bloodshed, had lost all courage and pulled back from Henry House Hill. Although there was no coordinated Confederate pursuit (in General Joseph Johnston's words, "Our army was more disorganized by victory than that of the United States by defeat"),[35] heavy fighting would continue for another hour or so, while the Union's thrashing rapidly degenerated from frenzy into an undeniable rout.

FOUR HUNDRED EIGHTY-ONE Northern troops were killed outright at Bull Run, and another 1,011 were wounded. In addition, some 1,460 Union soldiers were missing in action. It was a scene of utter medical chaos. There was no organized evacuation of the injured, and no provisions had been made to have available adequate numbers of field hospitals or even simple first-aid encampments to handle casualties. Everything seemed to have been left to luck or divine intervention. Such short-sightedness is mirrored in medical director King's postfight summation: "My impression at the commencement of the battle was that there would be a brisk skirmish, and then the rebels would most probably fall back and take up a new position. I thought it would be a small task, therefore, to make out a list of the killed and wounded, and with notebook in hand

I began to count the number of each."[36] However, after viewing almost one hundred dead and wounded, King recognized that the absence of prebattle medical planning was having a serious impact on the troops' welfare. Galloping hither and thither, King was never in a position to exercise control over his medical personnel, nor, during this very long day, could he adequately supervise the evacuation of the wounded. King simply assumed that each regimental surgeon and assistant surgeon would tend to his own battle group's injured, without regard to the ultimate evacuation and disposition of their patients. This strategy was complicated by the fact that ingress passageways were so crowded, the bulk of Union medical supplies never arrived.

Here, as at Blackburn's Ford, King was dilatory in arranging care for the wounded. With large numbers of dead and injured scattered over the battlefield, it was several hours before he acknowledged the medical seriousness of the situation and dispatched his assistant, Magruder, to prepare a field hospital. Commandeering Sudley Church, Magruder had the church's pews removed, the floor covered with blankets, buckets of water brought in, and men sent off to the surrounding fields to gather hay for bedding. Thus, Sudley Church became the only formal field facility established that day for the treatment of Union wounded. By midafternoon, a smattering of physicians, including the Fifth Massachusetts Infantry's medical student–cum–surgeon, William Williams Keen, gathered at the building as a few ambulances unloaded their wounded, having no place else to carry them.

Within two hours, the improvised hospital was filled to capacity and Magruder was forced to take possession of three other unoccupied buildings, which were situated fifty yards farther down the road. He ordered that some of the wounded be placed under trees, in an apple grove immediately behind the church. So inept was the evacuation process that other than those wounded in the immediate vicinity of Sudley Church, it appears that few additional injured were taken from the field by ambulance. In most cases, the recently hired civilian ambulance drivers and stretcher bearers, afraid for their own lives, fled the killing grounds, never to be heard from again. With the Union lines disintegrating, those wounded who were unable to walk were left scattered over Bull Run's undulating terrain to await the secessionist enemy.

As the Confederates advanced on Sudley Church, Keen and other less experienced volunteer physicians were told to leave for Washington. With no Union defenders in sight and Magruder not providing any answers, several seasoned physicians offered to remain behind. "We at once raised a white flag, and commenced doing what we could for the wounded," reported one of them. "Shortly after the last of our troops passed the church, a company of the enemy's cavalry rode up and took possession."[37]

Hordes of panic-stricken Union soldiers, along with their abandoned equipment, blocked most escape routes. Those of the injured who were fortunate enough to leave the scene under their own power walked mile upon mile, begging for assistance at every doorway they passed. Washington's battlefield spectators were similarly terrified, and the tens of thousands of Northern soldiers soon became ensnared with their shocked civilian supporters, creating a mob scene. "The whole road, for a distance of three miles, presented but the most frightful spectacle of a dense, struggling multitude of fugitives, artillery, infantry, cavalry and baggage wagons, all blended in inextricable confusion,"[38] wrote one observer. The sorry spectacle was summed up by a Northern war correspondent's laconic telegram to his editor: "Bull Run, They Run, We Run!"[39]

BACK IN CENTREVILLE, surgical conditions were little better than those at the battlefield. Frank Hamilton, a highly regarded professor of military surgery at Manhattan's Bellevue Hospital who was serving as surgeon to the Thirty-first New York Infantry (also known as the Montezuma Battalion), told of mass confusion at the improvised hospital in the town's Stone Church. Forty-eight-year-old Hamilton was among the most erudite of America's surgeons. He had studied medicine in Europe and was politically active in the profession, having been elected president of the New York State Medical Society in 1855. Sporting a well-trimmed beard and mustache, the ever natty Hamilton was a prolific author who two months before had written a short book on military surgery.

Arriving in the dark, Hamilton and his retinue found hundreds of severely wounded men "lying upon every seat, between all the seats, and on every foot of the floor." So tightly packed was the throng that Hamilton felt he was "constantly in danger of treading upon the wounded, indeed, it was impossible to avoid doing so." By the light of little more than two or three tallow candles, Hamilton completed two amputations, one below the knee and one above the elbow. With unusual soul-baring frankness for any surgeon, he confessed that both of them "were done very badly, but I could, at the time, and under the circumstances, do no better. My back seemed broken and my hands were stiff with blood. We still had no sponges, and scarcely more water than was necessary to quench the thirst of the wounded men."

Outside, Hamilton encountered a soldier with a horribly injured arm. The extremity was nearly torn off at the shoulder, and the man was dying of blood loss. Hamilton gave him whiskey and water, awkwardly dressed the wound, and left him to his fate. Just as the candles flickered out, Hamilton, covered in gore, returned to Stone Church. Realizing he could "do no more," he lay down upon the wooden floor beside the 250 or so wounded. But he was too fearful of being captured to sleep, so he stood and addressed the injured: "Thank God, my boys, none of you are very seriously injured; you will probably all get well." One or two replied feebly, "Thank you, Doctor, thank you."[40] When he was ordered to retreat, Hamilton left, hoping that the Confederates would care for the Union injured better than he could.

No regiment of McDowell's forces was more unnerved by events at Bull Run than the Fire Zouaves. The unit's sole medical ambulance was commandeered by able-bodied men now fleeing the field, and the regiment's physicians were separated from the main contingent of Zouaves. Thirty-four-year-old private John Campbell of Company F, with a right ankle shattered by gunshot, was completely immobile. Unattended, he lay on Henry House Hill for several days, became a Confederate prisoner of war, and was not repatriated to his Northern comrades for another three months. For Colonel Farnham and twenty-three-year-old private Egbert Post of Company E, the nightmare was just beginning. Farnham was struck by a supposedly spent musket ball, which created a superficial wound to his scalp an inch or so above his left ear. Stunned, he fell from his horse and was knocked unconscious. Farnham was examined in the field by surgeon Hamilton and taken to the E Street Infirmary in Washington. Initially, Hamilton described the injury as "a very slight and superficial wound, which seemed to have taken off very little more than the hair," but seven days later, he noted ominously that Farnham, despite "doing very well . . . kept to his bed."[41]

Shot in the left shoulder blade, Post also became part of the Union army's rush back to its capital. But unlike his colonel, who was transported by horse, the lowly private, despite suffering excruciating pain and having difficulty breathing, walked the twenty-seven miles till he reached Alexandria's Hallowell's School, which had recently been turned into a general hospital. This damp, dark, and dirty building contained almost one hundred beds, some miserably located in third- and fourth-floor walk-ups. There was little to suggest that this structure, with no running water, narrow stairs, and outhouses more than forty yards away, had been configured with any thought toward patient comfort. Doctors were rarely present, medical supplies were scarce, and infections spread like wildfire.

In view of the wretched conditions at Hallowell's School, it is not surprising that Private Post's wound soon became red, swollen, and tender. In this preantibiotic and preantiseptic era, he was diagnosed as having erysipelas, a highly contagious and painful infection called "St. Anthony's Fire" or the "Rose." Not until three decades later, once a firm understanding of bacteriology was in place, did erysipelas assume a specific medical dictionary identity: an acute, inflammatory disease caused by streptococcal bacteria. Present-day surgeons would more accurately label Post's condition severe cellulitis, caused by a mixed infection of both staphylococcal and streptococcal bacteria and accompanied by a host of localized and constitutional symptoms, including abscess formation, fever, and malaise. If an abscess is surgically incised, allowing unimpeded drainage of its fetid contents, then natural immunologic defense mechanisms should ultimately overcome the bacteria and the infection will abate. However, Private Post received no definitive surgical care and was left, according to his case report, "in a state of profound exhaustion."[42] In just a few days, the untreated and rapidly expanding abscess began pouring out pus and bony spicules.

The decrepit Hallowell's School building was all too typical of the facilities to which the retreating Bull Run wounded were admitted. Other than several small structures built of logs during the War of 1812, the United States Army had no prior experience or seeming need to construct military hospitals. In the spring and summer of 1861, with prospects for little more than a ninety-day war on the horizon, the idea of expending large sums of money to build military hospitals seemed unreasonable. Such thinking springs from the fact that hospitals were an insignificant aspect of American civilian life at that time. What few facilities did exist were used mostly by the working poor, for no family of substance would ever allow its members to enter such a place. As one young New York physician put it, "The people who repair to hospitals are mostly very poor, and seldom go into them until driven to do so from a severe stress of circumstances. When they cross the threshold they are found not only suffering from disease, but in a half-starved condition, poor, broken-down wrecks of humanity, stranded on the cold, bleak shores of that most forbidding of all coasts, charity."[43]

With no civilian or military facilities to emulate, it is understandable that in July 1861, District of Columbia authorities had done nothing more than organize and inadequately equip a group of abandoned dwellings, churches, government buildings, seminaries, and warehouses to serve as military hospitals. Besides, a flood of sick and wounded of the magnitude of Bull Run was, at that point, unthinkable. Within four years, however, America's innovative and sophisticated new military hospitals would serve as praiseworthy models for the future development of civilian facilities. Overseen by members of the United States Sanitary Commission, the construction of innumerable military medical facilities became a major component of medicine's story during the Civil War.

THE CONFEDERATES MAY have sustained a military victory at Manassas, but medical circumstances were equally miserable on their side. Confederate generals Johnston and Beauregard reported 387 killed, 1,582 wounded, and 13 missing, but battlefield carnage is sometimes best appreciated at the regimental level. For instance, Jackson's Thirty-third Virginia Infantry, the first to take on the two Union artillery batteries, experienced casualties of 30 percent. Even more dramatic was what happened to Johnston's four individual brigade commanders. Barnard Bee (who in an effort to rally his own troops at Bull Run pointed toward the stalwart Southern line and shouted, "Yonder stands Jackson like a stone wall. Let us go to his assistance")[44] was now dead, as was Francis Bartow. Edmund Smith was badly injured, though he would survive, while Stonewall Jackson's left middle finger was almost severed by a musket ball, probably fired by a Fire Zouave.

With the Confederate army controlling not only the Union's improvised hospitals at Sudley Church and Centreville's Stone Church, but the entire Manassas battlefield and surrounding area, Southern medical personnel were confronted with an unexpected and unwanted responsibility. Inadequately prepared to provide even a modicum of surgical care for their own disabled troops, rebel surgeons were now burdened with the obligation of rendering medical assistance to hundreds of the captured enemy. This was all the more difficult because the Southern medical effort, paralleling its Northern counterpart, was plagued by the appointment of incompetent physicians, the induction of recruits unfit for military service, and a lack of central command. There were few coordinated arrangements for care of the wounded, which was further underscored by a dearth of ambulances of any description. "In speaking of the inefficiency of the medical department of that period, I do not mean to cast the slightest reflection upon the individuals who composed it; for more competent, devoted and patriotic men never honored any service. I only mean to imply that they were small in number, deficient in organization, and unsupplied with such materials as the exigencies of the situation demanded," wrote Edward Warren, soon to be named North Carolina's surgeon general.

The Jefferson Medical School–educated Warren visited Virginia two weeks after the battle at Manassas. According to him, "Large numbers of disabled soldiers were still being sent from the field or its vicinity, most of whom had received only the scantiest attention." Disgusted with the professional incompetence he witnessed, Warren was of the decided opinion that many of the wounded were near death, as they had not undergone needed amputations. Scrounging about for any enclosed space to serve as a makeshift hospital, the Confederates faced a medical crisis of unprecedented proportion. "From what I could gather," wrote Warren, "the whole country, from Manassas Junction to Richmond in one direction, and to Lynchburg in another, was one vast hospital, filled to repletion with the sick and wounded of Beauregard's victorious army." Scattered throughout churches, hotels, private dwellings, and public halls, wherever a blanket and hay could be spread, the wounded and sick dotted the countryside. In the town of Charlottesville alone, Warren told of "more than twelve hundred cases of typho-malarial fever." Reeking from lack of personal hygiene, lice-infested hair, diarrheal stools, and gangrenous wounds pouring out malodorous discharges, Manassas's winners were a sorry spectacle.

Staring up vacantly at the Thomas Jefferson–designed Rotunda at the University of Virginia, Private Elisha Wolf of Stonewall Jackson's Fourth Virginia was in complete circulatory collapse. His upper thighbone had been shattered from a Union musket ball, and four weeks of watchful waiting had finally given way to blood poisoning. Emaciated, jaundiced, racked by chills, fever, and diarrhea, Wolf had not reached Charlottesville's most recently designated military hospital until three days after Manassas, receiving little in the way of initial care. Although it was hoped that his fracture would heal itself, this country boy (who, according to Warren's account, "at the first tap of the drum had left the plough in the furrow") was told that what little chance there was of saving him would necessitate the removal of his leg at the hip joint. Taking Warren's hand as tears ran down his wasted cheeks, Wolf lamented, "I am not afraid to die, doctor, but amputate for my mother's sake, for she would like to see her boy again."

Operative surgery, especially the amputation of an arm or leg, had forever been a speed event in which a surgeon's ego and a patient's suffering were intimately bound up with how fast the former could relieve the latter of his extremity. Tissues were incised, bones sawed, and blood vessels tied all in a few minutes to minimize blood loss and lessen a patient's anguish and pain. Despite the introduction of general anesthesia a decade and a half earlier, surgical expediency remained a hallmark of Civil War amputations. Using dirty instruments, feeling about with unwashed hands, Edward Warren completed Wolf's amputation in just three minutes. Amputation at the hip joint is a technically demanding and rarely performed surgical operation, and Warren's completion of the procedure in just 180 seconds was a medical tour de force.

For fifteen hours everything went well, and Warren's heart, according to notes in his diary, "began to thrill with hope and exultation."[45] At hour thirty, however, Private Wolf was dead. Warren confessed that he was not surprised by the fatal conclusion, knowing full well that all hip joint amputations performed by English surgeons during Europe's recent Crimean War had ended in death. What he could not reconcile was the lack of hygiene and timely care that together compelled the operating surgeon to become, in effect, a soldier's ultimate executioner.

If victorious Southern troops received such a poor level of care, what could their Northern captives anticipate? Monday, July 22, the day following the battle at Bull Run, dawned with a cold, driving rain that would last for the next forty-eight hours. Unable to provide inside shelter for most of the Sudley Church contingent, captured twenty-three-year-old assistant surgeon George Sternberg (who would later become president of the American Medical Association as well as surgeon general of the United States Army) obtained a detail of men from the Confederate cavalry officer in charge, constructed a wooden frame about thirty feet by twenty feet, and covered it with abandoned rubber blankets to protect soldiers lying outside. As for sustenance, Sternberg said, "A small quantity of corn meal was obtained from a house near the church, and some gruel was made. A cup of this was given to nearly every man, and this was all the food we were able to obtain for them."[46] That evening, the Union medical officers were moved eight miles to Manassas Junction for interrogation by General Beauregard's staff.

There were no customs concerning immunity for captured doctors, and the Yankees were asked to sign a "parole" or "word of honor" not to serve again during the war. All but a few agreed, and by Wednesday most of the surgeons had returned to Sudley Church. Sternberg, one of the refusers, was allowed to attend the wounded only upon pledging not to attempt to escape for five days. On Saturday, his parole having expired, George Sternberg made his getaway and hiked the twenty-five or so miles back to Washington. Other captured physicians were not so fortunate, including one who remained a prisoner for more than a year until he was repatriated under a flag of truce.

At Sudley Church, a scorching sun and continuing lack of surgical care brought about, according to an eyewitness, "wounds completely alive with the larvae deposited there by the flies." Of the amputations performed during this time, most terminated fatally within twenty-four hours. In many instances, stated one of the captured surgeons, the Northern wounded "were placed in the hands of ignorant pretenders to experiment upon. Some of these self-styled doctors had no knowledge of their profession, were intentionally cruel to those whom they called damned Yankees, and hacked off legs and arms in the most frightful manner."[47]

Following his release from Confederate jail in fall 1861, Joseph Homiston, physician to the Fourteenth New York Infantry (also known as the First Oneida Regiment), testified before a joint committee of the Senate and House of the United States Congress concerning barbarous surgical conditions he encountered following Bull Run. Relating the story of Corporal Charles Prescott, "a young man of accomplished character and liberal education," who had been wounded, Homiston told of begging Southern authorities to allow him to amputate Prescott's badly mangled leg. Rebuffed, Homiston was forced to watch the operation performed by rebel "tormentors":

> The assistants were pulling on the flesh at each side, trying to get flap enough to cover the bone. They had sawed off the bone without leaving any of the flesh to form the flaps to cover it, and, with all the force they could use, they could not get flap enough to cover the bone. They were then obliged to saw off about an inch more of the bone, and even then, when they came to put in the stitches, they could not approximate the edges within less than an inch and a half of each other. Of course, as soon as there was any swelling, the stitches tore out, and the bone stuck through again. Another operation was soon performed, but the unhappy young man, under such treatment, sank away and died.[48]

Not until Thursday, July 25, did the Sudley Church wounded and other Union injured begin to be moved to Richmond. The prisoners of war were barracked in a former tobacco warehouse, Richmond's almshouse, and other squalid buildings. Crowding was inevitable, and one Union surgeon wrote that he "witnessed suffering which I shudder to remember."[49]

Some of the captured wounded, who were no longer believed able to engage in active combat, were released to Union authorities in the fall. Among them was Fire Zouave private Campbell, who was stated to be "in bad condition," hobbling about, with his entire foot "swollen and painful, with discharge from several sinuses." In late October, Union surgeons removed decayed splinters of bone from his ankle, and by February 1862, Campbell was euphemistically described as having "recovered the use of his foot." He returned home to New York City, where he was pensioned. After twelve years, during which time he was undoubtedly an invalid, Campbell's wound was characterized as "open and connecting with dead bone."[50] In 1875, his orthopedic difficulty necessitated the removal of a large portion of ankle bone, engendering a painful rehabilitation.

FOR DAYS FOLLOWING Bull Run, all of Washington was in a state of confusion as frightened citizens watched stragglers and walking wounded fill their city. "The worst sight of all," wrote one newspaper correspondent, "was the ambulances, coming back empty, or with only tired soldiers in them. As the rain poured and the darkness drew on, our thoughts would go out to the hundreds of gallant fellows who were lying wounded and uncared for in the bushes, under the rocks and the forest trees, along the ravine of Bull's Run."[51] Among the most perturbed of observers was thirty-nine-year-old Frederick Law Olmsted, recently named executive secretary of the United States Sanitary Commission. He told of streets filled with "a most woe-begone rabble, which had perhaps clothed itself with the garments of dead soldiers left on a hard-fought battle-field . . . all were alike excessively dirty, unshaven, unkempt, and dank with dew." Watching soldiers begging for food, Olmsted described some who "appeared ferocious, others only sick and dejected, all excessively weak, hungry, and selfish." Olmsted found the higher-ups ensconced in a more luxurious setting at Willard's Hotel. According to him, they too were "dirty and in ill-condition" but "appeared indifferent, reckless, and shameless, rather than dejected and morose."[52]

A native of Hartford, Connecticut, Olmsted was an organizer extraordinaire, and the Sanitary Commission needed such a man. Henry Whitney Bellows, president of the commission, said of his newest hire, "Mr. F. L. Olmsted is, of all men I know, the most comprehensive, thorough & minutely particular organizer." Bellows added, "He is equally wonderful in the management of principles & of details. His mind is patient in meditation, capable & acute, his will inflexible, his devotion to his principles & methods, confident & unflinching."[53] Olmsted's credentials were impressive. He had traveled to China on a merchant ship at the age of twenty-one, was managing editor and part owner of *Putnam's* magazine, was a widely recognized author, and, having made several fact-finding horseback trips through the American South, became an effective literary voice against slavery. Not least, he was both architect and construction superintendent of the soon-to-be-completed Central Park project in New York City.

Olmsted firmly believed that sanitary reform was essential, and not just a parochial concern of army camps: To him, slovenliness was a national vice. "If five hundred thousand of our young men could be made to acquire something of the characteristic habits of soldiers in respect to the care of their habitations, their persons, and their clothing, by the training of this war," Olmsted wrote, "the good which they would afterwards do as unconscious missionaries of a healthful reform throughout the country, would be by no means valueless to the nation."[54]

Olmsted's concern probably stemmed from his personal experience with the vagaries of that era's surgical care. In September 1860, Olmsted was in a horrific carriage accident. Examining the broken bone protruding from the torn flesh of his thigh, several surgeons concluded that immediate amputation at the hip joint was necessary before gangrene set in. Other medical men cautioned that Olmsted was so weakened, he might not survive the operation. Surgical conservatism, in the form of a wait-and-see approach, won out, even though Olmsted's chances of survival were deemed small. Yet nine months after the accident, he was alive and, despite a permanently shortened leg and marked limp, he was walking and working.

In the weeks following Bull Run, the sick and wounded inundated Washington's two main military hospitals, the recently extemporized E Street Infirmary and its tumbledown counterpart, the Union Hotel. Numerous houses of worship were temporarily appropriated as medical shelters, as were the Capitol building, the U.S. Patent Office, Saint Elizabeth's Insane Asylum, and hundreds of private residences. Surgeons streamed in from as far away as New York City in an effort to help the wounded, but there was no one to coordinate these efforts in any official capacity.

Samuel Gross, the renowned professor of surgery at Philadelphia's Jefferson Medical College, found soldiers "lying in the streets in great numbers, some on their knapsacks, others on the bare earth, and horses and wagons were often seen in every direction, apparently without any one in charge of them. The whole city, indeed, seemed to be completely demoralized."[55] In Georgetown and then Alexandria, Gross inspected numerous hospitals and found surgical treatment consisting only of simple dressing changes. According to Charles S. Tripler, King's soon-to-be-named successor as medical director of the Army of the Potomac, the disorder was made worse because "every regimental surgeon sent what men he pleased to the general hospitals without knowing whether there was room for them or not, and men were discharged from the hospitals with no means provided to ensure their return to their regiments."[56]

The military's efforts to find and treat the injured left behind at Bull Run would soon end. Several days after the battle, medical director King organized a relief detachment of thirty-nine ambulances. But the convoy wandered aimlessly around the Virginia countryside, as permission allowing safe access to the battlefield was repeatedly denied by Confederate authorities. Fearful that the ambulances, with their supplies, would be captured, King ordered the carriages to return to Washington. A short time later, owing to his managerial shortcomings, King was replaced by Tripler.

AS A COMBAT regiment, the Fire Zouaves were dispersed, with only three hundred of the original contingent returning to their old camps. Not surprisingly, a sizable number of the firemen deserted, while others brought tidings of the defeat, albeit with wild stories emphasizing their own prowess under fire. DISASTER TO THE NATIONAL ARMY, blared a *New York Times* headline, although its reporter duly noted, "The men that seem to be 'jolly under the most difficult circumstances,' are the red-shirted Fire Zouaves. Some of them marched in last night after a walk of twenty-five miles . . . they were cracking their slang-jokes at one another, and seemed not the least disheartened."[57] However, a later account in *Harper's Pictorial History of the Civil War* labeled the Eleventh New York as "arrant cowards."[58] Remnants of the regiment were immediately reassigned to simpler duty guarding New York City's harbor. Eventually deployed to Newport News, Virginia, the Eleventh New York saw little in the way of further serious combat, and the Fire Zouaves were mustered out of service in June 1862.

Perhaps if Colonel Farnham had been able to speak up for his men, things would have been different. Unfortunately, by early August Farnham's head injury caused him to become irritable and essentially noncommunicative. A few days later, he suffered a paralyzing stroke followed by coma, and on August 14 he was found dead in bed. Autopsy disclosed bleeding in his brain and the formation of an "abscess, the size of an English walnut." Civil War physicians termed Farnham's problem "chronic irritability of the brain,"[59] but modern surgeons would label it an acute subdural hematoma or, simply put, an expanding pool of blood caught between the brain and its unyielding protective covering, the

dura membrane. A subdural hematoma is created by broken blood vessels bleeding on the surface of the brain, caused in Farnham's case by
the impact of the bullet bouncing off his skull or, more likely, by striking
his head on the ground when he fell off his horse. The growing collection of blood crowded and compressed the fragile brain tissue, with
death an end result.

Zouave private Post's date with a surgeon's scalpel at Hallowell's
School hospital did not come until August 18, almost a full month after
Bull Run. In "profound exhaustion,"[60] suffering from a dislocated shoulder, multiple fractures of his shoulder blade, and a pus-and-bone-
spewing abscess on his upper back, Post had a portion of his shoulder
blade removed and the abscess drained. He was fortunate that once the
abscess was opened, his natural healing powers proved satisfactory, and
three weeks later, he was sent home to New York City. However, Post's
convalescence was interrupted by continuing medical problems that
necessitated a series of surgical operations. Post finally succumbed to
his Bull Run injury in November 1865. For tens of thousands of others
like him, the process of dying from wounds proved a lengthy and ago-
nizing affair. Often it was not even officially recorded that such deaths
were a direct result of battlefield injuries.

CHAPTER TWO

"The people of this state have been bled long enough"

WHILE FIGHTING AT WHITE OAK SWAMP in Virginia in 1862, William Goodell, a private in the Sixth Vermont Infantry, was knocked unconscious by a shell that exploded behind him. When he awoke, a doctor observed that although there were no visible injuries, Goodell "could move his tongue perfectly in every way, but he could not speak; and he was totally insensible to all sound." The symptoms suggested a brain injury, and Goodell's physician had little doubt about how to treat the problem. Ice was placed on the soldier's head, veins in his neck were opened to remove blood, purgatives were given to induce vomiting and diarrhea, and blisters were created on his legs and behind his ears to allow "poisonous" body fluids to ooze from the raw skin surface. These treatments, lasting several weeks, were meant to decrease "congestion," or "inflammation," in Goodell's body. Communication was maintained between Goodell and his doctor by use of a writing slate.

In the 1860s, this therapeutic regimen was standard medical fare for all forms of illness. When Goodell remained "deaf and dumb," his physician thought the symptoms might be feigned. The recently discovered process of etherization—anesthesia was used for the first time in 1846—was employed to test Goodell's senses in a less guarded state. Dripping ether onto a sponge held at Goodell's nose, and paying no attention to his heart or breathing rates, the doctor repeatedly questioned Goodell as he drifted toward insensibility. As stated in his case report, "The operation only confirmed the reality of the symptoms."[1]

The following week, Goodell received jolts of electricity in an attempt to undo his body's "excitement." The shock therapy accomplished little beyond sapping his strength. After six months of what was considered modern medical treatment, Goodell's physician sent him home with no discernible improvement in his condition. Fifteen years later, Goodell's hometown physician wrote to a pension board that Goodell was totally incapacitated.

Goodell's story is illustrative of the state of medical knowledge during the Civil War. At that time, no doctor could conceive of diseases and treatments in anything resembling today's scientific terms. The mid-nineteenth-century physician's materia medica (the drugs and other therapeutic substances used in medicine) consisted of herbal and mineral concoctions similar to those used since the time of Hippocrates. The fact that there would soon be fundamental developments, such as antisepsis, bacteriology, public health, and radiology, was beside the point. Nor did it matter that the most important qualities of modern medical thought—scientific attitude, a willingness to question authority, a desire to learn from clinical experience, and a drive to modify therapeutic practices accordingly—would be mainstays of late-nineteenth-century clinical practice. In the 1860s, medicine stood on the cusp of a major revolution, which would be heralded within a decade or two by the likes of Claude Bernard, Charles Darwin, Joseph Lister, and Louis Pasteur. Unfortunately, Civil War–era physicians and combatants would not benefit one iota from this coming reformation. Filth, diseases, and ancient remedies prevailed. For American doctors, the teachings of one man, Benjamin Rush (1745–1813), largely set the standards for their practice of medicine.

Today, Rush's name conjures none of the controversy that once surrounded his every thought and deed. Some hailed him as the father of American medicine, but others substituted the words *vampire* and *slayer* for father, arguing that from the 1780s to the 1880s, Rush's concept of bleeding, blistering, and purging for every imaginable ailment led to tens, if not hundreds of thousands, of unnecessary deaths. Abolitionist, advocate for the insane, antiwar propagandist, prison reformer, signer of the Declaration of Independence, and treasurer of the United States Mint, Rush became the most celebrated American healer of his generation. "He was a physician of no common cast. His prescriptions were not confined to doses of medicine, but to the regulation of the diet, air, dress, exercise and mental actions of his patients," declared an early biographer. "In the treatment of disease he was eminently successful and in describing their symptoms and explaining their causes, he was uncommonly accurate." So encompassing was Rush's knowledge, he was said by the same writer to be "minutely acquainted with the histories of diseases of all ages, countries and occupations."[2]

But some suspected a dark side to his character. One medical historian found Rush's social passions "perhaps not entirely dissociated from a personal interest in increasing his practice."[3] Others felt his therapeutic convictions were based on the most arbitrary of clinical reasons. Extremely sensitive to the criticism that embroiled his public life, Rush expurgated his personal papers and wrote the most self-righteous of autobiographies. Still, to many of his contemporaries, this politically powerful man remained a medical saint.

In 1766, having received a BA from the College of New Jersey (renamed Princeton University in 1896) and served six years as a physician's apprentice, Rush settled in Edinburgh, Scotland, to complete his formal education by obtaining a doctor of medicine degree. His three years in Europe not only provided a medical diploma, but also transformed Rush's core political beliefs with regard to the matters of royalty. Having befriended an English antimonarchist and having observed the dauphin behaving badly at a banquet in Paris, Rush returned to America imbued with a growing social conscience and resolved to become involved in the debates surrounding the Colonies' drive to independence. As one of his acquaintances noted, "Three great political subjects, for the time being, engrossed his whole soul; the independence of his country; the establishment of a constitution for the United States and for his own particular state; and to enlighten the public mind and to diffuse correct ideas. On these important disquisitions he labored night and day."[4]

Rush was appointed professor of chemistry at the College of Philadelphia, the first medical faculty to exist in the Colonies, but political aspirations were his priority. In 1774, he founded the country's earliest antislavery society and two years later became a member of the Continental Congress. At the start of the Revolutionary War, Rush was named "Surgeon-General of the Hospitals in the Middle Department of the Continental Army." But Rush's military career and political ambitions ended in ruin less than two years later, when, during the grim winter of 1777–1778 at Valley Forge, he was found to have been an active participant in the ill-fated Conway conspiracy to bring about Washington's dismissal. Rush's situation was complicated by his involvement in another plot to force the resignation of William Shippen, Washington's choice as director general of the Continental army's Hospital Department. Attempting to disgrace Shippen, Rush unjustly accused him of financial improprieties relating to the procurement of wartime medical supplies. Accusations ran rampant, with at least one of Rush's contemporaries bluntly conceding that he "was capable of lying in the worst sense of that word" and calling Rush "an unprincipled man."[5]

Discredited by his attacks on Washington, Rush resigned his military post and resumed his medical practice in Philadelphia. Despite the political blot on his name, Rush played an active role in the daily life of the city. He became a founder of both the Dispensary for the Poor and the Young Ladies Academy, a finishing school for teenage girls. Rush also served as manager of the Philadelphia Humane Society and as vice-president of the American Philosophical Society. St. Thomas' Episcopal Church, a house of worship for African Americans, was established through his auspices, and Rush himself became an active member of the Philadelphia Bible Society. Working and writing with unflagging energy, Rush argued for ratification of the Constitution, attacked tobacco use as a cause of madness, opposed all forms of corporal punishment, and protested discrimination against Tories remaining in the city.

On his return to Philadelphia, Rush noted that "from the filth left by the British army in all the streets the city became sickly and I was suddenly engaged in an extensive and profitable business."[6] Rededicating himself to the practice of medicine, he wrote to a friend: "Medicine is my wife; science is my mistress; books are my companions; my study is my grave: there I lie buried, the world 'forgetting, by the world forgot.'" But he was not to be forgotten. Soon Rush was elected physician to the Pennsylvania Hospital, followed by his appointment as professor of medicine in the University of Pennsylvania. Staking his renewed reputation on a fresh theory of disease causation and therapeutics, he used his lectern as a bully pulpit. What set Rush apart from his medical peers was the resolve of his clinical convictions and the strength of his writings. His essays on various medical subjects were prolific and considered so original that a contemporary concluded, "They should be carefully perused by every medical student; for they unfold true principles, which will lead the physician of genius to correct, efficient, and energetic practice. To the American student they are of incalculable value."[7]

Referred to as the American Hippocrates, Rush was revered by medical students, who came from long distances to hear him speak. "I was enrapt," wrote Charles D. Meigs, later to become Philadelphia's preeminent professor of midwifery and diseases of women and children. "[Rush's] voice, sweeter than any flute, fell on my ears like droppings from a sanctuary, and the spectacle of his beautiful, radiant countenance, with his earnest, most sincere, most persuasive accents, sunk so deep into my heart that neither time nor change could eradicate them."[8] James Thacher, an early-nineteenth-century medical biographer, calculated that Rush instructed more than 2,250 prospective doctors during the course of his academic career. In turn, these students "extended the blessings of his instructions and improvement in the theory and practice of medicine, over the United States, and in a few instances to South America, the West Indies, and the eastern continent."[9] Rush's influence is all the more pervasive considering that at this time, the University of Pennsylvania's medical school graduated more men than all the other existing American institutions combined. Physicians and laymen throughout the country constantly sought his clinical advice. More often than not, Rush wrote back urging them to bleed, blister, and purge.

Basing his system of healing on the fever doctrine, one of the oldest and most popular explanations of sickness, Rush stated in 1790, "There is but one exciting cause of fever and that is stimulus; and that consists in a preternatural and convulsive action of the blood vessels." Rush simplified and streamlined prior theories by indicting excess activity in blood vessels as the root cause of human sickness. "It follows, of course, that all those local affections we call pleurisy, angina, phrenitis, internal dropsy of the brain, pulmonary consumption, and inflammation of the liver, stomach, bowels and limbs, are symptoms only of an original and primary disease in the sanguiferous system."[10] Arguing that hyperactivity in the vascular system was the essence of all illnesses, Rush promoted elimination of blood and other bodily fluids as the only means to heal. Copious bloodletting, administering drugs to induce diarrhea, salivation, sweating, and vomiting, and drawing out body fluids by blistering the skin served as the mainstays of Rush's approach. Called "heroic therapy" because of the strength of its combined actions, Rush's bleed, blister, and purge gambit remained the backbone of American medical therapeutics for almost one hundred years.

Since thermometers and the concept of measuring one's warmth or coldness did not yet exist, the term *fever* did not refer just to a simple increase or decrease in body temperature. Instead, it was a catchall phrase to designate all forms of acute and chronic disease. Whether cancer, cardiac failure, dysentery, emphysema, malaria, smallpox, or tuberculosis, the presence of an illness was viewed as a form of fever. Indeed, by focusing on fevers and bodily fluids, Rush was doing little more than providing an eighteenth-century update to a Greco-Roman formula relating health and sickness to an imbalance among four elemental bodily fluids or personality-affecting humors: black bile (melancholy), blood (sanguine), phlegm (phlegmatic), and yellow bile (choleric). Although the humors were naturally present in the body, an abnormal change of one over the other was associated with illness or fever.

Blood was the most abundant humor and the one most closely associated with life itself. The fact that blood could be lost without necessarily causing death probably explains the Greek practice of bloodletting as a means of reestablishing health. Through his actions and quill, Rush became known as medicine's premier interventionist. He stated, and most of his colleagues readily accepted, that without intrusion of heroic therapies, illnesses would inevitably worsen, leading to death. Rush's system rejected "undue reliance upon the powers of Nature, and teaches instantly to wrest the cure of all violent and febrile diseases out of her hands."[11] Henceforth, sick chambers would be under the strict purview of physicians only and their therapeutic renderings.

Rush's heroic therapy seemed to prove its own point, for when made to bleed, blister, cough, defecate, sweat, or vomit long enough, any patient would inevitably become relaxed, if not unconscious. With "fever" apparently out of his system, a patient now had time to recuperate. Although Rush's European mentors believed in various degrees of bloodletting, Americans carried bleeding and depleting further than had ever been done before. "It is believed that no man understood the human pulse better than Dr. Rush," said James Thacher, his biographer. According to Thacher, Rush was the ultimate salesman, a great proselytizer of his ideas: "Instead of making a profitable secret of his innovations in practice, he came forward boldly; taught them to his numerous pupils; published them to the world, and defended them with his pen."[12] Speculative and unempirical as Rush's system was, American physicians wanted to believe in an American system of medicine, and they considered the Philadelphian's opinions to be authoritative and state-of-the-art.

What patients looked for in physicians was a self-assured manner and an air of confidence about their therapies. James Thomas Flexner, a well-known medical historian, wrote of this era, "A Svengali who could hypnotize himself, his patients, and above all his colleagues into believing he was right was certain to be regarded as a great scientist. Rush was such a man."[13] Some of Rush's contemporaries did not agree with his depletive therapy and found his fondness for the bleeder's lancet intolerable. But Rush was such a renowned patriot and dedicated citizen, such a commanding and energetic person, such a prolific writer and inspiring lecturer, that his influence became far-reaching and long-lived.

RUSH'S HEROIC MEDICINE spread rapidly throughout the country and produced a deep and lasting impression upon the American practice of medicine. In fact, the early to middle decades of the nineteenth century were described by one social historian as marked by a "prow-wave of extensive and intensive bloodletting."[14] Citizens went on to suffer needlessly from its various effects. In an age when the simple measurements of blood pressure and body temperature were unknown and the importance of determining heart and respiratory rates was not understood, physicians had no parameters to prevent them from harming their patients.

Bleeding, or phlebotomy and venesection, as it was also called, rapidly filled all therapeutic voids and was regarded as the prescription of choice for every imaginable human illness. Not only did venesection dominate everyday use, but a fascinating willingness developed to voluntarily withdraw one's essential life force in large quantities at certain times of the year. For example, Philadelphia's Samuel Gross, the same surgeon who went to Washington to treat the casualties following Bull Run, noted, "Bleeding in the spring and autumn was very common, as a means, as was believed, of purifying the blood and relieving congestion."[15] This banal observation becomes more riveting when it is realized that Gross, a doyen of American surgery, was describing the siphoning off of a person's blood as treatment for nothing more than seasonal allergies and symptoms of nasal stuffiness and postnasal drip.

After a bloodletting session, if tension or congestion in the blood vessels was believed still present, Rush's system called for further depletive therapy in the form of gastrointestinal catharsis, specifically vomiting and laxation. Calomel became a panacea for mankind's medical miseries and the country's preeminent dual-action cathartic. Considered a wonder drug, this ivory-colored, tasteless powder degraded in the gut into highly poisonous components that caused explosive evacuation of the bowels accompanied by volcanic vomiting. This odious preparation of mercurous chloride was particularly distinguished for its latent side effects. Repeated doses of calomel would accumulate in the body, resulting in toxic aftereffects, from sore teeth and extreme salivation, with spittle pouring out at a rate of two to four pints a day, to gangrene of the facial tissues.

Supplementing calomel's checkered performance was a white-powdered mixture of antimony and potassium known as tartar emetic.

Usually ingested with magnesium sulfate dissolved in water, this all-purpose depletive was a poison. In small amounts it produced disabling vomiting and in larger quantities reduced heart activity to dangerously low levels. Together, calomel and tartar emetic proved dehydrating and ultimately debilitating, but in the 1800s, for both patient and physician, they were the latest in modern medicine. So adamant was Rush about the advantages of these particular cathartics that James Thacher told of how Rush named calomel the "Samson" of drugs. Rush's critics concurred in the propriety of the name Samson, but this was, according to Thacher, because "it has slain its thousands."[16] Still, at a time when the appellation "Rush's system" evoked a sense of medical patriotism, and it was commonly believed that without such intervention the inevitable conclusion of disease was death, Rush's heroic treatments offered genuine psychological relief.

PHYSICIANS' EMBRACE OF Benjamin Rush's heroic medicine is partially explained by the haphazard process of early American medical schooling and the disorganized state of the profession. The system of apprentice-based training, sometimes supplemented by a lecture term or two at one of the country's fledgling medical schools, produced practitioners unbeholden to standards and guidelines. It was an era of American individualism, in which each physician practiced his own brand of clinical medicine, prescribing unregulated doses of Rush's depletive therapies while passing on nothing more than suppositional knowledge to any student willing to pay and listen. Indeed, any physician or quack could formulate new therapeutic schemes while vilifying those of his competitors. The unscientific basis of medical practice made it impossible to prove or disprove the soundness of specific claims. As reported in the *New York Monthly Chronicle of Medicine and Surgery* in 1825: "No body of men are less in concert, or seem less influenced by the *espirit du corps*, than physicians ... the quarrels of physicians are proverbially frequent and bitter, and their hatred, in intensity and duration, seems to exceed that of other men."[17]

In the 1820s, a novel type of medical college began to dot the nation's landscape. Initially located in more rural settings, with faculties composed of local practitioners, these institutions were chartered as independent educational facilities legally authorized to award a doctor of medicine degree. No longer would small-town physicians impart knowledge on a time-consuming one-to-one or apprenticeship basis. Instead, doctors united by renting a room or two for academic lectures and anatomical demonstrations and made certain to charge appropriate matriculation and course fees. It was as if an entrepreneurial spirit suddenly engulfed American medicine, but with business interests ruling the day.

These proprietary medical schools became a powerful educational and political force and were soon found in virtually every major city as well. Competing institutions cropped up down the street from one another as economic considerations seemed to transcend academic standards. Even "if a student applies for admission into one of our colleges six weeks after the commencement of the term," one faculty member declared, he should not be refused matriculation "lest he turn on his heel and walk directly into the halls of some rival institution."[18]

At this point in our nation's medical past, neither the federal government nor the state legislatures were directly involved in issuing individual doctors their medical licenses. Instead, licensing laws typically placed responsibility in the hands of physician-managed county and state medical societies. However, lobbying efforts directed by proprietary medical school owners changed the situation. Newly enacted statutes stipulated that a diploma from a proprietary medical college was to be the equivalent of a license granted by a county or state medical society. As a result, the proprietary medical school graduate was free to roam the American countryside and practice medicine however he chose. "Each roll of parchment endorses its possessor as '*vir ornatissimus*' [a man of distinction]," declared the chairman of the American Medical Association's Committee on Medical Education, "and he goes forth amid the sound of martial music and rich bouquets showered upon him by the hands of fair ones, an accredited agent for life or death, endowed with all the paraphernalia of a 'Doctor of Medicine,' but destitute of the brains."[19]

By the time of the Civil War, almost fifty medical colleges provided instruction on an MD-granting basis, with 6,849 students having graduated during the 1830s, 11,828 individuals through the 1840s, and 17,213 in the 1850s. Indeed, neither literacy nor prior academic achievements nor good moral standing was of consequence as long as there was an ability to pay the necessary matriculation fees. Any method to increase enrollment and profits was countenanced, including, according to one president of the American Medical Association, faculty members visiting prisons to recruit medical students from among the inmates. It almost seemed as if every community's riffraff could subsist through the part-time practice of medicine.

Honorary degrees were bestowed on countless physicians as an enticement to send their apprentices and other young men to proprietary medical schools. Professors of anatomy, chemistry, materia medica, midwifery, and clinical surgery abounded, with the title holder having few academic qualifications beyond a pecuniary interest in a particular facility. Nathan Smith Davis, president of the American Medical Association during the Civil War, commented, "Every professional man who became ambitious of distinction as a teacher, sought a [medical] professorship in some [proprietary] college as the only position in which that ambition could be gratified. And as there are always more such men than there are places for them to fill, the constant and inevitable tendency is to the creation of more places."[20]

Sitting uncomfortably upright in a cramped, dank, amphitheater-like room, students endured six to eight hours of monotonous lectures per day. Whether at one of the new proprietary schools or an older institution with a nominal university affiliation—medical departments were founded at the University of Pennsylvania in 1765, King's College (now Columbia) in 1767, Harvard in 1782, Dartmouth in 1797, and the University of Maryland in 1807—course content was essentially the same. With no patients for clinical examination or surgical observation, lecture upon laborious lecture was given by preceptors turned pedagogues. Consisting of two four-month sessions, each identical in content to the other, the standard curriculum comprised anatomy; physiology and pathology; materia medica, therapeutics, and pharmacy; chemistry and medical jurisprudence; theory and practice of medicine; principles and practice of surgery; and obstetrics and the diseases of women and children. There was no consideration of scientific research or other nonpractical matters. Rote memory of textbooks served students best, as faculty members were too busy or too inept to devise written examinations. "Endless varieties of facts and reasonings are presented to his bewildered intellect which are rarely comprehended, never digested, and which leave the mind more confused at the close than at the opening of the session," complained Christopher Cox, chairman of the American Medical Association's Committee on Medical Education.[21]

Standards for a complete medical education did not even exist. Some students left after only two sessions (one year), having earned a bachelor of medicine, while others returned for a second year of repeat lectures to receive a doctor of medicine. Since a considerable graduation fee was due upon completion of studies, it behooved owner-teachers to pass all examinees regardless of their proficiency. Condemning the direct effects of proprietary medical education, a disillusioned Davis declared:

Every faculty of professors, so far from being disinterested and impartial examiners of their own classes, are under the direct influence of the strongest motive to swell, as far as possible, the list of successful candidates. These motives are nothing less than personal reputation and pecuniary gain, stimulated by the direct competition of rival institutions. Hence, every faculty of professors who resolve themselves into a board of examination, to sit in judgment on the qualification of their own students, are placed in such a position, that their own personal interests are in direct collision with their duty to the whole community, and their regard for the honor and welfare of the profession to which they belong.[22]

In mid-1863, Cox reported that a prominent medical college faculty had recently awarded a diploma to every student who managed to pay a graduation fee. Shortly thereafter, some of the newly anointed physicians registered to serve as army surgeons. At this time in 1863, two years into the war effort, the military had begun to apply a stricter set of standards to new physician recruits. All the neophyte physicians were summarily rejected as being ill prepared educationally for the clinical rigors, let alone the increased physical difficulties of military life. Of course, no matter how progressive medical education and its related institutions might have been, without a basic understanding of diseases and their treatment, physicians were stymied in their efforts to doctor their fellow man.

RUSH DIED IN 1813, succumbing to what was apparently tuberculosis plus the side effects of his own system of multiple bleedings and purges. He was eulogized as having added "more facts to the science of medicine, than all who had preceded him in his native country."[23] Even though Rush's bleed, blister, and purge system would remain a mainstay of therapeutics through the Civil War, it was not long before its status as medicine's holy grail of treatments was beginning to be questioned.

Rush's critics had long insisted that many diseases could be self-limiting in their course without the necessity of medical intervention. For example, discussing typhoid fever, Nathan Smith (no relation to Nathan Smith Davis), founder of medical schools at Dartmouth and Yale, declared that during the "whole course of my practice I have never been satisfied that I have cut short a single case." According to Smith, typhoid "has a natural termination like other diseases which arise from specific causes."[24] With this brief declarative statement, Smith placed himself at odds with Rush's strict interventionist approach and embraced, instead, the concept of self-limited illness. Trumpeting the successful treatment of typhoid patients with milk and water, Smith signaled that Mother Nature must always be welcomed in the sick chamber.

By the 1840s, criticism of Rush's theories had become part of everyday conversation in sophisticated medical circles. As greater numbers of American medical students flocked to Paris instead of Edinburgh and London, the rote prescribing of depletives was increasingly shunned and focus shifted to listening to and observing patients. Discussions about self-limited diseases and the realization of the physicians' limitations led to a growing respect for the healing power of nature. A good day's work, a restful night's sleep, and a diet of plants and meat, unencumbered by a doctor's intervention, were deemed what most individuals needed in their quest for health. Patients were urged to assume control of their own lives. For those afflictions whose final outcome was inevitably death, the physician and patient had to accept their fate and acquiesce to comfort care that was free of medical intervention.

In an era colored by the tenets of Jacksonian thinking, democratic ideas were beginning to influence the art of healing. Celebrating virtues of the common man, the eight years of Andrew Jackson's presidency (1829–1837) provided a steady improvement of social conditions, while a laissez-faire acceptance of all manner of healing became commonplace. After all, what could have been more reflective of self-help Jacksonian democracy than the decision to take charge of one's health?

Opposition to Rush's heroic therapies coalesced into a growing social and economic movement. "The people of this state have been bled long enough in their bodies and pockets," bellowed a state senator from New York, and "it was time they should do as the men of the Revolution did; resolve to sit down and enjoy the freedom for which they bled."[25] Rushing into this therapeutic void came cultists, quacks, and other medical miscreants who practiced what became known as unorthodox medicine. Their theories, which promised cures by methods at odds with the beliefs of the traditional or "regular physicians," seemed compelling to laypeople.

Each nontraditional or sectarian group had its own idiosyncratic theory of disease causation and treatment. Botanical medicine used only herbs, roots, and tree bark. Homeopaths prescribed infinitesimal doses of drugs that supposedly provoked symptoms and ultimately cured them. For hydropathic or water cure physicians, Adam's ale, externally and internally, was the treatment of choice. Thomas Graham and his followers employed vegetarianism as their basis for health reform; they insisted that a change in dietary habits, including steady ingestion of Graham's whole-grain cracker, would curb sexual urges, specifically masturbation and pre- and extramarital relations.

Established in 1847, the American Medical Association attempted to create a unified medical profession in direct opposition to the sectarian or unorthodox groups. In its attempt to upgrade admission standards at the nation's medical schools, its physician-founders proposed that every student should have a good English education, a knowledge of natural philosophy, an elementary understanding of mathematics, including geometry and algebra, and an acquaintance with Greek and Latin. Well-intentioned as these recommendations were, the number of students, especially from the frontier, who could have fulfilled these new, stricter requirements was so small that the concept seemed ludicrous to the physician-owners of proprietary schools.

Content with their revenues, they were not about to shut down their lucrative operations. Indeed, lobbyists never allowed the proposal to be seriously considered, and as a result, the association's earliest attempts to reform medical education proved fruitless. With committees on medical education, medical literature, medical sciences, practical medicine, obstetrics, surgery, and publications, the early meetings of the association were tumultuous. Displays of temper could be heard throughout the meeting halls, while actual voting sessions were riotous displays of the factionalism endemic to the era.

What doctors, particularly through membership in the American Medical Association, could agree on were ways to repudiate all non-orthodox thinking. A code of medical ethics was introduced forbidding regular physicians from consulting with sectarian practitioners or treating any patient under a nonorthodox doctor's care. But with an increasingly wary citizenry, it became impossible to suppress the sectarians. Certain movements, like Thomsonism, became wildly popular. Drawing on the philosophies of Samuel Thomson, a self-taught herbalist, Thomsonians proclaimed that disease was due to an excess of cold in the body. Thomsonians neutralized the cold with hot baths and employed a mild vegetative-based remedy to induce perspiration.

Thomson, a convincing salesman, began hawking rights to his methods. Especially popular on the southern and western frontiers among less educated country folk, Thomsonism started to rival orthodox medicine in influence and respect. With the establishment of infirmaries where steam-based treatments were administered, Thomsonism evolved from a self-help initiative to a movement dominated by full-time healers. But by the mid-1840s, professional Thomsonians and other herbal-oriented physicians were squabbling and split into a number of frag-mented botanical movements. Emerging from the fray were the eclectics.

By establishing botanical-based medical colleges in the South and Midwest, some even with MD-granting status, the new sect produced a group of healers trained in subjects similar to those taught at orthodox medical institutions. What distinguished these graduates was a strict re-liance on botanical equivalents of heroic therapy drugs and an absolute rejection of Rush's bloodletting approach. Eclectic physicians might have been looked down upon by their regular brethren, but they be-came an important and sometimes sole source of health care in many communities. However, within a decade and a half, botanical medicine lost much of its popular appeal because patients sought less harsh alter-natives to Rush's heroic therapeutics, not heroic botanical substitutes. By the start of the Civil War, the National Eclectic Medical Association, established in 1848, had suspended its activities.

The next threat to orthodox medicine came in the form of homeo-pathy. Most of the early homeopathic physicians received their initial medical education as members of the regular profession. Later in their careers, these orthodox doctors began to embrace homeopathic tenets. Such physicians knew orthodox medical thinking inside out, and by em-phasizing their new, gentler clinical approach, they were able to attract a more affluent and sophisticated clientele. Homeopathy was based on ex-perimental pharmacology as performed by a German physician, Samuel Hahnemann. Hahnemann hypothesized that certain diseases could be cured by prescribing very small doses of a drug that in large doses in a healthy person would produce symptoms like those of the disease. This hypothesis is stated in the first law of homeopathy: *Similia similibus curantur*, or "Like is cured by like." Since heroic doses of drugs were thought to aggravate illness, the second principle of homeopathy, the law of infinitesimals, stated that smaller doses are more effective in support-ing the vital spirit of the body. In other words, drugs gain potency through massive dilution. Hahnemann carried this concept to an ex-treme, believing that dilutions as small as one one-millionth of a normal dose were effective. Such dilutions worked, he claimed, because the body in illness was more sensitive to drug therapy than it was in health.

The tenets of homeopathy's gentler therapeutics were spread mainly through the influx of German-speaking immigrants who had set-tled in eastern Pennsylvania. By 1848, a state-chartered homeopathic medical school had opened in Philadelphia, and homeopaths with and without medical degrees began to spread their ideas throughout Amer-ica. Homeopaths called themselves the New School and did not hesitate to denounce their orthodox colleagues, arguing as one professor did that "we are the regular physicians, for the practice of the old school [heroic therapies] is very irregular, and in consequence its practitioners are irregular also."[26]

At first, some regular physicians welcomed homeopathic teachings as a viable alternative to Rush's principles. Indeed, homeopathic practitioners held membership in regular medical societies, since many of them were graduates of orthodox medical colleges. Samuel Hahnemann, having never set foot on American soil, received honorary membership in the Medical Society of the County of New York in 1832. However, orthodox physicians soon came to recognize the ideological and financial threats symbolized by the growth of homeopathy.

Although orthodox physicians were in the midst of their own fratricidal debates concerning the validity of Benjamin Rush's heroic dosaging, most members of the orthodox establishment agreed that the medicines prescribed by homeopaths were too small to have any effect. Ultimately, these regular or allopathic physicians would be proved correct in their fundamental thinking about the objective of medical therapeutics. Allopathy, or the treatment of disease by remedies that produce effects different from or opposite to those produced by the disease, would by the late 1880s become the basis of the scientific practice of medicine. However, in the years leading up to this breakthrough, the regulars' crusade of disparagement and innuendo only strengthened the homeopathic position.

State legislators, in a frenzy of self-help democratic ideology and stoked by homeopathic arm-twisting, responded to the perceived exclusivity of orthodox physicians by repealing virtually all medical licensing laws. Now, medical schools under any healing group's sponsorship could secure charters and authorize graduates to practice. Since sectarians usually went by the title of "Doctor," and legal distinctions between regular physicians and other healers no longer existed, the unschooled layperson had little to guide him or her in choosing a clinical practitioner.

At the start of the Civil War, there were almost 2,500 full-time homeopathic healers, supported by a national medical society, six medical colleges, and five monthly journals. With sectarian forces further bolstered by several thousand nostrum salesmen and quack self-help gurus, the nation's thirty thousand–plus orthodox physicians were on the defensive, seemingly unable to stem the sectarian tide. Some regular leaders now considered the MD degree so debased as to suggest abandoning it altogether.

So bitter were the antagonisms between regulars and irregulars that as the country divided into a Union and a Confederacy, allopathic and homeopathic physicians prepared to fight their own civil war. When President Lincoln's call went out for doctors to serve as Union army volunteers, the regulars who dominated the United States Army Medical Corps systematically denied entry to any known or suspected homeopath. These orthodox physicians unilaterally determined that medical care in the army should remain nonsectarian in nature. "Public authorities who deliberately consign the helpless and confiding sick to the charge of medical men practising a system so inefficient [as homeopathy], incur a fearful responsibility," suggested surgeon/editor Stephen Smith in his *American Medical Times*. "And that responsibility," he continued, "assumes a tenfold importance when the sick, who are to be subjected to this experiment, are the citizen soldiers who have sacrificed the comforts of home in defense of their country. Around them Government should throw its protecting care, and tenderly guard their sick beds from the ruthless hand of medical charlatanism."[27]

Early in the war, some regulars believed the question of homeopaths serving in the military had been settled. In fact, some homeopaths chose to enlist as army physicians and temporarily forgo clinical homeopathy in a "don't ask, don't tell" scenario. A number of homeopathic physicians joined Union regiments as simple soldiers rather than medical officers. An article in the *Chicago Medical Journal* declared, "Homeopathy attempted [to gain access to] the army and has found its Waterloo. It must henceforth conceal itself in the shades of private life—continue to dance attendance upon dyspeptic persons, vaporous dowagers, and neuralgic spinsters. The atmosphere of the camps is too harsh for its delicate tissues, and the poor moth must quietly prey upon the curtains and carpets of a *parvenu* aristocracy, and not tempt destruction by approach to the torch of military glory."[28]

The writer was mistaken, for it was not long before homeopathic activists questioned whether a government fighting for the rights of slaves could overlook the civil liberties of its own physicians. "Are personal rights abrogated by the Constitution in time of war? Has a soldier no right to think for himself, and to ask for that relief from suffering and death which his experience for years has taught him is best? Has Congress a right to establish a privileged order in medicine in violation of the spirit and genius of our government?"[29] asked a faculty member at the Homeopathic Medical College of Missouri. Such political questions had never before been framed in terms of an individual's right to choose a system of medical care. Faced with continued exclusion from the

army, Northern homeopaths launched an aggressive campaign questioning the constitutionality of the government's right to support one
system of medical care over all others.

Yet to justifiably criticize sectarians, the orthodox profession would
have to shed its own unscientific past by renouncing most of its prior
therapeutic endeavors, especially Rush's heroic therapies, and invoking
formalized education and scientific inquiry as the only acceptable
approach to medicine. As a result, not until the waning years of the
nineteenth century, when the scientific principles of bacteriology, im-
munology, pathology, physiology, and other basic ideas became entrenched in medical thinking, would the professional authority of
allopathic medicine be firmly established in America. For now, regulars
and irregulars appeared as equals in the court of public opinion.

INTERESTINGLY, A COMMON clinical ground did exist between allopathic
and homeopathic practitioners in their technical practice of surgery. As
one homeopathic clinician stated, "So far as the manual operations of
surgery are concerned, the homeopath most cheerfully records his approval and admiration of the perfection to which they have been
brought by the scientific investigation, ingenuity, and untiring industry
of the profession, and on all necessary occasions will promptly resort
to them."[30]

This growing admiration for surgery was due in part to the recent
discovery of anesthesia. To be able to free a patient from pain during a
surgical procedure was a remarkable scientific achievement. By the
early 1830s, ether and nitrous oxide had been discovered, and people
were amusing themselves with the pleasant side effects of these com-
pounds. It soon became evident that the pain-relieving qualities of these
gases might be applicable to surgical operations and tooth extractions.
In October 1846, William Morton, a twenty-seven-year-old Boston dentist, persuaded John Collins Warren, the eminent professor of surgery at
Harvard's Massachusetts General Hospital, to let him administer sulfu-
ric ether to a surgical patient. This allowed the skeptical Warren to pain-
lessly remove a small growth from a man's neck. After the operation,
Warren uttered five of the most famous words in American medicine:
"Gentlemen, this is no humbug."[31]

News of the momentous event spread rapidly throughout North
America and Europe. "No single announcement ever created so great
and general excitement in so short a time. Surgeons, sufferers, scientific
men, everybody, united in simultaneous demonstration of heartfelt
mutual congratulation," recalled Henry Bigelow, a witness to Warren's

astonishment.[32] Yet no matter how much it contributed to the relief of pain, the discovery did not immediately further the scope or safety of surgery. It could not bring forth the final step of the surgical revolution: all-important hygienic reforms.

In many respects, the recognition and acceptance of antisepsis (preventing infection by inhibiting the action of microorganisms) by the late 1880s was a more crucial event in surgical history than the advent of anesthesia. Even without anesthesia, a surgical procedure could still be performed. However, without antisepsis, major surgical operations typically ended in death following an overwhelming infection. Clearly, surgery needed both anesthesia and antisepsis (although antisepsis proved to have a greater impact).

Anesthesia would bring about profound technical changes in the manner in which an operation was conducted. Unfortunately, at the start of the Civil War, the mechanics of etherization and chloroform anesthesia remained very crude, and the often chaotic logistics of the war meant that these agents were sometimes unavailable. As a result, many surgical procedures continued to be performed in a preanesthetic fashion in the compromised setting of a battlefield or field hospital. This meant that clinical concerns were often of less consequence than the swiftness of the surgeon's knife.

Describing one preanesthetic amputation scene, a surgeon at Harvard told of how the flummoxed patient was brought to the operating theater and unceremoniously placed upon a table. The merciless surgeon stood with his hands behind his back and asked, "Will you have your leg off, or will you not have it off?" Saying "No" meant the individual had lost courage and was carried back to his ward bed. If the reply was "Yes," then he was immediately held down by a number of assistants and the operation went on regardless of whatever else was uttered. Even if the patient's courage failed after his initial assent, it was too late. According to the surgeon, "It was found to be the only practicable method by which such an operation could be performed under the gruesome conditions which prevailed before the advent of anesthesia."[33]

Not surprisingly, the scope of preanesthetic surgery remained quite limited. Surgeons treated only simple fractures and dislocations. Amputations were performed with high mortality rates. Limb fractures where fragments of bone pierced the skin were mostly unmanageable, with morbidity from infection a likely postsurgical outcome. More resolute surgeons managed to tie off a blood vessel or two for aneurysms and made valiant attempts to excise external tumors. Abscesses were drained, and some individuals even focused on the treatment of bladder stones, cataracts, and hernias. A few intrepid knife wielders endeavored to open the abdomen and chest, but such invasion inevitably ended with a dead patient. Neurosurgery and cardiac surgery did not exist. Wound care was an undisciplined art, noted more for its attendant complications than its long-term successes.

Despite the damning consequences, preanesthetic-era surgery was considered an important and medically valid therapy. This seeming paradox is explained by the simple fact that most operations were performed for external difficulties—that is, they proceeded from an objective anatomical diagnosis. Surgeons could see what needed to be fixed (for instance, abscesses, broken bones, bulging tumors, cataracts, hernias, and so on) and treated the problem in as rational a manner as the times permitted. The physician, however, was forced to render care for diseases that were neither visible nor understood. For instance, it is impossible to treat symptoms of illnesses such as allergies, arthritis, asthma, diabetes, and heart failure when there is no scientific understanding of what constitutes the disease's pathological and physiological underpinnings. For these reasons, when contrasted with his physician counterpart, the prescientific surgeon, despite the limitations of technical know-how, seemed occasionally to cure with a brutal confidence.

Even when anesthesia was available, Civil War surgery remained mired in filth and muck. "We operated in old blood-stained and often pus-stained coats," reminisced an eighty-one-year-old William Williams Keen. "We operated with clean hands in the social sense, but they were undisinfected hands. We used undisinfected instruments from undisinfected plush-lined cases, and still worse, used marine sponges which had been used in prior pus cases and had been only washed in tap water. If a sponge or an instrument fell on the floor it was washed and squeezed in a basin of tap water and used as if it were clean." Acknowledging the general ignorance of germs, Keen recalled, "If there was any difficulty in threading the needle we moistened it with saliva, and rolled it between bacteria-infected fingers. We dressed the wounds with clean but undisinfected sheets, shirts, tablecloths, or other old soft linen rescued from the family rag bag." Keen further described how, following his return to Jefferson Medical College after the debacle at Bull Run, the school's illustrious professor of surgery, Samuel Gross, "operated on the same table on which the cadaver was demonstrated by the professor of anatomy. Often the surgical assistants spent the morning in the dissecting room and at noon were assisting at operations."[34]

By THE EVE of the Civil War, the American practice of medicine had become a hodgepodge of therapeutic philosophies colored by a growing skepticism in matters clinical. Writing in his *History of Medical Education*, Nathan Smith Davis was plain: "Every species of medical delusion and imposition is allowed to spring up and grow without any legal restraint. The public press, that engine all powerful alike for good or evil, lends itself freely as the hired vehicle, for heralding every variety of pretended medicinal compound or nostrum, that the ingenuity of man can invent."[35] Describing the world as "doctored too much," one Philadelphia physician wrote, "There is scarcely a dwelling in the land, but what, upon emergency, could muster a host of empty bottles and pill boxes, as evidences of the fact." Doctors "keen upon the scent of the penny distribute the worthless but not harmless nostrums to all whose credulity or imaginary ailments demand them."[36] The confusion and distrust were summed up by Oliver Wendell Holmes, the renowned physician essayist, who said, "I firmly believe if the whole materia medica, as now used, could be sunk to the bottom of the sea, it would be all the better for mankind—and all the worse for the fishes."[37] Ultimately, the carnage of the Civil War would prove an enormous emotional and physical burden for the poorly educated, inadequately trained, and ineffectually organized physicians of that era.

CHAPTER THREE

"It is a good big work I have in hand"

A SSEMBLED IN THE TREASURY BUILDING in Washington in a room with a long, green-covered table and official stationery in front of each chair, the Sanitary Commission's board of managers listened as their executive secretary, Frederick Olmsted, discussed the Union's defeat at Bull Run. It was early September 1861, a mere seven weeks since the military disaster in Virginia, and Olmsted delivered a scathing rebuke. "No pack of whining, snarling, illfed, vagabond street dogs in an oriental city ever more strongly produced the impression of forlorn, outcast, helpless, hopeless misery," he recounted. "They entered the field of battle with no pretense of any but the most elementary and imperfect military organization and, in respect of discipline, little better than a mob, which does not know its leaders." Taking direct aim at the military brass, the executive secretary stated, "The majority of the officers had known nothing more of their duties than the privates whom they should have been able to lead, instruct, and protect."

Olmsted pointed to other problems. The march to the battlefield was too quick. Arms and equipment were thrown away with little consideration of later needs. Medical supplies never reached the front lines. And the health of the volunteer troops was abysmal: "blistered feet, rheumatic pains, aching limbs, diarrhoea, and nervous debility being prevalent,"[1] stated Olmsted.

Among those listening to the sordid details was Henry Whitney Bellows, the Sanitary Commission's founder and president. He held the pastorate of the First Congregational Church (Unitarian) in New York City and was a social reformer, renowned lecturer, and one of Manhattan's more prominent men of letters. Public-spirited and self-sacrificing, Bellows regarded himself as a mediator who could mollify political opposition to the commission and settle its internal differences.

On hearing Olmsted's criticism, especially that the army's Medical Department was considered wholly inept, Bellows understood the divisions that would inevitably ensue among the committee's civilian and military members. From the time of Lincoln's call to arms, when Bellows first expressed concern that the medical horrors of Europe's Crimean War not be repeated in America's Civil War, to Olmsted's denunciation of military misadventures at Bull Run, the establishment of the Sanitary Commission was mired in politics. Beginning on April 25, 1861, with a chance meeting in Manhattan between Bellows and Elisha Harris, who was physician in charge of the quarantine hospital on Staten Island, and continuing through the signing of papers creating the United States Sanitary Commission by President Lincoln on June 13, Bellows's efforts were viewed by Washington officials with a great deal of suspicion.

Bellows and Harris's brief encounter had led to their attending a soldiers aid society meeting at the New York Infirmary for Women. With armed conflict threatening their husbands and sons, women throughout the United States were forming societies to assist recruits and furnish men with homespun comforts. Some fifty women were present when Bellows was asked to be the chairman, which was in keeping with the contemporary practice of having men lead women's organizations. Bellows did most of the talking and proposed the establishment of a city-wide association embracing the churches, schools, and societies of women engaged in relief efforts. On April 29, in the great hall of New York City's Cooper Institute, a constitution prepared by Bellows was signed by ninety-two women to create the Women's Central Association of Relief. Declaring that the association would "establish recognized relations with the Medical Staff, and act as auxiliary to it; that they will maintain a central depôt of stores, and open a bureau for the examination and registration of nurses,"[2] the constitution embodied many of the principles that would shortly be incorporated into Bellows's concept of a nationwide relief effort.

After urging his female constituents to "find out first what the Government *will* do, and *can* do, and then help it by working *with it* and doing what it cannot,"[3] Bellows arranged a meeting with Richard Satterlee, the army's medical purveyor in New York. Satterlee's position was especially influential since his office supplied medical provisions to the troops. Unsympathetic to civilian interference in military matters, Satterlee rebuffed Bellows's proposals of assistance and insisted that the enthusiasm of the women and their male supporters was "superfluous, obtrusive, and likely to grow troublesome." More to the point, Satterlee predicted that the "sphere of the public in the work of aiding and relieving the army was predestined to be a very small one."[4] Not so easily dismissed, Bellows decided to seek a more satisfactory response by traveling to Washington to visit campsites, inspect troops, lobby politicians and military men, and see for himself what actually needed to be done.

Joining Bellows in his mission south were Harris and two other physicians. William Van Buren, an ex–army surgeon who held the chair of anatomy at the University of the City of New York, represented the Advisory Committee of the Boards of Physicians and Surgeons of the Hospitals of New York. Jacob Harsen, described in the official history of the Sanitary Commission as "an excellent and public-spirited man,"[5] was a member of the New York Medical Association for Furnishing Hospital Supplies in Aid of the Army, which was colloquially known as the Lint and Bandage Association. The four set out for Washington on May 15 and anticipated reaching the capital the following day.

An arduous sixteen-hour train ride left the committee men plenty of time to discuss the political events of the day. The firing on Fort Sumter, which had been preceded by the secession of seven Southern states (South Carolina, Mississippi, Florida, Alabama, Georgia, Louisiana, and Texas) from the Union, was barely one month old. Firebrand orators on both sides of the Mason-Dixon line could be heard exacerbating an already tense situation as Virginia, Arkansas, and North Carolina soon joined the secession movement. Arriving in Washington on Thursday, May 16, the Bellows party found everything in chaos. Northern troops were gathering, but no adequate preparations had been made for their reception or care.

As TWENTY THOUSAND troops crowded Washington's already garbage-strewn streets, Bellows's delegation grew concerned that the army's undermanned Medical Department could not possibly defend against the problems of inadequate sanitation in a force soon to number seventy-five thousand. With disease rates rising, the government appeared helpless in coordinating health care needs for its recruits.

Washington's disorder caused Bellows to plan for a far larger relief and sanitary effort with a more extensive supply system than had been originally anticipated. Harris urged that "the only true system which would cover the whole ground, and reach the seat of the evil, was the preventive system, founded upon the same principles, and administered by a Commission similar to that whose labors had produced such happy results in the Crimea."[6] Impressed with Harris's ideas, Bellows later recalled in a letter to Charles Stillé, the Sanitary Commission's historian, "The first idea of a Sanitary Commission, which certainly had not entered my head when we left New York, was started between us in the cars twixt Philadelphia and Baltimore—in a long and earnest conversation."[7]

THE CRIMEA IS a ten-thousand-square-mile peninsula that juts from the southern part of present-day Ukraine into the Black Sea and the Sea of Azov. The scene of the infamous Yalta conference between President Franklin Roosevelt, Prime Minister Winston Churchill, and Premier Joseph Stalin, the Crimean peninsula and the nearby countryside served for centuries as a battleground for conflicting national interests. Among these many hostilities was the 1854–1856 Crimean War, fought by Great Britain, France, Turkey, and Sardinia against Russia over the domination of southeastern Europe.

The Crimean War suffered some of the greatest losses from disease of all wars. For example, of the twenty-five thousand men who made up the initial English expeditionary force, eighteen thousand were dead at the end of twelve months, mostly from cholera, dysentery, scurvy, and other illnesses. More English soldiers lay in hospitals dying from malnutrition and sundry physical infirmities than were on active duty. This misery was compounded by a lack of adequate food supplies, warm clothes, evacuation and transportation systems, and sanitary service. Even when supplies were available, roads proved impassable owing to inclement weather or obstruction by men crowding the passageways.

When this lowly state of affairs became known in England, a concerted humanitarian effort was initiated by Parliament and the British public. Queen Victoria appointed a Sanitary Commission to coordinate medical relief efforts. Receiving a broad political and societal mandate, the British Sanitary Commission brought vast improvements to a soldier's day-to-day existence. Dirty camps, filthy hospitals, bad food, and ineffective nursing were replaced by a new regard for the advantages of proper sanitation and personal hygiene. Sick soldiers were no longer crowded together as they received more rest and better nutrition.

Coordinating much of this British relief effort was Florence Nightingale and her unit of thirty-seven nurses. Before long, they had ten thousand sick and wounded under their immediate care, as Nightingale attacked every aspect of patients' needs in the filth-encrusted English barrack hospital at Scutari (now known as Üsküdar). Sanitary reforms with insistence on cleanliness were called for, as was the establishment of kitchen, laundry, and recreation rooms to comfort her charges. The decrease in deaths from disease was phenomenal, and Nightingale became immortal.

OF THE 114 doctors serving in the U.S. Army in January 1861, 24 had resigned by spring of that year to join Confederate forces, and 3 more were dismissed for disloyalty. Consequently, the North's medical corps was left with only 87 physicians to begin its wartime service, far too small a cadre of military surgeons to care for a growing combat force. Furthermore, the Medical Department was in complete administrative disarray since its elderly chief, Surgeon General Thomas Lawson, had died the day Bellows and his fellow committee members set out for Washington.

Over eighty years old, Lawson had been surgeon general since 1836, when he was appointed by Andrew Jackson; unfortunately, his long-standing physical infirmities and lack of effective leadership contributed to the general lassitude of the Medical Department. Accustomed to handling health-related problems on small and isolated frontier posts, Lawson–era military doctors never needed grandiose plans for evacuating, hospitalizing, and caring for vast numbers of sick and wounded. Adding to the Medical Department's managerial woes was the simple fact that the rival and independent Quartermaster Corps built and equipped military hospitals and transported sick and wounded soldiers, while the Subsistence Department had sole charge of food and medical supplies. The decentralized Medical Department, with little bureaucratic leverage, was, according to the Sanitary Commission's treasurer, George Templeton Strong, run by old codgers "paralyzed by the routine habits acquired in long dealing with an army of ten or fifteen thousand and utterly unequal to their present work."[8]

During a series of meetings with Washington political and military officials, Bellows and his three companions lobbied for the establishment of a United States Sanitary Commission and also proposed a number of immediate medical reforms. On May 18, Bellows wrote to Secretary of

War Simon Cameron, asking that a "mixed Commission of civilians distinguished for their philanthropic experience and acquaintance with sanitary matters, of medical men, and of military officers, be appointed by the Government." Declaring that they wished to "prevent the evils that England and France could only investigate and deplore," the four New Yorkers suggested Cameron view the American conflict as "essentially a people's war." They reminded the secretary of war, "The hearts and minds, the bodies and souls, of the whole people and of both sexes throughout the loyal States are in it. The rush of volunteers to arms is equalled by the enthusiasm and zeal of the women of the nation, and the clerical and medical professions vie with each other in their ardor to contribute in some manner to the success of our noble and sacred cause."[9] Bellows concluded his letter with four items of imminent concern: more circumspect examination of volunteer troops to weed out physical misfits; training of regimental cooks under the aegis of the Women's Central Association of Relief, utilization of one hundred women to become nurses in the hospitals of the army; and establishment of a corps of volunteer medical students to work as wound dressers.

Unbeknownst to Bellows and his lobbying partners, President Lincoln was in the process of appointing Clement Alexander Finley, the most senior medical officer in the army, to be Lawson's successor. Once described as the handsomest physician in the army, with blue eyes, a ruddy complexion, and whiskers extending from the tips of his ears to the corners of his mouth, Finley was the picture of military bearing. A medical graduate of the University of Pennsylvania, he served at various army posts in the East and the West, including a stint as General Zachary Taylor's medical director during the Mexican War. Deeply religious and unfailingly blunt, Finley was an enemy of innovation. He particularly disliked Bellows's radical idea to employ female nurses in an all-male army hospital and the delegation's obsession with military hygiene and sanitary conditions.

After lengthy negotiations, Finley consented to the Sanitary Commission's creation, as long as their activities involved only volunteer troops. Grudgingly, Secretary of War Cameron gave his approval on June 9. Four days later, a hesitant Lincoln, who regarded the commission's establishment as adding a "fifth wheel to the coach," signed an executive order bringing the venture to life.[10] In just a few months, Bellows and his followers would control a volunteer empire, with more than seven thousand local auxiliaries actively raising funds and funneling donated clothing, food, and medical supplies to ten regional depots. For now, without specific organizational schemes in place, Bellows's concept seemed more braggadocio than substance, especially when he wrote to a friend, "Our plans have a breadth and height and depth which no similar military philanthropic undertaking ever had, since the world began."[11]

IN ASSEMBLING THE Sanitary Commission's initial board of managers, Bellows chose eleven socially prominent men with solid professional credentials. Alexander Dallas Bache, the vice president, was a West Pointer and descendant of Benjamin Franklin. Holding a lifetime appointment as superintendent of the United States Coast Survey, Bache was also professor of natural philosophy and chemistry at the University of Pennsylvania. The treasurer, George Templeton Strong, was a Wall Street lawyer of considerable reputation. He is best remembered for starting a diary at age twenty and, during the course of his lifetime, filling its thousands of pages with pithy anecdotes and frank, often acerbic comments about acquaintances, public figures, and current events. Elisha Harris was named corresponding secretary. Among the physicians on the board were William Van Buren and Cornelius Rea Agnew, surgeon general of the New York State Militia. Balancing the nine civilian appointees were three career army officers: George Washington Cullum, aide-de-camp to General Winfield Scott; Alexander Eakin Shiras, a major on the staff of the Subsistence Department; and Robert Crooke Wood, a thirty-five-year veteran of the Medical Department and husband of President Zachary Taylor's eldest daughter.

The Sanitary Commission's workings were bureaucratic and businesslike. Four- and five-day meetings were initially held in Washington every six weeks, but the work soon proved so overwhelming that standing committees were established. Constantly changing to meet the demands made upon it, the Sanitary Commission's growing bureaucracy functioned through hundreds of auxiliary branches that exercised local autonomy, although the commission's board of managers remained the ultimate authority over all major financial and supply matters. Eventually the commission would rival the federal government in scope and size and extend its work beyond the shores of North America. In November 1863 and March 1864, branches were established in Paris and London by expatriate Americans. These foreign branches, with others in Montreal and Toronto, aided the overall relief work by raising funds and, most important, lobbying the North's cause to Europeans and Canadians.

Various names were suggested for the position of the executive secretary, an appointment that would place a man in total command of the commission's growing, and as yet unstructured, national bureaucracy. Most prominent among them was the reform-minded Unitarian minister Edward Everett Hale, but Bellows's choice and the obvious front-runner was an obstinate, misanthropic, but brilliant New Yorker, Frederick Law Olmsted. Olmsted never received a formal college degree, though he held honorary ones from Amherst, Harvard, and Yale. He came to the Sanitary Commission with outstanding administrative credentials, gained mainly through his labors in creating New York City's defining public space, Central Park. As superintendent of construction, he oversaw the work of fifteen thousand men and the expenditure of millions of dollars. Not incidentally, Olmsted had extensive knowledge of the up-and-coming applied sciences of the day, sanitation and its twin, public hygiene. And most important to the Sanitary Commission's efforts was Olmsted's unflagging sense of patriotism. He believed that the Sanitary Commission would help further civilize the American people by providing up-to-date medical knowledge to army physicians and securing adequate hygiene and sanitation measures for soldiers. Writing to his half-sister Bertha, Olmsted confessed, "It is a good big work I have in hand, giving me absorbing occupation and that sort of connection with the work of the nation without which I should be very uncomfortable."[12]

A man of firm convictions and a strong work ethic, Olmsted would in modern terms be considered a workaholic. George Templeton Strong wrote: "He works like a dog all day and sits up nearly all night, doesn't go home to his family (now established in Washington) for five days and nights together, works with steady, feverish intensity till four in the morning, sleeps on a sofa in his clothes, and breakfasts on *strong coffee and pickles*!!!"[13] After arriving in Washington on June 27, 1861, Olmsted had Bellows immediately dispatched to chair a fact-finding mission in Ohio and inspect an army camp in Cairo, Illinois. Transformed from a strategically important but small railway junction into a Northern army garrison teeming with six thousand Union troops, Cairo was, according to the area's medical director, John Brinton, "not altogether a pleasant place," swarming with merchants, peddlers, produce dealers, and all sorts of camp followers. Brinton noted how "violent remittent, intermittent and low typhoid fevers invaded the camps, and many died. The general hygiene was bad, the company and regimental officers did not know how to care for their men, and the men themselves seemed to be perfectly helpless."[14]

Olmsted was not finding conditions any better in the East. Assisted by Elisha Harris, he investigated the condition of twenty camps of volunteers near Washington, taking particular notice of the lack of hygiene. He wrote that "a complete system of drains, so essential to the health of the men, did not exist in any of the camps, the tents were so crowded at night that the men were poisoned by the vitiated atmosphere, the sinks were unnecessarily and disgustingly offensive, personal cleanliness among the men was wholly unattended to, and the clothing was of bad material and almost always filthy to the last degree."[15] Any semblance of a wholesome diet was impossible, as the United States Army's Subsistence Department provided only beef and pork and refused to furnish vegetables or fruits. The officers of the Medical Department were particularly rude and never hid their resentment at the intrusion of civilians into military medical life.

The alarming state of affairs revealed by Olmsted and Bellows provoked differing reactions among the members of the Sanitary Commission. Civilian members fought with military members. Government backers, like Alexander Bache, grew suspicious of nonfederal employees. In one of his frequent letters to his wife, Mary, Olmsted lamented, "I do not get on very well; do not accomplish much & shall not I fear." Fiercely critical of the commission's three military appointments, Olmsted told Mary, "They do nothing but discourage & obstruct, & so of all officials. The official machinery is utterly and absurdly inadequate for the emergency & there is no time to think of enlarging it. I feel that the whole business is exceedingly uncertain & should not be much surprised to get up & find Jeff Davis in the White House." In late July, a divided commission urged government and military leaders to mend their ways. Not unexpectedly, few of the executive board's seemingly banal recommendations, including increased food supplies with improved cooking, greater camp discipline, and establishment of a ration system to better distribute provisions, were regarded in a favorable light. An unempathetic United States Congress refused to support measures deemed offensive to the army's Medical Department. A discouraged Olmsted returned to New York City not knowing what his future held. Newspaper reports made him aware that two mobs, now termed armies, were approaching each other near a stream called Bull Run, nestled in the Virginia foothills, adjacent to a hamlet known as Manassas.

AS NEWS OF the crushing defeat of Northern troops at Bull Run reached New York City, Olmsted hurried back to Washington. Demoralized soldiers, increasingly savage in their actions, filled the capital. Meanwhile, the Sanitary Commission members feared for the safety of Washington's citizens; Olmsted toured the streets and visited the army's ramshackle hospitals. "We are in a frightful condition here," he told Mary, "ten times as bad as anyone dare say publicly." He wondered if a less than unified Northern government, exemplified by Lincoln's administration and the nonstop carping of various state legislatures, was equal to the task of subduing a stubborn South. Only three weeks earlier, Olmsted saw Lincoln walking with some aides from the White House to the War Department building at Seventeenth Street and Pennsylvania Avenue. He condescendingly described the president to Mary as "dressed in a cheap & nasty French black cloth suit just out of a tight carpet bag."

Writing about the calamitous retreat at Bull Run, Olmsted told William Cullen Bryant, poet, co-owner of the *New York Evening Post*, and an acquaintance from Olmsted's days in New York's literary world, "that many officers, and even medical officers did act in the most dastardly manner there can be little question." Olmsted was convinced that radical measures needed to be taken: "A vast improvement in the character of our officers, and a complete reformation in respect of discipline, is a matter of vital necessity," he suggested to Bryant. Cautioning the newspaper editor that "we never shall succeed without it," Olmsted organized a team of seven young inspectors, including four physicians and one statistician, to determine what went wrong, medically and militarily, at Bull Run. Armed with a list of seventy-five questions that he prepared, the men were told to obtain answers from only the most intelligent officers and doctors of those regiments involved.

On September 5, 1861, almost seven weeks after Bull Run, Olmsted presented his *Report on the Demoralization of the Volunteers* to Bellows and the Sanitary Commission's board of managers. Like its author, the report was a model of common sense and practicality and was clearly intended to summon a visible reaction from the board members. Olmsted blamed the demoralization and rout of troops on the incompetency of political and military leadership. Speaking specifically to the three military members of the board, Olmsted asked, "When a man who has, through patriotic impulse, volunteered to serve his country in the field of battle, falls dangerously ill, or has a leg shot off, he cannot feel that it is right that an adequate supply—a generous supply—of proper clothing, delicate and nourishing food, wine, surgical attendance, nursing, or of anything else which will materially contribute to the reasonable assurance of saving his life, should be dependent on the success of any number of persons who are obliged to solicit the means to procure these articles and these services as if for charity." Olmsted concluded that the commission needed to expand its role beyond just investigating the army's sanitary conditions. "It will unquestionably become its duty to undertake a far larger business than its present organization is adapted to meet."[16]

Alexander Bache and the three army officers threatened to resign if the report was released to the public. Even George Templeton Strong noted in his diary that the report's "publication would have done mischief—would have retarded recruiting."[17] "My general Report somewhat startled them," Olmsted wrote to his wife. "I traced the disaster—demoralization of the troops which was the real disaster—not to Bull Run but to the imbecility of the government & the poorness of our system of government for this purpose. They all admit that I carry their convictions, but they dare not have it published—saying that it would be the severest & most effective attack ever made on the government." Bellows asked Olmsted to tone down his denunciations, and a revised, moderated account was printed. Writing to his father, Olmsted crowed, "So it will become a historical document. Meantime the practical measures which I urged have practically been all adopted and we have started a pretty row."

On the strength of Olmsted's survey, with its elaborate use of statistics, Bellows and the other civilian members of the Sanitary Commission were more convinced than ever that government agencies in charge of caring for the sick and wounded were lacking any sense of structure and function. The army's Medical Department was considered particularly inept. This was especially worrisome since Olmsted advised the members, "It is no longer right for the Commission to proceed on the supposition that it is meeting a wholly temporary emergency."[18]

The exigencies of four years of war would transform the role of the commission: From protector of the health of the volunteer army, it would expand into an agency existing outside official government circles but participating in virtually all wartime medical activities. For now, every military camp and hospital needed immediate in-depth inspection, and medical transport services had to be hurriedly organized. Issues of hygiene and sanitation were paramount, and the construction of modern military hospitals had to be addressed. But Olmsted realized that true remedies would take place only with the complete reform of the Medical Department. Only through an efficient medical corps could soldiers receive adequate clinical care. Soon, Olmsted and the Sanitary Commission began receiving the endorsement of various physicians and their professional societies.

Among the most prominent of these supporters was Stephen Smith, avowed crusader for improvements in public sanitation. Smith was the full-time editor and proprietor of the widely circulated *American Medical Times* and became the commission's best-known editorial booster. Older, more established medical journals rarely contained editorial comments.

Smith forged a new style by writing columns concerned with the role of medicine in modern society, including socioeconomic issues and wartime problems. Since he was a New Yorker, Smith devoted much of his time and editorial space to that city's health care problems—especially the need for legislation to improve sanitary conditions and for physicians to become active in the sanitary reform movement. In one of his earliest pieces of propaganda for the commission, Smith emphasized the role that physicians would have to willingly assume within this new organization:

> Unless the Commission is heartily sustained, unless thorough-bred physicians and surgeons, who are also high-toned men, are placed in positions of trust, and endowed with substantial rank and plenary powers, the same scenes of devastating pestilence will be witnessed among our troops which were witnessed in the Crimea, and which came near ruining the allied cause; and the same confusion, loss, and neglect of wounded, hopeless abandonment, and wasted courage, which complete the sad and bloody picture of our recent battle.[19]

CHAPTER FOUR

"He is our man"

ABRAHAM LINCOLN ISSUED A CALL for Northern troops on April 15, 1861. The first fully equipped unit sent south was the Sixth Massachusetts Militia, headquartered in Lowell. The eight hundred soldiers boarded a train in Boston, expecting to reach Washington two days later, in the late afternoon of April 19. At ten on the morning of April 19, Baltimore's President Street Station was in sight. But steam engines were not allowed to traverse certain sections of the city. The railroad cars were therefore separated and drawn individually along the Pratt Street tracks by horse. They were to be rejoined with a new engine a mile and a half away.

Baltimore was a city aflame with secessionist passions, and public officials feared that the presence of Northern troops, especially from a state regarded as the leader in the abolitionist movement, would create civil unrest. Indeed, a pro-slavery mob, poorly controlled by police, awaited the soldiers with threats and curses. The first nine railcars moved through the crowd unscathed, but horses were seized and anchors thrown upon the tracks as the last two cars came to a halt. Forced to scramble for their lives, the hundred-odd soldiers formed marching columns. Meanwhile, the mob threatened death to every "white nigger" and became a surging mass eight thousand strong.[1] People rushed toward Pratt Street, looting stores and armories, while several protesters further inflamed the crowd by crying, "Baltimoreans to the rescue! The war has commenced! The troops have fired upon the citizens! Our brothers are being murdered! Let us avenge them!"[2] Stones and bricks hailed down, shots were fired, pandemonium ensued, and by the time the Massachusetts men fought their way to the Camden Street depot, nine citizens and two soldiers lay dead, with another twenty-five of the militia wounded. One enlistee, Private Sumner Needham, was so severely injured by a brick to his forehead that he was taken to the Baltimore University Infirmary for medical treatment.

William Alexander Hammond, the infirmary's physician, was among the country's more acclaimed doctors, having received a major academic prize from the American Medical Association. Standing six feet two inches tall and weighing nearly 250 pounds, the thirty-two-year-old Hammond was a forceful, irascible, and vituperative man. Destined to become one of the era's best-known physicians, Hammond would sustain a career that closely paralleled the development of mid-nineteenth-century medicine. For instance, in a country distinguished by its indifference to the basic sciences, Hammond spent the 1850s conducting a series of physiological experiments that secured his reputation as one of the nation's earliest medical researchers. His 1865 decision to treat only patients suffering from diseases of the nervous system lent validity to the overall process of specialization in American medicine. In the mid-1880s, Hammond's avocation as an author led him to write nine widely praised works of fiction that highlighted the emergence of physicians as respected professionals who could make important contributions to nonmedical aspects of American cultural life. A man who later in his career supported rejuvenation therapy, spiritualism, and women's rights, Hammond was controversial, but he was also a leader, and individuals rallied to his causes.

For now, crowned by a thinning head of hair but with a full beard and mustache, Hammond was the newly named professor of anatomy and physiology at the University of Maryland and staff surgeon to the Baltimore University Infirmary. Standing over Private Needham, Hammond found the soldier comatose and hyperventilating from an injury to the head. The brick had fractured Needham's skull and caused bleeding into the brain. Needham's soft brain tissue was slowly being compressed by an expanding pool of blood. Knowing there was little to do except elevate the piece of indented skull bone, control the bleeding, and, hopefully, remove the offending blood clot, Hammond performed one of that era's most well-recognized surgical operations, trephination. Without anesthesia or any antiseptic measures whatever, Hammond took a trephine, or crown saw, a hollow metal cylinder with jagged teeth on the circular bottom edge, and went about removing a disk of bone from Needham's fractured skull. Grasping the ebony wooden handle of the slender instrument while assistants held the soldier's head motionless and pressing his considerable weight downward, Hammond twisted the saw back and forth to bore through the thick bone. Despite the surgeon's success in elevating the indented bone and removing the clotted blood, the soldier was apparently beyond hope, for according to Hammond's case report, "The symptoms were not relieved, and the patient died in a few hours."[3] Thus, the young militiaman became the Civil War's first casualty following a physician's attempt at surgical intervention.

It was seventeen years since Hammond began his formal medical studies as an apprentice in the New York City medical office of William Van Buren. Only nine years older than Hammond, Van Buren was a rising star in New York City medicine. It was this same Van Buren who in June 1861 would accompany Henry Bellows to Washington and help organize the United States Sanitary Commission. "Of lofty stature, well proportioned, gentle in his voice, bland and courtly in his manners, and scrupulously neat in his dress," according to Samuel Gross, professor of surgery at Philadelphia's Jefferson Medical College, Van Buren "operated well but not brilliantly, having an eye to the safety of his patient rather than to effect," wrote Gross.[4] Van Buren exerted a profound influence over Hammond's career and was always one of his closest confidants.

While serving as Van Buren's trainee, Hammond attended a two-year series of lectures at the Medical Department of the University of the City of New York, from which he received a doctor of medicine degree in 1848. At Van Buren's urging, Hammond tested successfully for a commission as a medical officer in the army's Medical Department. Assigned to frontier posts in the New Mexico and Kansas territories, he remained in the military for most of the 1850s. It was during these years, living in the uncharted West, that Hammond participated in several early natural history surveys, including those of the Smithsonian Institution and Philadelphia's Academy of Natural Sciences. A growing fascination with the natural sciences resulted in Hammond's establishing a physiology laboratory in Kansas to aid in his study of animal metabolism. His experimental successes stamped him as one of the country's first medical scientists and would set him apart from his fellow physicians.

Hammond also became involved in local politics while stationed at Fort Riley in Kansas Territory, which was at the front line of the nation's struggle over slavery. As pro- and antislavery settlers poured into the territory, land speculators flocked to the area and local politics drew everyone's attention. One controversial project centered around Pawnee, a site conveniently located near Fort Riley that some thought would become the state capital. Hammond and a group of men including Andrew Reeder, a Pennsylvanian appointed by President Franklin Pierce to be the first governor of Kansas Territory, established the Pawnee Town Association. As the land was carved up with abandon, abolitionist forces began to spread rumors that the moderately proslavery Reeder was taking advantage of his powerful position. Charges were soon brought against Reeder, and a trial resulted in his losing the acreage he received in the deal, based somewhat on the testimony of a politically naïve Hammond, who agreed that the Pawnee land project had become corrupt. Hammond found himself with a lifelong political enemy.

It was also while working on the western frontier that Hammond began to suffer disabling neurological attacks that apparently rendered him among other things cataleptic. A co-worker described Hammond treating a soldier's dislocated leg when the malady overcame him and "in a minute or two he was helpless, speechless, and . . . quite senseless." After thirty minutes, Hammond felt well enough to resume his duties. Then, standing by the patient, he was overcome a second time and became "entirely insensible" for an hour. Hammond initially speculated that these attacks were due to fatty degeneration of his heart or an unknown spinal cord disorder. He would later attest that "mental emotions and physical exertions both produce an attack."[5] Whether there was an underlying pathological basis to Hammond's problem or it was more hysterical in nature is unknown, but this on-again, off-again disorder affected him for years to come. From temporary paralysis of his legs to outright nervous breakdowns, Hammond was periodically forced to take weeks and even months off from routine activities.

In October 1857, Hammond had an episode so disabling that he was deemed unable to perform his clinical responsibilities and was granted extended leave from military duties. Back in Philadelphia with his family, he recuperated gradually as he adjusted to a more leisurely daily schedule. Increasingly involved with Philadelphia's sophisticated scientific community, Hammond began to conduct research experiments on a wide variety of topics and spent considerable time organizing a citywide biological society. By May 1858, he felt well enough to make a long-awaited trip to Europe. Traveling for almost three months, Hammond met the Continent's leading physicians and also inspected various public and military hospitals. Upon his return to America, he was regarded as an expert on hospital construction.

Seeking to continue the more settled life of a civilian practitioner, Hammond resigned from the United States Army's Medical Department in fall 1859 and moved to Baltimore, where he accepted the professorship of anatomy and physiology at the University of Maryland. Despite his disapproval of the city's secessionist leanings, Hammond stayed at his new position until shortly after the riots of April 19, 1861, and the death of Private Needham. After turning down an offer to serve as a physician in a Southern militia regiment, Hammond decided to show his loyalty to the North by reenlisting in the army. He appeared before a medical board, again easily passed the army's entrance examination, and was assigned to the Department of the Shenandoah.

Charged with the organization of general hospitals at Chambersburg, Pennsylvania, and Hagerstown and Frederick, Maryland, Hammond relentlessly requisitioned supplies from Surgeon General Finley's office and medical purveyor Satterlee's bureau. Though considered a nuisance, Hammond was quickly recognized for his managerial abilities. In September 1861, he was reassigned to organize a military hospital in Baltimore, and he began calling for such reformist measures as the employment of civilian cooks, female nurses, and medical students. Creating controversy wherever he was stationed, Hammond, renowned medical scientist, budding politician, and closet abolitionist, soon attracted the attention of members of the U.S. Sanitary Commission, especially Frederick Olmsted.

By late summer 1861, Olmsted was convinced that the Medical Department, under Surgeon General Finley's brief tenure, had not demonstrated sufficient interest in the basic principles of camp hygiene or in the science of sanitation. Besides an obvious personality conflict between Olmsted and Finley, the former having described the latter as a "self-satisfied, supercilious, bigoted blockhead,"[6] Finley did little to promote his own cause. When given an opportunity to lobby Secretary of War Cameron for additional military medical personnel, an organizational reform strongly urged by the Sanitary Commission, Finley revealed both his antipathy toward the commission's aims and a misunderstanding of wartime medical needs. Finley requested just twenty additional physicians for the Medical Department and fifty medical students to serve as wound dressers, and he proposed to employ civilian hospital attendants, but, in his own words, "not exceeding one to every ten beds."[7] Parsimonious to the extreme, he proudly indicated that for the fiscal year ending June 1861, the Medical Department managed to spend less than its budget. With little to recommend him for the surgeon general's post except his long career as an undistinguished army surgeon, Finley was, according to George Templeton Strong, the Sanitary Commission's secretary, "utterly ossified and useless."[8]

WITHIN A WEEK after the July 1861 debacle at Bull Run, Lincoln signed two acts authorizing the enlistment of one million three-year men. Eager volunteers crowded recruiting offices as newly formed regiments poured into the Washington area. In what was regarded as a bold military move, Lincoln summoned thirty-four-year-old George B. McClellan to take command of what would, hopefully, become the North's reinvigorated army. An 1846 graduate of West Point and veteran of the Mexican War, McClellan had served on an investigative board sent to Europe to study the conduct of the war in the Crimea. After resigning his military commission in 1857, McClellan settled into civilian life in Cincinnati as chief engineer and vice president of the Illinois Central Railroad and later president of the eastern branch of the Mississippi & Ohio Railroad. When the Civil War broke out, he was named major general of a three months' militia by the governor of Ohio but was rapidly promoted and placed in command of the Union army's Department of Ohio.

In late May, McClellan sent a small Union contingent across the Ohio River to disperse a gathering force of Confederate sympathizers. Following a number of rapid military successes, all gained in the space of eight days, McClellan's troops gained control of a portion of pro-slavery Virginia and renamed this liberated land the abolitionist-leaning West Virginia. Thus, Lincoln was presented with his first wholly successful military campaign and America had its newest war hero, complete with slicked-down jet black hair, drooping mustache, chin tuft, and wisp of a goatee.

McClellan was a superb organizer, and troops rallied around his every word. He instilled discipline and pride and, once called up by Lincoln, methodically forged the North's Army of the Potomac into a respectable fighting machine. To the members of the Sanitary Commission, it was McClellan's family background that proved particularly interesting, for the new commander in chief's father and brother were both physicians. Olmsted hoped that McClellan's natural sympathy for his army's health care plight would spell the end of Surgeon General Finley's unfortunate tenure. On a personal note, Olmsted's half-sisters, Mary and Bertha, were lifelong friends of McClellan's wife, Ellen.

By early September, Olmsted and Bellows had initiated a covert campaign to depose Finley, install a new surgeon general, and completely reform the Medical Department. Confidential letters were dispatched to McClellan and Secretary of War Cameron calling for Finley's retirement and seeking to expand McClellan's control over the medical care of his troops. McClellan was specifically asked to use his newfound influence to encourage the War Department to reform the Medical Department and to restructure the administration of medical affairs in the Army of the Potomac. Noting that stodgy septuagenarians controlled the Medical Department, Bellows wrote that the department's business "is usually carried on in a manner & style becoming a country apothecary, rather than a vast military Bureau." Taking direct aim at Cameron, Bellows reminded McClellan, "In the end the Nation will hold the Sec'y of War chiefly responsible for the slackness, the inability, & the defects of this Bureau."[9]

Particularly irksome to Olmsted and Bellows was Rule No. 1103 of the 1861 *Revised Regulations for the Army of the United States* ("Ambulances, and all the means of transport continue in charge of the proper officers of the Quartermaster's Department [Corps], under the control of the commanding officers"),[10] which divided responsibility between the Medical Department and the Quartermaster Corps. Medical officers might have been in charge of the wounded, but all two- and four-wheeled ambulances needed for evacuation and transportation of the injured and sick remained under Quartermaster General Montgomery Meigs's control.

At a private meeting on September 11, Olmsted and Bellows met with Cameron and McClellan to discuss the Sanitary Commission's requests. The secretary of war told Bellows, "You have never asked anything of me yet that you have not got—and you never will."[11] Listening intently, Cameron and McClellan seemed in apparent agreement with the commission's goals. But as Bellows and Olmsted would soon learn, Cameron was not to be trusted.

A former U.S. senator from Pennsylvania, Cameron was a Republican Party stalwart known for his heavy-handedness in political dealings. Corruption and mismanagement marked his tenure at the War Department, so much so that the cynical definition of an honest politician as "one who when he is bought will stay bought"[12] has always been associated with him. Double dealing was part of Cameron's political nature. In a characteristic move, he placed Olmsted and Bellows in an extremely embarrassing position when he gave Surgeon General Finley their confidential letter asking for his retirement. Finley was incensed, and his intense dislike of these civilian interlopers only increased. Thanks to Cameron's backroom machinations, McClellan sent Olmsted and Bellows a letter rejecting what they believed had previously been agreed to. According to the general, since the commission had no suitable candidate to replace Finley, it was best to leave him in place. Regarding purely medical matters, McClellan suggested he might be amenable to changing certain established routines within the Army of the Potomac.

Olmsted's and Bellows's reactions to McClellan's reply were a study in contrasts. Bellows, the more phlegmatic of the two, urged caution, while the impulsive Olmsted wanted immediate action. "I am not satisfied with the way things are going in any direction—least of all, perhaps, in the medical. I believe men are dying daily for the want of a tolerable Surgeon General. The whole business is miserably bad from the start," wrote an exasperated Olmsted. "It is a paltry business to be trying to remedy or palliate only details. This morning at daylight, the surgeon of a regiment which was under orders for an attack reported he had no ambulance and no stretcher and so on."

In October, Olmsted pressed his growing concern about the army's lackluster ambulance service when he warned McClellan that in the event of a battle, "the present want of any organized ambulance system, would fix a just stain upon our National Character for humanity and providence of life."[13] Olmsted attached a report that harshly criticized the two-wheeled "Finley" ambulance, most commonly used by the Army of the Potomac, as being particularly painful to wounded soldiers. Designed by Finley himself, it was flimsily constructed out of wood. The wagon contained two removable stretchers with a chassis resting on four elliptical metal springs. The least bit of motion was excruciating to an injured individual. Wounded men begged to be taken off Finley ambulances, and injured officers refused to get in. Finley's folly only strengthened the commission's resolve to force him out of office.

By mid-autumn of 1861, William Hammond's name was being circulated within the Sanitary Commission as a possible replacement for Finley. Olmsted had previously written to Bellows that he wished Charles Tripler, medical director of McClellan's Army of the Potomac, "could be shipped off to Missouri, Hammond put in his place, Van Buren made S. Genl."[14] However, William Van Buren demurred, and it was his protégé Hammond who became the commission's choice for the Medical Department's top job. According to Charles Stillé, the commission's historian, Hammond's "reputation was not merely that of a man of science and professional skill,"[15] but his military career was marked by an outstanding performance as a medical officer. Hammond's observation of European civilian and military hospitals in 1858, his knowledge of hospital construction, his military administrative work over the summer and fall of 1861, and his long-standing friendship with Sanitary Commission board member Van Buren recommended him as the individual of choice.

Secretary of War Cameron, however, took a strong dislike to the young doctor, spurred by a personal vendetta against the Hammond family. Before being named secretary of war, Cameron, the embodiment of boss rule in Pennsylvania, ran politics out of Harrisburg, the state capital. Hammond's father had been politically active in that locale, and the remnants of a Cameron-Hammond political squabble resurfaced when William Hammond's name was brought to Cameron's attention. With Cameron expressing disdain for any of Hammond's accomplishments, the latter's nomination became a tenuous proposition. Olmsted grew increasingly annoyed with Cameron's and Finley's actions and realized that the more diplomatic efforts of his fellow commissioners had produced few positive results. Writing to Bellows, Olmsted admitted that his "convictions sometimes boil up in exaggerated statements of what can be said." However, he added, "I really think I would die satisfied with my life, tomorrow, if I could put a live strong man with a humane big heart also—at the head of the Medical bureau—& give him a clear swing."

At nine A.M. on Thursday, October 17, 1861, Henry Bellows, Frederick Olmsted, George Templeton Strong, and several New York City bigwigs were ushered into the Cabinet Room of the White House. Having been granted a private audience with President Lincoln, they harangued the president for two hours about the inefficiencies of the Medical Department and their displeasure with Surgeon General Finley and Secretary of War Cameron. Clearly, the commission members had a delicate political task confronting them, considering the commission's official status as special adviser to the very department under scrutiny. Olmsted wrote to his wife that the exasperated chief of state "appeared older, more settled (or a man of more character) than I had before thought. . . . He was very awkward & ill at ease in attitude," according to Olmsted, "but spoke readily with a good vocabulary, & with directness and point."[16] Lincoln questioned the commission's motives. Strong noted in his diary that a seemingly annoyed president asked the commissioners whether they wanted "to run the machine."[17] Taken aback, the commissioners realized that any attempts at medical reform through official administration channels would prove an outright failure. Two weeks later, Olmsted took a new tack.

To ALL WHO knew him, thirty-one-year-old Cornelius Agnew's manage-rial abilities were as highly regarded as his ophthalmologic skills. Slen-der and dark, this son of a wealthy New York City merchant and youngest member of the Sanitary Commission's executive board quickly became one of Olmsted's major backers. Following the disappointing October meeting with Lincoln, Olmsted sought the young physician's advice regarding a strategy to discredit Finley. His intent was to plant stories in the recently founded *New York World*, a popular and respected daily. It was a nefarious scheme on the part of Olmsted, who knew the power of public relations from his work on Central Park. Manton Mar-ble, the *World*'s twenty-six-year-old managing editor, was Agnew's friend, and following some coaxing, he agreed to the plan. Soon, well-publicized exposés of military medical life appeared in the *World* with Cornelius Agnew's byline, while Marble wrote a series of editorials praising the work of the Sanitary Commission.

Much to Olmsted's dismay, other papers rushed to Finley's defense. In an editorial on November 25, Henry Raymond of *The New York Times* noted that Finley, although accused of allowing incompetent sur-geons to enter the military and of ignoring science in the construction of wartime hospitals, "has had a degree of experience in the medical care of armies to which none of the gentlemen composing the Sanitary Com-mission can for a moment pretend." Regarding the *World*'s recent charge that the "loss of life in the general hospitals of our army was due to neglect of sanitary precautions," the *Times* placed all responsibility on the Sanitary Commission's inefficiencies:

> The Sanitary Commission, which has assumed the special care of the camps, has it in its power to prevent a very large propor-tion of these deaths, by increasing its vigilance in urging sani-tary precautions there, and especially by causing the removal of the sick to the general hospitals, before all hope of their recov-ery has fled. This is the appropriate field of their duties—and they should never have allowed themselves to divert it for the more ostentatious service of passing resolutions and attempting to supersede the regular medical authorities of the service.

Soon a vitriolic letter to the *Times*'s editor, signed "Truth," attacked the commissioners, who were said to "have no more to do with the San-itary Commission's operations than the Sultan of Turkey." Furthermore, according to "Truth," any commission plans for building hospitals were proposed "only by the poorest kind of brains." Two days later, "Truth" struck again: "Surgeon General Finley understands the Sanitary Commissioners, and in the outset placed an effectual check upon their ambition—they, therefore, wish him out of the way." In his own letter to the *Times*, Olmsted attempted to rebut these accusations, insisting that three hundred individual inspections of camps by fifteen fully qualified men had just been sent to the War Department. Olmsted suggested that instead of hiding under the cloak of anonymity, "Truth" visit his office to verify that the Sanitary Commission was sending daily contributions valued at more than $1,000 to military hospitals. Undeterred, "Truth" charged in a further letter to the *Times* that Olmsted himself was never seen visiting any hospitals and that if he had only done so, he could "easily learn that the general hospitals in the City of Washington and vicinity have received but little, very little, of this 'thousand dollars a day' contributions."[18]

It was just prior to this war of printed words that General Thomas West Sherman organized an expedition against Southern military fortifications on Port Royal, an island lying off the South Carolina coast. With increasing numbers of Union troops encamped on Port Royal and one-third of Sherman's army already on the sick list, the area's medical director requested that a general hospital be built. Sherman concurred, but when the matter was brought before Finley, he countermanded the proposal based on his mistaken belief that South Carolina's mild winters made hospital construction an unnecessary expense. Little did it matter to Finley that four sick soldiers, housed in noninsulated tents, had frozen to death in the supposedly temperate South Carolina climate. When news of Finley's decision reached New York City, Horace Greeley, the well-known publisher of the powerful *New York Tribune*, decided he too should join in the attack on the surgeon general. In a scathing editorial, the *Tribune* noted that the Medical Department was "not accused of mis-feasance or malfeasance, but of non-feasance. It seems to have done nothing since the war began. It is simply inefficient and inert."[19]

Despite Greeley's support, Olmsted found himself and the commission the object of growing criticism. Writing to Bellows, Olmsted complained, "We have constant evidence of the harm the *Times'* articles are doing."[20] Even Olmsted's personal attempt at damage control, by arranging a private meeting with the *Times*'s Raymond, proved unsuccessful in convincing the editor that "Truth" was not accurately describing the commission's work. Olmsted recognized that the attacks by "Truth" had to be stopped and the tide of adverse publicity turned to the commission's side.

Following some background sleuthing, Olmsted and his associates discovered that "Truth" was twenty-six-year-old Elizabeth Powell and that the forty-one-year-old unhappily married Raymond was having an illicit love affair with her. As a volunteer nurse in a Washington military hospital, Powell had become impressed with Surgeon General Finley's solicitousness toward patients on his various visits to her facility. Unfortunately, she was less enamored of agents from the Sanitary Commission. Powell claimed the commissioners were unwilling to issue any shirts or socks to her hospital and, in what she perceived to be a major breach of ethics, had refused to answer questions about the commission's finances.

Whether Powell or Raymond was the instigator is unknown, but Raymond's infatuation with her certainly led to the publishing of her letters. As Olmsted wrote Bellows, "Miss Powell is doing much mischief propagating falsehood and slander very industriously. It is very desirable to squelch her." And squelched she was, when Olmsted saw to it that Mrs. Raymond was made aware of her husband's philandering. A few months later, George Templeton Strong provided some lively gossip to Olmsted. "I hear that Miss P. is found out," he wrote, "and that Raymond has had a grand scene with that lady which culminated in intervention by the police, who coerced the lady to quit Mr. Raymond's premises."[21]

WHAT ALSO HELPED turn around public opinion was a hastily composed ninety-six-page history of the Sanitary Commission's day-to-day and financial activities. Written at a time when the Sanitary Commission's actions and goals remained largely unknown to the public, Olmsted's *Report to the Secretary of War* was political lobbying at its best. Candid and exhaustive and leaked to the press, this white paper covered all aspects of a volunteer's camp life, including clothing, cooking, personal hygiene, and even recreation. More important, Olmsted presented statistics obtained by the commission's fifteen camp and hospital inspectors, and analyzed by an actuary, regarding sickness and death as well as detailed discussions about qualifications of physicians and the staffing, supplying, and construction of military hospitals. Uncompromising in its conclusions, the report, without specifically mentioning the surgeon general, implicitly criticized the Medical Department for its failures in assuring better care.

On December 21, 1861, the day of the report's release, Olmsted told Bellows, "I want that as soon as practicable after this is out, there should be a grand simultaneous expression of confidence in the Commission, which shall completely counteract the effect which has unquestionably been mischievous of the *Times'* & other attacks upon us."

Warning Bellows that "there is a *systematic* war on the Commission," Olmsted implored him to "get the editors *committed*."[22]

Within a few days, Greeley's *Tribune* and Marble's *World* showered editorial praise on Olmsted and the Sanitary Commission's past, present, and future plans. Joining in the flattery were two other important New York dailies—William Cullen Bryant's *Post* and James Gordon Bennett's *Herald*. Soon Raymond grudgingly agreed that the commission had done more than just quarrel with Medical Department physicians and volunteer nurses. As a *Times* editor noted, Olmsted's report was a description of "humanity ministering to wants and sufferings that would become horrors but for such merciful ministrations."[23]

OLMSTED MANAGED TO temporarily shield the Sanitary Commission from the ramifications of its criticisms of Finley and the Medical Bureau. But he and others continued to believe that Lincoln's administration, Congress, citizens, and even physicians remained wary of the commission's intentions to spark military medical reform. There was some truth in their concern. A damning editorial in Philadelphia's *Medical and Surgical Reporter* suggested that a financially flush commission would do little more than "make a cozy nest for some of its own adherents."[24] In his determination to thwart such thinking, Olmsted turned to grassroots political lobbying. Working with William Hammond, who was on military assignment administering hospitals in Baltimore, Olmsted had the politically savvy physician draft a bill promoting military medical reform to submit to influential congressmen and senators.

Seeking a revitalized Medical Department, Hammond and Olmsted called for the creation of a new group of medical officers (one inspector general and eight medical inspectors) who would assume responsibility for the sanitary condition of hospitals, military camps, and officer quarters. The bill further required that military hospital construction be based on plans recognized as modern and scientific by European standards and that the transportation service of the sick and wounded be switched from the Quartermaster Corps to the Medical Department. A revamped ambulance system, under the surgeon general's control, would also be organized. Finally, Hammond and Olmsted argued that merit and scientific accomplishments, rather than seniority, should be the primary criteria for future military medical appointments.

Among the most powerful politicians the commission approached was Senator Henry Wilson, a stocky man with a ruddy complexion and gray hair, who achieved prominence in Massachusetts politics successively as a Whig, a Free-Soiler, a Know-Nothing, and finally a Republican.

Wilson would later serve as vice president under President Grant, but for now he was chairman of the Senate Committee on Military Affairs. A consummate politician and independent-minded legislator, Wilson was considered an able debater, which is surprising since he had an inarticulate style that betrayed the poor education of his impoverished youth.

In December 1861, Wilson introduced Senate Bill 97, which embodied most of the major reforms sought by Hammond, Olmsted, and the Sanitary Commission. However, the bill's provisions proved controversial. So slow was its progress that Olmsted wrote to one of his fellow commissioners in January 1862, "There is no change in the drift of our affairs here and the machinery is working steadily. Evidences of virulent opposition and hatred increase. Slander and libels float and lodge in the majority of uninformed minds."[25]

While congressional action plodded along, the Sanitary Commission faced internal dissension. Divisions within the organization over the Wilson bill caused Olmsted to cancel a scheduled board meeting in January. Knowing that the executive board's three army men, George Cullum, Alexander Shiras, and Robert Wood, would oppose any attempt at outright Medical Department restructuring, Olmsted suggested that committee members come to Washington to lobby individually rather than as a group. Olmsted's ploy produced one significant effect. Cullum, Shiras, and Wood, recognizing their inability to control the board's drive toward military medical reform, quietly disappeared from the Sanitary Commission scene.

Another unanticipated benefit of the lobbying effort was Lincoln's asking Secretary of War Simon Cameron to resign in January 1862. Cameron had always been heavy-handed in his political dealings, and there was growing concern in Washington that his cronies had reaped enormous profits through favoritism in the awarding of government contracts, particularly in the Medical Department. As an astonished Lincoln was made more aware of Cameron's dishonesty and inappropriateness, egged on by Olmsted's and the commission's lobbying efforts, he requested Cameron's resignation. In mid-January, Edwin McMasters Stanton replaced Cameron as United States secretary of war. Stanton was a Democrat, a past attorney general under President James Buchanan, and a rude, vindictive, and violent-tempered person. Paranoid to the point that he carried a sheathed dagger under his waistcoat, Stanton was also regarded as an extremely hardworking, thoroughly honest, and able lawyer. Lincoln must have seen in him a genuine patriot and the makings of an outstanding war minister. Stanton, an asthmatic of medium height and stocky build who wore a patriarchal-looking beard of coarse,

graying whiskers, would greatly improve the efficiency of the War Department and eliminate the fraud and mismanagement that characterized his predecessor's efforts.

At first, Olmsted and other members of the Sanitary Commission
were pleased with Stanton's appointment. Three days after taking office,
the new secretary of war and General McClellan visited the Sanitary
Commission's central headquarters at 244 F Street in Washington and
promised to exert their influence on various congressmen to take action
on behalf of the medical reform bill. However, political matters suddenly
worsened when McClellan inexplicably delayed issuing an order recognizing the Sanitary Commission's right to inspect camps and hospitals.
With dwindling funds and medical reform on the distant horizon, Henry
Bellows, the commission's president, and George Templeton Strong,
treasurer, contemplated ending their organization's existence. So bad
was the situation that several of the commissioners prepared to submit
their resignations until Olmsted single-handedly talked them out of it.

With Hammond politically languishing in his new assignment as
medical purveyor of General William Starke Rosecrans's Union army of
occupation of West Virginia, Olmsted and other commissioners waited
impatiently for some measure of military medical reform as congressional hearings commenced for Henry Wilson's bill. Wartime injuries
and deaths mounted, and the proposed legislation began to receive a
great deal of attention as members of the Senate Committee on Military
Affairs listened to testimony on the merits of not only Wilson's proposal, but almost fifty other bills on the same subject. As Senator James
Nesmith of Oregon pointed out, "Every man who had any connection
with the military service in a medical capacity, seemed to be willing to
enlighten the committee on the subject of medicine and on the subject
of the proper organization of the corps of surgeons."[26] After six weeks of
discussion, Wilson's bill emerged from committee somewhat weaker
than the Sanitary Commission's original proposal. Still, it provided a
new structure for the future direction of medical work in the army—and
most important, it would impose uniform clinical standards on practitioners at a time when American physicians were accustomed to absolute noninterference.

The compromise legislation, renumbered Senate Bill 188, was introduced to the full floor of the Senate on the morning of February 27,
1862. Meeting in what is now called the Old Senate Chamber, dressed in
three-quarter-length black frock coats, the forty-two senators argued
passionately for and against the notion of medical reform. Much like the
troublesome question of individual states' rights versus collective

national interests that led to the Civil War itself, the spirited debate was centered on the vexing concern of individual versus group medical freedoms. Was it proper to permit national authorities to establish standards or otherwise control the clinical care provided to troops recruited, organized, and equipped on a local level? By whom would a sick and wounded soldier feel most comfortable being treated—a physician from his hometown who accompanied him into battle or a government-appointed practitioner totally unknown to the soldier?

James Grimes of Iowa noted that the vast majority of soldiers were volunteers. Therefore, he believed, "they would rather be physicked and dosed by their own neighbors and their own friends, men whose reputation they knew at home, who had been, in many instances, their own family physicians, who had reputations in their States." Countering this argument was Oregon's Nesmith: "To carry out that idea, every soldier must be permitted to take his own doctor into the Army with him. I know that in private life, it is very convenient for a man to select his own physician; but the thing is impossible and impracticable in the military service. The soldier must submit to discipline, and the Government must make provision for his care in sickness and in health." Nesmith pointedly added, "I myself very much doubt whether the Senator from Iowa, with all his knowledge—enlightened as I admit he is—would today be qualified to select for himself the best physician in the country; and I apprehend that if he was sick he would be about as likely to fare well—to be treated or to have his disease well treated—by a physician who was selected for him by the Government as by one whom he had selected for himself."[27]

In addition to determining the proper balance of individual versus group medical freedoms, the senators were at loggerheads on how to select the best men to fill the important new positions of medical inspectors and surgeon general. An eager William Hammond was Olmsted and the Sanitary Commission's choice for surgeon general; however, anticipating difficulty in securing his nomination (or that of other suitable persons), the commissioners attempted to place precautionary measures into Wilson's bill. For example, since Hammond and other career medical officers had demonstrated their clinical acumen by passing the army's difficult entrance examination, the commissioners suggested restricting these important appointments to members of the army's regular corps of physicians. This subterfuge caused confusion and political strife.

Whether or not Wilson was entirely on the commission's side during the effort to pass Medical Department reform is a matter of political perception. For instance, the senator agreed with merit-based appointees, and he approved of Hammond, but he opposed several of Olmsted's other requests, particularly the formation of an independent ambulance corps. Olmsted did not know what to make of the strong-willed Wilson and soon grew to distrust him, counting him among a group of administration leaders he described as "liars, pettifoggers and sneaks."[28]

Olmsted might not have appreciated Wilson's political machinations, but the senator remained true to his word to attempt to limit important appointments to career officers in the medical corps of the regular army. The majority of the senators, however, were not so accepting of this position. "I see no justice in it, no reason in it. I think it would be very impolitic. I think it ought to be opened to the volunteer corps," argued Lafayette Foster of Connecticut. Agreeing with Foster was Iowa's Grimes: "I do not want to say that if the President finds a man who stands head and shoulders among his fellows, a perfect Saul among the prophets, he shall not have the power to bring that man into the service, and to secure his abilities to the country." William Fessenden of Maine concurred: "I say if you want good officers enlarge your circle. If you want the best men you can get—and you do want them, or else the bill ought not to pass at all—do not confine the selection to a little knot of men, many of whom have not had the experience they should have had." Wilson had the final say and cautioned, "There are brigade surgeons of volunteers whom have, during the last five years, attended the sick-beds of more persons than all the surgeons of the Army have attended, and by the side of whose experience the experience of our Army surgeons is dwarfed into utter insignificance." However, he continued, "I think if you throw this door open, you will not obtain the services of these eminent gentlemen, who deserve all that can be bestowed upon them, certainly, but you are more likely to have the services of persons who have gone with the volunteer forces simply to advance their own personal interests, and certainly, we have had some of that class."[29]

THE ISSUES DEBATED before the Senate were complicated by a pervasive lack of clinical unanimity within the field of medicine. Physicians in the United States in 1862 simply did not form a cohesive professional community based on shared practice experiences, nor was there communal agreement as to what was accepted medical fact. Indeed, there were so many competing systems of health care and such a disparate range of clinical beliefs that whether it was in Massachusetts or Ohio, Philadelphia or Chicago, an urban setting or a rural one, there was no scientific basis on which to judge the merits of a medical man or his particular system of therapeutics. With regulars and sectarians, represented by allopaths and homeopaths, respectively, engaged in nonstop diatribes as to who was medically correct, the lay public had no reliable criteria to determine clinical successes. As a consequence, elected officials, with little knowledge of medicine, were similarly divided.

With battlefield and camp casualties mounting, the well-organized homeopathic physicians seized on the senatorial hearings to express their clinical differences with regular physicians and demand equal footing in the allopathic-dominated United States Army's Medical Department. Senator Grimes of Iowa, a longtime supporter of all things homeopathic, was about to introduce a bill placing some of the military hospitals in Washington under the sole jurisdiction of homeopathic adherents. Allopaths responded with pointed denunciations. An editorial in the *Boston Medical and Surgical Journal* termed homeopathy "one of the grossest and most barefaced systems of quackery that has ever disgraced the annals of medicine." The anonymous writer went on to argue that homeopaths wanted to be included in the medical corps only for the "prestige which such a public recognition of the claims of homeopathy would necessarily gain for it."[30]

Regular, also known as orthodox, medical institutions petitioned Congress and protested the potential employment of homeopaths as army physicians. The New York Academy of Medicine, for example, passed a set of resolutions in mid-January 1862 objecting to any use of homeopaths in the army by pointing to the exclusion of homeopathy in European armies. New York City's Stephen Smith, an allopathic surgeon, was particularly blunt: "I know of no system so indefensible as that which is engaging the attention of our honorable Senators." According to Smith, "Viewing the homeopathic system of practice from a rational, scientific standpoint, it must be regarded as the least worthy attention of any now popular in this country."[31]

Matters were further muddied by the senators' own uncertainty about the actual differences between allopathy and homeopathy. Was it the specific remedies employed, the size of the dose, or how the medicines were given? "I believe the difference between the two systems is the size of the dose, the homeopathists give less," said Nesmith. Grimes disagreed: "They have different medicines entirely." No one was certain as to the answers, least of all the senators debating the question. Confusion reigned as Nesmith related an incident that had occurred just a few days earlier during the hearings of the Senate Committee on Military Affairs. He told of how a spiritualist had come to the committee to "organize a corps of spiritual rappers [singers] to draw wagons out of the mud." Nesmith said that the individual even volunteered his corps of rappers to be used as clairvoyants. Moreover, the spiritualist was said to have sworn before the senators that "there were a great many spiritualists in the Army, and that that class of persons ought to be provided for by the selection of mediums." Declaring that it would be sheer insanity to "introduce clairvoyancers, spiritual rappers, homeopathists, and practicers of all other systems of medicine that are known at the present day, in order to gratify the caprice of every soldier who may happen to be in the Army," Nesmith lumped homeopathy with other fringe sects.

Of the allopaths' many arguments against homeopaths, the most valid was the need for simplicity and uniformity. Regardless of whose system it was, army surgeons and their patients were more likely to benefit from a standardized system of care. It was the very same concept of discipline and standards that the Sanitary Commission was advocating for the whole of American society. If forced to choose among competing therapeutic systems, especially in a high-pressure environment like a military hospital, physicians might make inappropriate split-second decisions. As the bill's sponsor, Henry Wilson pointed out, "I take it the fact is that the old school of practitioners have the control of the army's medical board, and they are jealous of the admission of any medical men of the new school." Admitting that "there is quite a difference in their practice," Wilson reminded his fellow senators, "If it were desirable to bring in medical men of the new school, as we have been asked to do this year by a large number of petitioners, some of them men of great eminence, the difficulty would be in having these diverse systems of practice in the Army. It would lead to great confusion. I think it better to have it all the one or all the other."[32]

At the end of a very long day, a roll-call vote was held on the question of limiting appointments of medical inspectors and the surgeon general to career medical officers. Wilson and the Sanitary Commission's position was defeated, 26 yeas to 16 nays. Senate debate on medical reform ended as the remainder of Wilson's legislation, including the creation of a new corps of medical inspectors with the power to impose uniform clinical standards, was passed essentially intact and sent to the House of Representatives. Allopathic physicians remained in control of the Medical Department, but their civilian political battles with homeopaths would only intensify.

The political fortunes of Olmsted and the Sanitary Commission suddenly seemed brighter, although Surgeon General Finley continued to try to thwart the commission's aims. In March, the now sixty-four-year-old Finley denied the Sanitary Commission any further use of

Medical Department records and banned inspectors associated with the commission from entering army hospitals. Finley termed the inspectors "irresponsible and ignorant pretenders"[33] who published distortions of the truth to embarrass him personally. Not unexpectedly, Finley also directed a behind-the-scenes attempt to derail the Wilson bill by dispatching army doctors to Congress to lobby against medical reform's very existence.

While the congressional hearings were in session, Finley appointed John Neill, an eminent surgeon from Philadelphia, to supervise the preparation of several army facilities for the care of sick and wounded. Neill had previously ingratiated himself with the surgeon general when, following the April 1861 fall of Fort Sumter, he took it upon himself to convert a civilian building in Philadelphia into a military-style hospital. Neill went so far as to telegraph Finley asking for authority to establish it as a branch of the United States Army. Unbeknownst to Neill, he had a well-connected professional enemy, a physician from Pittsburgh who was a longtime friend to Secretary of War Stanton. Learning of Neill's new position, the Pittsburgh doctor wrote Stanton asking how he could endorse Surgeon General Finley's choice of such a medical incompetent as John Neill. Stanton referred the supposedly private letter to Finley, expecting the surgeon general to investigate the charges and report back to him. Finley, however, had the letter copied and forwarded to Neil. The Philadelphian promptly instituted a suit for libel against the Pittsburgher, and the latter then wrote a second letter to Stanton informing him of the predicament. Stanton summoned Finley to his office, and according to the surgeon general's account, the following exchange took place: "Mr. Surgeon General, what has become of the letter I referred to you about the appointment of Dr. Neil as superintendent of Hospitals?" "Mr. Secretary, I sent the letter to Dr. Neill for report." "How dare you, sir, to so dispose of a letter I sent to you?" "The letter, Mr. Secretary, took the ordinary official course. There was no dare about it, and I do not permit myself to be spoken to in such a manner." "You don't, hey, I will show you about daring and permitting. Go back to your office and wait until you hear from me."[34] With Stanton's volatile temper unleashed, Finley was ordered to Boston to await reassignment. There the old soldier campaigned unsuccessfully to regain his post. He even appealed to President Lincoln for official protection against Stanton's injustice. Learning of the Neill affair, Olmsted and other commissioners stepped up their own calls for Finley's dismissal and Hammond's appointment. Disgraced and without formal redress, Finley chose a forced retirement effective mid-April 1862.

Finley's departure, although serendipitous, was an enormous victory for Olmsted and the Sanitary Commission. However, their most important triumph, final congressional approval of medical reform legislation, still faced political difficulties. On March 17, Henry Bellows, president of the Sanitary Commission, appeared before the House of Representatives' Committee on Military Defense. Despite Bellows's eloquence in detailing the suffering of soldiers from inadequate medical care, the commission's intentions were still viewed with suspicion. As one congressman stated, "I am informed that all these difficulties with regard to the medical department have arisen because of a conflict between the medical department and the sanitary commission; that the sanitary commission—a body I do not know how organized, or by whom appointed—have assumed to themselves to direct the medical department of the army."

Bellows, Hammond, and Olmsted needed a House ally, and an unexpected facilitator, the committee's chairman, Francis Preston Blair Jr., a Free-Soiler and Republican from Missouri, came to their assistance. A gifted speaker and younger brother of President Lincoln's postmaster general, Blair was about to accept a commission as colonel in the Union army and now vigorously opposed any attempts to thwart medical reform. This was a remarkable turnaround from just two months before, when Blair was supporting a competing bill that would impede change in the Medical Department. "We know," Blair stated, "that the sanitary commission grew up spontaneously in an effort on the part of our people to attend to the wants of the Army, and I believe that it is the testimony of all connected with the Army that that commission has been of very great service."

Some congressmen, like their senatorial counterparts, argued against the whole concept of health care reform: The army might need more knowledgeable medical officers, they conceded, but such physicians should be selected only at a local level, thereby protecting a soldier's individual rights. Socrates Norton Sherman, a Republican who had practiced medicine in Ogdensburg, New York, for almost four decades, was the most vocal critic. One of the few physicians serving in Congress, the sixty-one-year-old Sherman was about to enlist as a medical officer of the Thirty-fourth New York Infantry (also known as the Herkimer Regiment). A firm believer in locally sponsored military medical care, Sherman also predicted that the new medical inspectors called for in Blair's bill, "instead of supplying any deficiency in the medical corps, will be precisely what the drum major is to the band of a regiment, who marches before the band with his baton, but never strikes the drum." William Kellogg of Illinois concurred, "This bill will only swell the proportion of the medical corps of the Army without increasing its efficiency." Unfortunately, like others in Congress, Kellogg had little understanding of the breadth and brutality of the military struggle engulfing his country. He went on to exclaim, "At this time, when the rebellion is being so rapidly put down, and when, by the heavy blows it has received, it is near its extinction, I do not think that it is proper to be increasing the [medical] corps of the Army which will have soon to be largely reduced."

Despite the naysayers, no topic was generating greater congressional anxiety and public sympathy than the medical care of Union soldiers. Politicians were inundated with complaints from their constituents regarding inadequate military health care. "We need medical inspectors to inspect the sanitary condition of transports, quarters, and camps, and especially to inspect the field and general hospitals. Our soldiers have suffered incalculably from the incompetency, neglect, and, I am sorry to say, in some instances, the gross intemperance of some of the surgeons," declared one congressman. "I will vote for any bill calculated to give relief to our gallant soldiers who have so nobly endured and suffered." William Lehman, a wealthy Pennsylvania Democrat, concurred and insisted that medical reform be accomplished immediately and that appointments be open to anyone of merit. "Our hospitals," Lehman stated, "are filled with the sick and dying soldiers merely because routine and rank and seniority override what men of common sense and common discretion know to be the remedy for these things. If we are to have extended hospitals, and men who are fit to take charge of them, we must have physicians who have spent their lives in the hospitals of our large cities; men who know how to build hospitals and how to ventilate them; men who know how to construct the cooking department, and to furnish to the soldiers the most improved couches for their tortured and suffering frames to repose upon . . . and the best assistance, can be obtained from the ordinary corps of civilians of the medical profession, far better than can be obtained from the few men who constitute the medical department of the regular Army."[35]

Blair called for a vote, and on April 10, 1862, the House passed its version of medical reform legislation. A joint conference committee was needed to negotiate the Senate and House differences, and six days later, a bill to increase the efficiency of the U.S. Army's Medical Department was signed into law by President Lincoln. One key element of the Sanitary Commission's request, a substantially enlarged ambulance system controlled by the Medical Department, was not included in the final legislation. Its absence was conspicuous and would become the focus of a bitter and ongoing feud between Secretary of War Stanton and Frederick Olmsted and William Hammond. Also missing from the bill were any detailed plans regarding hospital construction. However, the legislation did provide increased rank and pay for officers of the Medical Department, and most important, the appointment of medical inspectors and the surgeon general would be based on merit rather than seniority. Olmsted and his commissioners considered passage of the medical reform bill their finest political achievement. An ecstatic Olmsted wrote to his father:

> As to the Sanitary Commission, our success is suddenly wonderfully complete . . . all of a sudden a bill which is just the thing we wanted quietly passes thro' both houses the same day and before we know it is a law, and this occurs at the moment the secy of war kicks the old Surgn Genl out of his seat, and all the staff, which, through espirit du corps has been regarding the Sanitary Commission as its enemy, suddenly opens its eyes to the fact that the San. Com. is its best friend.[36]

Reorganization of the Medical Department required a new surgeon general, and Stanton immediately invited William Van Buren, a friend and member of the Sanitary Commission's executive board, to Washington to discuss the situation. Although the secretary of war wanted Van Buren to be the next surgeon general, Van Buren turned down the nomination, refusing to act independently of the commission's and Olmsted's wishes. Van Buren, who was William Hammond's mentor, told Stanton that Hammond is "the best man for the place." Petitions for Hammond's nomination, signed by the most influential of American physicians, were presented to Stanton. Olmsted even enlisted General McClellan, who had grown more politically powerful as head of the North's Army of the Potomac, to lobby the secretary of war. "He is our man," McClellan said in reference to Hammond. "He is the only one of the whole corps, who has any just conception of the duties of such a position, and sufficient energy, faithfully to perform them."[37]

The Sanitary Commission's lobbying for Hammond was elaborate. Henry Bellows, the commission's president, visited President Lincoln early one morning while the chief executive was being shaved. Touting Hammond's credentials, Bellows must have impressed Lincoln because the president invited him back to the White House that afternoon. Carl Sandburg, Lincoln's biographer, tells of the president sitting at a desk piled high with legal documents waiting to be signed. Nodding to Bellows, Lincoln went about his business, while for fifteen minutes Bellows extolled the young physician's qualifications to the president. At last Lincoln spoke: "Shouldn't wonder if Hammond was at this moment 'Surgeon General,' and had been for some time." "You don't mean to say, Mr. President, that the appointment has been made?" said a startled Bellows. Looking up for the first time, Lincoln answered, "I may say to you that it *has*; only you needn't *tell* of it just yet."[38]

On April 25, 1862, a vote of the Senate confirmed Hammond's appointment. The next day, Stephen Smith wrote of the nomination, "The profession will hear of the confirmation of this appointment with the most sincere gratification. No man could be selected, who so happily combines in his professional relations, the confidence and esteem of both the Medical Staff of the army, and the profession of the country, as Dr. Hammond."[39]

But not everyone was thrilled. Several senior career army surgeons were outraged that they had been passed over. Some senators questioned whether Hammond, who had serious medical problems and a hypochondriacal nature, would be able to handle the physical demands of the office. Hammond was unfazed. He realized this was going to be an assignment unlike any other, in part because the rapidly growing volunteer army created untold medical management problems. He also knew that politics and medicine had rarely mingled on such a grand scale in the country's past.

CHAPTER FIVE

"The horror of war can never be known but on the field"

BELLOWS, OLMSTED, AND STRONG grew impatient with Stanton's failure to carry out promised medical reforms. The secretary of war had especially been dragging his heels on the appointment of the congressionally mandated medical inspectors. "I thoroughly hate that canting small politician," wrote Olmsted of Stanton to a member of the Sanitary Commission's staff. "I think, really, it is time the Sanitary Commission resigned and spoke its mind of him. He is more a fool than a knave, however, I believe, yet he is a big knave."[1]

Stanton's dawdling galled Olmsted, who had taken on a new and demanding responsibility: converting and equipping a ragtag collection of merchant vessels, river steamers, tugboats, and other rickety craft into a fleet of hospital ships that would transport northward the sick and wounded of McClellan's army. The need was paramount because beginning in the spring of 1862, more than 110,000 of McClellan's troops, 25,000 animals, 1,800 wagons, 44 batteries of artillery, and massive amounts of equipment had been moved southward by a flotilla of more than 400 ships to the tip of the Peninsula, a broad swath of Virginia territory bounded by the York River on the north and the James River on the south. McClellan strategized that with a secure seaborne supply line supported by the North, his men, having outflanked the Confederates, would simply march eighty or so miles up the Peninsula, capture Richmond, and end the rebels' cause without a serious tussle.

Unfortunately, it was not that easy. Not only had McClellan become alarmed at what appeared to be growing Southern military strength, but frequent rainstorms impeded the overall operation. The Peninsula was an inhospitable land with deeply indented shorelines covered with swampy forests where brackish streams expanded after every rain into marshy ponds. The roads, rudimentary and winding, were hardly usable at any time, and following a storm they became impassable for animal and vehicular traffic. One contemporary description told of McClellan's men and their horses "floundering through the miry roads," so often "bogged in the mud, interlaced with the roots of the forest-trees, as to render extrication extremely difficult. If any one attempted to escape from the slough of the roads, and turned aside into the woods, he found the undergrowth so dense, as to render it almost impossible to make any progress."[2]

The delays seemed endless, especially since the North nervously awaited its first major battlefield victory. Meanwhile, confusion ruled the camps as arrangements for the construction of field hospitals and the organization of medical strategies went awry. In case of battle, one doctor explained, some physicians were assigned to frontline positions but not allowed to take their surgical instruments. This would, according to him, create a situation "so that they have their hands tied as to performing any operation in which these [their instruments] would be used, no matter how urgent the necessity or how long the patients may be under their care. . . . This arrangement," warned the doctor, "is an insult."[3] As McClellan waited, the sick lists steadily increased, with large numbers of the soldiers suffering from respiratory illnesses and severe diarrhea. Uninspected campsites became a breeding ground for epidemic diseases, since the water supply in the swampy earth was easily contaminated by human waste. By the end of May, one-fifth of the troops were no longer physically fit to fight. McClellan himself was suffering from the lingering side effects of a case of dysentery that he had contracted the year before.

When Olmsted arrived on the Peninsula in late April 1862, he could scarcely have anticipated the confusion that awaited him. "There were few attendants, no clothing, no medicines, and the surgeons in charge seemed bewildered in their helplessness," wrote Charles Stillé, the Sanitary Commission's official historian.[4] To Olmsted, it was obvious that the higher-ups in the Medical Department had learned little from their disastrous experience nine months before at Bull Run. The sick and wounded were still dumped on riverbanks with little to no regard for their welfare. Olmsted, who expected to see some measure of medical reform in place on the Peninsula, became livid at the organizational chaos. The heat, humidity, pestilence, rain, and lack of adequate Medical Department services made the establishment of a viable hospital transport service extremely difficult. To make matters worse, certain physicians were said by Olmsted to be "mad with *surgical* fever."[5] These volunteer scalpel wielders were deserting their dysentery and typhoid patients to go to the front for the more exciting opportunity of performing an amputation or two. Conversely, according to Charles Tripler, McClellan's medical director, there were other physicians, "all sorts of doctors—even advertising quacks," who had never even seen, much less performed, a surgical operation and were incompetent in their own right.[6] Olmsted's nightmare seemed endless, and he indicated in his communications with the Sanitary Commission's Washington-based staff that something, including direct talks with Secretary of War Stanton himself, needed to be arranged if the Peninsula's medical crisis was to be properly managed.

AWARE OF OLMSTED'S mounting frustration, Henry Bellows prepared to see Stanton, who was not known to be a kindly person. George Gorham, Stanton's biographer, wrote that "he was regarded as tyrannical, arbitrary, and unjust."[7] Visitors were expected to make their case in the briefest terms, and according to Gorham, Stanton would answer "instantly and decisively, yes or no. . . . Having thus decided," Gorham added, "[Stanton] heeded no remonstrance, and tolerated no repetition of the request, but simply dismissed the case and the person together, hurried him on, and received the next one." On May 12, 1862, Bellows went to the secretary of war's office to urge the immediate appointment of an inspector general and eight medical inspectors as provided by the recently enacted medical reform legislation. When Bellows arrived, there were more than thirty other individuals also waiting to see Stanton. Questioning the delay, Bellows reminded Stanton that the newly appointed surgeon general, William Alexander Hammond, had submitted a list of men considered best qualified for the positions. According to Bellows, a clearly perturbed secretary of war snapped, "Doctor, I can't be catechized this way! The Government will act when it gets ready." Describing the three-minute meeting to his fellow commissioner William Van Buren, Bellows characterized Stanton as "a man with a brain in a very dangerous state of irritability, and one who in the use of his vast power forgets the rights and the position of his peers who chance to be in private life."[8]

The campaign for military medical reform received an additional setback when, only a few days after meeting with Bellows, Stanton invited Surgeon General Hammond to his office. Much like the secretary of war, Hammond had a dogmatic and pompous manner. He was often inconsiderate. The visit began with Stanton asking a simple question about the planned medical activities of the Sanitary Commission. But Hammond deemed Stanton's tone offensive. When the secretary of war went on to caution his subordinate, "If you have the enterprise, the knowledge, the intelligence, and the brains to run the Medical Department, I will assist you," the surgeon general became incensed. Hammond stood up and, towering over Stanton by nearly a foot, replied, "Mr. Secretary, I am not accustomed to be spoken to in that manner by any person, and I beg you will address me in more respectful terms....I will not permit you to speak to me in such language." Stanton, not one to shy away from a verbal dispute, snapped back, "Then, sir, you can leave my office immediately."[9] Hammond, not realizing the extent to which he had provoked Stanton's ire, had sown the seeds for his future difficulties as surgeon general.

Despite his clash with the secretary of war and its negative implications for the Sanitary Commission, Hammond continued to have praise heaped on him by Bellows and other commission members. In mid-June, Bellows wrote to Olmsted, "I am more and more pleased with Dr. Hammond. His views are large, his mind active & prompt—his action at present embarrassed by almost insuperable difficulties. But he is cutting his way out." Although he was glad to hear about Hammond, Olmsted, stuck amid the military and medical morass on the Peninsula, was enthusiastic about little else. The floating hospital transport service functioned poorly, owing primarily to Olmsted's struggles over who officially controlled the hospital ships. Was it the Quartermaster Corps, the Medical Department, or the Sanitary Commission? No one was certain, least of all Charles Tripler, medical director of the Army of the Potomac. Olmsted particularly resented the conflicting and dictatorial way in which Tripler issued orders to ships wholly equipped and staffed by commission members. In turn, Tripler was suspicious of civilians meddling in military matters and chafed at the mere presence of commission members on the Peninsula.

The continuing lack of medical reform and nebulous status of Sanitary Commission authority prompted Olmsted to warn Bellows, "If these armies keep their promises to fight, tomorrow ten thousand men will bleed to death and starve to death whose lives could have been saved if proper measures had been taken." Sensing the trouble to come unless the new surgeon general took vigorous action to change the tenor of military medicine, Olmsted urged that Hammond act to revolutionize the policies of the Medical Department: "Let him issue a manifesto. And don't let him wait another hour."[10]

REGARDLESS OF THE recent unpleasantness with Stanton, it took little more than Olmsted's coaxing and the rapidly deteriorating medical situation on the Peninsula to prompt Hammond to announce a series of bold steps toward Medical Department reform. Knowing that Stanton would act slowly in naming the eight medical inspectors, Hammond began instead to replace the aging and ineffectual medical directors of the army, who were under the authority of the surgeon general. At fifty-six, Charles Tripler was considered an old surgeon from the old army. He had become a man of excuses, and much to his discredit, he had not supported the organization of an effective ambulance corps or the establishment of adequate numbers of field hospitals. Arguing that existing regulations did not permit such initiatives, Tripler in his unyielding hesitancy typified the bureaucratic bungling of army medical life.

Hammond wanted medical directors who were "not quite so thickly incrusted with the habits, forms and traditions of the service."[11] Of these new administrators, the outstanding figure was Jonathan Letterman, a thirty-seven-year-old native Pennsylvanian and son of a physician, who would replace the faltering Tripler and help change the face of military medicine. A taciturn six-footer with a receding hairline, full goatee, and mustache, Letterman was said to have a good sense of humor and a generous disposition. But his health was not good—he was plagued by a chronic intestinal condition that left him ailing and poorly nourished.

Hammond's choice of Letterman was not surprising, given the latter's administrative capabilities and the fact that they were longtime friends. Both men had received commissions as medical officers in the U.S. Army's Medical Department in early summer 1849. Like Hammond, Letterman had initially been posted on the southern and western frontiers. He served in Florida in the campaign against the Seminole tribe and marched with troops from Fort Leavenworth, Kansas, to New Mexico. There he was stationed at Fort Defiance and fought against the Navajo and Gila Apaches. Like Hammond, he was scientifically curious and collected animal and plant specimens for the newly formed Smithsonian Institution. In 1858, Letterman returned east, first serving at Fort Monroe, located at the tip of Virginia's Peninsula, and then transferring as a novice medical purveyor to the office of Richard Satterlee, chief medical purveyor for the United States Army in New York City. With the start of the Civil War, Letterman was ordered to accompany troops from California to New York City, and in November 1861, he was placed on duty with the Army of the Potomac.

In June 1862, President Lincoln submitted Charles Tripler's name to the Senate as nominee for the important new medical post of inspector general. However, Tripler's reputation had clearly suffered as a result of his mismanagement during the early phase of the Peninsula campaign. This, coupled with the Sanitary Commission's effort to prevent any other important positions from being offered to Tripler, cost him a congressional confirmation. Tripler became a political liability, and Hammond took advantage of this fact by removing him as medical director of McClellan's army. A broken Tripler asked to be reassigned to the Midwest, where he served in several innocuous postings until the end of the war.

Within days of Tripler's downfall, Hammond met with McClellan and proposed his old friend Jonathan Letterman as the new medical director for the Army of the Potomac. McClellan and Letterman, who were both in their mid-thirties, probably knew of each other from their days in Philadelphia, where McClellan's father was dean of Jefferson Medical College, Letterman's alma mater. McClellan supported Hammond's recommendation, and Letterman arrived at Harrison's Landing on Virginia's James River the first week of July. Especially impressed by Letterman was Olmsted, who wrote of the new medical director, "I like him at first sight better than any Surgeon U.S.A. whom I have seen. He asks & offers cooperation, and will have it with all my heart, so far as it is worth-while to give it."[12] Letterman was a sanitarian in philosophy and, much like the members of the Sanitary Commission, worried about diet, discipline, and hygiene. And, like Olmsted, he believed the commission's hospital transport service should be restricted to the transport of sick and wounded men. Any other use of the ships constituted a breach of the Sanitary Commission's role and served only to lower the men's morale and decrease a fighting unit's effectiveness.

When Letterman took charge, McClellan's army was a medical mess. With tens of thousands of men close-quartered in highly contagious environments, sickness had become a crippling factor. Troops from more rural areas, most of whom had never been exposed to chicken pox, measles, or mumps, were promptly felled by these ailments. Even if the men managed to recover from the childhood diseases, the campsites were teeming with bedbugs, flies, lice, and all manner of vermin. Without refrigeration and other sanitary measures, inadequate culinary, galley, and scullery practices led to contaminated food supplies. Since the existence of invisible disease-causing microorganisms was not yet known, bathers, cattle, cooks, defecators, drinkers, and launderers would all share a campsite's water stores. The other little-discussed maladies were sexually transmitted diseases. As female followers flocked to campsites, cases of gonorrhea and syphilis became a serious impediment to troop health.

"The time has passed when the excuse of 'no supplies' will be accepted," wrote Hammond to Letterman at the time of his appointment. "I commit to you the health, the comfort, and the lives of thousands of our fellow-soldiers who are fighting for the maintenance of their liberties."[13] What Letterman found at Harrison's Landing on the Peninsula was not just an army sick from contagion and fatigued from heavy work and lack of sleep, but one that lacked fresh food and other basic provisions. Soon Letterman requested one thousand hospital tents and two hundred ambulances. The surgeon general quickly complied, and by August 1, tents and ambulances were in abundance. Letterman directed that Berkeley, the manor house of the Harrison's Landing's plantation and ancestral home of former president William Henry Harrison, be improvised into a hospital. As a result, tents were erected around the hospital and 1,200 patients were sheltered and cared for.

Compounding the physical hardships was a lack of adequate nutrition. Following months of monotonous meals of salted meats and no fresh fruits or vegetables, the men, according to Letterman, "do not feel sick, but yet their energy, their powers of endurance, and their willingness to undergo hardships, are in a great degree gone, and they know not why." Apparently, a massive outbreak of scurvy, or vitamin C deficiency, had occurred. This is an insidious disease that renders a person listless. Lethargy, malaise, and weakness prevail but are so slow in onset that the victim does not notice any physical deterioration. Knowing that scurvy also caused various degrees of mental depression and robbed a man of his courage, Letterman was quick to point out that "the fighting strength of the army was affected [by scurvy] to a much greater degree than was indicated."[14]

Frank Hamilton, the battle-tested surgeon of Bull Run and recently named medical director to Major General Erasmus D. Keyes's Fourth Corps, agreed with Letterman's assessment. A graduate of Union College and author of a popular textbook on military surgery, Hamilton was an expert on nutritional deficiencies and regarded as one of the most knowledgeable physicians on the Peninsula. He recalled that during the first five months McClellan's army was in Virginia, "probably not one full ration of fresh vegetables had been issued to the troops."[15]

Hamilton's opinions were highly valued, for not only was his brother-in-law Henry Wilson, chairman of the United States Senate Committee on Military Affairs, but Hamilton himself held the additional prestigious title of brigade surgeon. Brigade surgeons (also called "surgeons" and "assistant surgeons" of volunteers) were a select group of doctors who had been commissioned by Congress to supplement the work of the fewer than one hundred physicians who initially made up the regular staff of the medical corps (the latter were officially titled "surgeons" and "assistant surgeons" of the United States Army) and were usually assigned to administrative staff duty. Only 547 federal commissions were issued throughout the four years of the war, and applicants had to pass a rigorous examination of medical and surgical knowledge; as a result, brigade surgeons were considered the military's medical elite.

Hamilton placed second in the nation on his military entrance test and was from then on accorded kudos wherever he traveled. By the war's end, he was held in such high esteem by the Sanitary Commission that he was named editor of their two-volume text concerning surgical difficulties encountered during the conflict. As a brigade surgeon, Hamilton was no longer affiliated with an individual regiment. He became a medical ombudsman of sorts and was bureaucratically separate from the largest category of army surgeons, the regimental surgeons and regimental assistant surgeons, who were commissioned by state governors rather than by the president. Different from all the preceding groups were the acting assistant surgeons of the United States Army. These "contract surgeons" held no formal commission but received the pay of first lieutenants. They were employed chiefly in Northern general hospitals, which allowed them to continue their civilian practices.

Hamilton believed that twenty thousand soldiers on the Peninsula were suffering from scurvy and unfit to fight. Meeting at Harrison's Landing on July 7 with Hamilton and several other division and corps medical directors, Letterman acknowledged the situation and ordered the immediate shipment of foods to fend off scurvy. By mid-July, beets, cabbages, onions, potatoes, squashes, and tomatoes arrived in such abundance that some of the shipment was left to rot on a wharf. Large cauldrons for cooking and massive supplies of beef stock were made available along with fresh bread. As a final precaution, Letterman had the medical purveyor issue 1,500 boxes of fresh lemons to the various regimental hospitals. By mid-August, Letterman asserted that scurvy had disappeared from the Army of the Potomac. Hamilton was not so accepting. Even in mid-August, his regimental surgeons reported more than two thousand men still weak from scurvy and unable to march three miles an hour with their knapsacks.

More worrisome than nutritional deficiencies was a growing epidemic of communicable diseases, particularly pneumonias and the twin diarrhea producers dysentery and typhoid. Acute and chronic diarrhea, the so-called trots or two-step, was rampant, with almost fifty thousand cases reported. According to a doctor in the Fourth Maine Infantry, "The principal cause of diarrhoea in camp is the irregular manner in which the soldiers cook and eat their food. Some of them eat five or six fried dishes, or more properly messes, during the day. There is always an increased amount of diarrhoea after beans are issued to the men, especially in hot weather."[16] Complaining of back pain and headache that progressed to explosive diarrhea fifteen to twenty times a day, the soldier was soon emaciated and exhausted. Treatment was empirical, consisting of variations on Benjamin Rush's bleed, blister, and purge gambit, all in the false hope that health would return.

Tragically, these well-intentioned drug preparations, such as calomel and tartar emetic, accomplished little more than further dehydrating the patient. Along with their lack of knowledge concerning communicable diseases, Civil War–era physicians had no understanding of human physiology. This resulted in total disregard for a patient's fluid balance. The doctor's respected adage "Drink plenty of liquids," meant to be followed when an individual has fever or diarrhea, was an unthinkable remedy in 1862. The concept of maintaining bodily homeostasis through adequate fluid intake would not have occurred to physicians.

As infectious illnesses spread, Letterman was forced to institute a wide range of hygienic and sanitary measures. For instance, each company of one hundred or so men was ordered to name permanent cooks who would receive instructions on how to properly prepare soups and all other foods. Tents were moved to new ground weekly and their side flaps raised daily. Soldiers were no longer permitted to sleep on bare earth but instructed to gather pine needles to serve as rudimentary mattresses. Campsites could be situated near but not in woods to assure a freer circulation of air. Furthermore, a hearty breakfast was now required before any marching or physical labor could commence. Particular attention was given to personal hygiene. Troops were compelled to bathe once a week in a river for at least fifteen minutes. Pits were dug and used as latrines and six inches of fresh earth thrown into them daily. Once filled to within two feet of the surface, these excavations were covered up and started anew. Similar trenches were used for kitchen refuse, while animal dung was collected and buried two feet belowground or burned. As a final measure, regimental grounds were cleaned and inspected daily and all dead animals and the blood and entrails from slaughtered animals were buried at least four feet underground.

Letterman's plan was practical and necessary, as five months on Virginia's Peninsula had left the Union's troops decimated by disease. As McClellan reported to Stanton and Lincoln, "The service, labors, and privations of the troops had of course a great effect on the health of the army."[17] The numbers were simply staggering: In June, 24 percent of 103,000 Northern troops were listed as ill and no longer fit to fight. By July, the figure had increased to 29 percent. The sad reality for McClellan and his staff was that they knew the sick lists, lengthy as they were, represented an undercount of the ill. Stopped by sickness, the Army of the Potomac was no longer an effective fighting force.

BY LATE MAY, the Peninsula Campaign had degenerated into a cat-and-mouse struggle as McClellan's forces slowly advanced toward Richmond. Camped on both sides of the Chickahominy River, the Army of the Potomac was just seven miles or so outside the Confederate capital. Spring rains had turned what was an easily forded stream into a broad expanse of flooded swamplands. This made the stronger right wing of the Union army, stretched along the Chickahominy's north side away from Richmond, less vulnerable to any Confederate attack. The Northern army's left wing, consisting of thirty thousand men belonging to Major General Samuel Heintzelman's Third Corps and Major General Erasmus Keyes's Fourth Corps, had been sent across the river to a position that was more vulnerable on the south side. Keyes's troops led the advance and entrenched themselves near a crossroads village known as Seven Pines, midway between the Chickahominy and the city of Richmond. Major General Silas Casey's division, one of three that made up Keyes's Fourth Corps, was pushed a thousand yards beyond Seven Pines to Fair Oaks Station. Here there were several small farmhouses surrounded by a grove of oak trees. Casey's guards were advanced a further thousand yards to the edge of a dense forest, beyond which the Southern forces were camped. Trees were hastily cut down to form barricades, rifle pits were dug, and several redoubts were constructed for artillery units.

Knowing from his scout's report that McClellan's army was unevenly divided along both sides of the Chickahominy, Confederate general Joseph Johnston, prodded by Jefferson Davis, decided to attack the

Union's more isolated and numerically smaller left wing. During the late afternoon and into the evening of May 30, a series of violent thunderstorms swept over the area surrounding Richmond. This was excellent timing for the Southern cause. The Chickahominy, already full, became a raging torrent, and several makeshift bridges that provided the few links between a divided Army of the Potomac seemed ready to be swept away. Without a suitable route for retreat and no preparations in place to evacuate the wounded, the left wing of the Union army appeared doomed.

A few hours after Johnston's early afternoon attack on May 31, things seemed to be going the South's way. Casey's guards and their few supporting regiments had been surprised by a wave of Confederate forces that suddenly materialized through the screen of marshy woods. Confusion followed as the Union troops were immediately swept back to the division's main line of defense at Fair Oaks Station. Here Casey's men, scarcely five thousand strong, held their ground for more than two hours against fifteen thousand Confederates. Shells and bullets whistled through the air as casualties mounted. George Fisk, an eighteen-year-old private in Company H of the Eighty-first New York Infantry, was hit by a musket ball near his breastbone. Shot at an oblique angle, the bullet bounced off the bone, tunneled under Fisk's chest muscles, blasted into his upper arm bone, and exploded out the side. Bleeding uncontrollably, in terrible pain, and with a mangled limb, Fisk was in the middle of what was becoming a Union rout.

Under increasing enemy pressure in front, almost enveloped on both flanks, and having lost one-third of his troops, Casey and his men made a hasty decision to retreat to the Union's main line of defense at Seven Pines. An eyewitness to Casey's predicament was Frank Hamilton. Stationed near Fair Oaks Station, Hamilton was, by his own account, "able to see from where we stood the line of battle perfectly, and to note the fortitude with which, for more than two hours, General Casey's small division on the extreme front and left withstood the terrible assault which was made upon it."[18] As medical director for the entire Fourth Corps, Hamilton estimated that prior to the Confederate assault almost one-third of Casey's division was incapacitated from disease, leaving Casey just 3,500 effective men to hold off the almost 15,000-man Southern onslaught. Having received no further reinforcements, Casey's now decimated division was no longer capable of defending itself.

The lack of ambulances or other means of conveyance for the injured made matters even more difficult for Casey's troops. Hamilton had ordered the few available ambulances and their drivers toward the action. But two hours later, none appeared. As groups of soldiers using improvised litters to carry their wounded comrades passed by, a disgusted Hamilton rode off. Searching for his ambulances, he found the drivers a few miles away, gathered in a safe cluster, where they were, in his words, "under the grateful shelter of a hill, and entirely concealed from the sight and shot of the enemy."[19] This was not an unusual situation. During these first years of the Civil War, untrained ambulance drivers, unless closely watched, would head for the rear at first chance, especially once a wounded man had climbed on board.

With no organized evacuation of wounded possible, Hamilton left instructions for the stream of injured to be directed toward Savage's Station, a mile or so behind the defense lines at Seven Pines. The site contained a large two-story house shaded by oak trees and surrounded by fourteen other structures, including slave quarters, barns, corncribs, and woodsheds. Hamilton estimated the facility would furnish comfortable shelter for three to five hundred wounded. For the first few hours, supplies were limited, food was scarce, and "our corps of medical officers and of nurses was very inadequate," wrote Hamilton. The doctors could do little more than dress wounds, for they had no surgical instruments to perform operations. By late afternoon, medical supplies began to arrive along with two dozen or so additional physicians. Hamilton designated three areas (a barn, a tent, and beneath the shade of a tree in the rear of the house) where major operations were to be performed. Minor surgery would be completed in the open field. With an estimated one thousand men requiring some type of treatment during that first day and night, Hamilton confessed, "It cannot be supposed that, to some extent, all the wounded did not experience inconvenience, and that others did not actually suffer from delay or neglect."

Private Fisk was among those brought to Savage's Station for treatment. Hoping to preserve Fisk's left arm, the physician decided to forgo the usual amputation. Instead, a decision was made, probably at Fisk's urging, to complete the more technically demanding but less disfiguring removal of shattered bone—called an "exsection"—while preserving as many of the injured blood vessels, muscles, and nerves as possible. With Fisk under chloroform anesthesia, the doctor hacked away, oblivious to the need for cleanliness, gentleness, or technical precision. As a result, virtually every principle of scientific surgery and infection prevention was violated. The physician's fingers, with dirt layered beneath his fingernails and still covered with gore from his last patient, roughly pulled out splinters of bone, fragments of bullet, and embedded pieces of shirt fabric. There were no antibiotics to give or sterile water with which to rinse the wound. Instead, a dirtied dressing of cotton or lint was applied. In less than twenty minutes, the procedure was over. Fisk awoke in horrendous pain but knew that his arm was still attached to his body.

The main frustration for Fisk and scores of soldiers who had undergone a surgical operation was the interminable wait for railroad transportation back to McClellan's base camp at White House on the Pamunkey River, a branch of the York. There, Olmsted's hospital boats were supposed to whisk the men north to a waiting bed in one of several new general hospitals. However, the entire transportation process, from battlefront to field hospital to seaborne evacuation area to floating hospital to general hospital, was chaotic and mishandled. Fisk, for instance, would not reach Washington's Judiciary Square Hospital until June 4, four days after his operation. During those crucial ninety-six hours, he received little postoperative care as his wound became infected underneath an increasingly blood-encrusted and filthy bandage. Describing the situation at Savage's Station, Frank Hamilton noted in his official report, "The trains ordered to remove the wounded were not brought up as rapidly as the men were ready for removal, and, consequently, a large portion were compelled to remain one or two days after their wounds had been dressed, or their limbs had been amputated; some of whom had no covering whatever, not even blankets."[20]

From the beginning, the Battle of Fair Oaks (termed Seven Pines by Southerners) was a mismanaged struggle. The element of surprise provided the Confederates with an initial advantage, but their assault ended up disjointed and poorly coordinated. Southern strategy also anticipated that by noontime on May 31, the rapidly rising Chickahominy River would become impassable, leaving the Army of the Potomac permanently split. Early that morning, timbers from some of the Union's hastily built bridges were already seen floating down the river. However, the river crested four hours later than planned, and on the Union right, one of the corps commanders managed to get his divisions across the rain-swollen Chickahominy. Sloshing over the swaying "grapevine" bridge and guided by the sound of the firing, the Union troops pushed on to Fair Oaks Station, where they helped bring the rebels to a bloody halt under a setting sun. Fighting resumed again at seven in the morning but sputtered out four hours later. A reorganized Union response forced the Confederates to yield the ground they had won the day before, although the Northern forces became too scattered to plan any organized pursuit toward Richmond.

There were no real winners or losers in this two-day affair. The most prominent casualty was Confederate general Joseph Johnston, wounded by both a musket ball to his shoulder and a shell fragment to his chest wall. Examination revealed a broken shoulder blade and two fractured ribs, and the prescribed treatments were the usual bleeding, blistering, and purging. Enfeebled by his therapies and in constant pain, Johnston spent the remainder of the war in poor health. Replacing Johnston as commander of the soon-to-be-designated Army of Northern Virginia was a quiet Virginian, Robert E. Lee.

In the end, more than ten thousand men were lying upon a battlefield scarcely one mile square. Many had been mutilated by the trampling of countercharging squadrons. Unknown numbers, wounded early in the battle, perished from a lack of medical attention. Fighting in flooded lands, injured soldiers were propped against fences or tree stumps to prevent them from drowning in the swampy muck. Others crawled away from the two armies, leaving trails of blood behind them, to seek shelter beneath trees or shrubbery. Their groans attracted search parties, who bore them back to Savage's Station on stretchers, horses, or the occasional ambulance. Even medical director Hamilton himself went out looking for the wounded. "It is painful to state that so late as the third or fourth day wounded men were rescued from the marshes, who had lain all this time without succor," he wrote in a status report to the *American Medical Times*.

The exact number of wounded who passed through Hamilton's extemporized hospital during the first days after the battle is unknown, though it is generally thought to be at least three thousand. The disorderly manner in which the injured were taken care of never allowed for an accurate tally. Hamilton noted nothing more precise than that "many amputations were made."[21] One volunteer surgeon, John Swinburne of Albany, New York, was said to have completed twenty-six exsections of the shoulder and elbow joints in a day's work at Savage's Station. He was praised for managing to eat his hominy and drink coffee from an operating table, surrounded by exsected bones with their attached muscles and ligaments plus piles of amputated limbs.

IN THE DAYS following the Battle of Fair Oaks, the Union wounded began to pour into the army's main base of operations at White House. Arriving in boxcars or flatcars via the commandeered Richmond & York Railroad, the injured soldiers accumulated in makeshift hospitals or simply camped alongside the river. Although Olmsted had pressed all his available floating hospitals into service, many were poorly equipped and unable to accommodate the almost 7,000 sick and injured. For instance, the *Elm City*, a 760-ton steamer, could ferry only 450 to 500 men at a time to receiving hospitals thirty miles and several hours away at Yorktown. Barely 350 injured could squeeze on the *Daniel Webster*. The *Knickerbocker*, an old boat with no means of ventilation under the main deck, would, according to Olmsted, "breed a pestilence" wherever it went.

"The horror of war can never be known but on the field," Olmsted wrote home to his wife, Mary. "It is beyond, far beyond all imagination." Describing a "terrible week's work," Olmsted provided Henry Bellows with a graphic description of what he was facing:

> At the time of which I am now writing, Monday afternoon, wounded were arriving by every train, entirely unattended or with at most a detail of two soldiers to a train of two or three hundred of them. They were packed as closely as they could be stowed in the common freight cars, without beds, without straw, at most with a wisp of hay under their heads. They arrived, dead and alive together, in the same close box, many with awful wounds festering and alive with maggots. The stench was such as to produce vomiting with some of our strong men, habituated to the duty of attending the sick & wounded of the army.

Matters were made even worse by the declining health and mental state of Olmsted himself. He was despondent, having been out of touch with his wife for more than a month. The condition of his colleagues certainly contributed to his weariness. His most valued associate and closest friend in the commission, Frederick Knapp, a Unitarian minister in charge of provisioning the floating hospitals with clothing, food, and medical supplies, had contracted malaria and was sent home to recuperate in New York City. Another Sanitary Commission worker from Philadelphia became hysterical and apparently suffered a nervous breakdown. Many others on Olmsted's staff endured persistent diarrhea. Still, Olmsted felt he and his co-workers were making a difference. "If we had not been just where we were and just so well prepared as we were, I can not tell you what a horrible disgrace there would have been here to our country," he told Mary.[22]

While the wounded were gathered after the Fair Oaks fighting, Generals Lee and McClellan were planning their strategy anew. McClellan, ever the plodder and apologist, sent a steady stream of telegrams to Washington explaining why the Army of the Potomac was not ready to press on toward Richmond. Initially, it was due to the weather: "June 7th, The Chickahominy has risen so as to flood the entire bottom to the depth of three and four feet. I am pushing forward the bridges in spite of this; and the men are working night and day, up to their waists in water, to complete them. The whole face of the country is a perfect bog, entirely impassable for artillery or even cavalry, except directly in the narrow roads, which renders any movement either of this or the rebel army utterly out of the question until we have more favorable weather."[23] If it was not the weather, then it was the presumed size of the enemy's army. On June 25, McClellan wired Secretary of War Stanton, "The rebel force is stated at 200,000. . . . I shall have to contend against vastly superior odds." McClellan's unquestioning acceptance of these inflated figures (Southern strength was actually somewhere around eighty thousand to ninety thousand) suggests he welcomed them as a justification for failure: "I will do all that a general can do with the splendid army I have the honor to command, and if it is destroyed by overwhelming numbers, can at least die with it and share its fate. But if the result of the action, which will probably occur tomorrow, or within a short time, is a disaster, the responsibility cannot be thrown on my shoulders."[24] President Lincoln characterized McClellan as having the "slows."[25]

Conversely, Robert E. Lee was a doer. He sent Jeb Stuart, the famed cavalryman who had charged and broken the Fire Zouaves at First Bull Run, along with 1,200 of his men on a three-day reconnaissance mission behind Union lines. Stuart's troops quickly discovered the exact location of McClellan's right wing on the Chickahominy's north side. The area around the base camp at White House, with its burgeoning population of sick and wounded, was also scouted. Guided by men who had grown up near Richmond, the Confederate cavalry made a complete circuit around McClellan's army and captured 165 prisoners and 260 horses and mules.

Anticipating a reinforcement of thirty thousand of Stonewall Jackson's men, Lee's troops pounced on McClellan in a series of attacks called the Seven Days. It was a thrust-and-parry plan as the advantage shifted from rebel to Yankee and back again. After heavy Union losses at Gaines's Mill, where the third day of the battles was fought on June 27, a shaken McClellan hastily decided to move his operations base from White House to Harrison's Landing on the James River. Olmsted termed it the "skedaddle of the Pamunkey"[26] as a massive flotilla of ships, including all of the Sanitary Commission's hospital transport service, set sail on the Pamunkey River.

From a medical standpoint, the changing of bases proved complicated. Quickly the army had to march some fifteen miles to the James

River with ammunition, guns, and lengthy trains of supplies in tow. Concerned that a superior enemy was bearing down from the rear, McClellan decided that the sick and wounded who could not be carried or make the trek on their own would have to be left behind.

On Sunday, June 29, a battle broke out in the area of Savage's Station as Lee's men attacked the rear guard of the retreating Northern troops. The two hours of fighting were intense, with the opposing forces so close to each other that it was sometimes impossible to determine friends from foes. At a cost of more than one thousand men killed or wounded on each side, the Yankees won the fight and delayed the rebel advance.

Despite its supposed victory at Savage's Station, the Union army continued its retreat southward to Harrison's Landing. Consequently, a decision had to be made regarding the status of medical personnel and patients at Frank Hamilton's field hospital at Savage's Station. With the rebel army situated on the outskirts of the town and no spare ambulances or horses available to convey the growing number of Union injured, Generals McClellan and Heintzelman agreed there was little choice but to flee. However, all property that could not be removed was to be destroyed. Stores and provisions were piled in a great pyramid and set ablaze. Ammunition was heaped upon a train, which was sent down the rails toward the Chickahominy. Cars were set afire, and before they reached the river's bridge, shells began to explode. So great was the momentum that the engine and cars jumped the tracks, fell into the chasm, and exploded in a tangled heap on the river's bottom.

Holding a white flag of truce to stop the Confederate shelling, John Swinburne and approximately twenty other surgeons became voluntary captives while 2,500 Union wounded were made prisoners of war. Swinburne had been left in charge of Savage's Station. Contemporary accounts described the men as having a very hard time. "Nearly all the medicines were stolen by the rebels, and every bottle of liquor taken away. Every case of surgical instruments was taken,"[27] wrote one newspaper correspondent. The Confederates provided some food and medical supplies, but it was little more than maggot-ridden bacon and musty flour.

Swinburne wrote to Robert E. Lee asking that a mutual exchange of prisoners be arranged. Lee was unable to organize such a plan. As a result, Savage's Station was soon nothing more than a festering hellhole where infection and starvation were considered part of the daily routine. Two surgeons died from the hardships. Swinburne was released in late July as part of an arrangement allowing for the return of captured physicians.

The last of the Seven Days battles, Malvern Hill, was particularly ferocious, with 3,214 Union soldiers and more than 5,000 Confederate
men among the single day's casualties. Visiting Malvern House, an improvised hospital, one of the Union commanders of the day's fighting
told of injured men begging to be sent home or requesting that their
mothers or sisters be cared for. "We saw the amputated limbs and the
bodies of the dead hurried out of the room for burial," he recalled. "On
every side we heard the appeals of the unattended, the moans of the
dying, and the shrieks of those under the knife of the surgeon."[28]

The ferocity of the Seven Days campaign demonstrated the escalat-
ing level of military confrontation. The fighting was more savage than
ever, and there were increasing numbers of casualties. Recognizing the
futility of further attacks, Lee had his army regroup near Richmond.
Meanwhile, McClellan, still paralyzed by an unfounded fear of Lee's
supposed troop strength, ordered the Army of the Potomac to hurry up
with its hasty and disorderly retreat to Harrison's Landing.

SITTING IN HIS stateroom aboard the floating hospital *Wilson Small*, Frederick Olmsted surveyed the scene at Harrison's Landing. The Northern
fleet stretched two miles along the James River. Nearby, he could see the
gray turret of the Union's first ironclad, the *Monitor*, already famous following its March 1862 clash with the *Merrimac*. It was July 3, and the
exhausted Union forces were everywhere. Along the beach, thousands of
soldiers milled about, some bathing, some washing clothes, some doing
nothing, others reading newspapers that had just arrived from their
home cities. Many of the injured had their arms and legs in splints. On
the main pier, a dense crowd of wounded were being led onto one of numerous hospital boats to begin their journey northward. Situated at the
top of a nearby hill was Berkeley, the old brick mansion that Jonathan
Letterman had commandeered. It now served as the Yankees' central
hospital. Two of its four chimneys were capped by flimsy wooden structures that served as signal stations for the encamped Union forces.

"Our grand army is very nearly destroyed," Olmsted wrote home to
Mary. "It is striving bravely and cheerfully—heroically to the last, but
there is an end of human endurance."[29] What Olmsted saw was an army
abysmally depleted by combat, disease, loss of sleep, and poor nutrition. Having tramped for several days through swampy, vermin-infested
lands, almost one hundred thousand men were about to be crowded
into an area extending just three miles up and down the James River
and two miles inland. Malaria seemed everywhere, as did the onslaught
of scurvy. At this point the Union's Peninsula campaign ground to a

halt, since McClellan's army, enervated as it was by battle and sickness, was no longer an effective fighting force.

The only thing that seemed to function reasonably well was the Sanitary Commission's hospital transport service. Anticipating that the retreat from White House would degenerate into a medical nightmare, Olmsted had cautioned his crews and those of the army's own transports to be fully prepared for the conveyance northward of tens of thousands of wounded from Harrison's Landing. Thus, when Jonathan Letterman, McClellan's newly arrived medical director, visited Olmsted on the *Wilson Small,* Letterman wrote, "These vessels were fitted up with beds, bedding, medicines, hospital stores, food with many delicacies, and with arrangements for their preparation; everything, indeed, that was necessary for the comfort and well being of the wounded and sick." Surgeons, hospital stewards, and volunteer nurses were preassigned to each of the boats and remained on board wherever the craft traveled. "I doubt," Letterman recalled in his report to Hammond, "if ever vessels had been so completely fitted up for the transportation of sick and wounded of an army as these vessels had been."[30]

Letterman's arrival on the Peninsula must have seemed like a godsend to Olmsted. McClellan's new medical director was unflappable and an avowed enemy of bureaucratic red tape. This was extremely important, because Olmsted had grown tired of fighting what he regarded as the Medical Department's ambivalence toward soldiers' welfare and the lack of support for a dedicated ambulance corps. Meanwhile, Henry Bellows, the Sanitary Commission's president, urged the ailing Olmsted to leave the Peninsula. Responding to Bellows's request, Olmsted reasoned that recent appointments in the Medical Department would soon bring about needed changes. Besides, the hospital ships were costing the Sanitary Commission $20,000 a month; Olmsted felt the commissioners could better spend their dwindling cash reserves. "I am quite sure that our special transport service no longer pays what it costs, and that our position is not a dignified one," he wrote Bellows.[31] Bellows agreed and the hospital ships were soon turned over to the Quartermaster Corps. On July 16, Olmsted relinquished his post and set sail for New York City and a long-awaited reunion with Mary and the rest of his family.

THE UNION'S MILITARY campaign on the Peninsula was failing, and President Lincoln visited McClellan on July 7 to determine what could be done. The temporary hospitals were crowded with the sick, and their number was increasing. McClellan demanded reinforcements in order to press on, but some senior officers insisted that the army was in no medical condition to fight and should be withdrawn from the Peninsula. As Letterman, who had reported for duty at Harrison's Landing just a few days before, wrote, "The want of proper nourishment, the poisonous exhalations from the streams and swamps of the Peninsula, the labor undergone, and the anxiety felt, had undermined the strength and withered the spirits of a great many who were apparently well."[32]

Uncertain about what to do with McClellan and his troops, and desiring a new military adviser, Lincoln summoned Major General Henry W. Halleck from Mississippi to serve as general in chief of the United States Army. "Old Brains," as Halleck was called, not only graduated from both West Point and Union College, but was a practicing lawyer and author of a highly regarded book on the science of warfare. When Halleck visited McClellan on July 25, the army's medical situation had not changed substantively since Lincoln's visit eighteen days before. Making matters even more difficult, in mid-July numerous sickly and starving Yankee captives were released from the Richmond area in a prisoner exchange and arrived unexpectedly in Harrison's Landing in need of treatment and transportation north. Major General Keyes, commander of McClellan's Fourth Corps, recognized the growing problem of crowding the large army into a small space and the inevitable plague of diseases that would ensue. He warned that any raw troops from the North brought to the Peninsula at that time of year would "melt away and be ruined forever." Writing to Lincoln, whom he addressed as "his Excellency," Keyes told of his conviction that if the Army of the Potomac remained on Virginia's Peninsula, then by the middle of September "not more than 10,000 well men would have remained."[33]

Jonathan Letterman had another major concern. "The subject of the ambulances, after the health of the troops, became a matter of importance," he recalled.[34] To Letterman, it was obvious that the ability to complete a timely and well-organized evacuation of wounded was an integral function of a modern army. There was little doubt that when volunteer soldiers faced the prospect of being abandoned on the battlefield by their comrades, they were less willing to fight. In addition to saving lives, a well-structured ambulance system eliminated the need for able-bodied men to leave the front lines and carry wounded friends to safety. In 1861, and through the Peninsula campaign of 1862, this evacuation scheme did not exist.

That there was no formal ambulance corps at the start of the Civil War was not unusual, for few of the world's armies provided much in the way of medical care for their injured. Some fortunate wounded were carried to the rear by comrades, but most of the injured were left to die of exposure. The wounded were considered both an annoyance and an unnecessary burden, because once hurt they could no longer bear arms. That only the sick should care for the sick was acceptable military dogma. Medical assistance, if there was any, might not reach the battlefield until days after the fighting ended.

Not until the late eighteenth century did the French provide a more structured arrangement for evacuation of the wounded. Various horse-drawn wagons were organized into the *ambulance volantes*, or flying ambulance squadrons. These ambulances carried medical officers and their assistants right into the front line. The wounded were taken by stretcher bearers to the nearby medical officers, who waited for the ambulance wagon to arrive. With the physician present, the injured received surgical attention, including bullet extractions and even amputations. The treated victims were then transported in the ambulance wagon to a nearby field hospital.

By the time of the Crimean War, most of the major European armies employed some combination of trained stretcher bearers and ambulance wagons. The glaring exception was the British and their ill-conceived medical evacuation system. Having made the mistake of relying on regimental bandsmen to serve as litter bearers in previous wars, the British now turned to civilians. But civilians, lacking the resolve and training of military men, were more likely to run for their lives at the first sound of gunfire.

When British newspapermen reporting from the Crimea wrote home about the sufferings of the wounded, a public hue and cry led to an overhaul of the military's transportation system. Aware of these reforms, then United States secretary of war Jefferson Davis sent a military commission, which included a young captain, George McClellan, to travel to the Crimea and report on any novel concepts of warfare. Among the topics that interested Davis were new types of ambulances or other means of evacuating the sick and wounded. Reporting back to the secretary of war in 1857, McClellan and other members of the commission explained the use of a more structured ambulance transportation scheme in the Crimea.

Despite McClellan's testimony concerning the need for a better-organized ambulance system within the American military, when the Civil War began, army regulations still maintained a split responsibility between the Medical Department and the Quartermaster Corps with regard to transportation of the wounded. Quartermasters were to organize transportation of the injured and establish ambulance depots and field hospitals in the rear. Medical officers were to take care of a soldier's clinical needs. With little communication between the two departments, confusion reigned. To alleviate this difficulty, several ingenious designs for new types of ambulances were submitted to the government, including one vehicle that functioned as both evacuation wagon and doctor's hospital tent. Perhaps it might have bridged some of the coordination problems between quartermasters and physicians, but none of these so-called Moses ambulance wagons was ever built.

Instead, in the best of situations, a regiment of seven or eight hundred men would enter battle with half a dozen rickety two-wheeled ambulance wagons, perhaps one four-wheeled vehicle that doubled as a medical supply cart, and two or three tents. The "Finley" two-wheelers broke down almost immediately or quickly disappeared from the scene because the quartermaster used them for day-to-day transportation of officers instead of emergency medical needs. The one tent that served as a regiment's hospital was only fourteen by fourteen feet, and eleven feet high in the center, with side walls four and a half feet high. Designed to accommodate just eight men, the tent and its pins and poles weighed an imposing 217 pounds. Other types of tents were available, including a twelve-foot-high tepeelike contraption and a common wedge shelter, but their shape was considered impractical for hospital work. Complicating the health care problems was the fact that most regiments were usually short on medical supplies. Even simple stretchers to hand-carry the sick and wounded were difficult to find.

The smaller-size regiment remained the traditional unit to which medical treatment and hospitalization were directed. Friends wanted to serve and die with their friends, and the only physicians to be trusted were those from back home. The army brass was taught to think in terms of regimental ambulances, regimental fighting, regimental hospitals, regimental personnel, and regimental supplies. But as the British had learned in the Crimean War and the Americans would realize on Virginia's Peninsula, it was impossible during the chaos of combat to specifically direct the wounded to their own regimental hospital and physician. Care for the injured might have been centered on the needs of the regiment, but with no coordinated plans for ambulance evacuation, the regiment-only way of doing things wasted human lives.

Distressed at this lack of structured transportation services, the no-nonsense Letterman presented McClellan with a novel plan for an ambulance corps. He wanted to replace the smaller-scale regiment-only medical service with an organization of ambulances and attendants based on the army's larger-size units. The Union army was organized so that four or five infantry regiments (a combat-ready infantry regiment consisted of around one thousand men) constituted a brigade. Three or four brigades made up a division, totaling twelve thousand to fifteen thousand soldiers. Usually, three divisions constituted an army corps, with a single corps making up a small army and larger armies, including the Army of the Potomac, having two or more corps. In reality, owing to sickness and injuries, the average size of any given unit in the Union army was a third to a half of ideal numbers.

Letterman named a captain in each corps to be called commandant of the ambulance corps. Reporting to this commandant of the ambulance corps was a first lieutenant in charge of division ambulances, a second lieutenant serving brigades, and a sergeant for each regiment. By this simple trickle-down scheme, Letterman was able to divide each man's duties so that he was not overburdened by administrative details while preserving the captain's role as commander. For instance, part of a captain's responsibilities was teaching stretcher bearers how to properly carry a litter, "observing that the front man steps off with the left foot and the rear man with the right," according to Letterman. The first lieutenant was in charge of a traveling cavalry forge, a blacksmith, and a saddler so that the ambulance train would not break down for lengthy periods of time.

Letterman insisted that the officers in charge permit no one to ride in an ambulance without medical clearance. Rather than use regimental musicians as litter bearers, he ordered that only practical, physically fit soldiers be detailed and trained for this special type of work. Only members of the ambulance corps were to carry the sick or wounded from the battlefield. Letterman stipulated that when in camp, the ambulances for each division be parked near one another to prevent unscrupulous officers from using them for nonmedical reasons. "The system," according to Letterman, "was based upon the idea that they should not be under the immediate control of Medical officers, whose duties, especially on the day of battle, would prevent any proper supervision; but that other officers, appointed for that especial purpose, should have direct charge of the horses, harness, ambulances, etc." And in a bold attempt to emphasize the ambulance corps's uniqueness, Letterman mandated special uniforms and guns. Privates were authorized to wear a two-inch green band around their caps and a two-inch green half chevron on their upper arms, and they were to be armed with revolvers. Noncommissioned officers used the same cap band but were permitted full green chevrons with the V pointed toward their shoulder.

Letterman's plan was audacious, but he needed to guarantee more efficient battlefield evacuations. One way he achieved this was by relieving physicians and their staff of responsibility for physically placing wounded soldiers aboard an ambulance and transporting them, at the height of a battle, to a far-off field hospital. Ambulance corps drivers would now do this. Doctors could devote more time to their patients' needs. Basically, Letterman removed the responsibility for medical transportation from the Quartermaster Corps and placed it under his jurisdiction as medical director of the Army of the Potomac.

On August 2, McClellan implemented the Letterman plan as General Order No. 147 for the Army of the Potomac. As Letterman recalled, "Much labor was necessary to put it in operation."[35] This would be especially true because Old Brains Halleck had just reported back to Lincoln about the poor physical state of the Army of the Potomac. Halleck, suffering from chronic diarrhea that was made worse during his short stay at Harrison's Landing, was shocked by what he saw. Forty percent of the soldiers were unable to carry out their military duties. Yet only 4 percent of these were disabled because of combat wounds. Scores of new cases of dysentery, malaria, and typhoid were reported every day. According to one contemporary account, "The general feeling expressed by the officers was, that the army was not in a condition to fight, and that it should be withdrawn from the Peninsula."[36] A concerned Halleck wrote to McClellan, "To keep your army in its present position until it could be so re-enforced would almost destroy it in that climate. The months of August and September are almost fatal to whites who live on that part of James River."[37] With that season of the year coming on, Lincoln, Halleck, and others in the administration decided over McClellan's vigorous protests to withdraw the Yankee army.

The judgment to evacuate the Peninsula and end McClellan's quest to capture Richmond was an example of how easily common communicable diseases could disrupt military strategy in that era. Affected by the torrential Virginia rains of April and May and the unbearable humidity of June and July, the health of the Army of the Potomac had seriously deteriorated into a state of collapse by August. Would conditions have worsened in September? Using that era's scientific know-how, no one, not physician, politician, or soldier, knew the answer, nor could any of them fathom how to resolve the army's health care problem. Was the decision not to reinforce the Union army and abandon this land of pestilence and swamps medically valid? It would seem that it was. The incidence of dysentery, malaria, and typhoid, although varying from one regiment to the next, was on the rise. July and August's hot weather brought further fecal contamination of food and water supplies. A medical catastrophe that would lead to a military disaster was in the making, and it could be avoided only by the army's recall.

For ten days, sharp words passed between McClellan and Halleck, whom McClellan considered his intellectual inferior. Halleck responded to McClellan's barbs and apparent stalling: "The order will not be rescinded, and you will be expected to execute it with all possible promptness."[38] So commanded, McClellan initiated the mass evacuation of Harrison's Landing.

Letterman arranged sea transport for more than fourteen thousand sick and wounded to points north. On August 15 alone, 5,945 men were shipped out. The following day, the land movement of troops began. A long pontoon bridge was thrown across the Chickahominy near its mouth, and using this and other hastily constructed crossing sites, the Yankees departed. It took a full two days before the last rear guard was over and the bridges could be removed. McClellan congratulated himself on a safe passage, but the truth was that the whole Confederate force was a hundred miles away.

It was an arduous march from Harrison's Landing on the James River to Yorktown and then down to Fortress Monroe at the Peninsula's tip. When he saw lengthy wagon trains with ambulances in line, Letterman had his first opportunity to assess the beginnings of his ambulance corps. Although there had been little time for the implementation of his order, he was convinced that once fully operational, his ambulance plan would be of great service to the wounded and sick. Letterman soon left for Washington, where the political struggles over an armywide ambulance corps were only beginning.

Erasmus Keyes's Fourth Corps, along with his medical director, Frank Hamilton, moved from Harrison's Landing to a safer and hopefully healthier Yorktown. There, Keyes's troops were assigned to garrison duty and Hamilton was placed in charge of a temporary field hospital. For a few weeks, the dry and pleasant weather improved everybody's health and disposition. But by mid-September, the rains began again, mosquitoes swarmed, and malaria struck with a vengeance. On September 30, of Keyes's 8,168 men, only 4,764 were able to report to duty. In just thirty days, more than 40 percent of his command became sick. Considering that these troops had better living conditions than the Army of the Potomac had at Harrison's Landing and that the men at Yorktown were reasonably well fed, the extent of disease suggests that Lincoln and Halleck had been wise to prevent McClellan from remaining on the Peninsula.

CHAPTER SIX

"We get lousy! and dirty"

O N June 4, after a tedious four-day evacuation process following his gunshot wound at Fair Oaks, George Fisk of the Eighty-first New York Infantry was admitted to Washington's Judiciary Square Hospital. His now dirty, bloodstained dressing might have swaddled his shoulder, but the operative wound was already infected. Fisk's surgical procedure—removal of his shattered upper arm bone while leaving the major blood vessels, muscles, and nerves intact—had left a gap in his limb's skeletal continuity. His extremity now dangled unsupported from his shoulder and was functionally worthless. Fisk's doctor hoped that bone regeneration would occur and partial reuse of the limb would come about, but it was a false expectation. Without the ability to provide reconstructive skeletal support (for example, placement of a metal rod—a sophisticated surgical advance that would not occur until the mid-twentieth century), the operation was doomed from the start.

Even more grim was the fact that bone exsection or resection, the formal name for Fisk's operation, was a technically demanding feat and more difficult to perform than a straightforward amputation. As a result, exsection carried an extraordinary risk of infection, tissue necrosis, blood poisoning, hemorrhage, and death. Even if the patient survived these myriad postoperative complications, time would cause the loosely swinging and unmanageable arm to deteriorate. Turgidity set in, nerves could not conduct electrical messages, muscles lost the ability to contract, joints stiffened, fingers no longer functioned, and the limb, now useless, painful, and loathsome, needed to be amputated. Bone exsections were an exercise in unwarranted surgery fostered by overzealous physicians seeking surgical challenges. Not surprisingly, the procedure became less popular as the war progressed, especially once the results came to be regarded as poor, if not downright dangerous.

Fisk's shoulder was immobile, swollen, and tender, and the surrounding tissue was turning necrotic. Hungry, irritable, and growing weaker, he had to reckon with the fact that the appendage, though saved from a surgeon's amputation knife and aesthetically intact, now hung at his side like a dead weight. Worse, the physicians and nurses could do little to reduce his suffering. In an era when the presence of pus was mistakenly considered a positive part of the healing process and antibiotics and narcotic injections were unknown, all the staff could provide was some measure of comfort care. Weekly baths and twice daily washing of wounds were hardly equal to containing the infection that was taking possession of Fisk's body. Indeed, he had exactly sixty-four days till his wound would explode in a bloody eruption and end his life.

At least the sick house on Washington's Judiciary Square was new and clean. The building, though already overcrowded, represented the epitome of military medical construction, and its very presence created a change in the way Americans would view hospitals. Until the structure on Judiciary Square was completed in April 1862, the American hospital was considered an ignominious place to receive medical care, a facility of last resort. Essentially, it was a shelter for those who could not afford treatment at home, had no family to provide nursing needs, or lived in such adverse conditions that no space could be found for the sick or dying. No less an authority than Benjamin Rush, father of the country's bleed, blister, and purge style of medicine, labeled hospitals "the sinks of human life in an army." "They robbed the United States of more citizens than the sword," wrote Rush.[1] Few citizens, rich, poor, or otherwise, could ever imagine being admitted to such a place.

The status of America's military hospitals was no better. The army's far-flung network of log cabin infirmaries was ill equipped to handle the vast number of casualties from a prolonged war. Army officers had no experience working in larger hospitals because military regulations called for hospital accommodations in exact proportion to the number of men on a single regiment's roll. Providing hospital beds based on the larger size of a division or corps was simply unthinkable.

Critics of larger-size civilian hospitals pointed warily to the presence of "hospitalism," the concept that the building with its foul air, constantly degraded by bodily secretions and patients' breathing, was itself the cause of disease; a hospital's grimy walls and stale atmosphere caused illness, and the poisonous air or effluvia was thought to gain potency in direct ratio to the number of patients gathered together. But what if the crowded conditions and poisonous air could be tempered by new architectural designs? Officials were beginning to understand that large general hospitals had definite managerial and organizational advantages. Larger facilities could bring about more efficient day-to-day administration. For instance, multiple wards meant that the sick and wounded could be separated on the basis of their individual ailments, allowing for the administration of specialized medical and nursing care. Bigger and better-run kitchens provided more nutritious food. Larger bathrooms with better sanitary conditions could decrease odors. Fully equipped laundries assured fresh linens. And with expansive landscaped grounds, patients would be able to recuperate in the fresh air.

By the time of the Civil War, a growing emphasis on maximizing the circulation of air, along with a desire for cleanliness, spaciousness, and ventilation, had found architectural life in the form of pavilion hospitals. The country's embrace of pavilion-style architecture was a direct result of the recent British experience in the Crimean conflict, especially Florence Nightingale's pleas for sanitary reforms. Pavilion plans called for multiple wards branching out from a central interconnecting building, which housed moderate numbers of patients and was ventilated by numerous windows and doors. Pavilion design meant low, sprawling hospital complexes situated on wide-open grounds. In the best of circumstances, a flowing river or lake would be nearby to assure that cleansing breezes wafted through the buildings to constantly freshen the air.

Architects designed pavilion hospital complexes to minimize the accumulation of dirt. Smooth surfaces, few furnishings, decreased numbers of right-angle corners to lessen the accumulation of dust, and increased space between patients were major concerns. "Tidiness" and "commodious" became the code words for success. Combine all this with hygienic behavior, as exemplified by specific sanitary reforms— chamber pots emptied on time, commodes scrubbed daily, drainage ditches dug for human waste, refuse collected several times a day—and hospitalism would be eliminated.

What William Hammond observed as inspector of military hospitals in Maryland and western Virginia in early 1862 made him livid. "It is simply disgusting," was how he described a building recently extemporized into a military hospital. Its terrible condition, he told members of the United States Sanitary Commission, "does not exist in any other hospital in the civilized world, and this hospital is altogether worse than any which were appropriate to the allies in the Crimean War." Hammond knew what he was talking about. Only three and a half years earlier, he had visited Europe and inspected military and civilian hospitals. Knowledgeable about the minutiae of hospital construction and administration, from the preferred size of windows (six feet eight inches high and two feet seven inches in width) to the advantage of cotton over linen sheets (warmer in cold weather), Hammond was an advocate of Nightingale's precepts. In the Maryland and western Virginia situation, soldiers were packed together with as little as 84 cubic feet of space apiece, although pavilion hospital design required approximately 1,200 cubic feet for an individual's adequate ventilation. The sick troops were getting worse, according to Hammond, owing to "utmost confusion" in the hospitals' daily management, inadequate nutrition, and what he termed a "most disgusting want of cleanliness."[2]

Hammond suggested that the buildings in Maryland and western Virginia be abandoned and asked his longtime army friend Jonathan Letterman, then medical director of the military's Department of Western Virginia, to order the construction of several wooden huts based on a variation of the pavilion design. The first of these complexes was built at Parkersburg, Virginia (now West Virginia). The two wooden sheds measured 130 feet by 25 feet, with 14-foot-high ceilings, and were divided by transverse partitions into four wards containing twenty beds each. The unique architectural feature was a ventilation system of lengthy open spaces starting at the roofline and running along the sides of the building. Without a sash to close out the cold, these early ridge ventilators, as they were called, made it difficult to maintain any warmth within the structure. Once closable shutters were included in architectural plans, ridge ventilation became a fixture of military hospitals.

During the winter of 1861–1862, the Sanitary Commission received two lengthy reports from Hammond on the condition of military medical facilities. Relying on his recommendations, commission members urged the federal government to build a series of new hospitals based on the pavilion principle. The commission proposed five hospitals to house fifteen thousand soldiers and sent in elaborate plans estimated at $75 per bed. General McClellan, fearing dishonest contractors would take advantage of the chaotic military situation in Washington, objected to the project's total cost and reduced the number to two complexes of just two hundred beds each. Still, commission members viewed this compromise as an important first step toward establishing a national military hospital system. Soon, identical pavilion-style hospitals were being built in Washington—one on Judiciary Square and another on Mount Pleasant.

The two sprawling wooden complexes, consisting of ten separate pavilions containing twenty beds each, stood on three-foot-high cedar stilts. The crawl space, closed off by wooden slats, was supposedly well ventilated with numerous apertures. When combined with the roof's ridge ventilation system, the off-the-ground setting assured free circulation of air over, under, and through the building. Despite everyone's concerns with maintaining fresh ventilation, the buildings were soon enveloped in offensive smells from the water closets. These water closets, in proximity to each ward's kitchen, were nothing more than wooden commodes over holes in the ground where urinary and fecal matter percolated downward into a collecting sewer pipe. Higher partitions along with special ventilating shafts were built to fend off the bathroom smells, but the obsession with adequate air circulation was undermined by chronic fecal contamination.

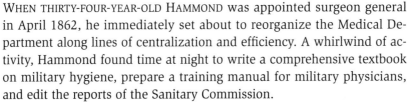

WHEN THIRTY-FOUR-YEAR-OLD HAMMOND was appointed surgeon general in April 1862, he immediately set about to reorganize the Medical Department along lines of centralization and efficiency. A whirlwind of activity, Hammond found time at night to write a comprehensive textbook on military hygiene, prepare a training manual for military physicians, and edit the reports of the Sanitary Commission.

Of Hammond's earliest projects, one of the most important was the construction of a massive military hospital in West Philadelphia. It was crucial that this be done expeditiously because it would serve as a model for a nationwide military hospital program and showcase Hammond's administrative and scientific capabilities. He wanted the Medical Department to be perceived as a powerful institution that transcended local interests. At the same time, it seemed as if every politician lobbied him to place a military hospital in his own jurisdiction. From White Hall, Pennsylvania, to Jeffersonville, Indiana, to Portsmouth Grove, Rhode Island, town fathers and city officials wanted to share in the boom to area business that a military facility would bring. Regional politics as well as sanitary issues had to be considered, but as Hammond warned one United States congressman, "all military hospitals should be entirely within the control of this Bureau—outside the hands of this Department all responsibility ceases." To a prominent Philadelphia surgeon, Hammond declared testily, "I intend to assume the entire control of these hospitals, and to employ the medical officers on duty with them not as State officers but as United States officers."[3]

Within a week of his appointment, Hammond drafted plans for what would later be named the Satterlee Hospital, after Richard Smith Satterlee, the army's elderly medical purveyor in New York. Located near Forty-fourth and Spruce streets (now the site of Clark Park), one-half mile outside Philadelphia's then city limits, Hammond approved a site on a slight hill "proven to be eminently healthy," according to his accounts, and only 250 feet from the rapidly flowing Mill Creek. Not one to waste time, Hammond was assured by the contractor that the complex could be completed in forty days. With twenty-eight pavilions containing 1,344 beds, two interconnecting corridors each measuring 740 feet in length, and a two-story administration building, Hammond's hospital was so massive that more than four acres of land would be covered by various structures. By June 9, seven of the wards were filled with patients, and a year later Hammond could justly claim, "The West Philadelphia Hospital is a credit to the army . . . the difficulties to contend with in the management of so vast an institution as this can scarcely be conceived by those who have not personally visited it and studied the system by which it is governed."

Hammond had every right to brag about his triumph. Its cost, exclusive of the furniture, exceeded $200,000. Not only was it expensive, but it was expansive: twelve and a half total acres of tree-dotted land enclosed by a fourteen-foot-high white picket fence. With barbershops, laundries, a pharmacy, and smoking rooms, the complex was a city unto itself, and following further additions, by war's end bed capacity reached an amazing 3,519. Hammond authoritatively claimed that with one exception, Satterlee was "the largest [military hospital] in the world intended solely for sick and wounded persons." Each bed had 1,141 cubic feet of ventilated space, and there were two hundred coal stoves for heating; washing machines, mangles, and wringers in every ward; fresh water pumped from the Schuylkill River; a printing press on the premises; a weekly in-house newspaper; and a large library and reading room. A slush fund was established, derived from the sale of animal bones, fat, flour barrels, manure, old newspapers, stale bread, slops, wastepaper, and a tax on purveyors of food and liquor. The moneys bought small luxury wares and recreational items for the men. The wards were also equipped with a new type of latrine—a twelve-foot-long cast-iron trough covered by a row of seat holes, with a water faucet at one end and a discharge hole at the other. In theory, the trough was supposed to be one-third filled with water and the collected ordure let off every hour into a general sewer pipe by elevating a lever controlled by lock and key. To save water, the tap was sometimes turned off until a great quantity of feces and urine had built up along with a suffocating odor. More commonly, the individual in charge of elevating the discharge lever was late for the task.

So involved was Hammond in the daily administration of the hospital that he personally picked its initial complement of physicians and other caregivers. According to his plan, one responsible medical officer would supervise each pavilion. There would be no meddling lay board of managers as found in civilian hospitals. Satterlee, and all other military hospitals, would be controlled by physicians and considered first and foremost a medical, not a charity-based, institution.

Hammond named thirty-year-old Isaac Israel Hayes, surgeon, naturalist, and renowned Arctic explorer, as overall physician in charge and ordered him to obtain the services of forty nuns to assist in nursing care. Chaplains were brought in on a permanent basis. Medical students were asked to volunteer their services and assist both physicians and nurses. Each ward was assigned one surgeon, one nun, three male nurses, and a medical student. Above all, Hammond wanted order. "The discipline has always been excellent, and the patients have been well cared for," he would later write.

Hammond became recognized as a master hospital planner and administrator. His book *A Treatise on Hygiene* contained almost 150 pages on the principles of hospital construction, from building materials to heating, lighting, and ventilation. "In the Judiciary Square Hospital in Washington City a great mistake was committed in closing this space," he wrote, referring to the thirty-six-inch crawl area between the ground and the wooden flooring. "It cannot too strongly be impressed upon the student of hygiene that confined air is always deleterious to those subjected to its influence." Even Satterlee was not exempt from criticism. "The West Philadelphia Hospital is by no means a perfect structure," Hammond lamented. "The corridors are too close together, and the distance between the pavilions should be at least ten feet greater than at present. The water-closets are constructed after a bad plan, and though the trough may be regularly emptied every hour, the excreta remain in it that long, and render the air of the wards more or less impure."[4]

FREDERICK LAW OLMSTED returned from Virginia's Peninsula in mid-July 1862, in poor health. Within a few weeks, he had an obvious case of jaundice, probably caused by hepatitis. "I grew daily more yellow, until I could have passed for rather a dark mulatto; the whites of my eyes gave place to a queer glistening saffron colored substance, and my skin became flabby leather, dry and dead. I itched furiously and where I plowed the surface with my fingerends, it presently became purple." Olmsted spent the end of July with his family on Staten Island, New York, but with little improvement in his condition. Seeking an even healthier environment, he traveled to Walpole, New Hampshire, to join his good friend Frederick Knapp, who was recuperating from the malaria he had contracted on the Peninsula. After showing no signs of improvement, Olmsted returned to his boyhood home in Hartford, Connecticut. Alarmed at Olmsted's deteriorating appearance, Cornelius Agnew, one of the physicians on the Sanitary Commission's executive committee, took him to a sanatorium in Saratoga Springs, New York. However, Olmsted had little time for a lengthy convalescence. After ten days, he boarded a train to Washington. Writing to a friend, Olmsted reflected, "I have been ill, and still am far from well. Being very deeply jaundiced, but avoiding acute illness by every dodge to which with the best medical advice, I can from hour to hour, resort."[5]

Following his return to the commission's central office, Olmsted engaged in a series of regular meetings with William Hammond. Acting on an earlier suggestion of Agnew's, Olmsted urged the surgeon general to immediately organize a special inspection corps of distinguished physicians to visit military hospitals and recommend changes. Hammond was enthusiastic in his support, regarding this as a prime opportunity to effect simultaneous reform throughout the entire hospital system. From October 1862 through April 1863, sixty of the most prominent men in American medicine visited military facilities in every part of the country. The results were somewhat surprising: According to Charles Stillé, the Sanitary Commission's official historian, "The hospitals were found, in general, in a far more satisfactory condition than had been anticipated."[6]

Florence Nightingale's mantra regarding cleanliness, now enforced by Hammond's previous orders during the spring and summer months, seemed to be working. Hospital filth was on the decline, and the inspectors noted that the majority of facilities were dirty in only one place: their plumbing. However, having looked at hundreds of hospitals located in all manner of buildings, from rooming houses to hotels and churches, the inspectors agreed on one major recommendation: the critical importance of establishing general hospitals only in structures erected specifically for such a purpose.

Hammond needed no further encouragement for expanding the pavilion system, and with Olmsted and the Sanitary Commission plus the nation's medical establishment backing his goals, the construction of new military hospitals became the country's largest coordinated construction project. So much had been learned in the building program of 1862 that by early 1863, the hospitals were already more comfortable for patients. The construction of the pavilions—wood and plaster with shingled roofs; improved lighting, heating, and ventilation; and upgraded bathrooms—was becoming standardized. In July 1864, architectural guidelines detailing mandatory elements of a pavilion hospital complex were issued. From choosing the site to the arrangement of pavilions in converging lines forming a V, with an administration building at the apex of the V—or, instead, pavilions radiating from the periphery of a circle, ellipse, or rounded oblong—all hospital complexes were to have the same basic design. The wards were to be 187 feet long and 24 feet wide, with a 14-foot ceiling. Various offices such as commissary, knapsack storage area, quartermaster storeroom, guardhouse, quarters for female nurses, chapel, operating rooms, records room, and a dead house, located, according to the plans, "so as not to be observed from the wards," were fully described.[7]

So massive and formalized had the hospital construction program become that by June 1863, there were eighty-four thousand beds in 182 facilities. One year later, the number of beds increased by nearly forty thousand. By the war's end, more than two hundred military hospitals could be found in every major Northern city and even in areas of the occupied South. In fact, Hammond's building program grew to such an extent that Olmsted became concerned that the Medical Department could not tell a wounded soldier's family where their son or father or husband was being treated or whether he was even dead or alive. This became especially evident in mid-1862 following the Peninsula campaign, the Second Battle of Bull Run, and Antietam. A steady stream of letters from the relatives and friends of the sick and wounded flooded the offices of the Sanitary Commission. "I think you will know my boy; he is fair-haired, straight, and slender, with a fair skin and delicate hands," wrote one mother. "Tell me he is living, and has done well, and I care for nothing else." The plea of a wife, typical among thousands, went unanswered: "Give him back to me dead, if he is dead, for I must see him."[8] Seeking some type of solution, Olmsted proposed the creation of a hospital directory to aid persons wishing to learn the location of sick or wounded soldiers. Some members of the Sanitary Commission balked at the projected cost, but Olmsted, writing to his wife, said, "I 'cuss'd and swore', so about it, that they yielded to my will until I got half an hour to deliberate upon it."[9] As usual, Olmsted had his way, and in November 1862, a hospital directory with 19,084 registered names was completed for the District of Columbia. By June 1863, Olmsted's registration plan covered all the army's general hospitals and eventually listed more than 215,000 soldiers.

Ultimately, contemporaries came to see the Civil War hospitals, despite their occasional design flaws, as a triumph of sanitary reason. With more than a million men treated as inpatients and an overall mortality rate of less than 10 percent, the army's general hospitals were regarded as invaluable and necessary public institutions. No longer were hospitals sanctuaries only for the destitute and insane. Instead, men from all walks of life acknowledged the hospital as integral to the nation's burgeoning health care system. For the first time, bankers, carpenters, clerks, lawyers, miners, policemen, and shopkeepers experienced the realities of institutional medical treatment. And, surprisingly, they found a quality of care far higher than it had once been. With massive wards maintained in scrupulous order and fresh linen and healthy foods, getting well within a hospital was becoming part of the American experience.

It was the Civil War that fostered the beginning of hospitals as big business and helped shape medical reformers' ideas as to what constituted a good facility. So insistent had activists, physicians, and even common citizens become on Nightingalian principles that pavilion-style hospitals were now considered sacrosanct. Frank Hamilton, the Bull Run battle-tested surgeon from New York City, had even gone so far as to suggest that if proper buildings could not be built in a healthy setting, then "it would be far better that the sick should remain without shelter."[10] Hamilton, who remained on Virginia's Peninsula with the men of Erasmus Keyes's Fourth Corps through September 1862, had resumed his professorship of military surgery and hygiene and of fractures and dislocations in Bellevue Medical College. On returning to Manhattan, Hamilton also renewed his relationship with the lay board of that city's Central Park Hospital. The hospital had been founded in January 1862 when New York City aldermen arranged to take over buildings of the Mount St. Vincent Academy in Central Park to serve as an emergency military hospital; now, thanks to Hamilton's efforts, it was assumed that Central Park Hospital would have a new ventilation plan. And if redesigning the buildings was not possible, Hamilton's alternative was to erect large tents with open side walls and raised flaps for doors that would be floored and strung together on the adjacent grounds. Yet despite his best intentions and implementation of the new ventilation system, smells from water closets on the two upper floors of the hospital were a source of frequent complaints.

Hamilton's drive for sanitary improvements did not stop in Central Park. He insisted that New York City's commissioners of public charities support a fever ward, composed entirely of well-ventilated tents, to be placed on isolated Blackwell's Island (now Roosevelt Island) in the middle of the East River. In this way, Hamilton wrote, "we shall now be able to ascertain how much pure air alone can accomplish in typhus and typhoid fevers."[11] Hamilton's work with New York City officials typified what was beginning to occur throughout the rest of the country, for it was not only the United States Army that was now building pavilion-style hospitals. Boston officials had agreed to construct a pavilion-style city hospital to be completed in May 1864.

The Civil War might not have brought about great changes in therapeutics or diagnostics, but the physical and administrative structure of the American hospital was being transformed. None of the pavilion hospitals built during the war years still exist, but structures like Armory Square and Harewood in Washington; Haddington, Mower, and Satterlee in Philadelphia; and Jarvis in Baltimore, each with more than one thousand beds, exerted a profound influence on the development of America's hospital system. The Civil War hospital was not yet dominated by a scientifically trained medical profession, nor was there a group of administrators to manage its day-to-day needs. This would not begin until the first decades of the twentieth century, when hospitals would come to be regarded as large, centralized structures that provided sophisticated medical care under the direction of well-educated and -trained physicians. What the Civil War experience did provide, however, by exposing millions of Americans to a coordinated hospital system, was an all-important sense of the promise of the future of medical care.

UNFORTUNATELY FOR GEORGE FISK, despite treatment in a pavilion-style hospital, he would not live to see the end of the summer of 1862. Almost two months had passed since Fisk's bullet injury at Fair Oaks, removal of his upper arm bone at Savage's Station, and evacuation to Washington's Judiciary Square Hospital. Fisk's case report from Judiciary Square describes the events of his hospital stay as follows: "The man entered hospital June 4th; did well till August 5th, when bleeding commenced at the interior wound. August 7th, profuse hemorrhage. On attempting to reach the artery by laying open the track of the original wound, and finding the vessel, the bleeding was so profuse that the patient died while operating."[12] This terse report glosses over the gory details of Fisk's demise. Malnourished and in constant pain, he suffered endlessly throughout his hospitalization. During a slow and torturous process, Fisk's operative wound became infected and the surrounding tissues turned gangrenous. This was neither an unusual nor a dreaded situation, since in this preantiseptic era, traumatic wounds were believed to be lined with dead tissue that was expelled in the form of pus. When a wound healed satisfactorily without an abundant flow of pus, it was considered an aberration. Not until later in the war, when enough wounds healed without the presence of pus, did some physicians begin to question the then classic theory of wound maturation.

With no knowledge of how to prevent or treat postoperative infection, a surgeon could do little to ameliorate a patient's suffering. In Fisk's case, the infection caused his incision to open and then deepen. The exposed muscles turned an ugly shade of oxygen-deprived reddish brown. Next, the once iridescent fasciae and ligaments, which attach muscle to bone, melted away. Eating their way downward, the bacteria and other putrid elements soon attacked life-nourishing blood vessels. Surrounding the arm's main artery, in the area of the armpit, or axilla, where it narrows and begins to branch out, the pulsating vessel was now stretched across a growing divide. Minute ulcers appeared on the artery's surface, creating areas of microscopic hemorrhage. On August 5, a sentinel bleed took place. This sudden presence of a small amount of bright red arterial blood was an indication that things were awry. In response, the modern surgeon would immediately act to suture closed a necrotic blood vessel. The Civil War surgeon had no idea what was occurring. Two days later, with the stench of decay permeating Fisk's clothes and bedding, the ulcers coalesced and his axillary artery exploded in a torrent of blood. Fisk rapidly lost consciousness.

At this point, any female nurses present were banished back to their rooms. Their presence was deemed a distraction, as most were untrained and considered incapable of providing emergency surgical care. Meanwhile, working at Fisk's unlit bedside (there were no operating rooms at Judiciary Square Hospital), the surgeon struggled to find the source of the bleeding. The gangrene, however, had turned Fisk's upper arm into a gelatinous mass of unidentifiable tissue. Normal anatomical landmarks were no longer present. Therefore, the artery was never located and Fisk eventually died. All of this happened in full view of other wounded men in Fisk's ward, who lay helpless on narrow iron bedsteads and straw mattresses. After nurses returned to the floor to assist the more able-bodied convalescing soldiers clean up the mess, Fisk's body was carried away on a handheld litter.

Located at the far corner of the Judiciary Square complex was the "dead house," a square fifteen-foot shack where corpses were stored. The building had no refrigeration, and few efforts were made to retard putrefaction. The smell of death filled the structure. Fisk's body was placed on a crude wooden bench, covered with a blood-soaked white cloth, and surrounded by other Union dead. But his travails with Civil War medicine were not yet over. The hospital's medical cadets (minimally educated medical students on leave from school or an apprenticeship) were asked by the head physician to perform an autopsy to document the manner of Fisk's death. Proceeding with abandon, the cadets hacked away at Fisk's body and removed what was left of the bones of his shoulder joint along with attached blood vessels, ligaments, muscles, and nerves. Further dissection revealed the axillary artery to have a large ulcerous opening from which Fisk bled to death. Having established the cause of his demise, the hospital at last dispatched Fisk's remains north to New York State for burial.

What Fisk's family did not know was that the removed shoulder joint and its attached tissues were handed over to John Brinton, the recently named first curator of the United States Army Medical Museum. The museum, one of Surgeon General Hammond's earliest initiatives, displayed pathological specimens as part of an ongoing endeavor to better educate physicians and improve medical care. From infected organs to fractured bones, thousands of items, many pickled in alcohol or mummified by sunlight, found their way to the museum's shelves. Fisk's shoulder was permanently assigned Case No. 1062.

As UNPLEASANT AS Fisk's story is, his treatment by novice medical students, poorly skilled surgeons, and untrained nurses was not atypical. At this early stage of the Civil War, providing an experienced on-site hospital staff was a much-discussed issue. Since the founding of the country, a hospital's nursing and housekeeping chores were traditionally undertaken by convalescents or even past patients who remained in the facility for lack of anywhere else to call home. America's military hospitals functioned in a similar manner, with recuperating soldiers, who were themselves frequently unable to maneuver around the cots, providing the bulk of nursing care. The situation among female nurses in military hospitals was particularly difficult both for the volunteers and the administrators under whom they served. Unlike the country's conglomerate of medical schools, no scholastic or vocational institutes offered programs in nursing education. There were no nursing diplomas to earn or professional credentials to collect. Most of the women who served as nurses during the Civil War were amateur caregivers relying on practical experience. Their best, and often only, resolve was a sincere desire to relieve the suffering of the soldiers they tended.

That women were capable of performing nursing duties was undeniable. Various Catholic and Protestant sisterhoods already stressed nursing as an avocation, but none of their novitiates' experience centered on the new Nightingale style of sanitary-based nursing care. Proper nursing, according to Nightingale's values, consisted of the formal schooling of nurses and involved principles of cleanliness, diet, drainage, lighting, quiet, warmth, and ventilation without disturbing a sick patient. Instead, the sisterhoods provided less structured learning while praying and working in their own order's hospitals. Assisting in a patient's emotional care, distributing clean clothing and linen, and regulating what a convalescent could eat were the sisters' primary tasks. The integration of sanitary reform with an understanding of the nursing sciences was not part of the daily learning routine.

As early as June 1861, a Confederate surgeon despairing of poor hospital care informally asked the Catholic Sisters of Charity in Emmitsburg, Maryland, to aid in the treatment of the sick and wounded in Richmond. Trained in obedience and unusually efficient, the half-dozen or so nuns who traveled to Virginia were widely hailed. Knowing of the sisters' success in the South, the federal government made a formal request, in the spring of 1862, of the Mother Superior in Emmitsburg to aid in the North's war effort. Immediately, the subject of Catholic sisters serving in army hospitals came under discussion within the church's hierarchy. The archbishop of New York City expressed his displeasure to the archbishop of Baltimore: "I am now informed indirectly that the Sisters of Charity in the diocese would be willing to volunteer a force of from fifty to one hundred nurses. To this proposition I have very strong objections." Soon, the New York City archbishop withdrew his criticisms, prompted perhaps by his nomination by President Lincoln to serve on a highly publicized diplomatic mission to Europe. Thereafter, all sisters in his religious jurisdiction who wished to volunteer as nurses at military hospitals went with his blessings.

The archbishop's about-face proved particularly important to Surgeon General William Hammond. When Hammond's pet project, the Satterlee Military Hospital, was being built, he knew the massive facility would require a strong-willed administrator. Having received several recommendations regarding potential candidates, Hammond settled on

Sister Mary Gonzaga of the Sisters of Charity, the longtime directress of Philadelphia's renowned St. Joseph's Orphan Asylum. Fifty years old, Sister Gonzaga had been a schoolteacher, nurse, and Mother Superior and had spent a year in France in an administrative capacity at the original convent of the order. On June 9, 1862, Sister Gonzaga, accompanied by forty sisters gathered from all over the country, embarked upon duty at Satterlee. Amazed at the size of the facility, one sister remarked that "they could scarcely find the entrance."[13] Living in a wing of private rooms located on the second floor of a converted storehouse, Sister Gonzaga and her nuns proved more capable than even Hammond thought possible. In a few weeks, he wrote to Lincoln, "We found in the Sisters of Charity, a Corps of faithful, devoted and trained nurses ready to administer to the sick and wounded."[14]

Administering medicine, loosening a bandage, cooking and feeding, or assisting with the spiritual needs of a soldier, the Sisters of Charity remained at Satterlee through 1865. "To see Sister Gonzaga always calm, always ready, with modesty and fidelity, performing a Christian duty, as an administering angel when physicians, surgeons, friends and all human aid had failed," one wounded soldier wrote, "was a beautiful sight."[15] So grateful were her many patients that at the hospital's closing, a petition was signed asking that the furniture and ornaments in the chapel, purchased through a soldiers fund, be donated to the orphans at Sister Gonzaga's St. Joseph's Asylum.

THE EXACT NUMBER of women who volunteered as Civil War nurses is not known, but the several hundred Catholic nuns and Protestant sisters represented only a small portion of the total number of women who did eventually serve. It was the other female volunteers, those coming from private life (believed to be approximately three to five thousand individuals), with whom men most found fault. In this Victorian era, the sheer presence of a woman in a hospital ward crowded with male patients created concerns regarding motivation and propriety. Might not women faint at the first sight of blood and disturb wounded soldiers with their hysterics? And would women not be in the way if they could not lift patients? Perhaps young women were hoping to find love in a military hospital? "Imagine," wrote a physician to the influential *American Medical Times*, "a delicate refined woman assisting a rough soldier to the closet-stool, or supplying him with a bedpan, or adjusting the knots on a T-bandage employed in retaining a urinary catheter in position. . . .

Women, in my humble opinion, are utterly and decidedly unfit for such service."[16] Further aggravating the day-to-day situation was the civilian status of female volunteers. This suggested an unwillingness to listen to military authority and, at times, made cooperation with army surgeons awkward. As one doctor stated, "Can you fancy half a dozen or a dozen old hags, for that is what they are, surrounding a bewildered hospital surgeon, each one clamorous for her little wants?"[17]

Despite the confusion and even outright hostility regarding a woman's role in the war's medical effort, women searched for ways to assist their husbands and sons. For some, simple measures like urging the hometown doctor to enlist and accompany local troops into action were enough. Others organized soldiers aid societies to coordinate the collection and forwarding of bandages and other surgical supplies to the front lines. For the more activist minded, nursing provided the closest firsthand experience to what the armed struggle was all about. Seeking to regulate this confusion and fulfill the growing need for nursing assistance, Secretary of War Simon Cameron, in May 1861, appointed Dorothea Dix to organize an army nursing corps comprising female volunteers.

A lean sixty-year-old, Dix was looked upon as America's Florence Nightingale, with the comportment of a straight-backed, no-nonsense general. Blessed with great personal energy, she was renowned for her lengthy crusade for better treatment of paupers, the insane, and prison inmates. In 1854, she secured the passage of a congressional bill granting the states 12,250,000 acres of public lands to be used for the benefit of the insane, deaf, dumb, and blind. But the measure was considered unconstitutional and eventually vetoed by President Franklin Pierce. Dix's response to this political setback was to take a two-year grand tour of the hospitals and mental institutions of Europe and the Middle East. Familiarizing herself with Nightingale's precepts on nursing, Dix grew convinced that the nurse must become the patient's primary in-hospital advocate, which would ultimately elevate nursing to a respected calling for American women. Determined to use her experience in hospital administration and national lobbying to realize this goal, Dix used the Civil War as a perfect opportunity to display her skills.

News of Dix's appointment spread throughout the North as female volunteers descended on her H Street headquarters in Washington. Many of these aspiring nurses scandalized their friends back home by what seemed quixotic behavior. Some women even left their children for this great moral and religious crusade. "Now is the judgment of this world. Each man and woman is taking his or her measure," wrote one nurse in her diary. "As it is taken even so must it stand—it will be recorded." And so, America's women came to tend the sick, wounded, and dying.[18]

Nominally, Dix was superintendent of an army nursing corps, but without nursing schools and diplomas, the term *nurse* took on a vague meaning. Indeed, most women brought to their nursing activities the beliefs that had defined their domestic lives. In an era that stressed the notion of a woman's place being in the home, female nurses came to regard the male-dominated military hospital as an extension of their home and the soldiers as their sons. Since most of the soldiers were young men away for the first time, motherly treatment was more valued than formal nursing care. "Excuse me, ladies! I thought I was at home with my mother,"[19] a feverish soldier in Baltimore said to his nurses. They had done little more than wrap him in a warm blanket and applied hot bricks and heated wooden sticks to his feet and legs.

Eventually, the word *nurse* came to refer to a range of caregivers: a woman appointed by Dix, or a female agent attached to the Sanitary Commission or a state soldiers aid society, or a woman specifically requested by an individual surgeon to work at his hospital, or a nun from one of the Catholic sisterhoods. The term *nurse* could be applied to an officer's wife who accompanied him to the battlefield or the wife, sister, or mother who rushed to the hospital bedside of a husband, brother, or son and remained to care for him. Sometimes laundresses or other matrons attached to combat units assumed nursing duties in between housekeeping chores. Most often, however, the Civil War nurse was a convalescing male (the male to female ratio was at least five to one for both the North and the South) who had been attached to a particular regiment. The result was a confusing patchwork of titles.

FOR FIFTY-TWO-YEAR-OLD HANNAH ROPES, the national call for female nurses must have seemed like a gift from on high. The Maine-born divorced mother of two teenage children was an unrepentant crusader, constantly seeking out the next great social reform movement. When national tensions developed in the early 1850s over the question of allowing slavery in the Kansas and Nebraska territories, Ropes aligned herself with the abolitionists of New England. In 1855, she journeyed west under the probable sponsorship of the Massachusetts Emigrant Aid Company, a free-state advocacy group. After setting up a household, she soon began to experience the troubled and violent world of Lawrence, Kansas. Murders by beating, gunshot, and lynching became an everyday occurrence as pro- and antislavery forces battled for supremacy. In less than a year's time, Lawrence was sacked by pro-slavery forces that destroyed the town's printing offices and the free-state headquarters and pillaged private houses. Growing fearful for her children's lives and her own, Ropes returned to Massachusetts in mid-1856. As political differences heightened, she wrote a controversial Free-Soil tract, *Six Months in Kansas: By a Lady*. Hoping to exploit her newfound minor celebrity status, Ropes became increasingly involved in all matters of public policy. By the late 1850s, she had become a well-known antislavery activist who helped articulate the great sociopolitical issues that divided the country. Making the acquaintance of the politically powerful in Massachusetts, Ropes became a particular favorite of Henry Wilson, the state's senior United States senator and subsequent chairman of the influential Senate Military Affairs Committee.

In 1861, when Lincoln called the country to arms, Ropes searched for a more hands-on role in the civil conflict. It was around this time that she received a copy of Florence Nightingale's recently published *Notes on Nursing*. Writing that "every woman is a nurse," Nightingale declared that "if, then, every woman must at some time or other of her life become a nurse, *i.e.*, have charge of somebody's health, how immense and how valuable would be the produce of her united experience if every woman would think how to nurse."[20] That was all the coaxing Ropes needed. Within a few months, she settled her personal affairs in Massachusetts and traveled south, intent on offering her services to Dorothea Dix and the nation as a military hospital nurse.

Upon arriving in Washington in late June 1862, Ropes must have been shocked by the intensity of Dix's battles with army doctors and members of the Sanitary Commission. What started out as a humanitarian partnership between Dix, the federal government, the U.S. Army Medical Department, and commission volunteers had quickly disintegrated. Both George Templeton Strong, the commission's diary-keeping treasurer, and Frederick Olmsted, its workaholic executive secretary, had quickly developed a strong dislike for Dix's management style. Strong recorded that in the summer of 1861, Dix, in "breathless excitement," interrupted a commission meeting "to say that a cow in the Smithsonian grounds was dying of sunstroke," and "she took it very ill that we did not adjourn instantly to look after the case."[21] In a letter to commission president Henry Bellows, Olmsted wrote, "Miss Dix held me for an hour today, and told me such a series of frightful stories, that I must believe her crazy [unable] to get any sleep tonight."[22] Further complicating Dix's relationship with the Sanitary Commission was her role in the founding of a rival organization, the Western Sanitary Commission. By encouraging friends in St. Louis to establish this alternative relief network, Dix bypassed the United States Sanitary Commission's western regional secretary.

Bellows, Olmsted, and Strong were incensed by Dix's actions and considered the formation of the Western Sanitary Commission an attempt to undermine the national unifying efforts of the United States Sanitary Commission. Indeed, the three men saw the two competing humanitarian ventures as emblematic of the central issue of the war: local rights versus national integrity. If the Confederate states' secession movement could split the country asunder, might not the Western Sanitary Commission do the same to the United States Sanitary Commission? Dix, however, was unmoved by their concerns and demonstrated continued support for the new initiative by delegating authority to one of the members of the Western Sanitary Commission to authorize the placement of military hospital nurses in the trans-Mississippi theater. Although the Western Sanitary Commission never rivaled the United States Sanitary Commission in its scope of activities, it became a formidable fund-raising competitor throughout the war years.

Convinced that Dix's plans should be thwarted, Olmsted decided to drop lobbying efforts to bolster her authority in the anticipated legislative endeavor to reorganize the U.S. Army Medical Department. At the same time, Charles Tripler, medical director of General McClellan's Army of the Potomac, was implementing his own plan to sabotage Dix. "We can get female nurses through Miss Dix and from among the [Catholic] Sisters of Charity," Tripler told McClellan, "but in the honest discharge of my duties, though a Protestant myself, I do not hesitate to declare that in my opinion the latter are far preferable to the former, being better disciplined, more discreet and judicious, and more reliable."[23]

Stepping up the campaign to marginalize Dix, Olmsted and Bellows put pressure on the officers of New York City's Women's Central Association of Relief to announce that they could no longer assume the obligation of financing Dix's program. Through November 1861, the association had sent thirty-two women to military hospitals. The reversal of policy forced Dix to begin to recruit her own nurses. From then on, Dix was compelled to rely on personal contacts as the primary source for her nurses. Recruiting thus became an arduous process. Though she remained superintendent of nurses, her interaction with the increasingly influential United States Sanitary Commission appears to have been limited after the late fall of 1861. A weary Dix would soon admit to a friend, "This dreadful civil war has as a huge beast consumed my whole of life."[24]

Dix's battle with Olmsted and Bellows meant that she was more isolated from the daily goings-on of the army Medical Department than she would have liked. Looking to protect her position, she plotted a strategy of maintaining personal ties with various high-ranking government and military officials. Edwin Stanton, the secretary of war and a foe of the Sanitary Commission, was known to have unflagging enthusiasm for Dix's efforts. Similarly, Quartermaster General Montgomery Meigs, responsible for the construction of hospitals and maintenance of the army's vast supply of provisions, was also a loyal supporter. Even these contacts, however, failed to quell the negative publicity that surrounded Dix's work. "It would seem that the whole responsibility of appointing female nurses, and systematizing their operations, rests with Miss Dix," wrote surgeon Stephen Smith in the *American Medical Times*. "It is a legitimate subject of inquiry," he continued, "why has not this most important duty been promptly and faithfully discharged? Many hospitals are suffering sadly from this neglect."[25]

By mid-1862, with only 250 or so nurses under her direct supervision in the Virginia and Washington areas, it appeared that Dix had been successfully separated from the Union's overall medical relief effort. However, she clung to the hope that William Hammond, the newly appointed surgeon general, would rally to her support and expand her authority. In an attempt to appease her, Hammond issued *Circular #7* on July 14, 1862, a written proclamation "to give greater utility to the acts of Miss D. L. Dix as 'Superintendent of Women Nurses.'" At the same time, however, Hammond authorized chief surgeons at army hospitals to dismiss any female nurses found to be, in his words, "incompetent, insubordinate, or otherwise unfit for their vocation."[26] In effect, Hammond made certain that Dix would never be able to maintain total control over her own nursing corps.

Adding to Dix's managerial woes were the daily reports of bitter encounters between volunteer nurses and hospital authorities. "Unfortunately, many of the surgeons in the hospitals do not work harmoniously with Miss Dix," reported one contemporary source. "They are jealous of her power, impatient of her authority, find fault with her nurses, and accuse her of being arbitrary, opinionated, severe and capricious."[27] Nurses were admonished for the most ridiculous of reasons—from keeping the wards too clean to working too hard. Physicians expected female nurses to meekly obey orders and keep to themselves their thoughts concerning more humane or novel ideas about treatments. At the Judiciary Square Hospital, one staff medical officer wrote to his superior, "Female nurses are, as a rule, of slight benefit." This doctor noted that "men can much better perform all the duties required and do much more work, and occasion far less trouble."[28]

Not surprisingly, the female volunteer nurses were equally displeased with the doctors. Nurses viewed the dictatorial commands of the medical officers and the army's bureaucratic methods as matters to be ignored, if not disobeyed. Nurses complained of drunkenness, incompetence, sexual harassment, and even thievery on the part of physicians. Cornelia Hancock, a young Quaker nurse, confided to her mother, "I cannot get used to the tyrannical sway of men in authority,"[29] while Mary Newcomb, a nurse from Illinois, told her surgeon, "You mind your business, and I will attend to mine."[30] Hannah Ropes, writing in her diary about the abuses she suffered from a surgeon, described him as a "nervous, irritable person." Certainly, she wrote, "the majesty of his shoulder straps seemed to have conveyed to his mind a sense of irresponsible power."[31]

Early in her command of the nursing corps, Dix confided to Frederick Olmsted (they were still speaking at the time) that the only women to receive the approval of their surgeons were "women of bad character." Dix pointed out that these nurses were "the mistresses of the doctors & this is the only reason they are retained."[32] Such beliefs led her to issue a set of rules intended to keep volunteer appointees above reproach. According to one contemporary account, "A woman must be mature in years, plain almost to homeliness in dress, and by no means liberally endowed with personal attractions, if she hoped to meet the approval of Miss Dix."[33] So rigid were Dix's requirements that she summarily rejected seemingly well-qualified applicants. The Sanitary Commission's executive secretary, Frederick Olmsted, sarcastically described her as a popular hero. Unfortunately, he said, she was great only at "beginnings and in promises and hopes."[34] Increasingly, her worst critics began to call her "Dragon Dix," and an embattled Dix spiraled downward in public standing.

This was not the case with Hannah Ropes and her relationship with Dix. When Ropes arrived in Washington in June 1862, she was assigned by Dix to the Union Hotel Hospital. Located in Georgetown near a bridge over Rock Creek, the structure was the first building known to be refashioned into a Union general hospital. There was a grand staircase on the first floor, but the hotel's upper-floor hallways were so narrow as to be torturous for the wounded to navigate. Bathrooms were inadequate in size and number, and proper ventilation was nonexistent. Much of the woodwork in the hotel was termite infested and decaying. The cellar was damp, with large pools of fetid water. There was no dead house. In fact, the facility was so inadequate to the needs of its two hundred or so patients that it was soon abandoned. However, with the beginning of the Seven Days battles on Virginia's Peninsula in the spring of 1862, and the pressing need for more Union hospital beds, it had to be reopened.

Strong-willed, politically savvy, and compassionate, Ropes immediately assumed the role of nurse and mother. "The fact is, the washing and putting of a man into a clean white shirt and drawers, and stretching him on a thoroughly white bed completely transforms him," she wrote to her daughter, Alice. "Wounded men are exposed from head to foot before the nurses and they object to anybody but an 'old mother,'" she explained. By mid-July, Ropes proclaimed to Alice, "I have learned now how to take care of a shoulder wound." But with no knowledge of bacteria or understanding of the role of antisepsis, Ropes was limited to changing the wounded soldier's dressings three times a day and providing him, each morning, with a new shirt. At a time when minimally soiled surgical bandages were often reused from one patient to the next, Ropes noted that at the Union Hotel Hospital, the soldiers' conditions were so awful that "all these shirts and bandages have to be thrown away, they are so offensive."

Twenty-one-year-old Alice, who had remained in Massachusetts, hoped to join her mother, but Ropes knew that Dix's criteria for appointment would prevent a reunion. "It is no place for young girls," she warned. "The surgeons are young and look upon nurses as their natural prey." As well, she cautioned, "We get lousy! and dirty. We run the gauntlet of disease from the disgusting itch to smallpox. My needle woman found nine body lice inside of her flannel waistcoat. And I caught two inside the binding of my drawers! I don't know of any price that would induce me to have you here!"

In the fall of 1862, Ropes was named matron in charge of nurses at the Union Hotel Hospital. It was a position she felt well suited for. "I am strong in the knowledge at least which comes with age," Ropes confided in her diary. Headstrong and wanting to right any perceived social wrong, she complained to Surgeon General Hammond, for instance, about the avarice of the hospital steward, who was there "to make all the money he could out of the hospital." Hospital stewards were non-commissioned officers with a variety of responsibilities. Some had pharmaceutical backgrounds and were in charge of the medical dispensary. Others functioned as a facility's individual quartermaster who issued and kept track of supplies such as clothing and blankets. Still other stewards managed rations. Hospital stewards were poorly supervised, and it was not unusual to hear about thievery within their ranks. In Ropes's case, the Union Hotel Hospital steward stole three trunks of patient clothes and later sold them for his own benefit.

Hammond refused to act on Ropes's charges and summarily referred the letter back to the hospital's chief medical officer. This was the very same doctor Ropes had described in her diary as "ignorant of hospital routine, ignorant of life outside of the practice in a country town . . . a weak man with good intentions." What Hammond failed to realize was the extent of Ropes's political connections in the highest echelons of government. When Ropes first arrived in Washington, she spent two weeks at the bedside of her mentor, Massachusetts senator Henry Wilson, who was recovering from an asthmatic attack. During those days, Ropes told of how the nation's ranking military officers and government officials were "at the door in squads every day to see him." This was Ropes's introduction to official Washington.

At the end of October 1862, Ropes decided to personally call on Hammond, who had little knowledge of her political connections. She sat in a stiff wooden chair outside Hammond's office and watched incredulously as Hammond walked by without so much as a nod. Indignant, Ropes asked for an immediate meeting but was put off by Hammond's assistant. "To help the oppressed did not seem at all the sphere of this place where we sat," she noted in her diary. Enraged by Hammond's unwillingness to punish the hospital steward and by Hammond's lack of courtesy, Ropes wrote in her diary, "Two rebuffs seemed about enough for a woman of half a century to accept without compromising her own dignity." Ropes made a beeline across Washington for Secretary of War Stanton's office.

Stanton's dislike for Hammond was well-known, and the secretary was only too ready to investigate Ropes's charges. "Go to the Union Hospital with this lady," Stanton ordered the provost marshal, "then arrest the steward and take him to a cell in the Old Capitol Prison."

Ropes returned to a hospital that was soon swarming with lawyers, military personnel, politicians, and, a few days later, Thomas Perley, the medical inspector general himself. Perley, a graduate of Bowdoin College and the Medical School of Maine, had limited military experience. His selection was attributed entirely to the political influence of Senator William Fessenden of Maine, a close friend of Stanton's and a leading abolitionist. Perley's work was said to be characterized by its foolishness and his inability to understand the various reports written by his staff. Perley's presence, however, demonstrated Ropes's political clout and was a measure of her commitment to her patients. Of course, it didn't hurt that Ropes was sometimes a guest at Perley's house for Sabbath dinner. Ultimately, Ropes was triumphant in her ability to negate the influence of Hammond by a clever use of wire-pulling. "Today the whole house began to brighten," Ropes wrote in her diary in early November 1862. "Each day has added something to the hope or assurance that the old state of things was played out."[35]

IT WAS EARLY September 1862, and Robert E. Lee's forces had just regained almost all of Virginia following a brilliant victory over Major General John Pope's newly formed Army of Virginia at the Second Battle of Bull Run. This repeat defeat of Northern forces at Manassas was particularly discouraging, especially from a medical standpoint. As had been the case on the Peninsula, there were few medical supplies, an appalling lack of equipment, and only a fraction of the necessary ambulances. Overwhelmed, Pope's physician staff issued frantic pleas for civilian medical volunteers. McClellan and his Army of the Potomac, still dazed from their retreat from the Peninsula, were attempting to make a mad dash northward to come to Pope's assistance. But McClellan's efforts, once again, were too little, too late.

When Lee realized that the bulk of McClellan's troops were bogged down and could not swiftly join Pope's force, he ordered Jackson to swing around behind Pope's army and descend on his rear units. On August 26, the daring flank march of Jackson's corps ended at Manassas Station, adjacent to the previous year's Bull Run battlefield. For two days, Robert E. Lee's Army of Northern Virginia outmaneuvered and outfought John Pope's Army of Virginia and a small and straggly contingent of McClellan's Army of the Potomac. When an overwhelming Confederate counterattack swept the Union forces from the field, almost five thousand Northerners were left in need of evacuation and medical attention.

Because Jonathan Letterman had not yet secured an ambulance service, there was no possibility of an efficient medical evacuation. Instead, the chaotic attempts to retrieve and treat the Union wounded at Second Bull Run in 1862 rivaled those of First Bull Run in 1861 for inexpediency, ineptitude, and consequent suffering. Fearing for the safety of Washington, the Northern high command soon ordered the whole army to retreat and take shelter behind the defense lines of the city. Official Washington was in a state of confusion. The army was dispirited, exhausted, and shattered by the disastrous events of Pope's campaign. Public disgust with the government was high. Meanwhile, the weather had turned miserable as a cold, driving rainstorm drenched Bull Run. The wounded dotted the battlefield, with no planned rescue in sight.

On September 2, Pope was relieved of his command and the Army of Virginia soon ceased to exist. Less than a month before, General Halleck had been in a bitter feud with McClellan regarding the latter's lack of leadership skills on the Peninsula. McClellan, however, had always enjoyed the confidence of the men in his army, and a now chagrined Halleck pleaded with him to take command of Pope's leaderless flock and combine them with his Army of the Potomac: "I beg of you to assist me in this crisis with your ability and experience."[36] The ever cagey McClellan was only too happy to oblige.

If official Washington was in a state of confusion, medical Washington was in a panic. The North's hospitals were rapidly filling to capacity as the war effort grew larger with each passing day. Soldiers were dying, and the reorganization of the North's Medical Department, along with continued pleas by the Sanitary Commission and Jonathan Letterman for recognition of a formal ambulance service, was not yet in place. Even Secretary of War Stanton publicly appealed for volunteer nurses, male or female, to assist in the care of the Bull Run wounded. Hammond, who remained busy with his various projects—an army medical school and a military medical museum were being developed, case reports and statistics for a medical history of the war needed to be compiled, books and papers on camp hygiene and sanitary reform were waiting to be written—was about to be tested.

CHAPTER SEVEN

"In Heaven's name let it be done"

WHEREVER HENRY INGERSOLL BOWDITCH WENT, he told a tale of overwhelming personal grief. His eldest son, Lieutenant Nathaniel Bowditch of the First Massachusetts Cavalry, had been fatally wounded during a charge at Kelly's Ford in Virginia in March 1863. There was a terrible irony to Henry Bowditch's saga that caught the public's attention. Over the previous six months, he had become the country's most outspoken civilian regarding the need for a United States Army ambulance corps. Now, Bowditch confronted the sad reality that the very reforms he had been championing might have prevented the torturous death of his son, who had lain helpless on the ground for hours, begging for medical assistance. "Resting," as he said, "under the solemn cloud-shadow of a great but benignant sorrow," the older Bowditch intensified his ongoing battle against Congress, the War Department, and the military. He lectured constantly, traveled wherever citizens would listen to his pleas, wrote pamphlets, and joined forces with members of the Sanitary Commission as they called for reorganization of the United States Army Medical Department.

A Boston Brahmin, Bowditch was the son of Nathaniel Bowditch, the country's most celebrated mathematician. More important, Henry

Bowditch was Jackson Professor of Clinical Medicine at the Harvard Medical School and the country's pioneer specialist in diseases of the chest. He lived in a mansion on Boylston Street, opposite the Public Garden, and was among the nation's best-known abolitionists and physicians, a man of deep religious conviction whose ancestors fought in the Revolution. However, the death of his son forced Bowditch to challenge his own assumptions regarding the sanctity of government. He would tell his audiences that he no longer appealed to "any one man, or to Congress, but to our Imperial 'Caesar,' the People!" The public was forced to listen, because if such a tragedy could befall the Bowditches, it could happen to any American family. "If any government under Heaven ought to be paternal, the United States authority, deriving, as it does, all its powers from the people, should surely be such," Bowditch wrote, "and should dispense that power, in full streams of benignant mercy upon its soldiers, when wounded in its defence."[1]

Bowditch's initial concerns about the ambulance system stemmed from a request by Surgeon General Hammond that he accompany a squadron of ambulances searching for Union wounded. It was early September 1862, and according to Hammond, the army's ability to remove the injured following the Second Battle of Bull Run was in a "frightful state of disorder."[2] As in the First Battle of Bull Run, anarchy reigned over the battlefield surgical work. For several of the North's medical personnel, the confusion undoubtedly evoked a feeling of déjà vu.

William Williams Keen, who served as a volunteer physician at First Bull Run while still a medical student, had returned to his studies and graduated from Jefferson Medical School in Philadelphia in March 1862. He immediately reenlisted in the army and was posted to Washington, where he spent several months preparing the Ascension Episcopal Church and the Eighth Street Methodist Church for use as military hospitals. During the waning days of August, Keen was sent from the capital to meet Pope's army with a supply train filled with 12 sets of surgical instruments, 600 cases of canned soup, 800 suits of undergarments, 2,600 blankets, and 4,800 bottles of brandy, sherry, and whiskey. Seventy-two hours later, most of the items were in the hands of marauding Southern troops and Keen was without an assignment. In a manner similar to his misadventures thirteen months earlier, Keen was abandoned and had no idea where to go or what to do. "The army left, and left me practically stranded," he recalled. "Again, nobody gave me orders."[3] In nearby Centreville, Keen found an extemporized hospital filled with roughly one hundred severely wounded men. There he performed several amputations using his penknife. Two days later, he hitched a return ride back to Washington on the very ambulance train that Henry Bowditch was accompanying.

Second Bull Run was another affront to the nation's collective medical conscience. As an eyewitness commented, "The sufferings of the wounded after this battle have probably not been equalled, at least not exceeded, during this war."[4] The best medically equipped Northern corps had a total of just 45 mule-driven ambulances instead of the requested 170. To make matters even worse, in the extensive maneuvering leading up to the conflict, most of these rickety vehicles had broken down and been abandoned. Whole divisions again went into battle without any means to rescue wounded combatants. The problem was compounded when civilians hired by the Quartermaster Corps to drive the army's ambulances panicked and ran away at the first sound of gunfire. According to Bowditch, "The drivers were men of the lowest character, evidently taken from the vilest purlieus [neighborhoods] of Washington, merely as common drivers, and for no other qualification." In addition, strategic battlefield decisions concerning the placement of provisions were poor. Forty-three wagons brimming with medical supplies, including Keen's, had been prematurely moved to forward positions and were captured by the Confederates when Union forces retreated. Railroad lines that were meant to evacuate the wounded from the battlefield were destroyed, and the patient load became too great for the few field hospitals of the area. Those unable to walk lay on the ground unattended for days.

The forty-eight hours that Henry Bowditch spent as part of a fifty-carriage ambulance train were so dispiriting that he immediately complained about the situation in a lengthy letter to Surgeon General Hammond. Bowditch told of fearful drivers abandoning their ambulances before they reached enemy lines and of men who "sulked or swore or laughed" but did little to assist the injured. Most disturbing was the drivers' heavy drinking. At one point, Bowditch himself was forced to take over the reins and drive through the night with one hand while using the other to prevent a drunk and snoring driver from falling backward onto a wounded soldier.

Bowditch was so appalled by the ambulance situation that upon his return to Boston, he reported his troubling experience to a meeting of the city's influential Society for Medical Improvement. What made the society particularly powerful was its close relationship with the widely hailed *Boston Medical and Surgical Journal*. Read by many in the profession, the *Boston Medical and Surgical Journal* was governed by an editorial board consisting almost entirely of members of the Society for

Medical Improvement. And whenever the society wanted an important issue brought before a national audience, it relied on the pages of the *Boston Medical and Surgical Journal* to communicate its views.

Within two weeks of his return to Boston, Bowditch was using the journal's prestigious pages to disseminate his thoughts concerning a military ambulance system. "I want now through this Society, to create a public sentiment that will compel the Government to attend to this matter, and to have a real ambulance corps,"[5] Bowditch stated. The editors of the journal agreed, and during the fall of 1862, the *Boston Medical and Surgical Journal* published numerous reports on the failures of the ambulance system. "Need anything more be said to rouse the community to an imperative demand that such outrages shall be at once and forever put an end to?"[6] wrote one editor. In October, Bowditch intensified his lobbying efforts by returning to Washington to meet personally with Secretary of War Stanton, General in Chief Halleck, Major General McClellan, Surgeon General Hammond, and various members of the United States Sanitary Commission.

HAMMOND HAD BEEN surgeon general for only four months when, in late August 1862, he urged Stanton to approve the formation of an organized ambulance corps staffed by noncombatants. "In no battle yet have the wounded been properly looked after; men under pretence of carrying them off the field leave the ranks and seldom return to their proper duties. The adoption of this plan would do away with the necessity of taking men from the line of the army to perform the duties of nurses, cooks, and attendants, and thus return sixteen thousand men to duty in the ranks,"[7] wrote Hammond. The request seemed reasonable, especially since large numbers of Union soldiers had suffered and died from lack of an adequate battlefield evacuation system.

Stanton, however, hated Hammond, whose appointment he felt had been thrust upon him by members of the United States Sanitary Commission. In turn, Frederick Olmsted, executive secretary of the commission, disliked Stanton. "I know that Stanton is the meanest kind of small, cunning, short sighted, selfish politician, that he is the worst kind of a hypocrite, that he trades in prayer and devotion and is habitually the grossest possible blasphemer," Olmsted told one of his friends. "He is a bully and a liar."[8]

Hammond and Olmsted, along with most commission officials, were friends of McClellan's. McClellan had few kind words for Stanton, whom he described as "the most unmitigated scoundrel I ever knew, heard or read of." Not surprisingly, Stanton had little faith in McClellan's military skills and felt the West Pointer was simply the wrong person to fight a relentless, offensive war. Further complicating matters was Halleck. When he was named general in chief by President Lincoln and backed by Stanton's approval in July 1862, McClellan instantaneously became Halleck's subordinate. McClellan would constantly complain that he could not serve under an officer he considered his intellectual and military inferior. McClellan made it clear that he would do everything possible to undermine Halleck's authority. In return, Halleck had little use for McClellan's way of doing things and was convinced that McClellan's suspension was "a matter of absolute necessity." "In a few more weeks," Halleck later confided to his wife, "[McClellan] would have broken down the government."[9]

As Henry Bowditch was about to learn, Stanton's animus toward Hammond, McClellan, Olmsted, and the Sanitary Commission was particularly evident when it came to discussions concerning an ambulance system. Within eight days of receiving Hammond's request to organize a noncombatant-based ambulance corps, Stanton, abetted by what he referred to as Halleck's "views adverse to the project," responded with a flat-out no. Ten days later, in the wake of Second Bull Run, Hammond again pleaded with Stanton for the establishment of some type of battlefield evacuation system. This time Stanton had Halleck answer directly: "It is proper to remark that the enemy have provided for their wounded on every battle-field with not one-half the ambulances and other facilities provided for our armies."[10]

Whether Stanton and Halleck truly believed the existing ambulance system to be satisfactory or were merely enacting a political vendetta remains historical conjecture. Halleck, who was more follower than doer, shares with Stanton the blame for condemning opportunities meant to bring newer methods and abler personnel into the medical corps. But the ultimate responsibility for lack of action was Stanton's.

While thousands of Union soldiers were dying from neglect, the proponents of a new ambulance system were stonewalled by Stanton and Halleck. Members of the Sanitary Commission, led by Olmsted, proposed that they change Halleck's attitude by personal persuasion. Despite an initial hesitancy, Halleck agreed to meet with commission members on the evening of September 17. As the hour for the meeting approached, tensions were heightened by scattered reports of a massive battle being fought on the banks of Antietam Creek, near the village of Sharpsburg, Maryland. Robert E. Lee's Army of Northern Virginia and George McClellan's Army of the Potomac were fighting in what is now regarded as the bloodiest day in American history. The fact that Antietam, with its staggering toll of dead and wounded, was ending just as the commission's meeting was beginning had little significance for Halleck.

A short, swarthy man with a double chin and flabby cheeks fringed by a crescent of withered gray whiskers, Old Brains Halleck was a difficult person to get along with. He was gruff and cantankerous, with large, blazing eyes that bulged out beneath a balding head. He also had an unnerving habit of constantly scratching his elbows. Speaking in a rapid fashion, Halleck explained that he respected the aims of the Sanitary Commission, but not those humanitarian gestures that caused difficulties with the efficient running of an army. Soldiers did not need fancy shoes, shirts, and trousers because these were "effeminating comforts,"[11] according to Halleck, that made fighting men weak and self-indulgent. Increasing the number of ambulances was a luxury, he declared, and men's suffering was an unfortunate result of war.

The commissioners were aghast. George Bellows, the commission's president, and George Templeton Strong, its treasurer, found Halleck off-putting. The general in chief was not the man they expected. Olmsted put it more bluntly: "I have seen Halleck. Heaven help us."[12] When Hammond learned of the evening's events, he despaired of ever establishing a formal, noncombatant-run ambulance corps while Halleck remained in command and Stanton was in office.

It was at this juncture in the lobbying campaign that Henry Bowditch arrived in Washington. It was early October 1862, and being neither a military man nor a government official, Bowditch could do and say things that would normally hamstring Hammond and the commission. Hammond and Olmsted particularly welcomed Bowditch because the Boston physician was closely aligned with the Sanitary Commission and would soon participate as a member of the commission's special inspection team of military general hospitals. Most impressive was the fact that Bowditch had gained the attention of the medical profession regarding his stand on the ambulance issue. Editorials supporting Bowditch's position could be found in medical journals in most major cities. In Philadelphia, the editor of the *Medical and Surgical Reporter* wrote, "We are told, over and over again, that all this 'is to be changed,' that the ambulance corps is 'being reorganized on an entirely new plan,' etc., etc. In Heaven's name let it be done, and that speedily, before another great battle is fought."[13] In New York City, Stephen Smith, physician-owner of the influential *American Medical Times* and the most prominent civilian propagandist for the Sanitary Commission, offered his editorial support: "In mercy's name, we protest against the barbarous and disorderly management of the ambulance trains, the brutal conduct of the wagon-drivers, and the unfitness of the existing system of field and general transportation of the wounded."[14] Word of the ambulance dilemma also began to spread to the public arena. The National War Committee of the Citizens of New York recommended the formation of an independent ambulance corps to Lincoln and Stanton. In Boston, the city's board of trade offered its support for Bowditch's initiative.

The medical profession and the lay public might have been roused, but in the fall and early winter of 1862, Bowditch would prove no match for the political machinations of Stanton and Halleck. Bowditch requested and was granted a meeting with both men and received assurances from them regarding their willingness to back his proposals. Stanton said he would support whatever Halleck recommended, and Halleck said he was waiting to hear from Stanton. Meanwhile, Bowditch obtained a letter from McClellan giving his opinion: "I regard the formation of a well organized ambulance corps as one of the great desiderata for our armies."[15] So it went, back and forth. But in the end, Bowditch's shuttle lobbying proved futile. For Stanton and Halleck, as long as Hammond, McClellan, and the Sanitary Commission were in favor of reorganizing the ambulance corps, the proposal was unlikely to receive their backing. By the middle of November, Olmsted and other members of the commission recognized the futility of expending so much time on the ambulance question. Reluctantly, Bowditch agreed and returned to Boston to focus his attention on promoting his ideas more directly to the people.

IDEALLY, THE PRO-AMBULANCE forces had hoped to gain approval of a United States Army–wide ambulance corps, staffed by specially trained noncombatants, under the sole charge of the Medical Department. The concept was laudable, but its implementation, at this rocky stage of the war effort, would have been difficult. Since the North's fighting forces were divided into several geographically distinct armies (in October 1862, the Union's principal units were George McClellan's Army of the Potomac, Ulysses S. Grant's Army of the Tennessee, and Don Carlos Buell's Army of the Ohio), attempts to coordinate basic health care services across the entire United States Army proved next to impossible. The medical organization within each individual army still more closely reflected the personality of its commanding general than the desires of a Washington-based surgeon general.

At the one extreme was Buell, a West Pointer and career military officer, who was considered a tyrant with little regard for the welfare of his men. Disdainful of advice given by his medical director, Robert

Murray, Buell begrudged the assignment of soldiers to battlefield evacuation teams or as nurses for their ailing comrades. He was even said to have withheld strategic information that would have assisted in the medical staff's preparedness. In Buell's words, "The medical department should be self sustaining—that the sick should care for the sick."[16] Buell's indifference toward the health of his men was noted in one volunteer surgeon's observation following the October 8 battle of Perryville, Kentucky: "It is proper here to remark that previous to starting from Louisville, the different surgeons of the army were directed by Surgeon R. Murray, U.S.A., medical director, to procure full supplies of medicines, hospital stores, dressings, bedding, etc., but no sooner were the supplies procured than they were ordered to be left behind by General Buell, who directed that only one wagon should be furnished to each brigade for the transportation of medical and hospital stores." Perryville proved a medical debacle as Buell left the sick and wounded without bedding, blankets, or tents.

The surrounding countryside became a spectacle of unnecessary suffering, and only the prompt efforts of the United States Sanitary Commission to supply basic necessities prevented even greater misery. As the volunteer surgeon made clear, "But for the timely arrival of these [agents of the Sanitary Commission], many lives would, undoubtedly, have been sacrificed."[17] Buell's conduct resulted in a formal investigation into his fitness to command. In late October, he was relieved of his duties.

Whereas Buell maintained an arm's-length relationship with his medical staff, George McClellan, in contrast, had a close association with Jonathan Letterman, medical director of the Army of the Potomac. "I saw immediately that Letterman was the man for the occasion, and at once gave him my unbounded confidence," said McClellan. Letterman had joined McClellan during the tail end of the Peninsula campaign in July 1862. At once, the two men engaged in a series of lengthy meetings concerning Letterman's duties. Medical conditions in the Army of the Potomac were so dire that the new medical director had to take immediate corrective actions.

With a remarkable ability to focus on a problem and solve it in a practical and timely fashion, Letterman was a bona fide genius when it came to strategizing and improving field medical tactics, especially an ambulance corps. McClellan backed all of the decisions, and years later he would write of Letterman, "I never met with his superior in power of organization and executive ability."[18]

August through mid-September 1862 was a dismal time for McClellan and his forces. The Army of the Potomac had been defeated, and the flag of the Confederacy, especially following the Union debacle at Second Bull Run, now flew almost within sight of the dome on the Capitol. As difficult as the military situation was, the organization of the medical unit of the Army of the Potomac and the care of its troops were improving. Stanton and Halleck might have said no to Hammond's plea for a United States Army–wide ambulance corps, but this disapproval had little real effect on the Army of the Potomac. Letterman's ambulance plan, conceived on Virginia's Peninsula, was in place, his relationship with McClellan was strong, and for the first time his ideas would be tested in actual combat.

BUOYED BY ITS recent battlefield success at Manassas, Robert E. Lee's Army of Northern Virginia invaded southwestern Maryland on September 4, crossing the Potomac River midway between Harpers Ferry and Washington. The Confederates were now on Union soil. Many Northerners viewed this as a calamity and one that was certain to bring about the secession of Maryland. If the rebels' military and political strategy worked, then other border states, especially Kentucky and Missouri, might also leave the Union. Meanwhile, Jefferson Davis, president of the Confederate States of America, additionally hoped that a decisive victory would facilitate British diplomatic recognition of his cause. Further aggravating the Union's concerns was the geographic reality that if Maryland fell, then an isolated Washington could no longer function as the North's capital. To accomplish his goals, Lee decided to first divide his army and send Stonewall Jackson and his corps to capture the strategically important town of Harpers Ferry, where a sizable Union force was based along with an ample cache of supplies. Almost immediately, the Union soldiers capitulated, and although only 80 Northerners were killed, 11,583 Yankees were now officially listed as missing in action and presumed prisoners of war. With their assignment completed, Jackson's twenty-five thousand men hurriedly rejoined the rest of Lee's troops.

Abraham Lincoln saw in his enemy's audacity a serendipitous opportunity to cripple the Southern army far from its home base. By striking such a blow, he could bring the rebellion to a rapid conclusion. Lincoln again asked McClellan and his now reconstituted army—having been combined with elements of John Pope's disbanded force—to move against the Southerners and, at the very least, repel the invasion. Lincoln also suggested that, if possible, McClellan should destroy the rebel army.

Once again, McClellan set about readying the depleted Army of the Potomac for combat. On September 7, he took the field in Maryland in person and, with a force of nearly eighty-four thousand men, began a slow march toward Lee's fifty-five thousand. As the army moved forward, attempts were made to complete its outfitting, particularly in accordance with Jonathan Letterman's medical specifications. Letterman ordered a number of well-stocked hospital wagons for distribution to the various corps. Ambulances, however, were in short supply, as many were being used to remove the wounded from Bull Run. On September 12, while camped in Frederick, Maryland, Letterman finally received two hundred new ambulances. All seemed in readiness, and four days later, McClellan and his army found themselves positioned on the left bank of Antietam Creek, a mile or so from Lee's yet-to-be-fortified location on the opposite side.

The Battle of Antietam (called Sharpsburg by the Confederates) was among the most brutal of the war. It began on Wednesday morning, September 17, and ended fifteen hours later when nearly five thousand men lay dead or dying; another twenty thousand wounded groaned in agony or suffered in silence. The carnage was overwhelming. Half the officers of the Thirty-fourth New York Infantry were injured or dead and every one of their color guard wounded. Only thirty-four of that whole regiment could be brought together after the fight. The Fifteenth Massachusetts Infantry went into the battle with seventeen officers and six hundred men. They came out with nine officers and one hundred thirty-four men. Robert E. Lee was told of losses of 50 percent or more in several Southern brigades. Scarcely thirty thousand rebels remained alive and well.

By most accounts, Antietam was a drawn battle. At the close of the fighting, the positions of the armies were nearly the same as at its start. While Confederates had inflicted a greater absolute loss than they had suffered, in terms of percentages, the Southerners had lost more men. Nevertheless, the Army of Northern Virginia maintained its position the next day, almost as if to dare the Army of the Potomac to renew the assault. McClellan, ever fearful of Lee's supposedly limitless legions, remained stationary. The Union campaign in the East, McClellan reasoned, depended on his army; if he committed his troops to further combat and lost, the East Coast and its major cities would be Lee's for the taking. But McClellan was doing little more than rationalizing his own fears in arguing against continued pursuit. Without further Union interference, the men of the Army of Northern Virginia soon abandoned their location and found shelter in Virginia's Shenandoah Valley.

From the perspective of repelling an invasion in the North, protecting the nation's capital, and stopping British diplomatic recognition of the Confederacy, Antietam can be regarded as a Union victory. Lee's offensive had come to an end, and only twice more, Gettysburg in 1863 and Nashville in 1864, did the forces of the South strike out on Northern soil. For Abraham Lincoln, this was the moment he had long been waiting for as he announced the preliminary Emancipation Proclamation on September 22. McClellan considered Antietam one of the greatest military triumphs of all time. He wired Halleck, "Our victory was complete. The enemy is driven back into Virginia. Maryland and Pennsylvania are now safe."[19]

"Complete" had a different connotation for Lincoln, who had wanted the rebel army destroyed. Lincoln had assumed that McClellan would follow up the victory with renewed attacks on Lee's battalions, especially in view of the fact that McClellan had fresh troops almost equal in number to Lee's entire remaining force. But the slow-moving McClellan demanded more clothing, food, and, above all, reinforcements before he would carry out additional assaults. Six weeks passed with almost total inaction as the tension between McClellan and Lincoln intensified.

While McClellan argued with Lincoln, Letterman was faced with his own set of problems. Because of time constraints, the instruction of members of the new ambulance corps prior to the fighting at Antietam had been spotty. As Letterman stated in a formal report to his friend William Hammond, "A portion of the ambulances of some of the corps arrived just prior to the battle; a large number had been distributed in other corps but were yet unorganized, and was not expected that they would prove as efficient as was desired." Still, the evacuation of the wounded at Antietam was completed in a more efficient manner than in any previous battle. The injured were sent, via caravans of fifty ambulances, to newly established hospitals in Frederick, Maryland, and then beyond, by railroad, to Baltimore, Philadelphia, and Washington. In his usual understated way, Letterman confirmed to Hammond that "with rare exceptions, all the wounded whose safety would not be jeopardized by the journey, were sent carefully and comfortably away."[20]

The new ambulance system was hailed as an unqualified success. As one surgeon on the scene noted, "After the battle of Antietam the wounded were more promptly and properly cared for than ever before, notwithstanding the large number to be provided for. This is owing, in a great measure, to the beneficial change in the ambulance service. . . . The surgeons also are more energetic and capable."[21] In an attempt to ensure that the ambulance corps functioned as efficiently as possible, Letterman even took time to meet the crusading Henry Bowditch. On a personal level Letterman found Bowditch boring, but he was interested in hearing about the Boston physician's plan for noncombatants to staff the corps.

Although the evacuation effort at Antietam had been well organized, the opposite resulted during the delivery and dispersal of medical
supplies. Letterman had telegraphed for provisions several days prior to
the battle, and they were promptly sent from the medical purveyor in
Baltimore. But once the supplies were turned over to the Quartermaster
Corps for railroad transportation, the situation was totally out of Letterman's control. As it happened, a railroad bridge over the Monocacy
River, between Frederick and Baltimore, had been destroyed by Confederate troops, making it necessary to remove the provisions from the
train at that point. Regimental officers and their medical staff were
therefore told to pick up the supplies and, as had been done countless
times in the past, assume control of transporting them to the battlefield.
Letterman recounted, "A great deal of confusion and delay was the consequence, which seriously embarrassed the medical department . . . large
amounts of medical supplies had been lost, and in various ways wasted,
and, not unfrequently, all the supplies for a regiment had been thrown
away for want of transportation, and, of course, were not on hand when
wanted."[22] Cornelius Rea Agnew, a physician and member of the United
States Sanitary Commission's executive committee, was an eyewitness
to the chaos: "Blame for the non-arrival of stores lies in the fact that of
all the forty or more surgeons sent, not one considered himself charged
with the function of hurrying anything forward but himself, the result
being that plenty of surgeons got upon the ground, but almost destitute
of necessary appliances. This I attribute, not so much to want of zeal on
the part of the surgeons, or of ability to recognize the emergency, but to
inability on the part of the central bureau to command the necessary
transportation."[23] Not even the genius of the telegraph, Agnew quipped,
could bring "one one-hundreth part"[24] of what a medical officer needed.

The Sanitary Commission had long urged that authority to maintain
an independent transportation service be given to the Medical Department. But no one in official Washington had been willing to act on this
concern. Frederick Olmsted, however, as a civilian, reacted quickly once
he realized the magnitude of the approaching supply problem. "I sent
agents & $3500 into Pennsylvania to purchase & push thro' stimulants
from the North," he wrote to his wife, Mary. "But fearing the trains
would choke the road bought, hired & borrowed wagons & horses and
sent them through by the turnpike ('National road')."[25] Olmsted was
brilliant in his foresight, for the Sanitary Commission's private wagon
trains, filled to the maximum, arrived at Antietam almost forty-eight
hours ahead of anything the government was able to send. "What the
condition of the wounded at Antietam would have been, without the

timely succor furnished by the Sanitary Commission and other volunteer organizations, it is horrible to imagine," wrote Charles Stillé, the commission's historian. "Chloroform, opiates, instruments, bed-pans, everything, in fact, required for the treatment of the wounded, was wanting."[26] Within a week after the battle, the commission's staff had distributed 10 pounds of chloroform; 20 to 30 tons of crackers, fruit, sugar, and tea; 120 bales of blankets; 2,620 pounds of condensed milk; 3,000 bottles of wine and cordials; 3,188 pounds of farina; 4,000 hospital gowns; 5,000 pounds of beef stock and canned meats; and 28,763 pieces of cloth mattress cases, dry goods, pillows, shorts, and towels. It was an amazing effort that brought the commission's humanitarian goals to the attention of the nation. "All the world comes to our office now to enquire about hospitals, wounded men &c,"[27] Olmsted told Mary.

Letterman's frustrations led him to conclude that a drastic change in the method of distribution would reduce losses, especially when troops were on the move. Before he became medical director, each regiment had de facto an independent medical service with its own regimental hospital. The regiment's wounded were treated by its own doctors, while nonphysician officers customarily used the regimental medical transport to carry their personal belongings. But while this regimental-based system sufficed in smaller wars, the scheme was disastrous when several hundred regiments were thrown into battle.

With the Army of the Potomac bivouacked in Maryland, Letterman decided in early October to reorganize the medical supply system on a brigade basis and avoid the waste and confusion of regimental issues. "Before the adoption of this system," he wrote in his memoirs, "one and sometimes two wagons were required to transport the medical supplies of a regiment, another to carry the hospital tents, cooking utensils, baggage of Medical officers, etc., and were frequently diverted from their legitimate use." In the new system, Letterman placed the brigade surgeon in charge of distributing medical supplies to the individual regiments. Receipts were issued and strict accounting measures instituted. Letterman even determined the precise manner in which the larger hospital and smaller transport wagons were to be stocked. Bedding, books, dressings, furniture, hospital stores, instruments, and medicines—each article had its designated packing instructions. To make the system more foolproof, regimental physicians were furnished with fully loaded medicine chests that were designed to be carried on horseback. Letterman even provided knapsacks filled with essential bandages, instruments, and medicines that were small enough to be carried by an orderly into combat.

HAVING REORGANIZED THE ambulance and supply system, Letterman took on the management of a field hospital system. As with his supply plan, he preferred to organize at a level higher than the regiment. In this case, he chose the division. His orders provided for a well-defined division of labor among the medical officers, ensuring that each person would know precisely what his assignment was. Under Letterman's new plan, one physician from each regiment would establish a dressing station, near the front, to render first aid. The remainder of the medical staff were to gather at the division's field hospital. One medical officer would keep records, according to Letterman, "of every case brought to the hospital, giving the name, rank, company, and regiment, the seat and character of injury, the treatment, the operation, if any be performed, and the result."[28] If the injured soldier died, then this same medical officer was to oversee the burial detail and assure that the grave was properly marked. Another physician was in charge of pitching hospital tents and providing blankets, fuel, straw, and water. Once this assignment was completed, the same person would organize the kitchen. Other physicians functioned as wound dressers.

In his boldest initiative of all, Letterman decided that surgical operations should be performed only by three physicians in each division with the most surgical experience. Though every military doctor might have been given the title of "surgeon," gone were the days when any physician, whether possessing surgical skills or not, attempted to perform surgical procedures. Letterman's action was prompted, at least in part, by articles he had read in several medical journals that described botched operations by incompetent army surgeons at Antietam.

John Brinton, one of Ulysses S. Grant's medical directors and a highly regarded Philadelphia surgeon, told of a "surgeon" who early in the war needed to perform a leg amputation on a severely wounded soldier. The "surgeon" came to Brinton's office to confess that though he had been named a regimental surgeon, he had never seen nor did he know how to perform the operation. He begged Brinton to assist him at the operation. "On the following morning I did so, and he operated very well, and to the satisfaction of the lookers on. Somehow or the other this amputation established his reputation." Several months later, Brinton was directing battlefield medical services when a hospital steward informed him that "a great surgeon" was busy operating in a nearby field hospital. Curious to meet this master surgeon, Brinton rode his horse to a little country house where the wounded were being carried. There, bloodstained footprints stamped the wooden floor, while upstairs in a small second-story room stood Brinton's "surgeon" friend of old, surrounded by mounds of amputated arms and legs. The man himself was smeared with blood, and according to Brinton, the scene was "ghastly beyond all limits of surgical propriety." "Ah, Doctor," said the new-fledged surgeon to Brinton, "I am getting on, just look at these," as he pointed to his surgical trophies littering the room.[29]

Letterman's decision was groundbreaking: Any physician under his command who wanted to perform surgical operations would be expected to have a level of technical expertise commensurate with his title, "operating surgeon." For the first time in the history of medicine in the United States, specialized skills within the field of surgery were a prerequisite to formal recognition of proficiency. At the time, Letterman's concept was regarded as a novel attempt to raise the level of care for the Army of the Potomac. In hindsight, however, it should be viewed as one of the most momentous medical reforms to come out of the Civil War.

IN THE WEEKS of battlefield inactivity following Antietam, President Lincoln was able to focus on McClellan's unsuitability for military high command. Everything that Lincoln said about McClellan was dominated by one word—"slow." The general was too slow before Antietam. He was too slow during Antietam. And he was too slow after Antietam. Hoping to spur McClellan on, Lincoln visited the Army of the Potomac during the first days of October. In scenes of colorful military pageantry, unending lines of men were ordered out for review as the booming of cannon announced the approach of the commander in chief of the armies of the United States of America. Each day the president, accompanied by McClellan, other personages, and an immense retinue, inspected various corps. In the end, in early November, Lincoln removed McClellan from command.

For Letterman, McClellan's discharge was awkward. They were friends, and as Letterman explained in his official report, "Amidst the most pressing engagements, [McClellan] found time to give his attention to every suggestion for [the soldiers'] benefit which I had to offer, and I feel the most grateful remembrance of the unvarying confidence and support which he heartily gave me in everything which I considered conducive to that end."[30] Making the situation even more difficult were the medical-political ramifications of the dismissal. With McClellan gone, Surgeon General Hammond, and to a lesser extent Frederick Olmsted and the Sanitary Commission, could no longer count on a relatively friendly link to the highest levels of the military and federal government.

Replacing McClellan was a genial six-footer, Ambrose Burnside. His handsome face was covered by a growth of heavy whiskers, which his men called "sidewhiskers" or "burnsides," and soon an anagram came about: "sideburns." A West Pointer, Burnside seemed bold, and he was. He sounded intelligent, but he was not. As much as McClellan was dilatory in his thinking, Burnside was impulsive in his actions. This brashness would shortly bring about a bloody and spectacular military failure in Fredericksburg, a small city located on Virginia's Rappahannock River.

The impatient Burnside decided on the necessity of a direct and massive assault on Richmond, the capital of the Confederacy. He opted for an overland advance in the direction of the Richmond, Fredericksburg & Potomac Railroad, which ran between Fredericksburg and the Confederate seat of government. Time was of the essence, and Burnside moved the army of now more than one hundred thousand men with uncommon speed to Falmouth, a village lying on the north side of the Rappahannock, opposite Fredericksburg. The strategy was to advance quickly across the river, seize the heights west and southwest of Fredericksburg, and then march on Richmond. Two Union corps reached Falmouth on November 17, time enough before Robert E. Lee could shift troops to prevent the Federals from crossing the river. Burnside had supposedly made arrangements to have pontoons available for the two corps to bridge the river, but no equipment was forthcoming for a week.

Burnside blamed Henry Halleck. Halleck blamed the Quartermaster Corps. Quartermaster General Montgomery Meigs blamed Burnside for issuing an unclear order. The end result was that Lee had his seventy-five thousand troops entrenched along an eight-mile-long front on the heights behind Fredericksburg by the time the pontoons arrived. Particularly fortified was Marye's Heights, which was located directly behind the city. As one of Lee's artillery officers stated, "We cover that ground now so well that we will comb it as with a fine-tooth comb. A chicken could not live on that field when we open on it."[31]

With the element of surprise lost and the chilly storms of December descending upon Virginia, Burnside watched as his engineers refurbished a railway landing at Aquia Creek (a tributary of the Potomac River) where a supply depot was established. Thus, the Army of the Potomac was provided a direct line of combined railway and river transportation back to Washington; the whole distance, about seventy-five miles, required a seventeen-hour journey.

Lee could bide his time. For political realities, Burnside could not afford to wait. Lincoln and the public wanted an offensive. Unfortunately, Burnside had lost the element of surprise. Correctly assuming that the Union forces would storm his virtually impregnable position on Marye's Heights, Lee decided to provide, at the time of the battle, just enough resistance on the flanks to confuse Burnside into thinking that he was shifting Southern troops away from the city and the area of Marye's Heights. Burnside was only days away from a disastrous defeat.

AS POORLY MANAGED as the Federals' fighting at Fredericksburg was from a military perspective, it represented a turning point in the medical treatment of combat casualties. For the first time in a great battle, three cardinal components of military medicine (evacuation measures, supply concerns, and hospitalization needs) were planned and facilitated in advance. Thus, the Battle of Fredericksburg is of singular significance to the history of military medicine. Ineptness and slowness might have lost the battle for Burnside, but the wasted weeks provided Letterman with an opportunity to sharpen his plans while ensuring that the Army of the Potomac was supplied with everything he thought would be medically necessary. "Ample supplies of medicines, instruments, stimulants, and anaesthetics were ordered from New York and Washington," according to Letterman, and "large quantities, over and above what were required for issue, of beef stock, dressings, milk, coffee, tea, blankets, and underclothing."[32] The army's medical purveyor established a vast storehouse of supplies at Aquia Creek and a subdepot at the railway station at Falmouth. Letterman made certain his staff knew of the storage facilities and that they need only send in a simple request to obtain what they required. Five hundred hospital tents were kept in reserve, and 254 fully loaded medical knapsacks, one for each regiment, were available. At the time of the battle, almost one thousand ambulances were in waiting—one for every 120 or so men. The delay in action allowed ambulance officers to drill and practice while harnesses, horses, lanterns, stretchers, and all that was necessary for putting the ambulance trains in service were procured.

Situated on the southern bank of the Rappahannock River, sixty miles north of Richmond and fifty-five miles southwest of Washington, Fredericksburg, despite its small size, was an important city in Spotsylvania County, Virginia. With a canal, a railway, and several dirt highways branching from the city, in addition to the Rappahannock, the area once proved a prosperous hub for commercial traffic. However, by December 1862, the tides of conflict had reduced Fredericksburg to a shell of its former economic self. With a wartime population of only four thousand inhabitants and its commercial worth destroyed, the city and its surrounding countryside were now most valued for their geographic importance.

In the predawn, fog-shrouded darkness of December 11, Union engineers began building pontoon bridges at Fredericksburg proper and a site a few miles downstream. The out-of-town effort was completed without much difficulty. But the bridges opposite the city were only two-thirds done when the sun rose. As daylight increased and the fog dispersed, two regiments of Mississippi sharpshooters, staked out in Fredericksburg's brick houses and behind its riverfront businesses, began to pick off the engineers. In this way, the rebels prevented attempts to complete the bridges. Shortly after noon, a frustrated Burnside ordered every available artillery piece—150 guns—to shell the hapless town (most civilians had already been evacuated) to suppress the sniping. Two hours and more than five thousand projectiles later, the town was wrecked, but the bombardment failed to dislodge the Southern shooters, who simply took advantage of new shelters created by the rubble.

When Union officers reported that the bridge work could not be completed, soldiers from three infantry regiments volunteered to cross the Rappahannock in open boats and undertake an amphibious assault. In midafternoon, as tens of thousands of anxious Union soldiers watched from the north bank, the volunteer infantrymen rowed into the river. One by one the oarsmen fell from enemy fire, but with the river only two hundred yards wide, the Northerners managed to reach shelter on the opposite bluffs and, after thirty minutes of house-to-house fighting, secured the town as the defenders were pushed back to their main lines on the heights behind the city. The rest of the day, and all of December 12, was spent in a tedious movement of the Union army over the pontoon bridges and in the deployment of its men.

Jonathan Letterman and members of his medical staff crossed the Rappahannock's pontoon bridges on the afternoon of December 12. Their mission was to find undamaged structures that could function as temporary field hospitals. Being near the Southern front lines, these facilities had to be easy to evacuate; they were intended to augment the larger division hospitals that were mostly on the protected north side of the river.

Letterman found desolation everywhere, but a cluster of buildings centered around the courthouse and several nearby churches were deemed suitable. Furniture was rearranged and mattresses and beds taken from adjacent dwellings. Straw was spread on the floor as candles, dressings, food, instruments, and stimulants were stocked. Operating rooms were extemporized, including one in the courthouse's main hearing room.

Burnside had divided his force of 120,000 men into three sections. There was a left wing (consisting of the First and Sixth Corps) that would engage the Confederates several miles downstream of Fredericksburg. The right wing (made up of the Second and Ninth Corps) would attack through Fredericksburg and storm Marye's Heights. A center force (formed by the Third and Fifth Corps) was to connect the two attacks and reinforce either at need. So spread out was the Union line (a total of 254 regiments divided into 18 divisions, with 3 divisions allotted to each corps) that the 18 division field hospitals were organized along a six-mile stretch of the Rappahannock. In an area three miles downriver from Fredericksburg, the Second Division of the Sixth Corps established its field hospital in a large stone mansion, known as Mansfield House, on the south bank of the Rappahannock. Charles O'Leary, medical director of the Sixth Corps, reported that this hospital had three operating tables staffed by operating surgeons and their assistants. "Instruments, dressings, and all necessary appliances, were arranged with an order, precision, and convenience rarely excelled in regular hospitals,"[33] reported O'Leary. A tent-only facility, for the First Division of the Ninth Corps, was established in a wooded ravine adjacent to Burnside's headquarters at a stately old home, the Phillips house, two-thirds of a mile from the river's north edge. A hospital for the First Division of the Third Corps was organized two miles northeast of the river near Falmouth, in a small farm called the White House, on the road to the hamlet of Belle Plain. With his fully staffed and stocked hospitals scattered throughout the countryside, Letterman believed his physicians capable of handling any number of Union wounded and being able to meet their needs for several weeks.

ON SATURDAY, DECEMBER 13, the Battle of Fredericksburg began in earnest in cold-weather conditions. The main battle was waged behind the town on the plain leading to Marye's Heights. Another, lesser conflict took place three miles downstream. Both would prove strategic fiascoes for Burnside. If managed correctly, the numerically stronger Union left wing, located at the downstream area, should have been able to crush Robert E. Lee's right wing, under the command of Stonewall Jackson. By noon, a force of Pennsylvanians had forged an opening through Jackson's line. It was now a simple fact of unleashing further force. However, Burnside issued an ambiguously worded order to send in more troops. William Buel Franklin, commander of the Union's left wing, misunderstood Burnside's intent and, failing on his own to appreciate the seriousness of the situation, did not throw in any reserves. Jackson had large numbers of his troops speed forward and counterattack.

The Pennsylvanians, finding themselves nearly surrounded, retreated back toward the Rappahannock with the Confederates in pursuit. Brigadier General David Birney's First Division of the Union's Third Corps was sent to assist the Pennsylvanians. Describing a scene of utter pandemonium, eyewitness accounts tell of fleeing Northern officers from the left wing shouting to Birney's men from the center force, "Go back! Go back!"[34] Disregarding these entreaties, the men of the First Division continued to advance. Among those leading the charge was a twenty-one-year-old corporal, James Quick of the Thirty-eighth New York Infantry (also known as the Second Scott's Life Guard). He could not know that Jackson's troops were in full force behind an upcoming embankment. Met by a hail of rifle fire so intense that it achieved the effect of machine guns, three hundred out of eight hundred charging Federals were wounded or killed within five minutes.

Quick was shot behind the left jaw, with the ball exiting through the left side of the nose. Dazed and bleeding profusely, he awaited evacuation to his division's field hospital at the White House farm. With the Union forces in full retreat, it was only a furious fire of Northern canister shot that eventually held the Confederates in check.

The fact that Franklin never brought more than half of his fifty-thousand-strong left wing into the fight was a serious blunder. Many of Franklin's troops had been relegated to simple picket duty, guarding the downstream pontoon bridges and the like, as typified by soldiers of the Fifth Vermont Infantry. Franklin's bungling of the battlefield situation meant that these Vermonters saw little skirmishing and were instead prime targets for the rebels' artillery shells. Among the first to be wounded was twenty-two-year-old Private John Coats of I Company. He was hit by a shell fragment, which glanced off his left shoe and struck his right shinbone, gouging out flesh and bone. Coats was quickly evacuated to his division's field hospital at Mansfield House. There, because his wound was not considered life threatening, he received little medical attention other than the wrapping of dirty lint bandages around his lower leg. Union physicians had more complicated cases to deal with, considering that 3,700 men were killed or wounded in this phase of the debacle at Fredericksburg.

Three miles away, a fiercely contested battle for Marye's Heights was raging, and the Union right wing was in a hopeless situation. Burnside had ordered the Second Corps to seize the heights directly behind Fredericksburg. It was a foolhardy assignment, because the Confederate position was overwhelmingly strong. Marye's Heights, covered with twenty-two Southern cannons, fell off abruptly toward Fredericksburg and ended in a road faced, on the city side, by a half-mile, four-foot-high stone wall. Various swales, positioned between the heights and the city, made this road invisible to the advancing Union troops. Indeed, the "sunken road" provided a perfect defensive position for the rebels.

Around noontime, wave after wave of Union Second Corps soldiers began to march out of the town toward Marye's Heights. They advanced at a brisk pace as shot and shell fell thickly about them, until they were within musket range of the base of the hill. From the rifle pits, behind the stone wall, a brigade of Georgians let loose a line of fire that decimated the Northerners.

The Yankees would fall back into the shelter of a swale and, reinforced by fresh infantry, would re-form and, at double quick with fixed bayonets, again face the murderous fire. But the Confederate guns were arranged so they could concentrate their aim instantly upon any position occupied by the assailing troops. This enfilading fire killed and wounded thousands of men. Whole regiments fell into disarray as the marching columns broke in the inevitable confusion, only to be rallied again and brought back into the fray.

Among the Second Corps's regiments surging forward, the Eighty-first Pennsylvania consisted of 16 commissioned officers and 245 enlisted men. As soon as this force advanced onto the muddy plain leading to the heights, it was exposed to the full onslaught of the rebels' musketry and artillery. According to the account of its brigade commander, "The fire here was terrific—the hottest I have ever seen. The men fell by hundreds."[35] Within sixty minutes, 12 officers and more than 160 enlisted men were killed or wounded. Among the injured was D Company private James Connor, who was hit by a musket ball that shattered his left thighbone and left him lying helpless on the battlefield. The battlefield situation was chaotic enough that Connor could not be brought immediately to his own division's field hospital; not until the next day was he admitted to the tent-only facility of the First Division of the Ninth Corps.

As the slaughter continued, the Second Corps's commander, Major General Darius Couch, climbed the steeple of the Fredericksburg Court House, the same building that was functioning as a Union field hospital. From above the haze and smoke, Couch had a clear view of the battleground. "I remember," he recalled, "that the whole plain was covered with men, prostrate and dropping, the live men running here and there, and in front closing upon each other, and the wounded coming back. The commands seemed to be mixed up. I had never before seen fighting like that, nothing approaching it in terrible uproar and destruction."[36] The Yankees battled through the darkening December afternoon, but not one Northerner made it over the stone wall. Nearly 13,000 Federals became casualties—most of them lying on the plain leading to Marye's Heights. Distraught, Burnside wanted to personally spearhead one last charge, but his staff warned against such a suicidal mission. All hope seemed lost for a defeated United States Army as, once again, another poorly planned drive on Richmond ended in calamity.

By nightfall, the streets of Fredericksburg were crowded with ambulances bearing the injured, and it was difficult to find any one spot that was totally safe from the sporadic but continuing Confederate fire. Ambulance activity was ceaseless as the wounded filled the courthouse, churches, private houses, schools, and stores, then the yards, and finally the sidewalks. Fragments of shells, minié balls, and shots of all kinds flew in at the doors and windows and whistled through the roofs.

The extemporized hospital's lantern lights became inviting targets for rebel guns. Blankets were fastened over windows to dim the flames' blazes. The surgeons worked through the night, completing amputation after amputation. As one observer said of the scene, "The sadness which prevailed throughout the whole army that night can neither be described nor imagined. The surgeons were the happiest of all; they were so busy they had no time to think of our terrible defeat."[37]

THAT THE SURGEONS within Fredericksburg proper were fully occupied was testimony to the efficiency of Letterman's ambulance corps. According to Letterman's official report on the Union's right wing, "Before daylight, all the wounded, save twenty, in a house outside of our pickets, beyond whose line the ambulances could not be permitted to go, were brought from the field." It was a relatively efficient evacuation since the wounded lay within a small space, on an open plain, immediately behind the city. The situation was different on the Federals' left wing, where the injured were scattered throughout the woods of Prospect Hill, a mile away from the banks of the Rappahannock. Because the forest was impenetrable for horse-drawn ambulances, stretcher bearers combed the area on foot, searching for the men. Rendezvous points were established where the litter carriers could bring the wounded. "Here the sufferers received such attendance as was absolutely necessary, and were conveyed thence by the ambulances to the field hospitals,"[38] Letterman recollected. Everyone's situation was eased by a change from the previous cold-weather conditions. A surgeon from the Sixth Corps observed, "A kind providence had favored them, for the weather had been delightful. Had such weather prevailed as we experienced a few days before, many of the wounded, faint and exhausted from the loss of blood, must have perished with the cold."[39]

By the morning of Sunday, December 14, all the wounded of the Union's left wing, except for approximately two hundred who lay close to or within Confederate lines, had been rescued. The predicament of these two hundred soldiers was resolved when a limited truce was arranged by Union major general Daniel Sickles and Confederate brigadier general Jubal Early. With a tacit though informal understanding in place, Sickles noted, "The ambulance men, frequently assisted by the enemy in pointing out our wounded and placing them on stretchers, brought off all of our men who had been left on the field."[40] Letterman was pleased enough with the actions of the ambulance corps that he made certain to note in his report, "The admirable manner in which [the ambulance corps] performed the duties required of it, fully justified and amply repaid the time and labor expended in its organization."[41] The corps's outstanding efforts were borne out by the fact that during the entire Battle of Fredericksburg, fewer than two dozen severely injured Yankees were taken as prisoners of war.

For Burnside, the relative calm of Sunday afternoon afforded little relief from a growing despair. One of his staff found him alone in his tent, pacing. "Oh! those men! Oh! those men!" Burnside muttered, sighing. When asked what he meant, the general pointed to the river and said, "Those men over there! I am thinking of them all the time."[42] That night, with the growing realization that he was in the midst of a military disaster, Burnside ordered all the wounded removed to the north side of the Rappahannock. On a dreary and rain-soaked Monday, December 15, the Confederates on Marye's Heights watched with what one eyewitness described as "awed fascination"[43] as endless lines of Union stretcher bearers and ambulances flying yellow flags transferred thousands of patients over the pontoon bridges. By midnight, most of the evacuation was complete. Then, under Letterman's personal direction, Fredericksburg was checked for any forgotten men. "Not one wounded or sick man was found," claimed Letterman.[44]

With all the wounded on safe ground, the remainder of the Army of the Potomac managed to slip away in the chill and darkness of early Tuesday morning. When the fog lifted from the valley, the rebels could see the whole Union force across the Rappahannock; the pontoon bridges were swung back, and the river once again separated the two armies. For the returning citizens of Fredericksburg, the city was in almost total ruin, and as one businessman was quick to point out, "ghastly were the numbers of amputated limbs found in great numbers in several places of the town."[45]

In planning for the battle at Fredericksburg, Letterman assumed that the very serious cases, such as wounds of the abdomen, chest, and head or those requiring amputation, could be adequately cared for within his newly created division hospital system (with its canvas tent complexes and hierarchy of operating surgeons and assisting physicians). Burnside, however, wanted to move the Army of the Potomac away from Fredericksburg and begin attacking anew. The wounded, who required nurses and physicians as well as large amounts of medical supplies, represented an impediment to his plans. It would be more efficient, he reasoned, to send the injured to the general hospitals in Washington and other Northern cities, thus freeing up the medical staff.

Letterman pleaded with Burnside not to expose the wounded to a lengthy trip in the winter cold. "I represented the matter to General Burnside, and informed him that these patients were as comfortable and as well taken care of as if they were then in Washington; that it was dangerous to remove them. The surgeons were taking the deepest interest in these cases," stressed Letterman. "Unless there was some military reason for removing these men, I wished to keep them where they were." A stubborn Burnside resisted Letterman's plea and issued an order for the immediate transportation of the wounded. Later, Letterman would note sarcastically, "I suppose this military reason did exist."[46]

Neither man was entirely right nor entirely wrong. In an era when mercy toward the wounded was not a fighting general's highest priority, Letterman, as a physician, would be expected to argue for the safety of his patients. However, he was also the innovator behind a new approach to battlefield health care. Letterman had a vested interest in the medical situation and, as a matter of course, assumed that care at Fredericksburg would be better than that after other battles. The wounded were certainly brought to field hospitals in a more expeditious manner, but improved evacuation methods and a better-organized hospital system could not change surgical treatments and their outcomes. Though Letterman made great strides toward eradicating battlefield neglect, without knowledge of germs and antisepsis, physicians were handicapped and infection remained a wounded soldier's main enemy. Even in the finest of the area's brick mansions serving as divisional hospitals, heaps of unwashed troops lay on filthy mattresses, wearing dirty, bloody uniforms. Amputation cases were positioned next to men dying from typhoid or tetanus. Outside the facility lay mounds of rotting amputated limbs. One soldier wrote home to his mother, "There is a hospital within thirty yards of us . . . about the building you could see the hogs belonging to the farm eating arms and other portions of the body."[47] The injured in Letterman's tent-only facilities were no better off. Crowding and a lack of cots were evidenced as row after row of amputees lay on blankets spread over boughs of pine and cedar for bedding while infections spread from one man to the next. The end result was that no matter how much good Letterman accomplished, his state-of-the-art ambulance corps, field hospitals, and medical supply scheme could not prevail against the medical primitiveness of the times.

IN THE FIGHTING at Fredericksburg, Union troops sustained almost 6,000 wounds of the upper and lower extremities, many causing bone fractures, but fewer than 1,200 gunshots to the abdomen, chest, and head. This pattern of injuries, like that for many Civil War battles, was fortunate because abdominal, thoracic, and cranial wounds were essentially untreatable. Surgeons did not have the technical expertise to open an abdomen and repair shrapnel-riddled intestines or stop the bleeding from a gunshot to the lung or excise a portion of the skull and operate safely on an injury to the brain. For those patients, recovery was based more on good fortune than medical know-how. However, surgeons did feel confident removing arms, fingers, legs, and toes.

For centuries, amputation had been among the accepted and chief forms of major surgery performed in medical practice. Samuel Gross, Philadelphia's renowned professor of surgery, wrote in his popular surgical textbook that if an extremity injury involved severe tissue destruction or the presence of fractured bone shards sticking through the skin, then "there is no choice; no question concerning a cure by mere therapeutic measures; the knife is the only remedy . . . the body, it is true, is mutilated, perhaps sadly disfigured, but life is safe, and surgery, science, and humanity have achieved a real triumph."[48] The result of such thinking, noted by a surgeon on the scene at Fredericksburg, was that "amputations were especially numerous, over one hundred being reported in the First Corps within the first forty-eight hours after the battle."[49]

The almost five hundred amputations performed on Northern soldiers at Fredericksburg may seem barbaric by today's standards, but Letterman was right to see that the wounded received immediate care. Men worn down by hardship and disease were poor operative risks but even poorer candidates if nothing was done. Badly torn tissue plus fractured bone provided an excellent environment for bacterial growth. Without a knowledge of antibiotics, doctors had difficulty treating the resulting bone and wound infections. Delay in treating shattered limbs, therefore, led to more pain for the patient, a higher chance of infection, and a decreased likelihood of survival. Adding to the justifiable worries about delayed amputation were the increased perils of transporting soldiers with broken bones sticking through their skin: the cruel jolting of army ambulances, further aggravation of fractures creating grossly deformed limbs, and a higher incidence of fatal hemorrhages.

There was also a growing awareness that death rates were lower if amputations were performed within the first forty-eight hours following injury (called "primary amputation"). Once forty-eight hours had passed, there was enough bacterial growth that any cutting would spread the germs through the bloodstream. The result was blood poisoning, which without antibiotics was almost invariably fatal. Stephen Smith, the well-known New York surgeon, pointed out the dilemma in his handbook on surgical operations: "Though the primary amputation is a violence, it is one the patient is likely to submit to with resignation, knowing that it is performed to remove parts which, if unremoved, will destroy life."[50] The soldiers' amputation quandary was voiced in this campfire ditty:

> To amputate, or not to amputate? That is the question.
> Whether 'tis nobler in the mind to suffer
> Th' unsymmetry of one-armed men, and draw
> A pension, thereby shuffling off a part
> Of mortal coil; or, trusting unhinged nature,
> Take arms against a cruel surgeon's knife,
> And, by opposing rusty theories,
> Risk a return to dust in the full shape of a man.[51]

Letterman's Fredericksburg transport scheme was unprecedented in the annals of medical history—no previous army had ever organized as efficient an ambulance service or delivered better medical care through its field hospitals and cadre of chosen operating surgeons. Battle tested, the ambulance and field hospital service designed by Letterman was so thorough and practical that it became a model for medical care in many of Europe's armies. By 1870, during the Franco-Prussian conflict, a massive Letterman–style canvas tent field hospital complex was erected on the outskirts of Paris. The facility was managed by John Swinburne of Albany, New York, the same surgeon who eight years earlier was a prisoner of war following the Union defeat at Savage's Station. Of all the visits of those who toured the complex, the most poignant was Ambrose Burnside, the recently retired governor of Rhode Island.

Despite Letterman's achievements at Fredericksburg, there were oversights. Hospital tents provided little insulation from the December cold, and Letterman, underestimating the possible number of wounded, had not ordered enough stoves. Consequently, many of the wounded suffered frostbite. "God knows how they endure the cold without perishing,"[52] wrote one physician to his sister. A lack of woolen hospital clothing added to the problem. The United States Sanitary Commission partially remedied the situation by providing hundreds of woolen blankets, quilts, shirts, stockings, and trousers.

Letterman's major misstep, however, was his insistence on keeping all the wounded on-site for as long as possible. It was a mistake to subject the injured to the harshness of a Virginia winter—housed in canvas tents and surrounded by filth—when they were less than a day's travel-time from the nation's capital. The general hospitals in Washington and cities beyond had undergone an impressive change since the first months of the war. No longer were ramshackle hotels and dingy warehouses the only buildings used to shelter the sick and wounded. Rapidly, they were being replaced by one-story barrack hospitals with modern ventilation and sanitation. The government was spending millions of dollars to build new facilities and Letterman should have incorporated them into his overall plan. Perhaps he believed the army's transportation capabilities were insufficiently organized to link field hospitals with far-flung general hospitals. Or perhaps he was uncertain as to what was clinically appropriate.

Letterman's lapses were downplayed by army surgeons and those who trusted him. Surgeon General Hammond toured the Fredericksburg campsite in mid-December and, according to one observer, was "well pleased with the medical arrangements, the hospital organizations, and the ambulance corps."[53] Letterman was also visited by Massachusetts senator Henry Wilson and members of the Congressional Committee on the Conduct of the War, who praised "the administration of the medical department."[54] Charles Stillé, the Sanitary Commission's official historian, rewrote history to protect Letterman's name: "It was the wise policy of the Medical Director to convey the wounded of this battle to the general military hospitals at Washington with the least possible delay."[55]

Among all this professional praise, there was one glaring dissenter. Medical inspector Thomas Perley visited the camps and hospitals in the Falmouth–Aquia Landing region during the first week of January 1863. He was appalled at what he found. "I do not believe I have ever seen greater misery from sickness than exists now," Perley wrote Hammond. Perley was critical of everything—lack of stoves, deficient hospital clothing, improper food, inefficient cooking arrangements, and, worst of all, poor management of the steamers used to transport the wounded northward. In reporting to the surgeon general, Perley informed Hammond that, in his opinion, very little had been medically correct at Fredericksburg. Without mentioning names, Perley raged that "the principal medical officer is not equal to his responsible station, and has failed in his duty, either from having too much to do or from neglect."[56]

Behind Perley's veiled denunciation of Letterman loomed the ongoing political feud between Secretary of War Stanton, Surgeon General Hammond, and their numerous surrogates. Perley was a man of dubious reputation who was indebted to Stanton for his position. Letterman, who was Hammond's appointee, found Perley unbearable. Perley returned to Washington eager to spread the word of Hammond's and Letterman's supposed failures. Hammond immediately demanded Perley's dismissal due to professional misconduct, but Stanton refused to comply.

Letterman's success at Fredericksburg was aided by the fact that Robert E. Lee did not counterattack on the morning of December 14. With the Army of the Potomac in disarray (President Lincoln would relieve Burnside of his command in January 1863), a successful advance by the Army of Northern Virginia could have dealt the North's war effort a serious setback. Letterman's field hospitals would have been overrun or at least bombarded by Confederate artillery, and he would have been accused of neglect in his planning. At Fredericksburg, the Southern troops were arranged only for a defensive battle. Any abrupt termination of this strategy by the Confederates could not have been anticipated, nor could Lee marshal his forces fast enough to begin an offensive operation.

Notwithstanding Letterman's motives in keeping the wounded at Fredericksburg, Burnside was correct, if for the wrong reason, when he ordered the injured moved. Burnside needed to repair a tattered military reputation and was resolved to cross the Rappahannock as soon as possible. Letterman's patients were in the way. Burnside understood the necessity of getting the men to Washington, but his rationale of military expediency was wrong. He should have transported the men for their medical needs.

On December 16, the removal of six thousand wounded began. It was a disorderly affair made worse because there was only a single railroad track from the Fredericksburg–Falmouth area to the Aquia Landing embarkation site, from which Potomac River steamers headed north to Washington. The army's failure to establish some kind of evacuation facility or way station compounded the chaos. If not for the Sanitary Commission organizing its own feeding and relief depot at Aquia Landing, the situation would have bordered on total neglect. The first night alone, the commission's agents fed and cared for six hundred wounded men. "What could we do here without the Sanitary commission," one soldier wrote home. "Many of our medicines, our stimulants, blankets, bedding, etc., come from the S.C. I would rather have Mr. Olmsted's fame than that of any General in this war since the beginning."[57]

While giving in to Burnside's wishes, Letterman insisted that those injured least be sent away first. This way the medical staff would maintain control of the more serious postsurgical cases for as long as possible. Regardless of the extent of a soldier's injury, the trip was a harrowing experience. Placed in rickety ambulances or walking if they could, the men were initially taken to the Falmouth railroad station and loaded onto railroad cars. According to one of the surgeons in charge, "Many of the cars consisted of simple platforms without covering, and were ill adapted for transporting men badly wounded, especially in midwinter; and, for this reason, some of these unfortunates suffered much."

There was no coordination between the trains' arrival at Aquia Landing and the steamboats' presence at the dock. The result was that the trains rarely connected with the boats and the wounded were left shelterless for hours at a time. The cold boat trip northward was itself a nightmare. "Nothing was provided for them to rest upon save the hard boards of the decks,"[58] related the surgeon in charge. Medical inspector Perley observed, "Only two of the transport were fitted up for the purpose; the others were taken from vessels lying in the creek, and in many instances no provisions seem to have been made for supplying food or even drink for the wounded, some of whom were frozen during the passage."[59]

Seventeen hours after leaving Fredericksburg, the troops arrived in Washington, where ambulances distributed them to various hospitals. By Christmas, the evacuation was finished. Letterman, in a not entirely honest description of the situation, wrote to Hammond, "I say, without fear of contradiction, that seldom, if ever, have wounded been so carefully transported, and felt assured that no more suffering was occasioned than the severity of the wounds, of necessity, entailed."[60]

ON DECEMBER 21, 1862, Hannah Ropes, abolitionist, social activist, and head nurse at the run-down Union Hotel Hospital, wrote to her daughter, Alice, "Today we are waiting for a fresh supply of worse wounded from the Fredericksburg battles, or murder ground I might say." It had been a difficult fall for Ropes, who described her hospital as a "terribly sick house." The men seemed to suffer increasingly serious injuries with each passing battle. At first there were only a dozen or so amputees, but every day brought more surgical cases, and by the last week of December, the building was filled with amputees. Supplies were short. Typhoid fever and other infectious diseases were spreading, and with the cold weather setting in, pneumonias began to appear.

These were also difficult times in the political life of the nation's capital. Military prospects appeared poor, and rumors were rife: Lincoln would leave; members of the cabinet threatened to resign; an embittered George McClellan was prepared to launch a coup and seek appeasement with the Confederates. Making matters worse was the presence of so many sick and wounded, who served to reinforce the medical misery the war had brought. The city grew crowded as wives, mothers, fathers, sons, and daughters journeyed to Washington to help care for their injured loved ones.

Despite the bleak and complicated medical situation, Hannah Ropes continued with her hospital work and maintained her many political contacts. "I dare say it looks worse to you in Boston than to us here," she wrote to Alice. "We are not going to smash up generally as a nation. We have reached the last quarter of the night preceding the dawn. And, as in nature, [though] that hour is the most cheerless it is not less hopeless because of the approach of the new day." Ropes had recently spent a Sunday evening at the home of her close friend, medical inspector Thomas Perley, discussing politics and medicine with other guests, among them the wife of Maine senator William Fessenden. "I had a pleasant visit," she assured her daughter. Another night was spent in the company of Massachusetts senator Henry Wilson and his wife.

Joining Ropes in mid-December as a volunteer nurse at the Union Hotel Hospital was a thirty-year-old writer for the *Atlantic Monthly*. "We are cheered by the arrival of Miss Alcott from Concord," Ropes confided to her diary. "The prospect of a really good nurse, a gentlewoman who can do more than merely keep the patients from falling out of bed, as some of them seem to consider the whole duty of a nurse."[61] Louisa May Alcott had already gained some literary recognition for her *Flower Fables*, written for the daughter of Ralph Waldo Emerson.

Ropes taught Alcott that bedpans were to be changed whenever used, that the soldiers' faces and hands must be cleaned with brown soap, and that the men's undergarments were to be replaced at least once a week. "My experiences had begun with a death," Alcott explained, "and owing to the defalcation [unanticipated leaving] of another nurse, a somewhat abrupt plunge into the superintendence of a ward containing forty beds, where I spent my shining hours washing faces, serving rations, giving medicine, and sitting in a very hard chair, with pneumonia on one side, diphtheria on the other, two typhoids opposite, and a dozen dilapidated patriots, hopping, lying, and lounging about, all staring more or less at the new 'nuss,' who suffered untold agonies."

Alcott's tenure at what she called "the Hurly-burly House" was not happy and would not last long. Her shared quarters were austere, with broken windowpanes, a bare wooden floor, and two narrow iron beds. The ineffective fireplace was so small that one end of the burning log jutted into the room, and, as Alcott described, "I tripped over it a dozen times a day, and flew up to poke it a dozen times at night." Rats and bugs were rampant. But as cold and uninviting as the accommodations were, the hospital's daily diet was worse. Alcott wrote that it "consisted of beef, evidently put down for the men of '76; pork, just in from the street; army bread, composed of saw-dust and saleratus; butter, salt as if churned by Lot's wife; and stewed blackberries, so much like preserved cockroaches, that only those devoid of imaginations could partake thereof with relish." Occasionally Alcott was forced to go without food altogether, because at mealtimes, the men (soldiers, surgeons, and male nurses alike) selfishly ate first and sometimes left nothing for the female nurses.

The wretchedness of the Union Hotel Hospital was most noticeable to Alcott when she visited the recently built Armory Square Hospital in Washington. Armory Square was a pavilion-style facility with airy, clean, and warm patient wards, and the sharp contrast in living and medical conditions between the two buildings was obvious. At Armory Square, Alcott felt "order, method, common sense and liberality seemed to rule in a style that did one's heart good to see." But at the Union Hotel Hospital, "disorder, discomfort, bad management, and no visible head, reduced things to a condition which I despair of describing."[62]

By the first week of January 1863, Alcott had contracted the early stages of pneumonia, with severe chills and a violent cough. Initially, Ropes believed Alcott to be hypochondriacal, but on January 11, Ropes became concerned enough that she ordered Alcott confined to her room with a mustard plaster on her chest. Having worked closely with the same patients, Ropes too became sick and wrote to her daughter that, like Alcott, she was staying in her room and that they both "suffered terribly."[63] Pneumonias were the most common cause of death at the Union Hotel Hospital, and the rampant typhoid fever was a known antecedent illness.

Among the most feared and often fatal of the terrible epidemic diseases in the nineteenth century, typhoid is an intestinal infection spread by ingesting food or water contaminated with the fecal bacteria *Salmonella typhi*. As the bacteria wander through the body, fever and a generalized fatigue develop, sometimes followed by diarrhea and, in the worst of cases, intestinal perforation and death. Typhoid can also cause bronchitis, leading to pneumonia. What was not understood, because of a lack of knowledge about microbiology, was that some individuals could also be infected with typhoid without having any gastrointestinal or pulmonary symptoms. Given the poor sanitation at the Union Hotel Hospital, with its adjacent latrines and kitchen, these unsuspecting typhoid carriers could easily have spread the organisms to more susceptible individuals. As Alcott said of the Union Hotel Hospital, "For a more perfect pestilence-box than this house I never saw—cold, damp, dirty, full of vile odors from wounds, kitchens, wash-rooms, and stables."[64]

With Alcott languishing in her room, physicians began to make daily visits, tapping at her chest to see if the pneumonia was resolving or spreading. In his journal, Alcott's father noted anxiously, "I fear [Louisa May's stint in Washington] will end in her breaking down presently."[65] But Alcott was determined to serve out her three-month commitment to the nursing corps.

She became delirious as typhoid attacked her senses. "Hours began to get confused; people looked odd; queer faces haunted the room, and the nights were one long fight with weariness and pain," Alcott recalled. Her hair began to fall out from the emotional and physical stress. During the third week of January, Alcott's father arrived in Washington, where he found his daughter near death and living in the most squalid of conditions. "At the sight of him, my resolution melted away," wrote Alcott. "My heart turned traitor to my boys, and, when he said, 'Come home,' I answered, 'Yes, father.'"[66] So ended Louisa May Alcott's forty-day career as an army nurse. She survived her illness, but not without a prolonged recovery. By August 1863, her letters home from the Hurly-burly House, plus additional recollections, were collected and published as *Hospital Sketches*, one of the truly great written works to come out of the Civil War.

Alcott's supervising matron, Hannah Ropes, would not fare as well. A rose-colored rash had appeared on her chest, accompanied by severe pains in her rib cage. Her breathing became hurried and shallow, and she began coughing up thick, foul-smelling phlegm. She suffered from uncontrollable diarrhea and was dehydrated. Ropes was bled, blistered, and purged, but soon she was having difficulty breathing and speaking. As she grew sicker, her daughter, Alice, was summoned to help care for her. Writing to her brother, Edward, Alice explained, "Mother has been ill for some weeks and indeed nearly all the nurses are ill." Medical inspector Thomas Perley visited every day, and Massachusetts senator Henry Wilson was there almost as often. Secretary of War Stanton personally sent for Ropes's son, who was a member of the Second Massachusetts Infantry, but his regiment was on a march and could not be located. On the evening of January 20, the same day that Louisa May Alcott's father was preparing to take his daughter back home to Concord, Hannah Ropes died in her room at Union Hotel Hospital. Edward did not arrive in Washington until January 28. His sister urged him to visit the Union Hotel Hospital, for "you would hear many pleasant things of mother from the nurses and her boys—you would see how they loved her."[67] Two months later, the impoverished facility, with its unsavory history of ubiquitous infectious diseases and staggering death rates, was permanently shuttered by medical authorities.

MUCH LIKE ALCOTT'S father, tens of thousands of citizens came to Washington's hospitals in search of sick and wounded family members. In mid-December 1862, forty-three-year-old Walt Whitman went looking for his brother, a captain in the Fifty-first New York Infantry (also known as Shepard's Rifles), who had been wounded at Fredericksburg. Whitman, already famous for *Leaves of Grass*, his volume of poetry, arrived in Washington and, after several days of fruitless rummaging about, decided to hitch a ride on a government steamer to Aquia Landing. Forty-eight hours later, he finally located his brother at an army base near Falmouth.

Although his brother's injury was slight, Whitman was shocked at the medical misery he encountered. "One of the first things that met my eyes in camp was a heap of feet, arms, legs, etc., under a tree in front of a hospital," he told his mother. Whitman recalled how, during his time in Falmouth, he would step out of his tent to wash his face and before him would be a stretcher holding a shapeless object covered by a dark gray blanket. "It is the corpse of some wounded or sick soldier of the reg't who died in the hospital tent during the night—perhaps there is a row of three or four of these corpses lying covered over," Whitman wrote in his diary. "No one makes an ado."[68]

Whitman's view darkened when he accompanied the injured back to Washington. Contradicting most of the United States Army's official reports, Whitman claimed that he saw many men die along the way. He told of feeble and sickly soldiers sent from Falmouth Station to Aquia Landing on open platform railroad cars, "such as hogs are transported." Too weak to sit up or help themselves, the men were unceremoniously dumped on the next northward-bound steamer. Once on board, Whitman observed that the soldiers were left to fend for themselves. Frequently, nothing was available to eat or drink. If the soldiers were cold and needed blankets or warmer clothes, they were often told to get the items themselves. Whitman described it as a "long train of exhaustion, deprivation, rudeness, no food, no friendly word or deed, but all kinds of upstart airs and impudent, unfeeling speeches and deeds from all kinds of small officials (and some big ones) cutting like razors into sensitive hearts."

After arriving in Washington, the sick and wounded were met at the wharves by enormous milling crowds. Confusion ruled; there was no nourishment waiting at the docks—not even crackers or water. There were no nurses or other health care workers. There were no structures to temporarily shelter the men. There were no governmental employees to determine to which hospitals the troops should be transported. Whether a particular soldier ended up at a new pavilion-style facility or a run-down extemporized hotel-hospital was entirely a matter of chance. Waiting ambulances simply whisked the men away without regard for their condition. Whitman was outraged at what he considered the callous care and governmental red tape. "In general, the officials—especially the new ones with their straps or badges—put on too many airs," he wrote.

Whitman's sympathy for the soldiers was so acute that he decided to remain in Washington and serve as a voluntary visitor to the wounded until the war was over. Supporting himself as a newspaper correspondent, he detailed his daily observations in dispatches to *The New York Times* and the *Brooklyn Eagle*. He called himself "a regular self-appointed missionary to these thousands and tens of thousands of wounded and sick young men here, left upon government hands, many of them languishing, many of them dying."

Early on, Whitman complained of ward masters who harshly ordered men dying from dysentery or disabled from gunshot wounds to care for themselves. "There are tyrants and shysters in all positions and especially those dressed in subordinate authority," he wrote. Whitman objected to certain groups of nurses. "I am compelled to say young ladies, however refined, educated, and benevolent, do not succeed as army nurses, though their motives are noble; neither do the Catholic nuns," he declared. Instead, according to him, "Mothers full of motherly feeling, and however illiterate but bringing reminiscences of home and with the magnetic touch of hands, are the true women nurses." Whitman described certain physicians as "careless, rude, capricious, and needlessly strict." He told of hospitals, in particular the extemporized second floor of the U.S. Patent Office building, that were crowded with rows of the sick and badly wounded. "It was a strange, solemn, and—with all its features of suffering and death—a sort of fascinating sight," he wrote. At the Judiciary Square facility, Whitman found "more impudence and more dandy doctorism and more needless airs than in all the two score other establishments in and around Washington." But there were also health care workers who impressed him. Several of the nurses at Armory Square were said to be "very good," especially one on Ward E, described by Whitman as "the best." Even at Judiciary Square, "some of the women nurses are excellent," he observed. A ward surgeon at Armory Square was "known to fight as hard for many a poor fellow's life under his charge as a lioness would fight for her young," according to Whitman.

Such personal observations made over the course of many months underscore the close relationships that Whitman developed with hospital personnel. "I go every day without fail and often at night—sometimes stay very late. No one interferes with me, guards, nurses, doctors, nor anyone. I am let to take my own course," he explained to his mother. To the soldiers, Whitman read poetry while providing words of comfort and a sympathetic smile. To many he was their scribe, penning letters home to an anxious family. Writing to his own mother, Whitman told her, "You can have no idea how these sick and dying youngsters cling to a fellow, and how fascinating it is, with all its hospital surroundings of sadness and scenes of repulsion and death."

From Whitman's war experiences came some of the nation's most renowned poetry. And it was not uncommon for his poems to contain medical themes. Several lines from "A March in the Ranks, Hard-Prest, and the Road Unknown," a poem in *Drum-Taps*, a collection of verse published in 1865, tell of surgeons and their work:

> Surgeons operating, attendants holding lights, the smell of ether,
>   the odor of blood;
> The crowd, O the crowd of the bloody forms—the yard outside
>   also fill'd;
> Some on the bare ground, some on planks or stretchers, some in
>   the death-spasm sweating;
> An occasional scream or cry, the doctor's shouted orders or calls;
> The glisten of the little steel instruments catching the glint of the
>   torches;
> These I resume as I chant—I see again the forms, I smell the odor;
> Then hear outside the orders given, Fall in, my men, Fall in....

Whitman was a great patriot, and his initial distress over governmental mismanagement of the medical situation began to lessen as he devoted more time to hospital volunteer work. Increasingly impressed with the military's effort to provide better health care delivery, he reported to *The New York Times* in late February 1863, "The government (which really tries, I think, to do the best and quickest it can for these sad necessities) is gradually settling down to adopt the plan of placing the hospitals in clusters of one-story wooden barracks, with their accompanying tents and sheds for cooking and all needed purposes. Taking all things into consideration, no doubt these are best adapted to the purpose, better than using churches and large public buildings like the Patent Office." One month later, Whitman reported to the readers of the *Brooklyn Eagle* "that the earnest and continued desire of the Government and much devoted labor are given to make the military hospitals here as good as they can be, considering all things. I find no expense spared and great anxiety manifested in the highest quarters to do well by the national sick."[69]

WHITMAN'S CHANGING ATTITUDE reflected the fact that military medical care had entered a new phase. Gone were the days of unpreparedness when the U.S. Army Medical Department's administrators failed to meet the demands of a rapidly growing army. No longer would managers be bound by archaic rules meant to regulate health care for a small, frontier-based fighting force. Gone too were questionably qualified physicians who practiced their own style of medicine without governmental oversight. And no longer would military hospitals be log cabin holes in the wall unable to provide up-to-date medical services.

By January 1863, the Medical Department's directors were younger and medically and managerially more sophisticated than their predecessors. Legislative reform of military health care had become federal law, and antiquated regulations were being replaced. The implementation of modern sanitary and hygienic measures led to noticeable decreases in contagious and nutritional deficiency diseases. More knowledgeable physicians were volunteering for military duty, and their battlefield experiences led to better clinical judgments and improvements in various treatment regimens. Innovative systems to evacuate wounded soldiers and ensure the availability of surgical supplies were in place. And more elaborate, well-staffed hospitals were dotting the country's urban and rural landscape.

Typical of this new phase in Civil War medical care was the treatment given to Private Coats of Vermont's Fifth Infantry. Within ten days of being wounded in his right shinbone at Fredericksburg, he had gone from his division's field hospital at Mansfield House on the Rappahannock River to Washington's 2,000-bed Harewood Hospital to Philadelphia's 3,500-bed Satterlee Hospital. The transfer from Washington to Philadelphia was intended to bring Coats closer to his home region of New England while still keeping him in the care of one of the military's new pavilion-style hospitals. Taking charge of Coats's case was William Williams Keen, who, following Second Bull Run and Antietam, had been posted to several hospitals in Frederick, Maryland, and in December 1862 was assigned to Satterlee.

When Coats was admitted to Satterlee, his leg wound was swollen and tender. Scalpel in hand, Keen incised the area to drain its bacteria-laden pus. However, without antibiotics, sterile dressings, and satisfactory wound care, the edges of Coats's incision soon turned an ominous ashy gray while surrounded by a bright red circle of inflammation. Keen suspected that Coats might have hospital gangrene, "the typhus of wounds," as he termed it—"a fearful and unwelcome guest in any hospital," according to the young physician, and one that "often puts to naught all the resources of the most skillful surgeons."[70]

Blood poisoning might have killed more men, but hospital gangrene was the disease that soldiers feared most. What began as a small darkened spot on a healing wound could, within a few days, turn a man's arm or leg into an evil-looking, exquisitely painful, putrid-smelling mass of decaying flesh. Contemporary descriptions tell of hospital gangrene advancing at the rate of half an inch an hour, destroying everything in its path while seeding itself to more distant areas of the body. Accompanied by a death rate of almost 50 percent, hospital gangrene, once present, spread quickly from patient to patient and from patient to caregiver. Rare in the first year of the war, the disease increased markedly during the second and third years, reaching more than 2,200 cases in Union forces from mid-1862 to mid-1864. Physicians were at a loss to explain its origins.

Frank Hamilton, the New York City surgeon who fought at First Bull Run and on the Peninsula, believed hospital gangrene was due to overcrowding of wounded soldiers in filthy camps and poorly ventilated barracks. William Keen thought it might be due to cramped living conditions but that the more likely culprit was adverse weather. "I pointed out repeatedly," he recalled, "that a few days of cold rainy weather requiring windows and doors to be closed, thus preventing a change in the atmosphere of suppuration, which then was normal, would be followed by an outbreak of hospital gangrene, and a few days of warm sunshine would promptly check its ravages."[71] Without an understanding of microbiology, it would have been impossible for Civil War–era doctors to know the exact bacteriologic etiology of hospital gangrene.

Remedies varied for halting hospital gangrene, but the usual treatment was to amputate the affected extremity and then, if the gangrene progressed, to remove the remaining stump and even more tissue as necessary. Additionally, hydrochloric or nitric acid was poured on the wound in a torturous effort to destroy any remaining infected tissues. With patients writhing in pain, both from the disease and its hoped-for cure, treatment became a deadly race to see how much tissue could be cut or melted away before the patient succumbed to either the ablative effects of therapy or the poisonous spread of the bacteria. As experience with hospital gangrene accumulated, doctors began to experiment with solutions of bromine instead of nitric acid to bathe the infected areas. Bromine is a close chemical cousin to chlorine and iodine, both of which provide the active chemico-biological ingredient for many of the most powerful antiseptic agents currently available to physicians. The trial-and-error use of bromine led to a rapid decline in cases of hospital gangrene, and the disease became rare by war's end. Thus, the combination of bromine washes, isolation of hospital gangrene patients, use of separate sponges and clean dressings for each new case, and nursing care that included handwashing in chlorinated soda marked the crucial first steps toward modern antiseptic wound care.

In Private Coats's case, Keen's use of the scalpel and gradual dilutions of a hydrochloric acid wash proved adequate to stave off an amputation. In late February 1863, left with a chronic, draining bone infection, Coats was returned to his home state of Vermont to be admitted to the Marine Hospital at Burlington. The rest of his days became an unending recovery process, with Coats checking in and out of various hospitals. The wound, according to his medical records, remained inflamed and "opens at any time the limb is much used in standing or walking." With a fused ankle joint that caused difficulty in getting about, Coats was reported by his physician, as late as 1878, to have continuing necrosis of his injured bone that "demands an operation."[72]

Coats was more fortunate than most of his fellow soldiers, both for the level of care he received and in the relative success of his therapy. Five days after being shot behind the jaw, Corporal Quick of the Thirty-eighth New York was admitted to Eckington Hospital in Washington. The entire left side of his face was swollen and black and blue, and his left eye was closed. There was little that surgeons could or knew how to do other than place Quick on bed rest, purge his intestines, and wash his face. One week later, as infection set in and bacteria attacked and ulcerated the numerous blood vessels within his skull, Quick began to bleed from his mouth and nostril. This first time he shed a quart of blood, but the hemorrhaging was controlled by shoving strips of dirty muslin inside his nose to act as a tampon. The next day Quick bled again, and a pressure dressing was fruitlessly placed over the side of his face. Without the technical capacity to perform delicate surgery on the bullet-injured structures deep within the bony crevices of his face, surgeons decided instead to tie off his left common carotid artery—one of the twin vessels that supply most of the blood to the head, neck, and brain.

Doctors hoped to lessen blood flow to the left side of Quick's face, thereby decreasing the bouts of hemorrhage. And since American physicians had half a century of experience with tying off all sorts of major arteries, it seemed a logical way to resolve Quick's needs. Unanesthetized, Quick moaned as surgeons, working at the side of the midneck, placed a single suture and tied it snugly around his half-inch-wide common carotid. Blood flow through Quick's artery ceased, but his struggle for life intensified. Diarrhea soon engulfed him, his mattress, sheets, blanket, and clothes. By New Year's Day, six days following the operation, Quick was described as "quite insensible" and "unable to swallow solids and feeling choked by swallowing liquids."[73] Three days later, he was comatose as his now infected incision began to drain pus and small amounts of blood. Soon the surgeon's wound let loose a torrent of blood. Quick was dead within minutes.

Quick's body was taken to the death house, where a crude autopsy took place. To no one's surprise, his carotid artery was found to have rotted through at the site of the previously placed suture. It was a sad reality that the very operation intended to suppress Quick's facial hemorrhaging was itself the cause of his fatal bleed. Physicians completed the postmortem examination by removing a six-inch section of Quick's common carotid artery, including the ulcerated portion. The blood vessel was sent to the curators of the recently established United States Army Medical Museum, where it became Specimen 898.

Both Coats and Quick were transferred to a Washington military hospital within six days of being wounded at Fredericksburg. For Private Connor of the Eighty-first Pennsylvania, evacuation to Washington's Stanton Hospital did not occur for almost two weeks after the gunshot wound that shattered his left thighbone. This delay occurred because those unable to walk were difficult to transport. When Connor finally reached Stanton on December 26, his leg was grossly swollen from the hip to the toes, and pus flowed freely from the bullet wound. Feverish and fidgety from a growing infection, Connor had one week to live. The infection was already severe enough that it had spread into the major veins in Connor's thigh and pelvis, and as a consequence, bacteria were being freely disbursed throughout his body. According to Connor's hospital records, "The case did pretty well till December 31st when symptoms of pyaemia showed themselves. He grew rapidly worse, and died January 2, 1863."[74]

Hospital gangrene might have been frightening, but pyemia—the presence of pus in the blood—proved a virtual death sentence. As the virulent bacteria multiplied in different areas of the body, septic shock and circulatory collapse, including kidney and lung shutdown, were the inevitable result. Connor had virtually no chance of surviving his plight. His only hope, and it was slim at best, would have been to undergo a primary amputation of his leg at the hip joint, but he was already beyond the critical forty-eight-hour time period when the operation needed to be completed.

Despite the grim statistics for all manner of amputations, many medical authorities argued against a nonsurgical or conservative approach to treating severe extremity injuries. "The popular opinion that the surgeons did a large amount of unnecessary amputating may have been justified in a few cases," admitted William Keen, "but, taking the army as a whole, I have no hesitation in saying that far more lives were lost from refusal to amputate than by amputation."[75] Written four decades after the war ended, Keen's statement is quite revealing. Clearly Keen, a brilliant and innovative surgeon and an expert on surgical infections—in 1892, he authored the first American surgery text based on the principles of antisepsis and asepsis—believed that the need for early amputation in the preantibiotic Civil War era outweighed the risk of not performing an amputation. Similarly, despite more than thirty thousand amputations performed on Union soldiers, Jonathan Letterman, in a report to William Hammond, wrote that he was also convinced "that if any fault was committed, it was that the knife was not used enough."[76] Private Connor finally did undergo an amputation of sorts, when the bones of his left hip joint and pelvic region, along with a bullet firmly impacted in them, were removed at autopsy and sent to the U.S. Army Medical Museum and labeled Specimen 622.

Although the United States Army was doing all it could to upgrade the treatment of the sick and wounded, hundreds of thousands of soldiers were still suffering and dying from the medical primitiveness of the times. Many of those who survived the ravages of their illness or injury returned home with their health permanently impaired by chronic disease and festering wounds. Surgeon General Hammond believed that some of this suffering could be relieved by upgrading the educational opportunities available to civilian and military physicians. By reducing medical incompetency and bringing knowledgeable doctors into army life, Hammond hoped to ameliorate some of the more intolerable practices of the profession.

William Williams Keen, 1863
COURTESY OF THE NATIONAL LIBRARY OF
MEDICINE

Sudley Church, Bull Run LIBRARY OF CONGRESS, PRINTS AND PHOTOGRAPHS DIVISION

Stone Church, Centreville LIBRARY OF CONGRESS, PRINTS AND PHOTOGRAPHS DIVISION

Frederick Law Olmsted, 1893

COURTESY OF THE NATIONAL PARK SERVICE,
FREDERICK LAW OLMSTED NATIONAL HISTORIC
SITE

William Alexander Hammond,
1863

Central office of the Sanitary Commission, Washington

Harewood General Hospital, Washington
LIBRARY OF CONGRESS, PRINTS AND PHOTOGRAPHS DIVISION

Wounded at field hospital, Savage Station
LIBRARY OF CONGRESS, PRINTS AND PHOTOGRAPHS DIVISION

Frame house division hospital, Fair Oaks

Jonathan Letterman (seated at left) and his staff

Ambulance crew demonstrating removal of wounded
LIBRARY OF CONGRESS, PRINTS AND PHOTOGRAPHS DIVISION

Fredericksburg, circa 1863 LIBRARY OF CONGRESS, PRINTS AND PHOTOGRAPHS DIVISION

Wounded at Fredericksburg
COURTESY OF THE NATIONAL LIBRARY OF MEDICINE

Hospital stewards LIBRARY OF CONGRESS, PRINTS AND PHOTOGRAPHS DIVISION

Surgeons LIBRARY OF CONGRESS, PRINTS AND PHOTOGRAPHS DIVISION

Log cabin field hospital, Brandy Station
LIBRARY OF CONGRESS, PRINTS AND PHOTOGRAPHS DIVISION

Cooking tent of the Sanitary Commission

Edwin McMasters Stanton, 1863

Henry Wilson, 1863
LIBRARY OF CONGRESS, PRINTS AND
PHOTOGRAPHS DIVISION

Paddleboat Daniel Webster COURTESY OF THE NATIONAL LIBRARY OF MEDICINE

Sanitary Commission wagons at a river landing, Belle Plain

Nurses and officers of the Sanitary Commission
LIBRARY OF CONGRESS, PRINTS AND PHOTOGRAPHS DIVISION

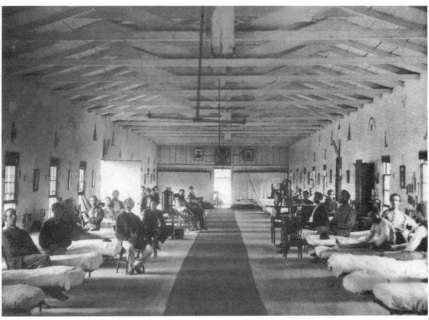

Patients at Armory Square Hospital, Washington
LIBRARY OF CONGRESS, PRINTS AND PHOTOGRAPHS DIVISION

Henry Wager Halleck, 1863
LIBRARY OF CONGRESS, PRINTS AND
PHOTOGRAPHS DIVISION

Ambulance wagons and drivers
LIBRARY OF CONGRESS, PRINTS AND PHOTOGRAPHS DIVISION

Stephen Smith, 1875
COURTESY OF THE NATIONAL LIBRARY OF MEDICINE

Henry Ingersoll Bowditch, 1865
AUTHOR'S COLLECTION

Joseph K. Barnes, 1863
LIBRARY OF CONGRESS, PRINTS AND PHOTOGRAPHS
DIVISION

Wounded at the Battle of the Wilderness LIBRARY OF CONGRESS, PRINTS AND PHOTOGRAPHS DIVISION

Medical supply boat, City Point LIBRARY OF CONGRESS, PRINTS AND PHOTOGRAPHS DIVISION

President Lincoln with George McClellan (sixth from left)
and Jonathan Letterman (eighth from left with hands on belt)
LIBRARY OF CONGRESS, PRINTS AND PHOTOGRAPHS DIVISION

CHAPTER EIGHT

"The profession of medicine has hitherto grievously failed"

THERE ARE FEW THINGS in my professional career in which I take more pride," wrote William Hammond in 1878, "than that the ideas of the Army Medical Museum and of the *Medical and Surgical History of the War of the Rebellion* were conceived by me."[1] Hammond's post–Civil War reflection highlights two of the most far-reaching Medical Department initiatives he instituted. Both provided ways to better educate the poorly schooled and often incapable medical men who populated the army.

According to the Sanitary Commission's historian, Charles Stillé, "The low standard of professional ability in the army at that time, was perhaps unavoidable, for the surgeons had been selected from civil life, in many cases, with hardly greater care than had been shown in the choice of the other officers of the Regiments."[2] Data compiled at the close of 1861 by a team of commission inspectors revealed that more than 20 percent of evaluated regimental doctors were considered having only "tolerable attentiveness" or could be placed in an even worse category, "negligent and inert."[3] By the end of the disastrous Peninsula campaign in the summer of 1862, Stephen Smith, an editorial voice for the country's more elite practicing physicians, noted in a column in the *American Medical Times*, "The sad results of incompetent, blundering, and inefficient surgery, are beginning to be apparent, and cannot longer escape notice."[4] Smith boldly suggested that volunteer physicians who lacked sufficient medical skills be immediately discharged and that Hammond implement measures to upgrade the basic knowledge and technical abilities of new physician recruits.

Physicians were criticized for more than just scientific ignorance. Character defects, especially the effects of drunkenness, and numerous incidents of neglect and mistreatment of patients were recorded in soldiers' diaries, in family letters, and even as headlines in hometown newspapers. "It was impossible to prevent all but worthy men from securing appointments, but one can but be amazed when he realizes that there are men who were army-surgeons to whose care we would not be willing to entrust a sick or disabled horse," wrote one soldier.[5] Writing to his wife, another physician told of "a storm brewing in the medical department of this regiment." He complained about his commanding surgeon, "I cannot, and will not stand it to have a drunken tyrant lord it over me."[6]

As regular army physicians who were serving prior to the start of the Civil War, Hammond and approximately one hundred other individuals had supposedly proved their medical ability by undergoing rigorous preenlistment written and oral examinations. It was a more severe ordeal than any medical school in antebellum America subjected its graduates to, and it represented the only way for a physician to obtain what was then considered a highly regarded appointment as a military physician. However, large numbers in this group of doctors, despite their lofty test-taking reputations, settled into what rapidly became a monotonous army life, with far-flung assignments that too often stifled their talent. At the start of the war, the hundred or so regular army physicians averaged twenty-three years of military service, and as Stillé wrote, "At these remote garrisons they were kept for at least five years, and the consequence was, that unless, in rare and exceptional cases, their professional ambition became deadened from the simple want of a stimulus to preserve it in proper activity."[7] To their credit, several of these regular army physicians, like William Hammond and Jonathan Letterman, were noted to be excellent managers and became medical directors of prestigious army units, staffed strategic appointments within the Medical Department, and made important contributions to the health care of soldiers. However, during the war's first months, the regular army physicians as a group did not engender the hoped-for respect.

In contrast with the regular army physicians, who had undergone some form of a screening process, medical practitioners applying to volunteer regiments were often appointed without proper assessment of experience or background. This practice stemmed from the view of traditional health care that emphasized physician familiarity with the family and a doctor's personal obligation to an individual patient. Considering the laissez-faire approach of American medical education and licensing procedures, it would have been unusual not to find incompetents, impostors, liars, scalawags, and even thieves among the thousands of volunteer physicians, appointed by scores of independent-minded politicians and their boosters. However, the lack of a credible credentialing process conflicted with the ideals of national medical authority, scientific discipline, and communitywide practice standards championed by Hammond, Frederick Olmsted, and other members of the United States Sanitary Commission.

In the fall of 1861, states began to establish examining boards for doctors accompanying the volunteer regiments. It was a disorganized system at best, with many governors unwilling to give up their powers of appointment. Even when politicians obliged the military authorities by having physician recruits take a test, the idea of a standardized examination was so novel to the rank and file of American physicians that chaos reigned in the test's administration. Not until Hammond's appointment would the confusion be addressed. Hammond insisted that any physician who wished to treat Union troops must pass an examination measuring his medical aptitude. In fact, he was so adamant about proper medical credentialing that he asked for the names of doctors, both regulars and volunteers, deemed incompetent in order to annul their existing contracts or at least force them to take one of the more stringent examinations.

Federally sponsored examining boards met in various cities for doctors seeking regular army commissions or promotions, while state examining committees oversaw physician appointments to the volunteer regiments. In some cases, the federal boards reexamined doctors who had been passed by the states' examining boards—in general, the federal examination was the more difficult test—to further eliminate unqualified individuals.

The organization and content of the examination could be haphazard, but in its most stringent form the test took several days and usually began with a short written autobiography to ascertain whether the candidate was functionally literate or not. Having passed this initial screening, the candidate had to write brief essays on anatomy, pharmacology (then called "materia medica"), medical therapeutics, and surgery. Following this, an oral quiz was administered on both basic and clinical sciences, including chemistry, hygiene, pathology, physiology, and toxicology. An examination of the candidate's clinical acumen might be conducted on live patients in actual hospital wards. A demonstration of surgical operations on a cadaver was also required in some instances. Hammond's toughening of standards generated considerable hostility among the examinees. Many physicians feared the disgrace of failure. These men generally refused to appear before an examining board and, although wishing to serve in the military, attempted to circumvent the testing system in any way possible. Not unexpectedly, better-educated physicians tended to support the new regulations, while rank-and-file doctors grew increasingly disgruntled with Hammond's interference in their practice of medicine.

In late summer of 1862, Secretary of War Edwin Stanton informed Hammond that more candidates needed to be passed or the boards would face suspension. Stanton, looking for any way to undercut Hammond's administrative powers, took it upon himself to represent certain individuals who had previously failed the examination and requested his personal intervention. The secretary of war strongly hinted that these men ought to pass the test or there would be ruinous political fallout for Hammond.

In theory, Hammond's examining boards were free of political and personal pressure. In reality, bribes, chicanery, and various methods of deception and influence peddling created a less than perfect system. The public outcry that surrounded the examining boards was further complicated when representatives of the nation's growing body of homeopathic and sectarian health care practitioners added their voices, denouncing allopathic examiners with special delight. As one homeopath wrote, "We must put to flight the combined hosts of the Philistines by the sight of truth and the artillery of facts—and our army be delivered from the cruel and barbarous treatment of allopathic ignorance and bigotry."[8]

The governor of Illinois complained to Hammond that the examining boards were made up of allopathists who refused to examine homeopathists. A spokesperson for the Medical Department could not hide the fact that this was an intentional strategy. As Joseph Smith, Hammond's personal assistant, explained to Governor Richard Yates, "This department, while straining every nerve to make every proper provision for the care of the sick and wounded, is clear in its conviction that rather than employ an incompetent officer it is preferable to employ none."[9]

By the end of 1862, Hammond ordered that passing grades be lowered, but sectarian physicians, including homeopaths, were prevented from appearing before the examination boards. Hostility, from both regular and irregular physicians, continued to mount toward Hammond, and although the concept of standardized qualifying examinations gradually became an accepted part of America's medical pysche and resulted in an increased number of better-educated army doctors, the military remained chronically short of experienced and knowledgeable physicians.

CONTINUED DISPLEASURE WITH the credentialing process prompted Hammond to institute other measures intended to increase the competency of military doctors. For instance, the U.S. Army Medical Museum was established in Washington in a building located on North H Street between Thirteenth and Fourteenth streets. Military personnel were instructed to obtain specimens from injured and diseased soldiers so that research could be conducted at the museum on the medical and surgical problems of wartime. Heading the collection effort was the museum's first curator, John Brinton, one of Grant's medical directors in the Army of the Tennessee. Brinton had previously run the military medical facilities in Cairo, Illinois, and later organized a large tent hospital on the battlefield at Shiloh.

A straitlaced thirty-year-old, Brinton had received his medical degree from Philadelphia's Jefferson Medical College ten years earlier. Brinton maintained a general medical and surgical practice in that city and also acted as a preceptor to numerous Jefferson medical students, including William Williams Keen. Almost immediately after the war's start, Brinton passed the army's rigorous examination to become a brigade surgeon. Considered a brilliant and perceptive physician, Brinton ranked fourth on what, in the spring of 1861, was still a nationally given test.

Brinton was a close friend to Surgeon General Hammond and a first cousin to George McClellan. These relationships made him suspect in the mind of Secretary of War Stanton, and such suspicion undoubtedly plagued early efforts to gain widespread government support for the museum. Brinton had recently returned east to serve as chairman of a federal medical examining board convened in Washington. Just a few months later, in August 1862, he was reassigned to his new post as curator. "My whole heart was in the Museum," wrote Brinton, "and I felt that if the medical officers in the field, and those in charge of hospitals, could only be fairly interested, its growth would be rapid. By it the results of the surgery of this war would be preserved for all time, and the education of future generations of military surgeons would be greatly assisted."[10]

Traveling from one battlefield to another, Brinton gathered mutilated limbs, organs from autopsies, and parts of bodies racked by disease—sometimes removing corpses from freshly dug graves to procure the needed specimen. It was a grisly task, with opponents deriding the project and demeaning the future museum as just "a collection of old bones." Hammond and Brinton were adamant, however, that the museum be considered not simply an assemblage of curiosities or objects of ghoulish interest, but an important adjunct to the education of the nation's physicians. Packed in kegs of alcohol, brine, or whiskey, the human bones and tissues were shipped to Washington, where anatomists cleaned and tagged them for public display.

Within two years, the museum became one of the more visited sites in Washington. Veterans and their families crowded into the facility to see what might possibly remain of an old friend or two. In some cases, wounded soldiers patriotically offered up their amputated extremity for viewing. Daniel Sickles, a well-known New York City politician–cum–major general, forwarded his leg bones (which had been crushed by a twelve-pound shot at Gettysburg and amputated at the thigh) in a makeshift coffin along with his calling card. Among those who flocked to the site were foreign dignitaries, including a contingent of surgeons and sailors from a Russian fleet anchored at Alexandria, Virginia.

Some viewers were also less than enthusiastic. In at least one instance, an amputee Union soldier, shocked to discover that his limb was on display, demanded its immediate return. A quick-witted museum official asked the man how long he had been enlisted. "For three years or the war," was the reply. "Then," explained the curator, "the contract is not yet terminated. Come back at the end of the war or at the expiration of your three years' service and you can have your bones. In the meantime, one detachment of you is stationed in this Museum on government duty, the other wherever you may be ordered. Such is the opinion of the Attorney General."[11] Not knowing what to say, the soldier left the museum while his bones remained in place.

By the end of 1862, Brinton's efforts yielded 1,349 objects. Four years later, when the *Catalogue of the Surgical Section of the United States Army Museum* was published, there were 4,719 specimens, ranging from injuries and diseases of the head to operations on soft tissues. At the conclusion of the war, the museum had outgrown its original building, and the medical assemblage was soon moved to a remodeled Ford's Theatre, the site of President Lincoln's 1865 assassination. Over the years, Hammond's museum has been transformed into the world-renowned National Museum of Health and Medicine of the Armed

Forces Institute of Pathology and is currently housed at the Walter Reed Army Medical Center. There, visitors can still see some of the same preserved specimens that Americans gawked at 150 years ago, including Dan Sickles's fractured tibia and fibula.

Hammond hoped that the museum would serve as the centerpiece for a postgraduate school of medicine, where physicians and others serving in the Medical Department could be kept abreast of advances in the sciences. Modeled on the medical schools of the English and French armies, the students would be those "seeking admission into the corps, who could receive such special instruction as would better fit them for commissions, and which they cannot obtain in the ordinary medical schools," according to Hammond.[12] Stephen Smith agreed with his friend Hammond's suggestion for this postgraduate-style institution: "No one who gives the subject a moment's thought can doubt that a special system of education for the duties of the army surgeon must be established in this country, if the Medical Staff is to keep pace with the reforms and improvements in the other branches of the army service."[13]

Plans called for classes to be conducted in a specially converted space in the basement of the museum's building. "I had fitted up the rooms beneath the main hall for teaching purposes," Brinton noted in his memoirs. "There was a charming lecture room, with sloping seats, a couple of convenient little retiring rooms or laboratories, a good stage to speak from, and a well constructed lecture and revolving table." Upstairs, the museum's collection of specimens, photographs, drawings, and illustrations would be available to supplement lectures by well-known members of the army's Medical Department.

By the early fall of 1863, all was ready and Hammond and Brinton anxiously awaited Edwin Stanton's personal approval. The secretary of war, or, as Brinton referred to him, "the dreadful Mr. Stanton," planned to stop at the museum on one of his morning drives from his home. After descending from his carriage, Stanton moved hastily through the museum's rooms and the downstairs lecture theater. Later, Stanton demanded to know whether the medical school's courses would be given in the evening in the lecture theater. Upon receiving an affirmative reply, Stanton growled, "They will go to the theater and neglect their duties. It shan't be."[14] Thus, the secretary of war abruptly canceled Hammond's plan to provide postgraduate educational opportunities for the military's physicians. In addition, Stanton turned down Hammond's accompanying request to fund a medical library in association with the museum. The museum, as a medical research institution, was left to develop on its own.

Fortunately, Hammond was able to implement two educational projects that did not need the secretary of war's overt permission. The first of
these was a medical history of the conflict, which he wished to publish at
the war's end. Hammond's authority over a huge corps of physicians provided him the opportunity to engage in this large-scale, collective medical
research project—something that the nation's physicians had never before been able to organize. Championing the cause, Stephen Smith set the
tone for the future work: "The profession will look on the undertaking
with great favor, and we hail it as the first fruits of reform. . . . If the country should reap no other additional advantage from the reorganization of
the Medical Department than this historical record, it will compensate for
all the effort required to effect the change."[15] The examination of hundreds of thousands of Civil War soldiers and their diseases and injuries,
using newly established, standardized protocols, provided so much data
that a six-part, fifty-five-pound compendium, *The Medical and Surgical
History of the War of the Rebellion*, was published over a period of eighteen years, 1870–1888. It was a remarkable scientific achievement that
listed and described tens of thousands of Union soldiers' wounds, injuries, and diseases. Even its accompanying tinted lithographs and en-
gravings were considered outstanding works of medical art.

On a more immediate basis, Hammond recognized that no prominent English-language work existed on the subject of military hygiene.
"If I had not believed that a great necessity existed for such a treatise,"
he wrote, "I certainly should not, in addition to my onerous public duties, have undertaken the task of preparing the present volume."[16]
Hammond's 600-page *Treatise on Hygiene*, published in mid-1863, received outstanding reviews and was soon considered one of the era's
standard medical textbooks. "Dr. Hammond's style," according to one
reviewer, "is uniformly easy, lucid, and agreeable, making what the
general as well as the professional reader will find a very readable
book."[17] That same year, Hammond also completed a 350-page book
on basic human physiology.

Hammond's literary forays did not end with his own writings. He
suggested to Joseph Woodward, a longtime friend who had recently enlisted and was assigned to the Office of the Surgeon General, that he
write a guide for hospital stewards and other medical attendants regarding their day-to-day responsibilities. Woodward soon followed *The Hospital Steward's Manual* with a second treatise detailing the diagnosis
and treatment of diseases prevailing in army camps. Meanwhile, Hammond ordered eight hundred copies of the recently revised *On Bandag-
ing and Other Operations of Minor Surgery* by Fitzwilliam Sargent, a

Philadelphia physician and father of painter John Singer Sargent. The manual was distributed to members of the Medical Department.

Hammond might have been headstrong, but this very resoluteness allowed him to proceed with his educational plans, despite the hue and cry that surrounded his every effort to upgrade the capabilities of doctors caring for Northern troops. Complaints about surgeons continued throughout the war, but by the end of 1863, Hammond's educational initiatives were beginning to show some hard results. Thomas Ellis, one of McClellan's medical directors, declared, "There is a marked improvement in the surgeons attached to the army in contrast with their inefficiency at the commencement of the rebellion."[18] Even Walt Whitman wrote back to a New York newspaper, "I must bear most emphatic testimony to the zeal, manliness, and professional spirit and capacity generally prevailing among the surgeons, many of them young men, in the hospitals and the army. I will not say much about the exceptions, for they are few. I never ceased to find the best young men. . . . They are full of genius, too, and this is my testimony."[19]

HAMMOND'S INTEREST IN medical education was closely tied to his desire to further scientific research. In 1857, he had been awarded a first-place medal from the American Medical Association for an exhaustive research project in which he varied his diet by eating at first only egg albumen, then starches, gelatins, and, last, gum arabic. Then he studied the resultant chemical composition of his own blood and urine. A few years later, while on extended leave from the army, Hammond founded the Philadelphia Biological Society, an organization intended to be a forum focused on the exchange of scientific ideas based strictly on new experimental research.

For Hammond, the concept of intertwining medical practice and clinical investigation grew increasingly important. He urged interested military physicians to learn how to use microscopes and to study the cellular makeup of organs affected by various diseases. Consequently, printed instructions on the care and use of microscopes were now circulated throughout the Medical Department. By the end of the war, important photomicrographs were published. Other new types of instruments for clinical investigations were listed in the department's standard supply table, including stethoscopes, speculums to look inside the ear, stomach pumps, hypodermic syringes, and even rudimentary thermometers.

The concept of conducting scientific research with a specialized clinical focus was viewed by some with the same suspicion as using standardized examinations as a prerequisite for entrance into the U.S. Army's Medical Department. Specialism did not exist within American medicine. Though some physicians acted as self-styled surgeons, surgery as a well-defined specialty was essentially unknown. Admittedly, there were doctors who treated only patients with eye and ear diseases, but other than these few self-declared specialists, there were no cardiologists, gynecologists, internists, neurologists, pediatricians, psychiatrists, rheumatologists, or surgeons. Wishing to change this situation, Hammond ordered the building of specialty hospitals and the organization of specialized wards within several of the military's medical facilities. He reasoned that by segregating patients with the same diseases or wounds, physicians would develop an expertise in these conditions that had not been previously obtainable.

A hospital dedicated only to smallpox victims and another for eye and ear patients were constructed in St. Louis. Others for skin disorders secondary to diseases such as typhoid were organized in Arkansas, Kentucky, and Washington, D.C. But the most renowned of the Civil War clinical research hospitals was Turner's Lane in north Philadelphia, designed according to the pavilion plan and formally known as the U.S. Army Hospital for Diseases of the Nervous System. Hammond had a long-standing interest in nervous maladies that probably related to his own difficulties with recurring and perplexing psychosomatic illnesses. From catalepsy to temporary paralysis of his legs, these on-again, off-again neurological disorders affected Hammond throughout his life. When he heard that a physician friend from Philadelphia, who was a contract surgeon to the army, had taken an interest in cases of nervous diseases, Hammond requested that a specialized hospital be established for these patients.

Hammond's physician friend was no ordinary doctor. In addition to becoming a world-renowned neurologist specializing in the treatment of hysteria and related disorders, S. Weir Mitchell gained recognition as a novelist and a poet. For now, this thirty-four-year-old's claim to fame were the various research projects in pharmacology, physiology, and toxicology that he pursued following his return from studying with Claude Bernard in Paris. Whether it was producing cataracts in frogs by the administration of sugar or an analysis of the effect of snake venom on the nervous system, Mitchell, like Hammond, considered scientific investigation the bedrock of a successful calling in medicine.

One other executive officer to the new facility was William Williams Keen, the same young doctor who treated the wounded at First and Second Bull Run. As a longtime faculty member at Jefferson Medical College,

Keen gained international recognition for his clinical acumen and became one of the founders of neurosurgery in America. (It was also an eighty-four-year-old William Keen who in 1921 misdiagnosed Franklin Roosevelt's acute case of lower-extremity paralysis as not being polio.)

The wide range of neurological conditions that Mitchell and Keen encountered at Turner's Lane Hospital provided unprecedented opportunities to study conditions rarely found in civilian practice. As a result, they were able to test clinical theories by observing injured humans without necessarily having to resort to laboratory experiments on animals. But of all the nervous conditions Keen and Mitchell encountered, it was the feigning of paralysis and other neuroinjuries that was of special interest to them. In a report to the country's most prestigious medical monthly, the *American Journal of the Medical Sciences*, Keen and Mitchell described faked aphonia, blindness, deafness, epilepsy, insanity, lameness, pain, and outright paralysis. Assigned the task of detecting the malingerers, Keen used ether anesthesia as a way to uncover the fraud. He told of testing blindness in one eye by etherizing the individual and covering the good eye with adhesive plaster. On recovering from the anesthetic, though not yet fully aware, the supposedly blind soldier would inevitably reach out for the water or whiskey being offered. In another instance, a man claiming the inability to talk was anesthetized and while still recovering from his ether-induced sleep found himself answering questions.

Mitchell and Keen's investigations at Turner's Lane were exhausting, marked by hours as late as midnight or one a.m. two or three times a week, but they were necessary to adequately compile the rapidly increasing number of case records. Gunshot Wounds and Other Injuries of Nerves, a monograph that summarized Mitchell and Keen's clinical experience, was published in 1864. An acknowledged classic of nineteenth-century American medicine, this work provides the first detailed study of traumatic neuroses and introduced the concept of causalgia, a burning sensation caused by inflamed nerves.

The Turner's Lane facility closed in fall 1864. Keen resigned his commission and traveled to Europe to obtain further medical training. Mitchell remained in Philadelphia, continuing with his neurological-based research while struggling to raise two young children following the unexpected death of his wife. Although short-lived, the specialized Civil War hospitals offered unprecedented opportunities for medical research that had not been previously available in America. They contributed significantly to the beginnings of the new clinical specialism that characterized the last decades of nineteenth-century American medicine.

BY MID-1863, THE tragic medical consequences of the war were evident to all. The expanding population of disease-afflicted and disabled Union veterans was receiving both a federally funded disability pension and an additional monetary allowance to obtain artificial limbs. With entrepreneurial finesse, prosthestic-limb manufacturers engaged in public relations efforts to focus attention on what should have been the government's continued medical responsibility toward the permanently injured. "To the mutilated soldier," wrote one industrialist, it is the government's indebtedness to care for "the army of gallant men, who, to save the nation from dismemberment, have sacrificed ten times a thousand of the noblest hands that ever brought so precious a tribute to the altar of Constitutional liberty."[20] Although various models of artificial limbs were available prior to the Civil War, the rapid increase in the number of men needing false arms and legs brought about startling innovations in prosthetic technology. From 1861 through 1873, close to 150 patents for limbs and assisting devices were issued, an almost threefold increase over the previous fifteen years. Additional products for the disabled also began to flood the market, from combination forks, knives, and spoons for arm amputees to hand-powered tricycles for those missing a leg. These devices, like the medicine being practiced, would seem crude by present-day standards, but at the time both the general public and physicians could not help but be impressed by the skill of the manufacturers. "In our time limb-making has been carried to such a state of perfection," wrote Stephen Smith, "that both in form and function they so completely resemble the natural extremity that those who wear them pass unobserved and unrecognized in walks of business and pleasure."[21]

The artificial-limb industry made fortunes for men like Augustus Marks of New York City and B. Franklin Palmer of Philadelphia. The manufacturers were a politically savvy lobby and managed to cast themselves more as humanitarians than businessmen. Marks lived an opulent lifestyle in a mansion on the banks of Long Island Sound. His namesake company, with its impressive Broadway address and street-level glass cases filled with dazzling arrays of merchandise, made its mark by covering lightweight willow or basswood legs and arms with painted and varnished parchment to resemble the various hues of human skin. Later, Marks enclosed his creations in an outside layer of India rubber meant to be more pleasant when the extremity came in contact with someone.

Marks was the ultimate businessman; Palmer was the public relations genius. An amputee at an early age, Palmer was a dentist by training who, at the start of the war, billed himself as an artist and artificial-limb maker. He wrote a heroic account of his own struggle against physical adversity. And in a most audacious stunt, Palmer personally contacted a panoply of renowned surgeons, including Surgeon General Hammond, asking for their support in choosing the Palmer artificial leg as the one to be recommended to maimed soldiers by the army and navy. He then described his efforts in a widely distributed forty-eight-page pamphlet that trumpeted his written correspondence with the surgeon general of the U.S. Army and the chief of the Bureau of Medicine and Surgery of the Navy. Many doctors agreed with Palmer's proclamation that his patented artificial arm and leg, with its various articulations consisting of detachable ball-and-socket joints meant to perform for months without need of oil or attention, was one of the most important medical advances of the war. "It is perhaps the best of the old style of artificial limbs," wrote one supporter, "and has hitherto enjoyed the approbation of the profession, generally for its lightness, the ingenuity displayed in its construction and finish, and for that essential desideratum, efficiency."[22] Following the war, Palmer extolled his role as a national benefactor by taking credit for assisting the government in issuing seven thousand artificial arms and legs to the country's so-called empty-sleevers.

THE DIFFICULTY OF caring for this growing population of invalid soldiers, along with the large number of doctors leaving civilian practice for military service, was having an adverse impact on physician manpower. Indeed, the 1861 and 1862 meetings of the American Medical Association were canceled at a time when the profession desperately needed more national organization, not less. Many physicians were simply unavailable to attend the meetings because of wartime commitments. In addition, increasing political animosities could not be ignored. Some physicians never wanted to mix politics with medicine. "We have no censures to pass upon our Southern brethren," was how one doctor expressed the sentiment. "That they have freely tendered their humane and scientific services to the armies of their own section, including, as they do, their sons, brothers, friends, and neighbors, was to have been expected."[23] Nathan Smith Davis, the Chicago-based president of the American Medical Association, stated a more inflammatory and widely held opinion: "The section animosity and wickedness which had been threatening the peace of our country for several years has culminated in an open, unjustifiable and monstrous rebellion."[24]

When the AMA resumed its annual meeting in June 1863, discussions went beyond scientific matters. Medical politics were now at the forefront. For instance, a committee was established to determine whether or not vaccination against smallpox, to counter the supposed threat of Southern terrorists spreading the disease through Northern cities, should be made compulsory. Murmurings were heard concerning the adequacy of William Hammond's performance as surgeon general. Did Hammond's headstrong standardizing of medical protocols and entrance examinations imply a lack of confidence in the skill of the nation's physicians? Did he side too often with homeopathic physicians in their battles against the allopathic doctors?

The AMA delegates, egged on by Henry Bowditch, also debated a resolution demanding the organization of an army ambulance corps. Following his disappointing meetings with federal and military officials in Washington in fall 1862, Bowditch grew only more determined to solve the ambulance issue. In February 1863, he thought he had succeeded when the United States House of Representatives unanimously passed an ambulance bill encompassing his ideas along with those of Jonathan Letterman and the United States Sanitary Commission. The legislation provided for a special enlistment of ten thousand men along with several hundred new officers to serve as first-aid noncombatants under the direction of the Medical Department. These men would devote their time and attention to the care of the wounded on the field, transportation of casualties from the battle site, and care of the injured and sick in field and general hospitals. It was estimated that formation of this new corps would in turn free between fifteen thousand and twenty thousand combat soldiers who were serving as ambulance drivers and hospital attendants. Following joint approval by Surgeon General Hammond and Quartermaster General Meigs, the bill was sent to the Senate. There, Massachusetts's Henry Wilson, chairman of the Committee on Military Affairs, promptly blocked its passage, stating it was an "impracticable measure to organize such a corps at this time."

Wilson never provided a more detailed explanation, but in the past he had refused to support legislation unwanted by Hammond's nemesis, Secretary of War Edwin Stanton. In response, Henry Bowditch launched a public relations campaign that included publication of an emotional pamphlet, *A Brief Plea for an Ambulance System*. Its pages included a public airing of the ongoing dispute with Wilson. Wilson, according to Bowditch, "seemed to deem the ambulance corps proposal a preposterous notion of an unpractical enthusiast."[25] Bringing his political beliefs and lobbying efforts to the AMA's annual meeting was the logical extension of Bowditch's campaign. He had been involved with the AMA since its inception and, in 1877, was asked to serve as the organization's twenty-ninth president.

For now, he enlisted his peers to pressure their own senators and congressmen to pass an ambulance bill. Meanwhile, Bowditch confronted Wilson with a series of impassioned letters, many of which were published in that era's medical journals. Medical editorialists also took up the cause: "It is very evident that personal feeling has a good deal to do with the opposition which has sprung up to this great movement. . . . We sincerely hope and believe that the petitions now circulating throughout the country in favor of an ambulance corps will bear with them to Washington such a burden of signatures that no public man will dare to oppose them."[26]

There is no doubt that personal animosities played a part in this drama. Bowditch was viewed by Wilson as sympathetic to the causes of the Sanitary Commission, as evidenced by Bowditch's recent appointment by Hammond as one of the commission's special inspectors of the military's general hospitals. Even more discrediting from Wilson's point of view was that prior to her death from typhoid in December 1862, Hannah Ropes, a clear favorite of Wilson's, had gone to great lengths to criticize Hammond's arrogance in handling a problem she had at the Union Hotel Hospital, where she was head nurse.

Public pressure on Wilson continued to mount, however, as Bowditch enlisted boards of trade and chambers of commerce in his cause. Petitions in favor of an ambulance corps circulated throughout the country, with signing drives coordinated by a group of individuals who called themselves "the Committee of Citizens Who Have in Charge the Sending of Petitions to Congress for the Establishment of a Thorough and Uniform Ambulance System in the Armies of the Republic."

Bowditch's campaign was markedly advanced following the ferocious fighting in July 1863 at Gettysburg, where the Sanitary Commission organized an enormous relief station with awnings, tents, and kitchens to care for thousands of the wounded at a moment when military services were sorely lacking. Aware of the Sanitary Commission's growing reputation in the public mind for expeditiously confronting lapses in military medicine, Wilson finally capitulated in late fall of 1863. As Bowditch noted in his diary, "To my utter astonishment and delight, Mr. Wilson *volunteered* to introduce a bill for an ambulance department of men drilled for the purpose of taking care of the wounded. And my end was accomplished, for I cared not what special arrangement was made, so long as a corps of drilled men was thereafter to be with every army of these United States."[27]

MUCH LIKE THE medico-political controversies that surrounded the establishment of an armywide ambulance corps, the supposed threat of Southern medical terrorism, and William Hammond's performance as surgeon general, the physicians' role in the Civil War draft process was a source of concern to many in the profession. By early 1863, the North's armies were depleted owing to battlefield casualties, camp diseases, the medical unfitness of soldiers who had disabilities prior to entering the military, the expiration of the tour of duty for which men had previously enlisted, and large-scale desertion. Lincoln and his political and military leaders knew that the worsening manpower situation would prevent further offensive operations from being sustained. Conscription, therefore, represented a last-ditch effort by the government to fill the ranks with the three hundred thousand men necessary to reinvigorate the army.

The Union's Enrollment Act of 1863, enacted on March 3, was guided through Congress by Senator Henry Wilson to implement a draft system in which each congressional district established a board of enrollment comprising three men, one of whom had to be a licensed practicing physician. Like many aspects of military medicine during the Civil War, the enrollment doctor's duties were vaguely defined. However, he was expected to participate in all administrative activities of the board and, most important, conduct physical examinations of each draftee, substitute, and volunteer. This was an important assignment, since his decision alone determined whether or not an individual was fit for military service.

Not surprisingly, few citizens liked the idea of a draft. There seemed something un-American about its coerciveness in a land founded on the concepts of individual liberty and fairness. As a result, physicians were forced to deal with a steady stream of bribers, bounty jumpers, and social malcontents. Draftees bribed enrollment doctors to find conditions or diseases that would exempt them from military service. Conversely, men who wished to enlist in the army in order to receive a cash bounty, planning all the while to immediately desert and reenlist under a different name so as to obtain another bounty and desert again, paid physicians to ignore medical problems that might keep them from serving in the army. Thus, the enrollment board doctor was under enormous pressure, financial, political, and otherwise, to rapidly interview and evaluate large numbers of men.

"I have examined, on a few occasions, one hundred and fifty men per day," stated a physician from Pennsylvania's Twelfth District. "They were volunteers, and did not require as much time as drafted men. Men who have always considered themselves healthy suddenly discover, after being drafted, that they are afflicted with some fearful malady, and are not satisfied with an examination unless considerable time is spent with them, and all the motions gone through with. To do this, *sixty* men per day are as many as one man can examine." A doctor from Troy, New York, countered, "In my opinion, only *fifty* men per day are as many as one surgeon can examine carefully and thoroughly." By all accounts, any doctor who evaluated seven men in an hour was unbelievably busy. To see fifteen individuals in an hour raised doubts about a physician's dedication to the process, his clinical decision-making abilities, and the financial motivation that probably explained his pace.

Regardless of the ideal soldiers-per-hour ratio, contemporary observers unanimously noted that even in the best of circumstances, undesirable men continued to slip through the system. The exasperating task of physically examining large numbers of soldiers-to-be became even more onerous when the government hired outside doctors to function as a board of inspection to review the enrollment surgeon's medical findings. Physicians' complaints about this second-opinion program were particularly acrimonious. Oramel Martin, the enrollment doctor in Massachusetts's Eighth District, noted, "Our professional decisions in this State were reviewed by three contract surgeons, selected, apparently, because they had nothing else to do, and recommended, I presume, by one who seemed to lose sight of the great cause in which we were engaged." In Connecticut, one physician accused the inspectors of treating "surgeons of the enrollment districts as if they were necessarily a set of bribed and unprincipled knaves." He wondered if, perhaps, the members of the inspection board itself were not financially tainted by recruits seeking discharges. The doctor from Iowa's First District summarized his understanding of the problem: "The boards of inspection were nothing more nor less than a board of censors to decide upon the medical and moral qualifications of surgeons of boards of enrollment."

Why would a physician, aware of the animus that surrounded the medical aspects of the draft, want to serve as an enrollment board doctor or even on a board of inspectors? Patriotism was certainly one factor. Abraham Rothrock, from Pennsylvania's Seventh District, declared, "I decided to accept the position as a change, and, once initiated, I became interested in the cause, and felt that, as we must all make sacrifices in putting down this terrible rebellion, I would do what I could toward the consummation of the great work." Yet despite the government's claim that the "busiest or most eminent practitioners of a district consented to serve upon the enrollment boards, though to the detriment of their private fortunes," enrollment board physicians were usually inexperienced and poorly educated. In general, the pay—equal to what the lowest-grade assistant surgeon in the army received a month ($100 to $130)—was not enough to induce more talented physicians to accept an appointment. So poor was the caliber of some of the enrollment doctors that several ended up being dismissed by general court-martial, while others were disgraced by having their appointment summarily revoked. Courageously, a few enrollment board physicians did complain in writing to the federal government about their peers: "Too many incompetent and dishonest men have been employed," wrote one distraught practitioner.

As pressures on enrollment board doctors grew, disputes between them and draftees and their families led to attempts at defamation or even physical attacks. "Under the most favorable circumstances, the surgeon cannot avoid giving great offense to many who fancy they have a claim upon him, based upon long years of professional patronage," claimed one enrollment board physician. "The surgeon must expect to submit to considerable abuse and to receive letters more pointed than polite from those of his neighbors whom his decision has rendered 'fit food for powder.'"[28]

Circumstances usually worsened in the weeks leading up to a draft call. It was not unusual to hear reports of scattered resistance along with threats of bodily harm directed at members of draft enrollment boards. As the designated day of the draft approached, tensions peaked and it took little to ignite a riot. The worst of such civil disorders occurred in New York City in July 1863. Several policemen were killed while officers of the city's draft enrollment boards feared for their lives, and at least one deputy was bludgeoned to unconsciousness. New York's physicians were similarly concerned. "After dinner [on the third day of the uprising] I thought I would take a row out on the East River with some of the doctors for our own health," related a physician at Bellevue Hospital. "My friend thought he heard a noise like a bullet whistling in the air over head, but I laughed at the idea of any attacks upon us. But a moment after, I heard something whistling too, and I thought it was best not to stay there any longer."[29]

The viciousness of the New York City draft riot revealed deep-seated class, ethnic, and racial divisions that political and civic leaders would need to respond to. For the doctors, the uprising by the mostly tenement-dwelling poor called attention to their wretched living conditions, their abysmal personal health, their sanitary plight, and their public health predicament, all of which generated medical hopelessness.

BEFORE THE CIVIL War, most physicians and their local medical communities demonstrated little personal or collective professional interest in matters of public health and sanitary reform. This was due to a combination of factors, especially a lack of understanding of the relationship between germs and diseases. Without knowledge of this interdependence—until the late 1880s, the public and medical professionals believed that disease was caused strictly by dirt—there was little reason to teach public health in the era's medical schools. Frank Hamilton, the battle-hardened New York City surgeon and professor at Bellevue Hospital Medical College, admitted that with regard to giving lessons on this subject, "the profession of medicine has hitherto grievously failed."[30] Without knowledge of the basic science of public health, physicians could not become advocates for improved sanitary and public health standards. This paucity of both professional and governmental interest in public health and hygiene reform was evidenced in New York City in the pre–Civil War period, when the powerful position of city inspector of the Board of Health was filled by incompetent political hacks instead of properly trained physicians.

Still, some individuals did spread the gospel of hygiene. Of these early health reformers, the one who became the most prominent sanitarian of them all was Stephen Smith—the same Stephen Smith who wrote provocative editorials in the weekly *American Medical Times* concerning the role of medicine and the medical profession in society. Smith's relentless goading of public officials to make New York City a safe and more sanitary place, along with his chairing an 1864 sanitary survey of Manhattan and dramatic testimony before the New York State Legislature, led to passage of the Metropolitan Health Bill. This legislation became the basis of civic sanitation laws throughout the United States and was instrumental in vastly improving the day-to-day lives of most Americans. As a result, Smith's efforts can be regarded as among the most important civilian-initiated medical advances to come out of the Civil War era.

An asthenic, short man, Smith was a native New Yorker, born in 1823 on a farm near Skaneateles in the Finger Lakes region. Destined to live six months short of one hundred years, Smith bridged the great medical milestones of the age, from discovery of anesthesia in 1846, to the acceptance of surgical antisepsis in the late 1880s, to the rise of American medicine to world prominence by the early 1920s. Smith received his medical degree from New York City's College of Physicians and Surgeons in 1850, and he interned at Bellevue Hospital, where he remained on active staff for sixty years. His father-in-law was a United States congressman. Indeed, Smith used his family's political influence to help found the Bellevue Hospital Medical College. Smith was a prolific writer: His *Hand-book of Surgical Operations*, designed as a pocket manual for Civil War field use, went through five editions, while his *Manual of the Principles and Practice of Operative Surgery*, first published in 1879, was a standard surgical textbook for almost two decades; in addition, he wrote two classic essays on the history of surgery in the United States. As a distinguished professor of surgery, Smith was among the first to introduce Joseph Lister's doctrine of antisepsis in surgery into New York City hospitals. An authority on hospital construction, Smith designed the Roosevelt Hospital in New York City in 1866, and nine years later he was one of five men invited to submit plans for the building of the Johns Hopkins Hospital in Baltimore.

As impressive as Smith's accomplishments were in clinical medicine, his greatest achievements came in the areas of public health, sanitary reform, and the treatment of the mentally ill. Over the last five decades of his life, he would serve, beginning in 1868, as commissioner of the Board of Health of New York City, organize the American Public Health Association in 1872, assist in founding in 1879 (at the request of President Rutherford B. Hayes) the short-lived National Board of Health, be appointed New York State commissioner in lunacy from 1882 to 1888, travel on behalf of President Grover Cleveland as a United States delegate to the ninth International Sanitary Conference in Paris in 1894, serve as vice president of the New York State Board of Charities from 1903 to 1913, and at the age of eighty-nine be asked to assume the presidency of the thirteenth New York State Conference of Charities and Corrections. Through it all, the genial Smith never seemed to lose the vitality and energy he had as a younger man.

As a New Yorker sensitive to the city's social conditions, and because his *American Medical Times* was published in Manhattan, Smith devoted editorials to local public health and sanitary problems, primarily advocating legislative reform and, in particular, the need for active participation on the part of the medical profession. "They scorn the knowledge of our political history and a familiarity with current political events," Smith said of the city's doctors, "as matters too vulgar to occupy the attention of minds devoted to the sacred calling of physic. Diseases and their remedies are never the themes of their thoughts and conversation. Health and preventive medicine, and all measures of public interest, are discarded as without the pale of their 'sacred calling.'"[31]

Smith's particular interest in civic hygiene and sanitary reform dated back to the early 1850s, when he was in charge of a typhus tent ward run by New York City's commissioners of charities on Blackwell's (now Roosevelt) Island. Smith found that large numbers of patients were continually admitted from a single building on East Twenty-second Street. To better understand the sanitary conditions in which these individuals lived, Smith did what few physicians of that era would do: He went to inspect the house. "The doors and windows were broken; the cellar was partly filled with filthy sewage; the floors were littered with decomposing straw, which the occupants used for bedding; every available place, from cellar to garret, was crowded with immigrants," he wrote in his memoirs. "The whole establishment was reeking with filth, and the atmosphere was heavy with the sickening odor of the deadly typhus, which reigned supreme in every room."[32] After attempting to have the building declared uninhabitable, Smith realized that the so-called city Health Department was an ineffectual branch of government. There was no sense in lodging sanitary-related complaints when such a department was incapable of responding to the simplest of hygiene problems. The police were also stymied, because no law permitted a building to be condemned solely on the presence of disease. Only after the house's owner was notified that Smith had taken the matter to William Cullen Bryant, editor of the *Evening Post*, and that Bryant was going to publish the details of this hazardous situation, did the landlord agree to rehabilitate the residence.

For Stephen Smith, this episode, so early in his professional career, sparked what became a passion for public health–related activities. In 1859, he founded the New York Sanitary Association, an organization that helped introduce sanitary-related bills for the city into the state legislature. The following year, his inaugural issue of the *American Medical Times* singled out public hygiene as an area that would receive vigilant and unrelenting editorial attention. Smith said of the supposedly reorganized New York City Health Department, "It does little for health, but much for disease and death."[33] This was a difficult time for political change, however, for most positions within the city government were dominated by Boss William Tweed and his Tammany cronies, who were not about to undo the system of political patronage they had concocted.

Recognizing that immediate prospects for a legislative fix of the city's hygiene problems were unlikely, Smith directed his quest for sanitary change to the nation's military. He volunteered his medical expertise and spent several weeks as an acting assistant surgeon at the Union's military base at Fort Monroe, Virginia. Disturbed by the poor hygiene conditions he observed in the camps and hospitals, he used his editorial pen to lobby for more adequate sanitary inspections in the army. "I make these remarks in no spirit of unfriendliness towards those gentlemen who now compose the Corps of Military Inspectors," wrote Smith upon his return to New York City, "but I may assure them that much is expected from their labors." At the same time, he came to be viewed as the chief civilian propagandist for the United States Sanitary Commission, "for whose good offices the country cannot be too grateful," Smith explained.[34] This was not an unexpected alliance, since Elisha Harris, one of the founding members of the commission and a leading sanitarian in New York, was a next-door neighbor and close friend to Smith. Through Harris, Smith became friendly with other members of the Sanitary Commission, including Frederick Law Olmsted.

If any event made clear to Stephen Smith how sanitary neglect threatened American society, it was the New York City draft riot of 1863. Ten days after the anarchy stopped, he wrote in the *American Medical Times*, "As long as New York disregards the homelife of this class of the poor, she nourishes in her bosom a viper which any day may inflict a fatal wound." Sanitarians like Harris and Olmsted held an absolute belief in the health-giving influence of pure air, cleanliness, sunlight, and personal thrift. For Smith, who adamantly believed in the same virtues as Harris and Olmsted, public and professional apathy were the major obstacles in the path of reform. In an effort to bring change, Smith took advantage of his editor's bully pulpit and wrote a series of articles concerning the prospect of health reform in New York City. He listed the anticipated effects from legislative action: the protection of citizens, the lengthening of life, and an increase in human happiness. "The great and patent prevention for riots like that which we have witnessed is radical reform of the homes of the poor," he told his readers. "No family circle can be practically virtuous which grovels in the cellar or the garret, deprived of the sunlight and fresh air."[35]

Slowly the sanitary reforms in the army, mediated largely through the efforts of the Sanitary Commission and Smith's sanitary campaign in New York City, were beginning to influence the civilian population. In December 1863, one hundred prominent New York lawyers and businessmen formed the Citizens' Association, a group organized to clean up the city government and reverse the effects of Tweed's corruption. Impressed with Smith's writings, the Citizens' Association saw new sanitary legislation as integral to their goals. Some of the leading physicians of the city, including Stephen Smith, Elisha Harris, and Frank Hamilton, were asked to form a council on hygiene and public health. The doctors decided that to convince the public and the state legislators of the necessity for new health laws, a detailed sanitary survey of the city should be completed. Smith was asked to supervise the project. Dividing New York City into thirty-one districts, each to be inspected by a trained physician, he completed the investigation, at a total cost of $22,000 to the Citizens' Association, by mid-November 1864.

Conditions were even more shocking than had been originally suspected. Slaughterhouses, with decomposing animal parts strewn about, stood next to crowded tenement buildings throughout the city. "In certain populous sections are fat-boiling, entrails-cleansing, and tripe-curing establishments, which poison the air for squares around with their stifling emanations," described Smith. One inspector told of a two-block stream of blood and liquid animal parts that stretched from a slaughterhouse on Thirty-ninth Street to the Hudson River. Overflowing toilets with sewage-filled basements were a common sight. The crowding tallied by Smith's team was simply staggering. Eight of New York City's thirty-four square miles housed a population of almost one million. One-half of these people were from the poor and laboring classes, and they were pressed into only two square miles.

Smith, with the help of Harris, collated the data and produced the five-hundred-page *Report of the Council of Hygiene and Public Health of the Citizens' Association of New York, upon the Sanitary Conditions of the City*, which brought about a great public outcry. Community leaders flocked to the reformers' cause, and the matter turned into a hot political issue that led to Stephen Smith's impassioned appearance before a joint session of the New York State Legislature in February 1865. Smith quoted statistics, provided graphs, showed pictures, dramatized and personalized the problems of poor sanitation, told of ongoing cholera, smallpox, and typhus epidemics, brought the horrors of filth, sickness, and disease to the floor of the New York State Legislature, and made certain that its members understood that Tammany Hall's use of political patronage in naming sanitary inspectors had to stop: "New York City is the only city in the civilized world which disregards the Platonic idea that in a model republic medical men should be selected to preserve and promote the public health." Smith's cause had become so widely known that *The New York Times* printed the entire speech and began to run editorials committing the paper to some measure of health reform. Smith himself had become a *cause célèbre*, and in the end the politicians listened. The Metropolitan Health Bill, which in large part had been drafted by Smith, became law in March 1866.

Much like Smith and Harris's earlier report, which ranks among the most important of nineteenth-century epidemiological studies, the new health law marked a pivotal point in the history of public health in New York City and the United States as a whole. It gave a great urban metropolis the beginnings of effective sanitation and provided civic hygiene laws that would be enforced by trained professionals. On a national scale, the sanitary reform in New York City set an example for other states to follow. The law was "declared, officially and judicially, to be the most complete piece of health legislation ever placed on the statute books," claimed Smith. "From that fountain of legal lore the whole country has been supplied with both the principles and the details of sanitary legislation."[36]

STEPHEN SMITH'S EFFORTS resulted in the merger of medical and civic responsibilities. They brought order to the disordered science of public health, dramatically improved the status of physicians and their profession, and stand as one of the most important episodes in our country's medical past. No individuals were more pleased with this turn of events than members of the United States Sanitary Commission. By 1863, the Sanitary Commission had become a large organization, with tens of thousands of citizens volunteering their services to the more than seven thousand local affiliates spread throughout the cities, towns, and villages of the North. And the commission had won enough popularity with soldiers and their families to gain substantial influence with state and federal officials. Frederick Olmsted had created an effective bureaucracy with himself at the head and three associate secretaries: one in charge of the work east of the Alleghenies plus New Orleans, one in charge of the area west of the Alleghenies, and one designated chief of sanitary inspection. Managed as a large governmental bureaucracy, the commission worked through regional branches and affiliated societies that maintained local autonomy but recognized Olmsted and the executive board as the ultimate authority.

For men like Frederick Olmsted, Henry Bellows, George Templeton Strong, and Cornelius Rea Agnew, the formation of the commission presented a serendipitous opportunity to transform a land born of individualism into an ordered and disciplined nation. Charles Stillé, in his official history, bluntly admitted that the commission "subordinated all its plans, even for the relief of suffering, to the maintenance of that discipline in its strictest form."[37] As Bellows told his son, the Civil War was "God's method of bringing order out of chaos."[38]

The men of the Sanitary Commission believed that knowing how to maintain personal hygiene while keeping clean camp and hospital sites would reinforce self-discipline and sustain morale through a long war. For this reason, the first important task of the commission was to inspect army camps and general hospitals for their sanitary fitness. From September 1862 until May 1863, when army physicians officially approved by Congress took over the function, Olmsted sent dozens of experienced medical men into the field as sanitary inspectors. Given checklists with almost two hundred items, these men were instructed to focus on sanitation and prevention. They reported on hospital locations and the nature of the soil and drainage, the number of medical officers and stewards and their educational backgrounds, and the quality and quantity of food available. They studied the soldiers' discipline, morale, and mortality rates. They counted blankets and clothes and noted the condition of tents. The reports were forwarded to Surgeon General Hammond's office, where any corrective or disciplinary action could be carried out. With all this information in hand, the commission began to publish its own broadsides, monographs, and pamphlets, most of them written by renowned physicians and sanitarians of the day, to disseminate their findings and update health care policies.

Assuring proper sanitary conditions and teaching soldiers good personal hygiene were important activities, but what drew the most public praise for the Sanitary Commission were the relief efforts to aid the soldiers. Once it became obvious that the army was incapable of attending to all the daily needs of the rapidly mobilized volunteer force, Olmsted began to establish depot centers from which relief agents could distribute supplies (all the efforts of the Sanitary Commission and its related agencies were termed relief, whether they concerned sanitary matters, food provisions, medical needs, or pension programs for the sick and disabled). The thousands of local organizations, usually supervised by women, collected, stored, and shipped to these depots all manner of baked goods, bandages, blankets, canned foods, and clothing. Local branches also raised funds to purchase other much-needed items, including alcoholic beverages, cots, medicines, wagons, and even horses and mules. The Sanitary Commission distributed its donations on such a massive scale that it was sometimes difficult to discern which was the soldier's primary source of supplies—the federal government or the commission.

By the spring of 1863, four and a half months after their disastrous defeat at Fredericksburg, the North's Army of the Potomac was once again on the move. Ambrose Burnside was out as commander, and Joseph Hooker—"Fighting Joe," as he was known—was in. Displaying energy and tenacity, Hooker reorganized his more than 120,000 troops, many of whom had lost hope of ever defeating the rebels, and attempted to flank Robert E. Lee's men, who continued to hold the Rappahannock River and the countryside surrounding Fredericksburg. Hooker's operations began well and seemed about to succeed. But Hooker, like McClellan and Burnside before him, hesitated, withdrew his troops to a defensive position, and became involved in the disastrous Battle of Chancellorsville. A brilliant victory for the Confederates, it came at the cost of Lee's ablest general, Stonewall Jackson. Accidentally shot in the left arm by one of his own men, and suffering from massive blood loss and splintering of bone, Jackson was forced to submit to the amputation of his arm two inches below the shoulder. For eight days he fought for his life, but without the benefit of surgical antisepsis and antibiotics, he died from pneumonia and blood poisoning.

Jackson's death would prove a staggering loss to Southern military leadership, but for now, Lee, brimming with confidence from the victory at Chancellorsville, decided to invade the North again. In early June, the Confederate army began their march up Virginia's Shenandoah Valley, through Maryland, and into Pennsylvania. On June 28, Hooker, having lost the backing of President Lincoln, resigned and was replaced by George C. Meade, who now led the Army of the Potomac.

Both sides moved toward Gettysburg, although neither Lee nor Meade planned to fight there. On July 1, 1863, the conflict began when a Confederate brigade, searching for badly needed supplies, inadvertently ran into Northern cavalry. All troops—a Northern army of 93,534 men and a Southern army of 70,226 men—then hurried to the unexpected battlefield at Gettysburg, and after a brutal three days, the Army of the Potomac emerged with a decisive victory.

Around 14,000 Union wounded needed treatment at Gettysburg—another 5,300 or so were missing, many of whom would eventually require surgical care—but a shortsighted Hooker, prior to his resignation, decreased the number of accompanying supply wagons to facilitate the movement of his army pursuing the invading Confederates. "The want of tents, cooking apparatus, etc., occasioned by the recent orders, was to me," Letterman noted, "in common with all the medical officers, a cause of the deepest regret, and to the wounded of much unnecessary suffering."[39]

JUST AS REBEL spies attempted to follow the movements of the Army of the Potomac, so did Sanitary Commission agents seek to determine where the next battle might occur so that commission supply depots could be established nearby. Such information proved invaluable at

Gettysburg, where commission stores reached the battlefield hours prior to and in more abundance than supplies from the government. "Thank God, here comes the Sanitary Commission; now we shall be able to do something," was how one exhausted surgeon explained the easing of the crisis to a group of wounded and untreated men. From Baltimore, Frederick, and Philadelphia, via railroad cars filled with ice, came tons of bread, butter, eggs, fish, milk, mutton, poultry, and vegetables. Thousands of napkins, shirts, shoes, stockings, towels, and underclothes, in addition to 110 barrels of old linen and bandages and 1,200 crutches, were also sent to Gettysburg. "It was a grand sight to see this exhibition of the tender care of the people for the people's brave," wrote Charles Stillé in his official history of the Sanitary Commission.[40] "It was a bit of home feeling, of home bounty, brought to the tent, and put into the hand of the wounded soldier."

The distribution of supplies to field hospitals was only one aspect of the Sanitary Commission's work at Gettysburg. An enormous lodge and feeding station was organized at the railroad station, which served as the departure point for injured being transported to general hospitals. Here commission agents set up 150 beds, kitchens, and tents; they fed 16,000, sheltered 1,200, and made certain that a surgeon examined the wounded and applied new dressings. The commission spent $20,000 in the first seven days after the battle, and by the end of July, the figure had jumped to $75,000. Costs were becoming a matter of concern, because as Frederick Olmsted noted to a friend, "our operations have been on a much larger scale than ever before."[41]

The difficulties of raising funds were a constant problem for the commission. There was always a fresh infusion of moneys following great battles like Fredericksburg, Chancellorsville, and Gettysburg. For instance, in July 1863, $28,863 in contributions was raised, but each great battle also produced a drain on the commission's coffers. During the last six months of 1863, the disbursements of the commission were twice its receipts, and in December alone, the commission spent $64,634. With the cost of distributions out of proportion to receipts, the commission entered 1864 with only $41,725 in its coffers. In an attempt to solve the ongoing financial crisis, the commission sponsored a series of sanitary fairs, held from the fall of 1863 for the duration of the war, and they became lucrative sources of fund-raising.

As described by one eyewitness, the opening ceremonies of the first fair, held in Chicago in late October 1863, had "banners flying, drums beating, and all manner of brazen instruments thrilling the listening ear, and stirring the hearts of the vast multitudes of people with exciting music. It was a mighty pageant." With a parade three miles long, the attention of Chicago's citizens centered on the exposition; businesses closed, courts delayed their cases, and schools suspended classes. Nine divisions of troops marched, children by the thousands sang "John Brown's body lies a-mouldering in the grave," and hundreds of farm wagons, overflowing with vegetables for the soldiers, passed in a colorful display down the parade route. Numerous buildings were packed with goods on display or for sale. Manufacturers Hall contained heavy machinery, while Bryan Hall, "transferred for the nonce into a bazar, rivalling those of the Orient in bewildering beauty," according to the fair's organizer, was a sales room for fancy wares.[42] A trophy room held captured Confederate flags, a shackle taken from the neck of a slave, and metal fragments from the wreck of the rebel ship the *Merrimac*. But the greatest sensation of the Chicago Sanitary Fair was Abraham Lincoln's gift of an original draft of the Emancipation Proclamation. Purchased by a philanthropist for $3,000, the proclamation was then lithographed and copies sold to raise money for a home for invalid soldiers. In the end, nearly $80,000 was brought in, an enormous sum. For the hundreds of fairs that followed, whether in small-town America or urban centers, the same pastiche of parades, speeches, and exhibits was used to stir enthusiasm and generate contributions. By mid-1865, which marked the end of the war, an astonishing $4,392,980 had been raised.

AS THE UNITED States Sanitary Commission grew in size, some of the hierarchical discipline that Frederick Olmsted had put in place began to break down. By 1863, regionalism emerged, with state agents insisting that contributions raised in their particular state should be used only for the relief of their soldiers. This spirit of localism greatly disturbed Olmsted, who always looked upon the commission as a national organization. After all, among the issues that instigated the Civil War, federal mandates versus states' rights was most prominent. To resolve this dilemma, Olmsted requested that the commission's executive committee further centralize his authority. "I think that you have no more right to do business in the free and easy, careless hasty inconsiderate way you do, than you have to leave your butcher's bills unpaid or to drop your lighted cigar end in the straw of a stable-door," he wrote to Bellows. "That is not the way that business is done successfully. Everything must, in one way or another, by one method or another, be thoroughly done, or trouble comes of it." The committee rejected Olmsted's advice, and funding issues between the national commission and its local organizations were never entirely resolved.

Increasingly disenchanted with the manner in which the Sanitary Commission was run, Olmsted promised his wife, Mary, he would resign in just six more months. By summer 1863, the six months were past and his frustrations had only mounted. "I believe," he complained to Bellows, "the Commission is not one tenth part as useful as it would be if the original plan of organization had been maintained. I am as certain that the Commission can not exist long with its present arrangements as I am that I should not exist if I tried and succeeded in making my heart and brain interchange duties."

Olmsted was in New York City when word of the battle at Gettysburg reached him. Departing for the battlefield, he traveled first to Philadelphia, where he coordinated the purchase of several tons of butter, chickens, eggs, fruit, milk, and mutton. The Sanitary Commission loaded these items onto a railroad car, along with a ton of ice, rented another car, and filled it with large tents and furniture. Both cars were attached to the first train through to Gettysburg. "Our men never behaved so well and I believe they fought better than the enemy—they were cool and steady and showed every good quality of veterans, and it was I suppose the best fought field of the war," he wrote Mary. "Its moral effect is incalculable.... I think we can hold our heads up with a good conscience again."[43] It was the last major assignment that Olmsted undertook as executive secretary. On September 1, 1863, he officially resigned from the Sanitary Commission. Just two weeks later, he was on his way to San Francisco, where he had accepted the position of manager of the Mariposa Estate.

Olmsted's tenure with the United States Sanitary Commission lasted slightly more than two years. During this time, he brought about the reorganization of the U.S. Army Medical Department, forcefully promoted the nomination of William Hammond as surgeon general, and became one of the nation's most vociferous advocates for an independent army ambulance corps. George Templeton Strong, the commission's treasurer, writing in his private diary concerning Olmsted's resignation, noted, "We can ill spare him."[44]

CHAPTER NINE

"There were none for whom it was impossible to provide"

F OR SURGEON GENERAL WILLIAM HAMMOND, the timing of Olmsted's departure could not have been worse. Since the beginning of 1863, Hammond's already strained relations with Secretary of War Edwin Stanton had markedly deteriorated. Prior to his leaving, Olmsted warned Henry Bellows, the Sanitary Commission's founder, that "the Surgeon General has got wind of an intrigue against him in the department."[1] Stanton had apparently found someone to replace the surgeon general.

Described as a "high-toned gentleman,"[2] Joseph K. Barnes had already served twenty-two years as an army physician when he reported for a new assignment in Washington in May 1862. Like so many of that era's leading doctors, he received his medical degree from the University of Pennsylvania and after two years of postgraduate training entered military service to begin a series of postings in frontier America. A tall, double-chinned man with receding wavy black hair and a thick droopy mustache that joined muttonchop side-whiskers, Barnes was considered down-to-earth. Although few personal accomplishments distinguished him from other career army doctors, he enjoyed a burgeoning friendship with Edwin Stanton. Barnes's last assignment before coming to Washington was as Henry Halleck's medical director of the Department of the

West. When Lincoln brought Halleck east in mid-July to serve as general in chief of the U.S. armies, the latter told Washington of Barnes's capabilities as a doctor, which led to his ascendancy.

Because of his bullying ways and heavyset build, Edwin Stanton did not seem sickly, but he was a chronically ill and perhaps even depressed individual. Suffering from asthma since childhood, he endured an increasing number of breathing attacks that caused him to be bedridden for days at a time. The asthma was complicated by accompanying congestive heart failure and cirrhosis of the liver. His waking existence was further strained by a permanent limp brought on by a long-standing, poorly healed fracture of the knee. It was the unassuming Barnes serving as personal physician to numerous army officers and War Department officials who was soon seeing Stanton on a daily basis. Barnes was constantly advising the secretary of war to rest, but it was not in Stanton's nature to be inactive. "Keep me alive until this rebellion is over and then I will take a rest—maybe a good long one,"[3] Stanton told Barnes.

As Stanton's health deteriorated, he became more dependent on Barnes's medical advice, and their personal relationship grew stronger. Indeed, their wives vacationed together. It was not long before Stanton realized that the genial Barnes would make a perfect foil to the overbearing Hammond. In February 1863, Stanton appointed Barnes a medical inspector with the rank of lieutenant colonel.

Despite Barnes's rapid rise within the military medical hierarchy, there is no evidence of friction between Barnes and Hammond. Certainly, Hammond appeared oblivious to Barnes's potential as a possible successor, and with Olmsted's departure and the Sanitary Commission in some disarray, there was no organized effort to thwart Stanton's plan to topple Hammond. In mid-1863, George Templeton Strong recorded in his diary a conversation heard between Stanton and another War Department official. "The fact is," said the secretary, "the Commission wanted Hammond to be Surgeon-General and I did not . . . the Commission beat me and got Hammond appointed. I'm not used to being beaten, and don't like it."[4] The politically tactless Hammond, who was frequently his own worst enemy, was about to fall victim to Stanton's machinations.

Of the many initiatives that Hammond introduced as surgeon general, none created the controversy of Circular No. 6, also called the Calomel and Tartar Emetic Order, or so readily delivered him into the clutches of Stanton. Beginning with the days of Benjamin Rush and his bleed, blister, and purge style of medical care, the employment of calomel (mercurous chloride) and tartar emetic (antimony and potassium) as cathartics had become an accepted part of the physician's pharmaceutical armamentarium. But beyond their renowned abilities to bring about explosive diarrhea and volcanic-like vomiting, both calomel and tartar emetic had more frightening long-term effects. A buildup of mercury in a patient's system could cause extreme salivation, with the gums and tongue becoming inflamed and painful. In the worst cases, ulcers formed in the mouth, and as these open sores coalesced they gradually ate away the bones and tissues of the face, leaving behind grotesque features. Antimony and potassium was such a poisonous combination that it could reduce the force and frequency of the heartbeat to levels occasionally incompatible with life.

The most bewildering aspect of the continued use of calomel and tartar emetic was that even though doctors recognized the awfulness of these side effects, they continued to prescribe the deadly minerals. There was a simple explanation for this seemingly bizarre therapeutic behavior: The scientific ignorance of the times was overwhelming, and the great mass of poorly educated physicians remained blindly devoted to old medical routines. Still, while the majority of healers might have been committed to this dangerous therapy, more elite physicians were beginning to express their concerns about the excesses of heroic therapies, and public opposition to the horrors of bleed, blister, and purge medicine was slowly emerging. Therapeutic battle lines were drawn as laypeople, opposed to the regular or allopathic medical profession's reliance on heroic therapy, joined forces with irregular or sectarian medical practitioners. The defining feature of this coalition was an unequivocal opposition to massive dosing with harsh mineral agents. In particular, sectarian doctors decried the allopaths' devotion to such therapy, with calomel and tartar emetic singled out for special condemnation.

By the time of the Civil War, the debate over the safety and efficacy of heroic therapy was transformed into a public referendum on professional credibility. Accusations were traded between allopaths and sectarians as each side extolled particular treatments while vilifying the other. To treat disease, sectarians chose less harsh therapeutics and were known to sometimes shy away from operative surgery for certain categories of wounds. From the allopathic point of view, this was too passive an approach to military medicine and ill suited for the battlefield. The arguments were unending, and orthodox and unorthodox interests eventually centered on the contentious issue of what therapeutic substances should be included in the army's standard list of medical supplies.

When William Hammond, an allopath, was named surgeon general, he received overwhelming support from the orthodox medical community. But like many of the nation's better-educated doctors, he harbored a growing skepticism toward the continued use of heroic therapy. "But while I do not wish to be understood as at all doubting the efficacy of proper medication in the treatment of disease," he wrote in the preface to his *Treatise on Hygiene,* "I am sure that . . . [calomel and tartar emetic], the traditional actions of which have been positively disproved by physiological and chemical researches, as well as by the soundest deductions from pathology, are too frequently administered through a strict adherence to the routine which hinders the development of medical science, and cramps the powers of those who labor for its advancement."[5]

In spring 1863, Hammond received reports from several medical inspectors indicating that under the imprimatur of heroic therapy, the administration of calomel and tartar emetic continued to be pushed to excess by military surgeons. Cases of profuse salivation and even mercurial-induced gangrene of the face abounded, with soldiers suffering more from the treatment than from the disease. In early May, Hammond, without giving much thought to the political ramifications of his actions, declared that the use of calomel and tartar emetic in the army was forbidden and that these mineral agents would be removed from the medical supply list.

The sectarians were elated, most regulars were aghast, and Hammond found himself in the middle of a controversy that would not end. "Surgeon General Hammond has thrown a perfect bomb shell into the ranks of old-fashioned allopathy," wrote John King, one of the country's best-known eclectic physicians.[6] Homeopaths joined the chorus, considering Hammond's order to be both timely and necessary. Even Stephen Smith, representing antimineral allopathic doctors, wrote that he was "compelled to regard the order of the Surgeon General as a judicious, and even a necessary measure . . . in no other way could the evil have been successfully reached."[7]

In wider allopathic medical circles, however, Hammond's order was viewed as not only insulting to the regulars, but providing unwarranted support for their sectarian enemies. A committee under the auspices of the American Medical Association condemned Circular No. 6 as "unwise and unnecessary"[8] and requested the surgeon general to modify it. The most violent criticism against Hammond came from the medical journals and members of the local, county, and state medical societies of the Midwest. With large numbers of sectarian practitioners in Ohio, regular physicians in that state, more so than anywhere else in the North, felt their livelihoods threatened by unorthodox competitors. "Dr.

Hammond has attempted to degrade his profession. He is the representative of the medical profession, and must, therefore, answer to it. . . . He must be removed," wrote the editor of the *Cincinnati Lancet*. Not only was Hammond personally attacked in this lengthy editorial, but the writer even lambasted Stephen Smith and his *American Medical Times*, labeling the magazine Hammond's "official organ."[9] Noting that Hammond had several hundred copies of the weekly *Times* sent gratis to military hospitals and regimental surgeons, he accused Smith of being little more than a paid propagandist for the surgeon general.

American medicine could not have been more contentious at the time of the Civil War. Allopaths hated sectarians and vice versa. Anti-heroic therapy allopaths fought with pro-heroic therapy allopaths. Homeopathic sectarians battled with eclectic sectarians. As one medical editor warned, "We intend to wage an unceasing opposition against quacks and quackery in the regular profession, who attempt to hide its ugly practices under the mantle of respectability."[10]

Hammond's Circular No. 6 certainly sparked professional discord, but with allopaths in complete control of Northern military medicine, the order did little to encourage medical pluralism in the army. If anything, it strengthened allopathic domination by condemning the most common, albeit increasingly scorned, allopathic treatment but not the practice of heroic therapy itself. Although calomel and tartar emetic were taken off the army's official supply list, they continued to be available by special request and remained among the favorite prescriptions of Union physicians. Ultimately, the Union army remained an institution decidedly against sectarian practitioners and their brand of therapeutics. Such animosities were not found in the Confederate army, where soldiers who desired nonorthodox treatment met with little opposition. At least in terms of official Southern policy, there was no discernible ill will between allopathic and sectarian practitioners.

The calomel and tartar emetic controversy brought to the surface deep, festering feelings about Hammond's performance as surgeon general. Sectarians might have been ecstatic about Circular No. 6, and better-educated orthodox physicians might have believed that scientific progress was being made, but for legions of older and more conservative regular physicians, this was the last straw: Hammond had to go. Apparently, Hammond had seriously underestimated the extent to which allopaths would defend their therapeutic beliefs. Disliked in influential army and governmental circles, Hammond was losing his already narrow base of support, and he was more vulnerable than ever to incriminations by politically vindictive enemies like Edwin Stanton.

SENSING HAMMOND'S POLITICAL weakness, Stanton appointed a special commission of three civilians in July 1863 to examine the management of the Medical Department. Heading the commission was Andrew Reeder, the same individual who in 1854 was territorial governor of Kansas when Hammond was stationed there as an army physician. At that time, Hammond testified against Reeder concerning accusations of corruption involving land transactions. Reeder was found guilty and ended up having to be secreted out of Kansas, and Hammond acquired a lifelong political enemy. When Stanton named Reeder to lead the investigation into Hammond's Medical Department, it was evident that the latter's decade-old biases would color the commission's outcome. "I never saw a man who entered more eagerly upon the discharge of the duties of his office," said Samuel Gross, the well-known professor of surgery at Philadelphia's Jefferson Medical College and a close friend to both Hammond and Reeder. "[Reeder's] object was to revenge himself upon his Kansas enemy, and how he acquitted himself the result only too clearly showed."[11]

Reeder's committee functioned like a grand jury, with closed sessions and secret depositions. One of the committee's main investigators had recently been turned down by Hammond for an appointment as inspector of liquors for the army. When told by the surgeon general that such a position did not even exist, the man complained to Stanton, who proceeded to get him the job with the Reeder commission. The fix was in as Reeder and his cronies went hunting for supposed evidence of Hammond's shoddy business practices.

By the end of the summer, a newspaper investigator gleaned enough information from Reeder's camp to report that "censure to a slight degree might possibly be attached by this commission to the Surgeon General or some of his subordinates; but everything adduced went to show that, so far as the appropriation for the purpose would admit, the wants of the sick and wounded of our armies had been supplied with most commendable promptness and completeness, both in the field and in the hospitals."[12] Most of Hammond's supporters, therefore, saw no immediate reason to intervene. After all, the charges seemed minor, especially in the context of the continuing horrors of the war. Besides, when Helen Hammond made a visit to the secretary of war, he assured her that he had no intention of dismissing her husband.

Meanwhile, Stanton was forging ahead to maneuver Hammond out of office. Several weeks later, in mid-August, Stanton promoted Barnes to the important post of medical inspector general. Barnes replaced the incompetent Thomas Perley, who was requesting immediate discharge to return home to Maine and attend to his sick wife. At the same time, Stanton ordered Hammond to take a tour of far-flung army posts, such as Hilton Head, New Orleans, and Nashville. George Templeton Strong recorded in his diary that Hammond recognized this as "the first step in a scheme of Stanton's to supersede him." Strong also noted that Hammond "is probably right. Stanton shook him by both hands when he bade him good-bye, and it is generally understood at Washington that that mark of cordiality is the invariable precursor of some stab or blow at its recipient."[13]

Additionally, Stanton ordered Hammond's chief assistant out of Washington to New Mexico to prevent him from giving testimony favorable to the surgeon general before Reeder's committee. Stanton then cited a little-known law from 1836, stating that when the surgeon general was on an extended tour of faraway military bases, an acting surgeon general could be named. On September 3, 1863, Joseph K. Barnes was named acting surgeon general and temporary head of the United States Army Medical Department. Whether or not the new acting surgeon general was pawn or player in Stanton's scheme remains unknown. In any event, with Hammond out of the picture, Stanton's machinations moved forward. Work was ordered stopped on the army medical school and plans for the medical museum were scaled back, while investigations into Hammond's comings and goings intensified.

THROUGH NOVEMBER, HAMMOND remained silent about the events in Washington. His friends, however, learned of his troubles and began to rally to his cause. Frank Hamilton, the war-hero surgeon from Bellevue Hospital, had been appointed by Hammond in July 1863 as a high-ranking medical inspector. Hamilton protested the injustice occurring to his friend by resigning his commission and returning to New York City a week or so after Hammond was banished from the nation's capital. Members of the recently formed Union League Club of New York City, a fraternal organization founded by Frederick Olmsted among others, circulated a petition on Hammond's behalf. Several renowned scientists conducted a letter-writing campaign meant to sway public opinion. Even foreign physicians were taking his side. "Dr. Hammond is not an unknown man," wrote the editor of London's *Medical Times*. "The voice of the country must prevent Dr. Hammond, if innocent, from being sacrificed, as others have been, to personal spite."[14]

In early December, Hammond completed his southern inspection tour, but Stanton refused to allow him to return to Washington in any official capacity. Isolated in Nashville, Hammond received a letter of reprimand from Stanton forbidding him to make any more purchases for the Medical Department and curtailing all of his remaining powers as surgeon general. A man of strong ego, Hammond was unable to fully comprehend the seriousness of Stanton's intent. It was difficult for him to believe that anybody could find fault with his running of military medicine. At a real disadvantage given his distance from Washington, Hammond was uncertain how to mount a credible offense. He asked for a copy of the Reeder report but never received one. His demands on Stanton went unanswered. Around Christmastime, Hammond received word that the Reeder committee findings had been submitted to President Lincoln. The testimony was said to be sufficient to bring about Hammond's immediate dismissal.

Hammond was under considerable stress when in December he tripped and fell down some steps while leaving a hospital in Nashville. He struck his head and lower back, but the injuries appeared minor. Soon, however, his lower legs were partially paralyzed. The incident necessitated his immediate return to the East Coast for medical evaluation. Stopping in Philadelphia, Hammond met with S. Weir Mitchell and William Williams Keen at the army's specialized Hospital for Diseases of the Nervous System. These men were friends of Hammond's and experts in nerve injuries, particularly hysterical reactions in response to mental stress. Mitchell and Keen's evaluation showed paralysis of the legs, but they were unable to determine the exact reason for the symptoms. In a short time and without treatment, Hammond's leg strength returned and he headed for Washington.

This episode parallels others that intermittently disabled Hammond during periods of great anguish in his life. He was a recognized hypochondriac. One of Hammond's biographers admitted there was "some 'whispering' about this paralysis, which does appear to have been convenient."[15] In late December, George Templeton Strong and other members of the Sanitary Commission recognized Hammond's desperateness and finally decided to intervene on his behalf. "The Commission did feel itself called upon to vindicate his administration upon the highest grounds," wrote Charles Stillé, "those which rest upon a belief that it was so conducted by him, that those who suffered through the casualties of war, received a skillful and humane treatment unexampled in military history."[16] The commission's executive committee had good reason to defend the surgeon general, for if he was dismissed, regardless of the veracity of the charges, then the commission would lose standing with official Washington. George Templeton Strong had letters published in the commission's widely read *Bulletin* questioning the legal basis for Hammond's banishment. As well, a testimonial signed by numerous eminent physicians and scientists was sent to every congressman. Stephen Smith joined the fray in a fiery editorial. "It is the duty, and should be the privilege of every physician, whether in civil or military life, to sustain by every influence which he can employ SURGEON GENERAL HAMMOND as the head of the medical staff of the army," implored Smith. "Whatever prejudices may have been created by any of his official acts should now be laid aside, and a united effort be made to restore him to his legitimate position, or secure him a fair and impartial hearing."[17]

The commission's voice was apparently heard, because Stanton told a senator that he might be willing to drop the investigation, a case of letting "bygones be bygones."[18] But Hammond insisted that the secretary of war issue a public apology or that his name be cleared by an immediate court-martial. The equally stubborn Stanton offered no apology, and on January 17, Hammond was placed under house arrest. "I received this announcement with joy," wrote Hammond. "I was confident that no unprejudiced court would convict me of wrongdoing."[19] He would soon find out how wrong he was. The trial began two days later.

THE SURGEON GENERAL was charged with a series of bureaucratic irregularities, most significantly that he exceeded his legal authority by personally purchasing blankets for the military rather than allowing a medical purveyor to complete the transaction. To make matters worse, according to Reeder's investigators, the blankets were overpriced, of inferior quality, and bought from suppliers known to be friendly to the surgeon general. The appearance of graft by a department head was considered a serious matter in wartime Washington, especially since Edwin Stanton had been named secretary of war, at least in part, to counter the accusations of fraud that swirled around his predecessor, Simon Cameron. Hammond denied any wrongdoing. Further, there was no evidence to suggest that he made a personal profit from the sale. Regarding the quality of the blankets, Hammond explained to the court that bureaucratic red tape needed to be circumvented in order to rush the needed coverlets to the battlefield. In such an emergency situation, the surgeon general argued, competitive bidding was not feasible.

The other major accusation against Hammond was that he lied to a fellow medical officer concerning that physician's staff assignment. George Cooper had been a medical purveyor in Philadelphia when he was allegedly told by Hammond that General in Chief Henry Halleck wanted him replaced. Halleck testified that he could not recollect all the facts concerning Cooper's dismissal but vigorously denied Hammond's version of the events. Hammond stated that a series of written notes was passed between him and Halleck that could have clarified the situation. However, the surgeon general claimed these documents were stolen from his desk while he was in the Midwest. Thus, it simply became a case of one man's word against another's, and there was little doubt that the respected general in chief of the U.S. armies commanded more trust than the despised surgeon general.

Hammond proved clueless not only to the guile of his adversaries, but also to the growing influence that national politics played in the conduct of the trial. It was 1864, a presidential election year, and George McClellan, the dismissed commander of the Army of the Potomac, was being touted as a possible opposition candidate to Lincoln's reelection bid. Naturally, McClellan's chance for electoral success could be boosted if scandal sullied the Lincoln administration. Stanton, therefore, conducted a campaign to preemptively discredit many of McClellan's supporters, of whom Hammond was among the more prominent. Stanton, cautioned George Templeton Strong, "is a ruffian and will always abuse the power of his great place to purposes of arbitrary, vindictive tyranny."[20]

From the outset of the court-martial, things looked bleak for the surgeon general. The chief judge was hostile to Hammond, who was never given sufficient time to mount an adequate response to the charges. In addition, evidentiary papers needed by Hammond's defense team mysteriously disappeared. Disappointingly, after drawing up a petition on Hammond's behalf, some of his supporters—distinguished men in the arts, education, medicine, and sciences—inexplicably denied their own signatures. And in a most glaring example of witness tampering, George Cooper, the star accuser, later confessed to John Brinton, whom Hammond had appointed curator of the U.S. Army Medical Museum, "I knew you were a friend of Hammond's. . . . Now, Doctor, I will tell you, in the late trial, it was Hammond's head or mine, and I saved mine."[21]

The trial lasted four months. At first, the goings-on attracted a moderate amount of press coverage, but as the days dragged into weeks, the events of the war, in addition to the presence of other, more exciting court-martials, overshadowed Hammond's predicament. Finally, on May 7, 1864, after less than two hours of jury deliberation, Hammond was found guilty of all charges. He was shocked and hurt, but the reality was that during the proceedings few individuals actively supported him. Hammond's lawyers did get the respected Jonathan Letterman to attest to Hammond's forthrightness, but it was a case of too little too late. Even the Sanitary Commission, growing more fearful of its declining influence and not wishing to further offend Stanton, did nothing to aid

Hammond. "As a Commission, whatever may have been the opinion and action of its individual members," wrote Charles Stillé, "it has refrained from defending Dr. Hammond, when his personal integrity, or the technical offence of exceeding his authority, were in question."[22]

On the day before the verdict was announced, George Templeton Strong and Cornelius Rea Agnew visited Stanton to apprise him of the Sanitary Commission's desire to continue performing public work. The subject of Hammond was raised, and a deal was made. Stanton could count on the commission's continued and needed support of the war effort, and the commissioners were assured that they would receive Stanton's renewed backing if he was allowed to get rid of Hammond. A few weeks later, Strong wrote to Henry Bellows, "We certainly stand well with the people—and the Secretary of War spoke well of us lately! We must remember to have a Feast of the Conversion of St. Stanton in the Sanitary Calendar."[23]

The court-martial verdict could not become official until reviewed by President Lincoln, and he did not act on it until August. In the meantime, Hammond and his family pressed to have the decision reversed. Hammond's wife went to the White House and requested a meeting with Lincoln. Her visiting card was returned with a note in Lincoln's handwriting: "Under the circumstances I should prefer not seeing Mrs. Hammond."[24] Hammond wrote a letter to the president asking for a personal interview but never received a reply. Meanwhile, Democratic Party officials opposed to the general policy of Lincoln's Republican administration chose McClellan as their presidential candidate. The party's platform denounced the war as a failure and proposed negotiating with the South for peace.

On August 18, 1864, the trial verdict was sustained by presidential review and thirty-six-year-old William Hammond was dismissed from the military service and forever forbidden to hold appointment in the federal government. Stephen Smith, in an editorial in the *American Medical Times*, expressed his "profound regret." He wanted Hammond to be remembered not just as a representative of American medicine, but also as a "man of science."[25] The editors of *The New York Times* were not so charitable. Hammond's discharge from government service was labeled an inadequate punishment for someone who had sunk to a state of "utter villainy, bartering away the comforts and periling the lives of the sick and wounded soldiers."[26]

Hammond was gone, his pride battered, his pocketbook nearly empty. Still, he printed and distributed at his own expense a seventy-three-page pamphlet defending his actions. The leaflet began to soften the profession's opinion about Hammond. "We think that, *a priori,*" wrote the editor of the *Boston Medical and Surgical Journal*, "there is much in the circumstances of the trial which should lead the community to accept the verdict rendered against Dr. Hammond with some hesitation as to its justice."[27] To the civilian medical establishment, Hammond was more and more seen as a victim of the unseemly influence of government on medicine. Yes, Hammond was technically guilty of some of the charges, but it was also obvious that he did what he considered necessary under wartime conditions. In such a circumstance, his supporters asked, would a more impartial secretary of war have placed formal charges against a surgeon general? Even the Sanitary Commission's Charles Stillé was forced to comment: "Hammond did a work while in that position, which will always be regarded by men of science and the friends of humanity as one of the proudest monuments of the civilization of our age and our country."[28]

Stanton would have none of this. He was not about to change his opinion of Hammond, nor was he going to allow the cashiered surgeon general to have any say in the future running of the Medical Department. His entreaties refused, Hammond moved his family to New York City. There he was embraced by the leadership of the city's medical societies and embarked on what would become a successful career unique among physicians of his era: a full-time specialty practice in nervous and mental diseases.

FOLLOWING WILLIAM HAMMOND'S arrest in January 1864, Joseph Barnes assumed full administrative control of the army's Medical Department. With Barnes in charge, Stanton's interest in medicine revived—after all, his father, brother, and brother-in-law were all physicians—and military health-related initiatives, previously suggested by Hammond but turned down or stopped by the War Department, were revitalized for implementation. Ironically, since Barnes lacked the creative vision and scientific expertise of his predecessor, many of Hammond's innovative ideas served as guidelines to lead the Barnes administration through a final year and a half of war. Foremost among the projects was congressional enactment of an armywide ambulance service.

True to his word to Henry Bowditch in late fall of 1863, Senator Henry Wilson of Massachusetts, chairman of the Committee on Military Affairs, introduced—with Stanton's approval—a congressional bill to create an independent armywide ambulance corps. The legislation was based upon Jonathan Letterman's plan, first introduced at Harrison's Landing on Virginia's Peninsula in August 1862. Wilson had Letterman testify about the pending legislation and incorporated the medical director's ideas into the new bill. Wilson stressed to his colleagues that General Ulysses Grant favored the concept and that another general had declared, "The system as embodied in the bill is almost practically perfect." "It extends to all our armies the system adopted eighteen months ago in the Army of the Potomac," said Wilson on the floor of the Senate, "and which at Fredericksburg, at Chancellorsville, and at Gettysburg, according to the testimony of our officers, worked most admirably."[29]

As Bowditch continued his lobbying efforts, the public outcry for an ambulance corps was increasingly heard. A political action committee had tens of thousands of copies of an article from the influential *Christian Examiner*, describing the merits of an ambulance system, reprinted and distributed throughout the country. The Massachusetts State Legislature passed a petition signed by the governor and presented it to Senator Wilson, stressing the need for an ambulance corps. With Stanton and Wilson indicating their firm support, the Ambulance Corps Act of 1864 was passed by both houses of Congress and became law on March 11.

The ambulance service was finally extended to all Union armies, and although there was to be no special enlistment, members of the Medical Department chose, trained, and examined the men detailed to the corps. To maintain the ambulance service's uniqueness, persons other than these special soldiers were forbidden to assist the wounded from the field. Further strengthening the corps's role was a strict prohibition against the use of ambulances for purposes other than the transportation of patients and, in an emergency, medical supplies. Punishments for disobeying these rules, including public reprimand and dismissal from the military, were written into the new law. Ultimately, the underlying principles of the Ambulance Corps Act were so well received that they became the basis for ambulance organization and evacuation of wounded for most armies of the world through World War I.

It was not only Hammond's ambulance plans that went forward under Barnes's regime. Increased public viewing hours for the U.S. Army Medical Museum were added. A father-and-son team of anatomists prepared bone and tissue specimens, and a microscopist joined the museum's staff as the scope of the collection was enlarged. Barnes employed illustrators and photographers to assist in the preparation of the multivolume *Medical and Surgical History of the War of the Rebellion*, and a physician was hired to collate the accumulating medical data coming from the camps and battlefields. All were ideas originating from Hammond's vision of military medicine. Furthermore, Stanton agreed to fund an army medical library—another of Hammond's concepts—and

Barnes brought John Shaw Billings to Washington. The twenty-six-year-old physician, who would become president of the American Public Health Association as well as director of the New York City Public Library, increased the size of the surgeon general's library from six hundred volumes in 1865 to fifty thousand just eight years later. An avid bibliophile and bibliographer, Billings started publication of the renowned *Index Medicus*, a monthly guide to the world's medical literature that is published to this day.

In July 1864, Barnes asked Stanton to issue instructions declaring that all future hospital construction must be completed on the "principle of detached pavilions, each ward being in a separate building, with beds for sixty patients,"[30] a pattern originally proposed by Hammond. Further demonstrating his willingness to support Barnes's implementation of Hammond's concepts, Stanton ruled that general hospitals were to be controlled exclusively by the surgeon general and that any doctors working in these facilities came under the jurisdiction of on-site medical officers and not local military commanders. Intended to add stature to the military's physicians, the ruling had been long sought by Hammond, to no avail.

Barnes looked to his predecessor's administration for solutions to other problem areas, in particular the nursing program run by Dorothea Dix. By now, Dix was over sixty years old, overworked, and weakened from malaria and pulmonary problems. Making matters worse, she remained authoritarian, unapproachable, and increasingly irritable. These character traits did little to endear her to military physicians, and opposition to her ways was intense. Since mid-1862, Hammond had looked to marginalize her influence by curtailing the number of nurses under her control. However, Stanton's early support of Dix, combined with his dislike of Hammond, made this impossible.

When Barnes assumed the position of surgeon general, he informed Stanton that some of Dix's charges were not performing to standards. Moreover, Dix would not respond to any of the Medical Department's concerns, and she refused to alter the criteria—only plain-looking women thirty years of age or older, with no bows, curls, hoop skirts, or jewelry—used to choose her appointees. Barnes stressed to Stanton that military doctors needed to have the right to hire or fire Dix's appointees without her approval or the soldiers' health would suffer. The secretary of war acquiesced to Barnes's appeals and General Order No. 351 was issued, stating that beginning in January 1864, no females could be employed in general hospitals unless specially appointed by the surgeon general. Moreover, women nurses were to be under the exclusive control of the senior medical officer of the hospital in which they served, and he would assign them their duties. More important, this physician could dismiss women nurses without notice when they were "considered supernumerary, or for incompetency, insubordination, or violation of his orders."[31] Dix's influence was further diluted when Stanton decreed that not more than one nurse be assigned to every thirty hospital beds. As well, Barnes gleefully pointed out that from then on, any woman requesting work as a nurse in a general hospital could be employed "irrespective of age, size or looks."[32] This, of course, was devastating to Dix, who for all practical purposes found her official position as superintendent of nurses completely undermined. By war's end, Dix wrote to a friend, "This is not the work I would have my life judged by!"[33] Once again, with Stanton's backing, Barnes had accomplished what Hammond could not.

ALTHOUGH DAILY ROUTINES under Surgeon General Barnes varied little from those of the Hammond regime, Barnes was not totally dependent upon his predecessor's ideas. He might not have had Hammond's intellectual strengths, but he was a better leader of men. Barnes developed mentor relationships with several of the personnel who worked for him. For instance, his principal assistant for almost two decades, Charles Henry Crane, succeeded him in the office of surgeon general. Barnes maintained a more democratic approach to the management of military medicine than did Hammond and demonstrated a greater affinity for the common physician. Barnes displayed this concern for physicians and soldiers when, in mid-1864, he assigned an assistant surgeon general to a permanent office in Louisville. This way, the Medical Department could more effectively oversee doctors in that area of the country, keep close supervision on military hospitals, and better control the distribution of medical supplies.

Barnes further underscored his independence from Hammond when he changed many of the higher-ranking personnel working with him in the Office of the Surgeon General. Among the first to be transferred was John Brinton, Hammond's curator of the U.S. Army Medical Museum. "In Washington, in bureau life at that time, everyone had enemies," recalled Brinton. "The 'outs' wanted to become the 'ins,' and everyone who was in, *ipso facto*, became a target for the malice of his enemies." Brinton was told that he was being sent west for reassignment. When asked if Barnes was dissatisfied with his current job performance, an aide simply said, "Doctor, what is General McClellan's middle name? George *Brinton* McClellan—that's all I can say."[34]

Political considerations clearly played a part in Barnes's running of the Office of the Surgeon General. Supported by Stanton, who reneged on his pledge to work amiably with the commission, Barnes and the secretary of war concluded that the revamped Medical Department could better manage its responsibilities by minimizing Sanitary Commission interference. They denied the commission further authorization to use the department's and adjutant general's records to compile a directory of hospitalized army patients and their locations. For several weeks in the spring of 1864, Barnes refused permission to allow the Sanitary Commission to move freely in the staging area where the Army of the Potomac prepared for a new offensive in Virginia. "In Surgeon General Barnes," wrote a historian of the Sanitary Commission, "the secretary [Stanton] found one who was 'jealous, uncooperative, and slyly injurious' to Sanitary plans."[35]

The diminishing influence of the Sanitary Commission was a prime indication of the growing strength of Barnes's role as leader of the United States Army Medical Department. But it was neither Barnes's medical acumen nor his ability to command men that brought about this change. Instead, it was the department's foundation, established by Hammond and championed by Stanton, that explained much of Barnes's success.

In 1864, physicians were still unable to defeat endemic and epidemic diseases. Postoperative infections remained widespread, and the manner in which wounds were handled was not substantively different from that of the start of the war. However, order, initially present under Hammond's leadership, characterized Barnes's running of the Medical Department. The success of the ambulance corps and triumphs of the field hospital system in evacuating, clothing, feeding, sheltering, and caring for the sick and wounded were striking. From now on, Barnes's most pressing concern would not be camp sanitary tactics, the presence of disease, incompetent physicians, or the abandonment of men on the battlefield. Instead, it was how to best use the organizational structures left by Hammond to expeditiously confront the military needs of an aggressively waged final year of war.

SIGNS WERE BEGINNING to point to a Northern victory in early 1864, when Lincoln promoted Ulysses S. Grant to the rank of lieutenant general and gave him command of all Northern armies. Grant, known as a determined warrior, coordinated a three-prong pincerlike offensive. A reconstituted Army of the Potomac, commanded by George Meade, was to confront Robert E. Lee's men in Virginia and occupy Richmond, the capital of the South. Grant established his headquarters with the Army of the Potomac and assisted Meade and his army in planning their movements. Also joining them was Phil Sheridan, a renowned horseman, who took charge of Meade's cavalry. William Tecumseh Sherman, designated by Grant to be his successor as commander of the North's western armies, was to take his troops and march toward the Atlantic seaboard from Tennessee into Georgia and along the way seize Atlanta, the arsenal of the South. Last, Nathaniel Banks would move his men from New Orleans through Montgomery to eventually join Sherman. This third part of the offensive never developed as Banks attempted to fight his way up to capture Shreveport. In a mishandled campaign, Banks, the politician—he was governor of Massachusetts from 1858 through 1861—turned general, was badly defeated.

Virginia was now destined to become the scene of the bloodiest fighting of the whole Civil War. It was also where the culmination of three years of Medical Department experimentation and planning, ranging from total confusion at Bull Run to comparative order at Gettysburg, would be showcased.

Thomas McParlin, Jonathan Letterman's replacement as medical director of the Army of the Potomac, thought he was thorough in his preparations for Grant's spring 1864 offensive. More than 600 ambulances were repaired, painted, and marked with the distinctive badges of their divisions and corps. The 60 officers and 2,300 men of the ambulance squad were drilled and redrilled. Nearly 700 medical officers were divided among the field hospitals. Two hundred and ninety-four hospital tents were readied. McParlin calculated that there were enough supplies to treat 20,000 wounded for almost one month. As a final measure of readiness, during the last days of April, the existing sick and wounded were transferred to Washington.

McParlin, who had served as medical director of John Pope's Army of Virginia and then as chief surgeon of the Naval School Hospital at Annapolis, was fortunate that the army he inherited was reasonably healthy. Clothing and bedding were abundant, and the morale of the troops was excellent. The men were well fed—during January, February, and March, millions of pounds of desiccated mixed vegetables, dried apples, onions, potatoes, and pickles were issued to the Army of the Potomac—and well rested, most having received a thirty-day furlough for visits to home and friends. The sick list was small, with few cases of epidemic diseases, and McParlin had even gone so far as to have the troops vaccinated when several cases of smallpox appeared.

This was no longer the army of 1861, when mobs of men went into battle without any reasonable preparation for battlefield casualties. After three years of medical misery, this outfit had been transformed into a re-laxed, fit, and splendidly equipped fighting force that maintained its own ambulance corps and contained a staff of increasingly well-trained and highly motivated physicians. The Army of the Potomac and its plan for medical preparedness were intended to be adaptable to whatever the military situation called for. And within two weeks, this scheme would begin to be tested to its limit.

In May 1864, Grant's 130,000-man Union force launched a major drive into a desolate area of northern Virginia known as the Wilderness. Stretching westward from Chancellorsville, this vast region of tangled forests and impenetrable underbrush was crisscrossed by swamps and hills and ridges. The Battle of the Wilderness raged for two days as troops stumbled through the landscape, which often permitted no more than a few yards of visibility. So intense was the fighting that at one point the underwood caught fire and two hundred trapped Yankee wounded died in the flames.

Though the stretcher bearers displayed great gallantry, McParlin re-ported to Barnes, they had "very little success, it being almost impossi-ble to find wounded men lying scattered through the dense thickets and the enemy firing at every moving light or even at the slightest noise."[36] For two days, members of the ambulance corps struggled to locate and remove the injured. Grant grew impatient with what was designed to be an orderly evacuation process from battlefield to field hospital to base depot hospital to general hospital. Consequently, he had Meade author-ize the wounded to be immediately sent back to Washington in one large wagon train.

Hundreds of supply wagons were hurriedly emptied and converted into makeshift ambulances, and almost five hundred regular ambu-lances joined them in an evacuation column stretching seven miles in length and containing more than seven thousand men. With all efforts focused on getting the already rescued to Washington, at least one thou-sand wounded soldiers were left behind in the Wilderness's maze of thickets. Twenty-four hours later, Grant and Meade changed their minds, fearing that rebel guerrillas might capture the poorly protected medical wagon train. Instead, they ordered the casualties to be taken twelve miles away, to Fredericksburg, scene of the infamous Burnside debacle in December 1862 but now under Union control.

Because of these altered plans, the thousands of injured spent a day and a half stuck in their ambulances, going nowhere as their wounds fes-tered and poisoned their bodies. Grant, however, was not about to slow down his offensive and wait for the Medical Department to bring all the injured to safety in Fredericksburg. And he was not overly concerned that the physicians who accompanied the wounded to Fredericksburg had to remain there to treat them. This unintended splitting of the health care staff between Fredericksburg and the front lines compounded the medical dilemmas, since the doctors remaining at the battle site were becoming overworked and fatigued. With large numbers of physicians needed in two locations, there were no longer enough practitioners available to treat all the injured and sick at either place. Despite the detailed advance planning, no one on the medical staff or in the Union's high command anticipated the ferociousness of the fighting or the overwhelming number of casualties that would result from Grant's push toward Richmond.

Grant lost more than seventeen thousand men at the Wilderness, while Lee's forces suffered eleven thousand casualties, but the rebels had prevented the Yankees from flanking their position. Unlike McClellan, Burnside, Hooker, and Meade before him, Grant was not about to let mounting casualties force him to abandon a well-planned strategy. He would keep on fighting until an acceptable endpoint was achieved.

Grant moved quickly and tried to reach Lee's right flank. Two days later, on May 8, a desperate ten-day battle began at Spotsylvania Court House. It was a vicious confrontation that resulted in another twenty thousand injured Union soldiers. According to McParlin's testimony, initially "all the ambulances were absent, being engaged in conveying the wounded of the battle of the Wilderness to Fredericksburg, and much confusion and delay in the collection of the wounded occurred in consequence." Responding to the situation, McParlin informed Meade that an emergency existed owing to the lack of regular ambulances. Realizing the gravity of the problem, Meade issued an order: "All vehicles and spring wagons, of every description whatever, now in use at any headquarters, or by any officer of the army, for the transportation of baggage or for any other purposes, will immediately be turned over to the medical director for the transportation of the wounded."[37]

Attitudes regarding evacuation and treatment of the wounded had changed. Unlike past battlefield crises, when quartermasters were reluctant to assign vans and wagons under their control to medical personnel, now McParlin received hundreds of however rickety two- and four-wheeled carts. Fifty-six spring-supported wagons, used to move staff officers' luggage, were also given to the medical corps. By the middle of May, McParlin estimated that 18,500 wounded soldiers had already gone through his field hospitals and were on their way to Fredericksburg via these extemporized vehicles and newly available regular ambulances. "Long trains of ambulances, dripping with their gory burdens, were continually arriving at the designated spots for field hospitals," reported an eyewitness to the scene at Spotsylvania. "Some of the sufferers were pale and silent, the life-blood nearly exhausted; some were mutilated with the most frightful wounds; prayers, sighs, groans were heard on all sides. The surgeons, bloodstained to the elbows, were busy with knife and probe. Piles of arms, legs, hands, feet, and fingers covered the ground. The utmost possible care was taken of the wounded."[38]

McParlin originally intended to establish a vast base depot hospital— a fully supplied facility that would function as a staging area from where injured soldiers could then be transferred to the North's general hospitals—at Brandy Station, a short distance from the Wilderness battle-fields. Grant's unexpected decision to move the tens of thousands of wounded to Fredericksburg tested the Medical Department's ability to adapt to strategic emergencies, especially since there were no stockpiles of supplies in that city. Unlike prior Union medical disasters, where chaos and confusion accompanied battlefield carnage, in May 1864, McParlin's medical staff was better prepared to respond to a fluid military situation. In telegraph communication with Surgeon General Barnes, McParlin requested extra surgeons and medical supplies. Barnes complied immediately as calls went out from Washington for members of the reserve medical corps.

This loosely organized system was established by William Hammond after Gettysburg, when continuing difficulties with volunteer civilian physicians, regarding their job descriptions, demonstrated a need for change. In cooperation with state governors, a reserve medical corps—thirty doctors per state—was formed. Its members' medical competence was vouched for by local authorities, and the corps's mandate was to be available on short notice in time of need. Under the new system, the civilians received a monthly salary of $100, were subject to the orders of the Medical Department, and had to remain at an assignment for at least two weeks. Within days, a multitude of practitioners descended on the Wilderness. Unlike earlier episodes, where disorder accompanied the arrival of civilian volunteers, this time reserve physicians primarily changed dressings, treated sick soldiers, and helped run the hastily organized field hospitals. Amputations and other complicated surgical procedures were left to army doctors, who had been previously selected for their skill with the knife.

FREDERICKSBURG WAS IN shambles from previous battles, but in early May, the few standing structurally sound buildings were extemporized into military installations. "The town was one vast hospital; every church, every store, every dwelling; every door-yard was crowded with wounded," recounted an eyewitness relief worker. "Even the side-walks were occupied in many places by exhausted soldiers on their way from the field in search of shelter and assistance."[39] Despite the unplanned move to Fredericksburg, within four days, McParlin reported, "the con-dition of the wounded was comparatively comfortable, and the supply of all necessary articles was abundant."[40] Only bedding straw and sta-tionery were said to be lacking. Even the Sanitary Commission, having momentarily settled its dispute with Surgeon General Barnes, had placed at the Medical Department's disposal two steamboats and two barges laden with two hundred tons of supplies as well as forty-four four-horse wagons to transport the goods to Fredericksburg. Receiving assistance from, among others, two hundred commission relief agents, the sick and injured from the Battles of the Wilderness and Spotsylvania received a level of care that was better organized, albeit still crude by present-day standards, than ever before.

At the end of the first week, a member of the Christian Commis-sion, one of the Sanitary Commission's rival aid organizations, wrote to *Harper's Weekly* concerning Fredericksburg, "The medical and sanitary work was thoroughly systematized." He went on to describe how on any given day, despite six thousand wounded in the hospitals and two thousand soldiers wandering the streets, "there were none for whom it was impossible to provide."[41] So impressive were the transportation ca-pabilities of the Medical Department that when Meade next ordered McParlin to abandon Fredericksburg and establish another base depot hospital twenty miles farther south at Port Royal, the medical director was able to have all of the wounded—twenty-five thousand over the twenty days that Fredericksburg served as a supply and medical center—either moved ahead to the next facility or taken northward by train and boat to general hospitals.

Grant's losses were now somewhere around forty thousand men, but continued Southern resistance only strengthened his determination to win. Telegraphing Henry Halleck in Washington, Grant wrote, "I propose to fight it out on this line if it takes all summer."[42] Again, Grant rapidly moved south toward Richmond. On June 3 at Cold Harbor, a few miles east of the Confederate capital and near the Chickahominy River, Grant initiated the last of his massive frontal assaults through open land. The rebel positions were exceedingly strong, consisting of well-engineered triple lines of breastworks that were not easily broached. The Union at-tack failed miserably as more than six thousand soldiers fell to murder-ous fire in less than one hour's fighting. Skirmishing continued for days as Grant's losses ended up totaling thirteen thousand. Still, he remained as resolute as ever, although his strategy was about to change.

For several weeks, medical director McParlin's unit had leapfrogged from one base depot hospital to another as the Army of the Potomac pursued the rebels. While boats were still being loaded with wounded troops at Port Royal, McParlin was told to close Port Royal and establish another facility forty-five miles to the southeast at White House on the James River, in proximity to the fighting at Cold Harbor. During the two weeks at White House, scurvy began to appear among the soldiers. "For over one month the men had no vegetables," McParlin reported, "and the beef used was from cattle which were exhausted by the long march through a country scantily provided with forage." But scurvy was not the only problem: Poor camp sanitation was again an issue as diarrhea spread through the troops. "The water now used by the troops is entirely derived from surface drainage, and is saturated with organic matter derived from decaying vegetable tissues," McParlin told Meade. "The ground around many camps is strewn with dead and decomposing horses and mules, and with the hides and offal of slaughtered beef cattle. Very few regiments have provided sinks for the men, and their excreta are deposited upon hill sides, to be washed thence into the streams, thus furnishing an additional source of contamination to the surface water."[43] Within days, a large shipment of fresh vegetables arrived at White House and campsites were cleaned up as offal was buried and sinks dug. A truce was even arranged with the general commanding the Confederate troops so that the wounded could be collected and thousands of rapidly decomposing dead could be buried to lessen sanitary concerns.

The Medical Department was systematized and better able to retrieve the sick and injured from the front lines than in the past. And most observers agreed that troops now received care in as timely a fashion as military events would permit. Despite this, death from disease still remained the most formidable enemy, with the chances of dying from illnesses such as pneumonia or typhoid twice as likely as from bullets and shells. Though the organization of military health care had changed, the day-to-day practice of medicine was scarcely different from that of centuries before. There were more ambulances available in 1864, but without effective pain medicines, soldiers faced a horrifying and rattling ride to safety. There were more hospital tents for shelter, but without antibiotics to quell communicable diseases, epidemics spread unchecked. There were better-trained physicians, but without an understanding of antisepsis, surgical operations led to death from infection.

While the usual story of Civil War medicine highlights bravery, caring, and organizational innovation, the reality of war for the wounded and sick was more sharply defined by agony, butchery, and loneliness than anything else. Yet little fault can be found in the performance of the Medical Department during the Battles of the Wilderness, Spotsylvania, and Cold Harbor. No military force in the 1860s could have cared more effectively for the fifty thousand casualties that occurred within one month's time than the revamped Union's Medical Department. The Letterman–designed ambulance corps functioned admirably; his field hospital system was as sophisticated as any conceived; and the efficiency of the evacuation and transportation scheme was unprecedented. What distinguished this change from earlier in the war was the new-found respect and authority accorded the Medical Department. With Secretary of War Stanton giving his full support to Surgeon General Barnes, who in turn provided McParlin as medical director with whatever supplies and manpower he requested, the positive changes were readily apparent. "It may be remarked that circumstances will rarely tax more severely the capabilities of the medical staff than those of this year have done," wrote McParlin. "When necessary, I received prompt, cordial and efficient cooperation from the chief quartermaster and other chiefs of departments whose operations were connected with my own. This complete official accord was as beneficial to the service as it was personally pleasureable."44

DURING THE THIRTY-NINE days from the Battle of the Wilderness on May 5 to the close of the fighting on the Chickahominy on June 12, Grant lost almost fifty-five thousand men, of whom forty-five thousand were dead or wounded (the other ten thousand were missing in action). Faced with such staggering casualty numbers, Grant realized that the taking of Richmond and destruction of Lee's army would not occur solely by direct battlefield confrontation. However, Southern resources appeared to be dwindling rapidly. Southern railroads had just about stopped running, and the Confederate government was having difficulty resupplying its armies. Temporarily concealing his movements from Lee, Grant marched his Army of the Potomac farther southward, crossed the James River, and advanced on Petersburg, an important railroad center near Richmond. Union troops dug miles of trenches around Petersburg as a stranglehold on the Richmond area began in earnest.

In midsummer 1864, Grant unleashed his brilliant cavalry commander "Little Phil" Sheridan against Confederate forces in the Shenandoah Valley. In a series of victories that took place through the fall,

Sheridan drove the Confederates from the region. The countryside was stripped bare of supplies as the grip on Richmond tightened. Months of cold weather set in, with trench warfare pinning Lee to a static defensive position and depleting his forces and their morale. The Confederates slowly withered away as Lee was unable to relax Grant's hold on Petersburg; this control would intensify until April 1865 and the end of the war. Grant's casualty lists in Virginia were unprecedented, but his resolve to continue fighting, through both assault and siege, made him the steadily prevailing force. "He is one of us," a soldier told a reporter, "this Unconditional Surrender General; and he will bring us through, God willing, just as surely as the sun shines."[45]

The other major Union campaign of mid-1864 was led by William Tecumseh Sherman, who took his sixty-two-thousand-man army and proceeded to march through Tennessee and north Georgia and carry the war into Atlanta. Much like Grant, Sherman was unrelenting in his drive to achieve victory and did not hesitate to repeatedly send his troops against heavily defended Southern entrenchments. And here, as had happened in the hectic days during the Battle of the Wilderness, numerous rapidly changing military situations caused many difficulties for medical planners. Following the June 27 confrontation at Kennesaw Mountain with its 2,500 Yankee wounded, Sherman ordered all casualties evacuated to the far rear within twenty-four hours. Under less frenetic circumstances, this number of injured could have been transported without difficulty by the regular ambulance corps. However, there were not enough available ambulances to complete the move within the allotted time. Hundreds of carts and wagons were soon appropriated and the transport was accomplished, but not without difficulty.

The fact that the evacuation was carried out at all on such short notice was one indication of the new adaptability of the Medical Department to respond to emergency situations. Unfortunately, many deaths resulted from the suddenness of this move. As Sherman's medical director stated, "The haste in which this transfer of wounded was made, caused, I doubt not, much suffering, and I regret to say that, in some cases, neither proper nor sufficient food was furnished the men." With the dirt roads almost impassable thanks to two weeks of constant rain, what should have been a twelve-hour ride became thirty-six hours and even longer, leaving the men chilled, hungry, and demoralized. Responding to the situation, the Sanitary Commission established three feeding stations along the evacuation route. Within days, the commission's agents had served more than seventeen thousand meals. As the medical director explained to Surgeon General Barnes, "It was impossible to do better than was done. The conveniences were few, the wounded many, and the stay-at-the-rear fault-finding patriots in excess. Everything at our command was made use of to mitigate the sufferings of our troops, and it was only where the medical department had no control that the wounded were subjected to unnecessary suffering."[46] By early September, Sherman's troops occupied Atlanta.

With Atlanta taken, Grant, Meade, and the Army of the Potomac settled in for their siege of Petersburg, Virginia. McParlin's team had established another base depot facility at City Point, located directly on the south side of the James River, nine miles northeast of Petersburg. With outstanding accessibility to the water, the City Point installation was quickly brought to full operational capacity. By November 1864, it was considered the most outstanding base depot hospital of the war. The encampment, initially consisting of 1,200 tents, covered two hundred acres. In the warmer months, when patients could stay outdoors, the facility was equipped to handle ten thousand troops. In colder months, when felt-insulated log house pavilions replaced many of the tents, the population was reduced to six thousand wounded and sick.

City Point's equipment and accommodations sounded positively luxurious. Bathhouses with warm water dotted the site. Cooking stoves, cauldrons, and portable ovens were found throughout. The avenues between buildings were graded and graveled, and sidewalks were corduroyed in wood. A network of shallow ditches surrounded each group of tents and conducted rain away from the living areas toward the river. A log-and-earth-covered, and supposedly bombproof, trench system was constructed to contain fireplaces and bunk beds for sentries. Two steam engines of four horsepower each pumped river water into a thirty-foot-high six-thousand-gallon holding tank. The water was then distributed by a system of underground pipes for bathing and laundry use. Wells were dug, and numerous springs in the vicinity afforded a plentiful supply of fresh water for drinking and cooking. On warm days, when dirt was kicked up by marching troops and passing wagon trains, eight specially constructed carts sprinkled water on the ground to keep the dust down. As well, a rail line ran through the center of the campus and carried soldiers from the railroad cars directly to their beds, bypassing the need for ambulances. Fine netting was hung on bed frames to keep away annoying mosquitoes and swarms of flies. Latrines were sprinkled with sulfate of iron, a crude form of disinfectant. Even the food seemed tasty and included a Christmas Day dinner of turkey, celery, and cranberry sauce. Special diet kitchens were organized and supervised by ladies who, in McParlin's words, "were of much more use than when employed as nurses in the wards."[47]

Evacuation and treatment of the sick and wounded was exceptional at City Point. Two pontoon wharves allowed vessels with a shallow draft to be easily loaded. This eliminated most of the need for extensive overland conveyance as the steamships traveled the inland waters unimpeded to Annapolis, Baltimore, and Washington. Indeed, the transportation process was so efficient that a continuous flow of wounded was always heading northward. From mid-May through October 1864, almost fifty thousand sick and wounded were transferred from the various base depot hospitals to general hospitals in the North, thus keeping open sufficient numbers of beds for City Point's new arrivals. Amazingly, in that same period, despite the prescientific foundation of the era's medical care, more than ten thousand hospitalized patients were returned to duty with their regiments in reasonably good health. As City Point's chief medical officer stated modestly, "The numbers who have recovered and been returned to duty within a few weeks after their admission, and without removal to a distance from the seat of war, have proved this hospital a most eligible one."[48]

In November 1864, Sherman and his troops left Atlanta in flames and marched on Savannah. It was the beginning of the last offensive of the Union's western armies, but ironically it occurred along the East Coast. Sherman resolved to push through Georgia, swing upward into the Carolinas toward Virginia, and lay waste to everything of military value along the way. There was enough concern about maintaining proper medical care during the march that when Savannah was occupied on December 21, four hospital steamboats were waiting in the city with supplies for five thousand sick and wounded. So well-equipped and staffed was Savannah's base depot hospital that when Sherman continued northward for a link with Grant and Meade in early 1865, he had no trepidation about leaving his injured behind and even sending additional sick back south, as long as the army remained within reach. "I cheerfully bear testimony to the skill and professional merits of the medical officers with this army," wrote Sherman. "Quiet, industrious, and most skillful, they attend the wounded almost on the skirmish line, move them to the field hospitals, and afterward transport them with a care that entitles them to all honor."[49]

In Virginia, Grant's siege of Petersburg intensified, and as milder spring weather enveloped the area, the final stage of the campaign began. Concerned about the possibility of increased numbers of wounded, McParlin ordered the capacity of the City Point base depot hospital increased by one thousand beds and maintained supplies to treat up to twelve thousand men. At the same time, he had extra hospital railroad cars stationed near City Point to improve the efficiency of transporting sick and wounded while hospitals were cleared of all patients, in case Grant ordered the army to suddenly move southward. In early April, Grant achieved his military goals when he outmaneuvered Lee's right flank and seized the railroads supplying Richmond. Casualties were fewer than expected, and the transfer northward of Union patients was so efficient that City Point's base depot hospital was rapidly reduced to just 2,500 beds, many of them unoccupied. Lee's army retreated westward, hoping to join forces with other Confederate troops in North Carolina. But with Sheridan's army ahead of them and Grant's men pressing them furiously from the rear, Southern surrender was inevitable.

On Sunday, April 9, Grant and Lee met in a farmhouse at Appomattox Court House and hostilities were brought to an end. Two weeks later, details of the capitulation reached North Carolina, and the remainder of the rebel forces in that area surrendered to Sherman. At City Point, the fewer than one thousand remaining sick and wounded were moved along with medical supplies to Alexandria, and within four weeks these men were dispersed to general hospitals. City Point ceased to exist, as did the Army of the Potomac on the last day of June 1865.

The evacuation, treatment, and transport service at City Point was considered such a success that McParlin boasted of 26,244 patients receiving care at the facility from January 1865 to its closing. In his opinion, this number was so large because, after four years of war, military officers were no longer suspicious of the Medical Department's services. Medical preparedness was finally at the center of military preparedness, and the United States Army's embrace of this fundamental concern for human welfare remains the real legacy of Civil War medicine. "An army that has witnessed its beneficial provisions," extolled McParlin, "is prepared to appreciate the justice and wisdom of committing to the medical department trusts and powers in some degree commensurate with the duties imposed."[50]

THAT THE CIVIL War occurred in the waning years of medicine's prescientific era heightened its tragedy. Physicians were essentially helpless when confronted with communicable illnesses and devastating wound infections. Yet within one decade of the war's end, an understanding of the role of microorganisms in producing disease and the principles of antiseptic surgery would become accepted everyday knowledge. The cruel circumstance of this timing added to the physical horror that constituted Civil War medicine. Such suffering should prevent the conflict from being viewed in terms of medical glory. With the untimely death of more than six hundred thousand young men and the debilitation and disfigurement of an equal number, the true medical aspects of the war were hopelessness, misery, and stench; while bravery and gallantry and pageantry and parade are readily recalled, the physical essence of the conflict, as is true for most wars, was the organized maiming and murder of other human beings for political purposes.

There were no astounding medical breakthroughs during the Civil War. Communicable diseases ran rampant. Wound infections spread unchecked. Surgery, despite the performance of tens of thousands of operations, remained as barbaric and crude in 1865 as it was in 1861. For the first time in military history, medical record keeping was voluminous, yet this information provided few clues to help prevent or cure epidemics that ravaged the army. But it was not only the combatants who suffered. Physicians also died in extraordinary numbers, and the position of medical officer was not one of comparative safety. According to George Otis, a Civil War–era medical statistician, doctors sustained a mortality record "proportionately larger than that of any other staff corps."[51]

The significant achievement of Civil War–era medicine has to do with its transformation in the administration and organization of military medical care, from an appalling lack of preparation and concern to readiness and sympathy for the patient in a war that was waged on a scale never before known. Discipline was imposed on what had been an undisciplined profession. "The constant mingling of men of high medical culture with the less educated had value," wrote S. Weir Mitchell, "and the general influence of the war on our art was, in this and other ways, of great service."[52] Mitchell's observation, written one-half century after the national conflict ended, highlights one of the most enduring aspects of the story of medicine during the Civil War. The lasting medical impact of the war experience was not measured by ingenious innovations or engrossing surgical victories. Instead, it derived from physicians' day-to-day caring for sick and injured human beings in the face of scientific ignorance, superstition, and political interference. Given its striking inability to offer innovations in the medical sciences, Civil War medicine may be best remembered for its effective organization and administration of health care. Medical education and licensure laws were strengthened and upgraded. The Civil War established the supremacy of a strong federal government, and this centralized authority ultimately drew states together to solve health care problems. By awakening public sentiment to the necessity of sanitation, proponents of hygiene facilitated swifter progress in the crucial arena of public health.

Through the horrors of the Civil War, a generation of doctors received a depth of clinical experience that they could not have obtained in peacetime. Physicians, for the first time in the history of American medicine, organized and directed large hospitals that were architecturally developed around new hygienic measures. Doctors learned that cleanliness and ventilation were essential to good health and that wound infections might be less apt to spread if sanitary guidelines were implemented. Physicians and nurses began to understand the principles of sound nutrition and came to realize that maintaining a patient's mental welfare was just as important as assuring his physical well-being.

On a practical note, an editor of the *Medical and Surgical History of the War of the Rebellion* pointed out that "before the war, there were few surgeons who chose to undertake operations on the great vessels, [but] there are now thousands who know well when and how a great artery shall be tied."[53] The Civil War medical experience made operating surgeons out of a large number of physicians who previously had minimal experience with a scalpel. This extensive hands-on training helped surgery spread throughout the whole of the United States, especially during the 1870s and 1880s, when asepsis and antisepsis became an accepted part of the surgeon's routine. As the number of successful surgical operations increased and surgery advanced in sophistication, even physicians from the most rural locations, having gained surgical experience during the Civil War, were able to bring their craft home. Similarly, doctors who had little prior background in treating complex illnesses such as congestive heart failure and cirrhosis of the liver, or the phalanx of sexually transmitted diseases, suddenly gained a lifetime of professional experience in four years of camping and marching. Subsequent to the war, these practitioners of internal medicine brought a wealth of new information to the cities and towns where they settled.

By maintaining an appropriate historical perspective, and understanding that Civil War–era physicians could not act on knowledge they did not possess, readers can accept the medical and sanitary records during the war years as generally satisfactory. There were deficiencies, and soldiers suffered, but what physicians did medically during the Civil War was as modern to them as anything doctors do today. The only difference is the year in which treatment was carried out.

Epilogue

IN 1878, HAVING MADE A GOOD DEAL OF MONEY from the private practice of medicine, William Hammond launched a public relations campaign to vindicate his earlier career as surgeon general. To the public, most of the personal animosities that plagued his time as the military's top doctor were fading memories, and many of the individuals involved in the various disputes were no longer alive.

In December 1869, Edwin Stanton was appointed by President Ulysses S. Grant to be an associate justice of the United States Supreme Court. Four days later, at the age of fifty-five, Stanton died unexpectedly of congestive heart failure brought on by repeated bouts of asthma. Surgeon General Joseph Barnes served as lead pallbearer at Stanton's funeral. Barnes remained surgeon general until he was forced to leave his position for reasons of age in 1882. Less than a year later, he was dead from kidney failure. Henry Halleck was commander of the military division of the South when he died, in 1872, at the age of fifty-seven. George McClellan, who lost the 1864 presidential election to Abraham Lincoln, served as governor of New Jersey from 1878 to 1881. He died of heart disease at the age of fifty-nine in 1885. Toward the end of the war, Jonathan Letterman moved to California and was elected coroner of San Francisco and appointed surgeon general of the state. His always precarious health worsened, and in 1872, Letterman expired from an undiagnosed gastrointestinal ailment. That same year, Henry Wilson was nominated by the Republicans to be President Grant's running mate in his reelection bid. Grant was successful, and Wilson became vice president of the United States. Three years later, before completing his term of office, Wilson was dead from a stroke at the age of sixty-three.

Not all of Hammond's acquaintances died so young. Frank Hamilton gained further renown when he treated President James Garfield following an assassination attempt in 1881. In almost constant attendance during Garfield's eighty-day lingering course, Hamilton passed away in 1886, at the age of seventy-three, from tuberculosis. Henry Bowditch was eighty-four years old when he died in 1892. It had been fifteen years since his influential treatise *Public Hygiene in America* called attention to what he considered the country's negligence in dealing with matters of public health and vital statistics. John Brinton served as a professor of surgery at Jefferson Medical College from 1882 to 1906. He was seventy-five years old when he expired in 1907. Six months shy of his one hundredth birthday, Stephen Smith died in 1922. William Williams Keen, who guided American surgeons into the antiseptic era, succumbed to old age in 1932 in his ninety-sixth year.

THE CRUSADE TO clear Hammond's name began in early 1878 when bills were introduced in the United States Senate to overturn the court-martial decision of 1864. Hammond, his attorneys, and others testified before the senators, and a report was issued authorizing President Rutherford B. Hayes to review the matter. To improve the likelihood that the prior verdict would be overturned, the prosperous Hammond insisted that no financial considerations or pension be included in any restoration of rank. President Hayes handed the matter over to a military board, which after several months of unhurried activity—mostly rereading the 1864 record while refusing to hear additional testimony on Hammond's behalf—recertified, in March 1879, the original trial outcome of guilty.

Not willing to accept the same verdict, Hammond rallied his supporters to lobby for the submission of newly acquired evidence. Another round of political activity ensued, including a second presidential commission. In the end, it took an act of Congress and an order by President Hayes to reverse the guilty verdict. Hammond's name was officially entered on the retired list of the army in August 1879, when he was breveted brigadier general with the stipulation that he could never receive a government pension.

A decade later, Hammond closed his well-to-do New York City neurology practice and relocated to Washington, where he built a lavish private sanitarium for the treatment of diseases of the nervous system. It was not long before his various business ventures proved too costly. By the late 1890s, he was broke and searching for monetary support. In 1899, Hammond petitioned Congress to reinstate his previously unwanted pension benefits, but five days into the new century, the seventy-two-year-old physician died from a heart attack. No action was taken by Congress on Hammond's monetary request, but the family did receive permission for the former surgeon general to be buried in Arlington National Cemetery.

FREDERICK OLMSTED WAS eighty-one when he died in 1903. Following his resignation from the United States Sanitary Commission, Olmsted was a consultant to numerous urban landscaping projects. George Templeton Strong passed away in 1875 at the age of fifty-five. He had remained a lawyer with offices on Wall Street until 1872, when he became comptroller of Trinity Church in New York City. Henry Bellows was sixty-eight when he died in 1882. Most of his later years were spent tending his Manhattan congregation and being involved in Unitarian and local political affairs. Elisha Harris died in 1884 when he was sixty years old. Following the Civil War, Harris was appointed sanitary superintendent of New York City. Charles Stillé became provost of the University of Pennsylvania. He was eighty when he passed away in 1899.

The United States Sanitary Commission officially closed its headquarters in the summer of 1865. The commission's files and papers were packed away and ended up at the main branch of the New York City Public Library, where they are currently stored. In 1866, a direct offshoot of the commission evolved when Henry Bellows was named president of the American Association for the Relief of Misery on the Battlefield. Many men who had worked with the Sanitary Commission were named to the board, including Frank Hamilton, Elisha Harris, Frederick Olmsted, Charles Stillé, and George Templeton Strong. The goal of the association was to give advice based on the Sanitary Commission's Civil War experiences to new war relief societies organized in Europe. It was also hoped that the United States government would sign the Treaty of Geneva, an agreement establishing a code for the treatment in wartime of the sick, the wounded, and prisoners of war, including the protection of ambulances, hospitals, nurses, and physicians. At the time, the United States Congress and President Grant declined to become a signatory, citing the fear of American involvement in ongoing and future European wars (it was a later Geneva Convention that was accepted by the United States). In 1870, the association ceased to exist, effectively ending any working remnants of the Sanitary Commission.

NOTES

CHAPTER ONE

1. W. W. Keen, *Addresses and Other Papers* (Philadelphia: W. B. Saunders, 1905), 421 ("up to that time"), 420 ("My preceptor"), 421 ("as green as"), 422 ("The rebs are"), and 423 ("broke away from").
2. H. Guernsey and H. W. Alden, eds., *Harper's Pictorial History of the Great Rebellion* (New York: Harper & Brothers, 1866), 157.
3. S. Smith, editorial, "The Profession and the Crisis," *American Medical Times* 3 (1861): 73.
4. Quoted in J. M. Gallman, *The North Fights the Civil War, the Home Front* (Chicago: Ivan R. Dee, 1994), 76.
5. Smith, "The Profession and the Crisis," 73.
6. *New York Times*, April 28, 1861.
7. Quoted in B. I. Wiley, *The Life of Billy Yank, the Common Soldier of the Union* (Indianapolis, IN: Bobbs-Merrill, 1952), 26.
8. W. Grace, *The Army Surgeon's Manual* (New York: Baillière Brothers, 1864), 27.
9. S. Smith, editorial, "Rank of Civil and Military Surgeons," *American Medical Times* 3 (1861): 56.
10. *The Medical and Surgical History of the War of the Rebellion* (Washington, DC: Government Printing Office, 1870–1888), appendix to vol. 1, pt. 1 (report of Charles S. Tripler), 45.
11. S. Smith, editorial, "The Right Man for the Right Place," *American Medical Times* 2 (1861): 404.
12. Editorial, "Surgeons for the Volunteers," *Boston Medical and Surgical Journal* 64 (1861): 293.
13. *Medical and Surgical History*, appendix to vol. 1, pt. 1 (report of Theodore Calhoun), 91.
14. *Revised Regulations for the Army of the United States* (Philadelphia: J. G. L. Brown, 1861), 285.
15. *Medical and Surgical History* (Charles S. Tripler), 47.
16. Ibid.
17. Wiley, *Life of Billy Yank*, 23.

18. *Medical and Surgical History* (Charles S. Tripler), 47.
19. J. S. C. Abbott, *The History of the Civil War in America* (New York: Ledyard Bill, 1863), vol. 1, 120.
20. M. A. Livermore, *My Story of the War: A Woman's Narrative of Four Years Personal Experience as a Nurse in the Union Army* (Hartford, CT: A. D. Worthington, 1887), 106.
21. *New York Times*, May 11, 1861.
22. *Medical and Surgical History*, appendix to vol. 1, pt. 1 (report of W. S. King), 1.
23. Quoted in G. W. Adams, *Doctors in Blue* (New York: Henry Schuman, 1952), 19.
24. *Medical and Surgical History* (Charles S. Tripler), 51.
25. E. E. Bryant, *History of the Third Regiment of Wisconsin Veterans Volunteer Infantry* (Madison, WI: Veterans Association, 1891), 445.
26. *Medical and Surgical History*, vol. 1, pt. 3 (report of Charles J. Nordquist), 155.
27. J. J. Woodward, *Outlines of the Chief Camp Diseases of the United States Armies, as Observed During the Present War* (Philadelphia: J. B. Lippincott, 1863), 30 ("subtle gas") and 42 ("When great numbers").
28. S. Smith, editorial, "War and Medicine," *American Medical Times* 2 (1861): 293 ("Every Army surgeon") and 293 ("Let this matter").
29. Abbott, *History of the Civil War*, 171.
30. *Medical and Surgical History*, appendix to vol. 1, pt. 1 (report of C. C. Gray), 6.
31. Ibid. (W. S. King), 3.
32. Quoted in W. C. Davis, *Battle at Bull Run: A History of the First Major Campaign of the Civil War* (New York: Doubleday, 1977), 206.
33. C. C. Buel and R. U. Johnson, eds., *Battles and Leaders of the Civil War*, vol. 1, *From Sumter to Shiloh* (New York: A. S. Barnes, 1888), 189.
34. *The War of the Rebellion: A Compilation of the Official Records of the Union and Confederate Armies* (Washington, DC: Government Printing Office, 1880–1901), ser. 1, vol. 2 (report of Andrew Porter), 385.
35. Buel and Johnson, eds., *Battles and Leaders*, 252.
36. *Medical and Surgical History* (W. S. King), 4.
37. Ibid., appendix to vol. 1, pt. 1 (report of G. M. Sternberg), 8.
38. Abbott, *History of the Civil War*, 180.
39. Keen, *Addresses and Other Papers*, 423.
40. F. H. Hamilton, "Battle of Bull Run: One Day's Experience on the Battlefield," *American Medical Times* 3 (1861): 78.
41. *Medical and Surgical History*, vol. 2, pt. 1, (Noah L. Farnham), 109.
42. Ibid., vol. 2, pt. 2 (Case 1463—Private E. Post), 493.
43. V. M. Francis, *A Thesis on Hospital Hygiene, for the Degree of Doctor of Medicine in the University of New York* (New York: J. F. Trow, 1859), 145.
44. W. M. Robins, "The Sobriquet 'Stonewall,' How It Was Acquired," *Southern Historical Society Papers* 19 (1891): 166.
45. E. Warren, *A Doctor's Experiences in Three Continents* (Baltimore: Cushings & Bailey, 1885), 271 ("In speaking of"), 270 ("Large numbers of"), 270 ("From what I"), 270 ("more than twelve"), 273 ("at the first tap"), 274 ("I am not afraid"), and 274 ("began to thrill").

46. *Medical and Surgical History* (G. M. Sternberg), 8.
47. Quoted in Abbott, *History of the Civil War*, 185 ("wounds completely alive") and 185 ("were placed in").
48. Ibid., 185.
49. *Medical and Surgical History* (C. C. Gray), 7.
50. Ibid., vol. 2, pt. 3 (Case 896—Private J. Campbell), 619.
51. *New York Times*, July 26, 1861.
52. Quoted in C. J. Stillé, *History of the United States Sanitary Commission* (Philadelphia: J. B. Lippincott, 1866), 91.
53. Quoted in W. Rybczynski, *A Clearing in the Distance: Frederick Law Olmsted and America in the Nineteenth Century* (New York: Scribner, 1999), 199.
54. Quoted in J. T. Censer, ed., *The Papers of Frederick Law Olmsted*, vol. 4, *Defending the Union* (Baltimore: Johns Hopkins University Press, 1986), 12.
55. S. D. Gross, *Autobiography of Samuel D. Gross, M.D.* (Philadelphia: George Barrie, 1887), vol. 1, 134.
56. *Medical and Surgical History* (Charles S. Tripler), 44.
57. *New York Times*, July 26, 1861.
58. Guernsey and Alden, eds., *Harper's Pictorial History*, 152.
59. *Medical and Surgical History* (Noah L. Farnham), 109.
60. Ibid., vol. 2, pt. 2 (Private E. Post), 493.

CHAPTER TWO
1. *The Medical and Surgical History of the War of the Rebellion* (Washington, DC: Government Printing Office, 1870–1888), vol. 2, pt. 3 (Case 1047—William C. Goodell), 707.
2. J. Thacher, *American Medical Biography: Or Memoirs of Eminent Physicians Who Have Flourished in America* (Boston: Richardson & Lord and Cottons & Barnard, 1828), vol. 2, 54.
3. F. H. Garrison, *An Introduction to the History of Medicine* (Philadelphia: W. B. Saunders, 1913), 379.
4. Thacher, *American Medical Biography*, 49.
5. Quoted in M. C. Gillett, *The Army Medical Department, 1775–1818* (Washington, DC: Center of Military History, 1981), 42.
6. Quoted in J. T. Flexner, *Doctors on Horseback: Pioneers of American Medicine* (New York: Viking, 1937), 89.
7. Thacher, *American Medical Biography*, 57 ("Medicine is my") and 45 ("They should be").
8. Quoted in Flexner, *Doctors on Horseback*, 110.
9. Thacher, *American Medical Biography*, 32.
10. Quoted in ibid., 36.
11. Quoted in Flexner, *Doctors on Horseback*, 102.
12. Thacher, *American Medical Biography*, 34.
13. Flexner, *Doctors on Horseback*, 110.
14. E Garrison, "The History of Bloodletting," *New York Medical Journal* 97 (1913): 500.
15. S. D. Gross, *Autobiography of Samuel D. Gross, M.D.* (Philadelphia: George Barrie, 1887), vol. 1, 152.
16. Thacher, *American Medical Biography*, 34.

17. Editorial, "Remarks on Medical Fees," *The New York Monthly Chronicle of Medicine and Surgery* 1 (1824–1825): 25.
18. Quoted in N. S. Davis, *History of Medical Education and Institutions in the United States, from the First Settlement of the British Colonies to the Year 1850* (Chicago: S. C. Griggs, 1851), 183.
19. C. C. Cox, "Report of the Committee on Medical Education," *Transactions of the American Medical Association* 14 (1863): 77.
20. Davis, *History of Medical Education and Institutions*, 117.
21. Cox, "Report of the Committee on Medical Education," 79.
22. Davis, *History of Medical Education and Institutions*, 188.
23. Thacher, *American Medical Biography*, 65.
24. N. R. Smith, *Medical and Surgical Memoirs, by Nathan Smith, M.D.* (Baltimore: William A. Francis, 1831), 70 ("whole course of") and 71 ("has a natural").
25. "Remarks Before the State Senate," *Transactions of the Medical Society of the State of New York, 1844, 1845, & 1846*, 6 (appendix) (1846), 71.
26. G. R. Starkey, *An Introductory to the Fifteenth Annual Course of Lectures in the Homeopathic Medical College of Pennsylvania* (Philadelphia: A. M. Spangler, 1862), 9.
27. S. Smith, editorial, "Homoeopathy in Military Hospitals," *American Medical Times* 4 (1862): 44.
28. Editorial, "The War and Homoeopathy," *Chicago Medical Journal* 5 (1862): 370.
29. J. T. Temple, editorial, "Humanity, Homeopathy and the War," *North American Journal of Homeopathy* II (1862): 161.
30. E. E. Marcy, editorial, "On Homeopathic Surgery," *North American Journal of Homeopathy* I (1851): 150.
31. Quoted in R. M. Hodges, *A Narrative of Events Connected with the Introduction of Sulphuric Ether into Surgical Use* (Boston: Little, Brown, 1891), 35.
32. E. H. Clarke, H. J. Bigelow, S. D. Gross, T. G. Thomas, and J. S. Billings, *A Century of American Medicine, 1776–1876* (Philadelphia: Henry C. Lea, 1876), 80.
33. Quoted in E. D. Churchill, *To Work in the Vineyard of Surgery: The Reminiscences of J. Collins Warren (1842–1927)* (Cambridge, MA: Harvard University Press, 1958), 37.
34. W. W. Keen, "Military Surgery in 1861 and in 1918," *Annals of the American Academy of Political and Social Science*, 80 (1918): 18.
35. Davis, *History of Medical Education and Institutions*, 163.
36. Editorial, "The World Is Doctored Too Much," *Medical and Surgical Reporter* 8 (1862): 528.
37. O. W. Holmes, *Currents and Counter-currents in Medical Science* (Boston: Ticknor & Fields, 1861), 39.

CHAPTER THREE
1. Quoted in J. T. Censer, ed., *The Papers of Frederick Law Olmsted*, vol. 4, *Defending the Union* (Baltimore: Johns Hopkins University Press, 1986), 165 ("No pack of"), 162 ("They entered the"), 162 ("The majority of"), and 161 ("blistered feet, rheumatic").
2. Quoted in C. J. Stillé, *History of the United States Sanitary Commission* (Philadelphia: J. B. Lippincott, 1866), 43.

3. K. P. Wormeley, *The United States Sanitary Commission: A Sketch of Its Purpose and Its Work* (Boston: Little, Brown, 1863), 3.
4. Stillé, *History of the United States Sanitary Commission*, 44.
5. Ibid., 46.
6. Ibid., 51.
7. W. Q. Maxwell, *Lincoln's Fifth Wheel: The Political History of the United States Sanitary Commission* (New York: Longmans, Green & Co., 1956), 5.
8. A. Nevins and M. H. Thomas, eds., *The Diary of George Templeton Strong*, vol. 3, *The Civil War 1860–1865* (New York: Macmillan, 1952), 181.
9. Stillé, *History of the United States Sanitary Commission*, 528 ("mixed commission of"), 528 ("prevent the evils"), 527 ("essentially a people's"), and 527 ("The hearts and minds").
10. Quoted in ibid., 58.
11. Maxwell, *Lincoln's Fifth Wheel*, 10.
12. Censer, ed., *Papers of Frederick Law Olmsted*, 256.
13. Nevins and Thomas, eds., *Diary of George Templeton Strong*, 291.
14. J. H. Brinton, *Personal Memoirs of John H. Brinton, Major and Surgeon U.S.V., 1861–1865* (New York: Neale, 1914), 68 ("not altogether a") and 61 ("violent remittent, intermittent").
15. Quoted in Stillé, *History of the United States Sanitary Commission*, 85.
16. Censer, ed., *Papers of Frederick Law Olmsted*, 125 ("I do not"), 125 ("They do nothing"), 130 ("We are in"), 126 ("dressed in a"), 133 ("that many officers"), 134 ("A vast improvement"), 134 ("we never shall"), 182 ("When a man"), and 185 ("It will unquestionably").
17. Nevins and Thomas, eds., *Diary of George Templeton Strong*, 180.
18. Censer, ed., *Papers of Frederick Law Olmsted*, 197 ("My general Report"), 195 ("So it will"), and 186 ("It is no longer").
19. S. Smith, editorial, "The Sanitary Commission," *American Medical Times* 3 (1861): 89.

CHAPTER FOUR
1. Quoted in A. H. Guernsey and H. W. Alden, eds., *Harper's Pictorial History of the Great Rebellion* (New York: Harper & Brothers, 1866), 86.
2. Quoted in E. Warren, *A Doctor's Experiences in Three Continents* (Baltimore: Cushings & Bailey, 1885), 250.
3. *The Medical and Surgical History of the War of the Rebellion* (Washington, DC: Government Printing Office, 1870–1888), vol. 2, pt. 1 (Case—Private Sumner H. Needham), 58.
4. S. D. Gross, *Autobiography of Samuel D. Gross, M.D.* (Philadelphia: George Barrie, 1887), vol. 2, 163.
5. Quoted in B. F. Blustein, *Preserve Your Love for Science: Life of William A. Hammond, American Neurologist* (New York: Cambridge University Press, 1991), 24 ("in a minute") and 25 ("mental emotions and").
6. Quoted in W. Rybczynski, *A Clearing in the Distance: Frederick Law Olmsted and America in the Nineteenth Century* (New York: Scribner, 1999), 204.
7. *The War of the Rebellion: A Compilation of the Official Records of the Union and Confederate Armies* (Washington, DC: Government Printing Office, 1880–1901), ser. 3, vol. 1, 633.

8. A. Nevins and M. H. Thomas, eds., *The Diary of George Templeton Strong*, vol. 3, *The Civil War 1860–1865* (New York: Macmillan, 1952), 181.

9. Quoted in W. Y Thompson, "The U.S. Sanitary Commission," *Civil War History* 2 (1956): 49.

10. *Revised Regulations for the Army of the United States, 1861* (Philadelphia: J.G.L. Brown, 1861), 164.

11. Quoted in J. T. Censer, ed., *The Papers of Frederick Law Olmsted*, vol. 4, *Defending the Union* (Baltimore: Johns Hopkins University Press, 1986), 150.

12. Quoted in *The Encyclopaedia Britannica* (New York: Encyclopaedia Britannica Inc., 1926), vol. 5, 109.

13. Censer, ed., *Papers of Frederick Law Olmsted*, 202 ("I am not") and 433 ("the present want").

14. Ibid., 312.

15. C. J. Stillé, *History of the United States Sanitary Commission* (Philadelphia: J. B. Lippincott, 1866), 129.

16. Censer, ed., *Papers of Frederick Law Olmsted*, 203 ("convictions sometimes boil") and 213 ("appeared older, more").

17. Quoted in Nevins and Thomas, eds., *Diary of George Templeton Strong*, 188.

18. *New York Times*, November 25, 1861 ("has had a," "loss of life," and "The Sanitary Commission"), December 4 ("have no more"), December 6 ("Surgeon General Finley"), and December 14 ("easily learn that").

19. Quoted in G. W. Adams, *Doctors in Blue* (New York: Henry Schuman, 1952), 29.

20. Censer, ed., *Papers of Frederick Law Olmsted*, 242.

21. Ibid., 244 ("Miss Powell is") and 245 ("I hear that").

22. Ibid., 246.

23. Quoted in W. Q. Maxwell, *Lincoln's Fifth Wheel: The Political History of the United States Sanitary Commission* (New York: Longmans, Green & Co., 1956), 115.

24. Editorial, "The Sanitary Commission—Cui Bono?" *Medical and Surgical Reporter* 7 (1862): 401.

25. Censer, ed., *Papers of Frederick Law Olmsted*, 250.

26. *The Congressional Globe: The Official Proceedings of Congress* (Washington, DC: John C. Rives, 1862), 987.

27. Ibid., 988 ("they would rather") and 996 ("To carry out").

28. Quoted in Censer, ed., *Papers of Frederick Law Olmsted*, 255.

29. *Congressional Globe*, 986 ("I see no"), 987 ("I do not want"), 995 ("I say if you"), and 987 ("There are brigades").

30. Editorial, *Boston Medical and Surgical Journal* 66 (1862): 33.

31. S. Smith, editorial, "Homoeopathy in Military Hospitals," *American Medical Times* 4 (1862): 42.

32. *Congressional Globe*, 997 ("I believe the"), 997 ("They have different"), 996 ("organize a corps"), 996 ("introduce clairvoyancers, spiritual"), and 997 ("I take it").

33. Quoted in Maxwell, *Lincoln's Fifth Wheel*, 126.

34. Quoted in J. E. Pilcher, "Brevet Brigadier General Clement Alexander Finley, Surgeon General of the United States Army, 1861–1862," *Military Surgery* 15 (1904): 64.

35. *Congressional Globe*, 1585 ("I am informed"), 1271 ("We know that"), 1270 ("instead of supplying"), 1273 ("This bill will"), 1587 ("We need medical"), and 1588 ("Our hospitals are").
36. Censer, ed., *Papers of Frederick Law Olmsted*, 310.
37. C. J. Stillé, *History of the United States Sanitary Commission* (Philadelphia: J. B. Lippincott, 1866), 133 ("the best man") and 131 ("He is our man").
38. C. Sandburg, *Abraham Lincoln: The War Years* (New York: Harcourt, Brace & Co., 1939), vol. 3, 434.
39. S. Smith, editorial, *American Medical Times* 4 (1862): 239.

CHAPTER FIVE

1. J. T. Censer, ed., *The Papers of Frederick Law Olmsted*, vol. 4, *Defending the Union* (Baltimore: Johns Hopkins University Press, 1986), 351.
2. J. S. C. Abbott, *The History of the Civil War in America* (New York: Ledyard Bill, 1865), vol. 2, 46.
3. G. B. Wilson, "Letter from Surg. Geo. B. Willson—March from Hampton to the Camp Before Yorktown," *Boston Medical and Surgical Journal* 66 (1862): 255.
4. C. J. Stillé, *History of the United States Sanitary Commission* (Philadelphia: J. B. Lippincott, 1866), 155.
5. Censer, ed., *Papers of Frederick Law Olmsted*, 320.
6. *The Medical and Surgical History of the War of the Rebellion* (Washington, DC: Government Printing Office, 1870–1888), appendix to vol. 1, pt. 1 (report of Charles S. Tripler), 58.
7. G. C. Gorham, *Life and Public Services of Edwin M. Stanton* (Boston: Houghton, Mifflin & Company, 1899), vol. 1, 247.
8. Quoted in W. Q. Maxwell, *Lincoln's Fifth Wheel: The Political History of the United States Sanitary Commission* (New York: Longmans, Green & Company, 1956), 142.
9. Quoted in M. C. Gillett, *The Army Medical Department, 1818–1865* (Washington, DC: Center of Military History; 1987), 177.
10. Censer, ed., *Papers of Frederick Law Olmsted*, 371 ("I am more"), 369 ("If these armies"), and 370 ("Let him issue").
11. Quoted in G. W. Adams, *Doctors in Blue* (New York: Henry Schuman, 1952), 32.
12. Censer, ed., *Papers of Frederick Law Olmsted*, 387.
13. B. A. Clements, "Memoirs of Jonathan Letterman," *Journal of the Military Service Institution of the United States* 4 (1883): 253.
14. J. Letterman, *Medical Recollections of the Army of the Potomac* (New York: D. Appleton & Company, 1866), 7.
15. F. H. Hamilton, *A Treatise on Military Surgery and Hygiene* (New York: Baillière Brothers, 1865), 80.
16. *Medical and Surgical History*, vol. 1, pt. 2 (report of George W. Martin), 73.
17. *The War of the Rebellion: A Compilation of the Official Records of the Union and Confederate Armies* (Washington, DC: Government Printing Office, 1880–1901), ser. 1, vol. 5 (report of George B. McClellan), 26.
18. Hamilton, *Treatise on Military Surgery*, 273.
19. F. H. Hamilton, "Battle of Fair Oaks," *American Medical Times* 5 (1862): 117.

20. *Medical and Surgical History*, appendix to vol. 1, pt. 1 (report of Frank H. Hamilton), 87.

21. Hamilton, "Battle of Fair Oaks," 118.

22. Censer, ed., *Papers of Frederick Law Olmsted*, 359 ("breed a pestilence"), 368 ("The horror of"), 368 ("terrible week's work"), 363 ("At the time"), and 368 ("If we had not").

23. A. H. Guernsey and H. W. Alden, eds., *Harper's Pictorial History of the Great Rebellion* (New York: Harper & Brothers, 1866), 356.

24. *War of the Rebellion*, ser. 1, vol. XI, pt. 1 (report of George B. McClellan), 51.

25. Quoted in T. H. Williams, *Lincoln and His Generals* (New York: Alfred A. Knopf, 1952), 177.

26. Censer, ed., *Papers of Frederick Law Olmsted*, 381.

27. Quoted in the Citizens' Association, *A Typical American; or, Incidents in the Life of Dr. John Swinburne of Albany, the Eminent Patriot, Surgeon, and Philanthropist* (Albany, NY: The Citizen Office, 1888), 29.

28. C. C. Buel and R. U. Johnson, eds., *Battles and Leaders of the Civil War*, vol. 2, *North to Antietam* (New York: A. S. Barnes, 1888), 426.

29. Censer, ed., *Papers of Frederick Law Olmsted*, 386.

30. *Medical and Surgical History*, appendix to vol. 1, pt. 1 (report of Jonathan Letterman), 93.

31. Censer, ed., *The Papers of Frederick Law Olmsted*, 404.

32. *Medical and Surgical History* (Jonathan Letterman), 95.

33. *War of the Rebellion*, ser. 1, vol. XI, pt. 3 (report of Erasmus Keyes), 313 ("melt away") and 383 ("not more than").

34. *Medical and Surgical History* (Jonathan Letterman), 95.

35. Letterman, *Medical Recollections*, 25 ("observing that the"), 23 ("The system was"), and 30 ("Much labor was").

36. Abbott, *History of the Civil War*, vol. 2, III.

37. *War of the Rebellion*, ser. 1, vol. XI, pt. 1 (report of Henry Halleck), 83.

38. Guernsey and Alden, eds., *Harper's Pictorial History*, p. 380.

CHAPTER SIX

1. B. Rush, *Medical Inquiries and Observations* (4 volumes in 2) (Philadelphia: E. Kimber & S. W. Conrad, 1815), vol. 1, 150.

2. Quoted in B. E. Blustein, *Preserve Your Love for Science: Life of William A. Hammond, American Neurologist* (New York: Cambridge University Press, 1991), 56.

3. Quoted in ibid., 65.

4. W. A. Hammond, *A Treatise on Hygiene with Special Reference to the Military Service* (Philadelphia: J. B. Lippincott, 1863), 364 ("proven to be"), 371 ("The West Philadelphia Hospital"), 370 ("the largest in"), 371 ("The discipline has"), 392 ("In the Judiciary Square"), and 371 ("The West Philadelphia Hospital").

5. Quoted in J. T. Censer, ed., *The Papers of Frederick Law Olmsted*, vol. 4, *Defending the Union* (Baltimore: Johns Hopkins University Press, 1986), 412 ("I grew daily") and 413 ("I have been").

6. C. J. Stillé, *History of the United States Sanitary Commission* (Philadelphia: J. B. Lippincott, 1866), 444.

7. *The Medical and Surgical History of the War of the Rebellion* (Washington, DC: Government Printing Office, 1870–1888), vol. 1, pt. 3, 945.

8. Quoted in K. P. Wormeley, *The United States Sanitary Commission: A Sketch of Its Purposes and Its Work* (Boston: Little, Brown, 1863), 95.

9. Censer, ed., *Papers of Frederick Law Olmsted*, 422.

10. F. H. Hamilton, *A Treatise on Military Surgery and Hygiene* (New York: Baillière Brothers, 1865), 123.

11. Ibid., 135.

12. *Medical and Surgical History*, vol. 2, pt. 2 (Case 1506—Private G. H. Fiske), 535.

13. Quoted in G. Barton, *Angels of the Battlefield* (Philadelphia: Catholic Art Publishing, 1897), 7 ("I am now") and 107 ("they could scarcely").

14. Quoted in Blustein, *Preserve Your Love for Science*, 67.

15. Barton, *Angels of the Battlefield*, 114.

16. Correspondence, "Duties of the Army Surgeon—Females Not Suitable for Nurses," *American Medical Times* 3 (1861): 30.

17. J. H. Brinton, *Personal Memoirs of John H. Brinton, Major and Surgeon U.S.V., 1861–1865* (New York: Neale Publishing, 1914), 44.

18. J. R. Brumgardt, *Civil War Nurse: The Diary and Letters of Hannah Ropes* (Knoxville: University of Tennessee Press, 1980), 113.

19. M. A. Livermore, *My Story of the War: A Woman's Narrative of Four Years of Personal Experience* (Hartford, CT: A. D. Worthington, 1887), 243.

20. F. Nightingale, *Notes on Nursing: What It Is, and What It Is Not* (New York: D. Appleton & Co., 1860), 3.

21. A. Nevins and M. H. Thomas, eds., *The Diary of George Templeton Strong*, vol. 3, *The Civil War, 1860–1865* (New York: Macmillan, 1952), 182.

22. Censer, ed., *Papers of Frederick Law Olmsted*, 202.

23. *The War of the Rebellion: A Compilation of the Official Records of the Union and Confederate Armies* (Washington, DC: Government Printing Office, 1880–1901), ser. 1, vol. 5, 103.

24. Quoted in T. J. Brown, *Dorothea Dix: New England Reformer* (Cambridge, MA: Harvard University Press, 1998), 301.

25. S. Smith, editorial, "Female Nurses in Hospitals," *American Medical Times* 5 (1862): 149.

26. Quoted in Brown, *Dorothea Dix*, 308.

27. Quoted in L. P. Brockett and M. C. Vaughan, eds., *Woman's Work in the Civil War: A Record of Heroism, Patriotism and Patience* (Philadelphia: Zeigler, McCurdy & Company, 1867), 103.

28. Quoted in Blustein, *Preserve Your Love for Science*, 68.

29. H. S. Jaquette, ed., *South After Gettysburg: Letters of Cornelia Hancock, 1863–1868* (New York: Thomas T. Crowell, 1937), 66.

30. M. A. Newcomb, *Four Years of Personal Reminiscences of the War* (Chicago: H. S. Mills, 1893), 34.

31. Brumgardt, *Civil War Nurse*, 87.

32. Censer, ed., *Papers of Frederick Law Olmsted*, 202.

33. Brockett and Vaughan, eds., *Woman's Work in the Civil War*, 101.
34. Censer, ed., *Papers of Frederick Law Olmsted*, 640.
35. Brumgardt, *Civil War Nurse*, 55 ("The fact is"), 58 ("I have learned"), 58 ("all these shirts"), 61 ("It is no place"), 115 ("We get lousy"), 73 ("I am strong"), 74 ("to make all"), 73 ("ignorant of hospital"), 51 ("at the door"), 83 ("To help the"), 83 ("Two rebuffs seemed"), 85 ("Go to the"), and 87 ("Today the whole").
36. Quoted in A. H. Guernsey and H. W. Alden, eds., *Harper's Pictorial History of the Great Rebellion* (New York: Harper & Brothers, 1866), 390.

CHAPTER SEVEN

1. H. I. Bowditch, *A Brief Plea for an Ambulance System for the Army of the United States* (Boston: Ticknor & Fields, 1863), 6 ("Resting"), 14 ("any one man"), and 15 ("If any government").
2. *The War of the Rebellion: A Compilation of the Official Records of the Union and Confederate Armies* (Washington, DC: Government Printing Office, 1880–1901), ser. 3, vol. 2 (letter of W. A. Hammond), 525.
3. W. W. Keen, *Addresses and Other Papers* (Philadelphia: W. B. Saunders & Co., 1905), 426.
4. K. P. Wormeley, *The United States Sanitary Commission: A Sketch of Its Purposes and Its Work* (Boston: Little, Brown, 1863), 97.
5. Quoted in S. L. Abbot, "Army Ambulances," *Boston Medical and Surgical Journal* 67 (1862): 165 ("The drivers were"), 166 ("sulked or swore"), and ("I want now").
6. "Dr. Gay's Report to Surgeon-General Dale," *Boston Medical and Surgical Journal* 67 (1862): 284.
7. *The Medical and Surgical History of the War of the Rebellion* (Washington, DC: Government Printing Office, 1870–1888), vol. 2, pt. 3, 933.
8. J. T. Censer, ed., *The Papers of Frederick Law Olmsted*, vol. 4, *Defending the Union* (Baltimore: Johns Hopkins University Press, 1986), 399.
9. Quoted in B. P. Thomas and H. M. Hyman, *Stanton: The Life and Times of Lincoln's Secretary of War* (New York: Alfred A. Knopf, 1962), 209 ("the most unmitigated") and 225 ("a matter of").
10. *Medical and Surgical History*, 933 ("views adverse") and 934 ("It is proper").
11. Quoted in W. Q. Maxwell, *Lincoln's Fifth Wheel: The Political History of the United States Sanitary Commission* (New York: Longmans, Green & Co., 1956), 177.
12. Censer, ed., *Papers of Frederick Law Olmsted*, 420.
13. Editorial, "The Ambulance System," *Medical and Surgical Reporter* 9 (1862): 43.
14. S. Smith, editorial, "The Wounded and the Ambulances of Our Army," *American Medical Times* 5 (1862): 247.
15. Bowditch, *Brief Plea for an Ambulance System*, 28.
16. Quoted in G. W. Adams, *Doctors in Blue* (New York: Henry Schuman, 1952), 62.
17. *Medical and Surgical History*, appendix to vol. 1, pt. 1 (report of G. G. Shumard), 252 ("It is proper") and 253 ("But for the").

18. B. A. Clements, "Memoirs of Jonathan Letterman," *Journal of the Military Service Institution of the United States* 4 (1883): 276.
19. *War of the Rebellion*, ser. 1, vol. 19 (letter of George B. McClellan), 330.
20. *Medical and Surgical History*, appendix to vol. 1, pt. 1 (report of Jonathan Letterman), 98.
21. T. T. Ellis, *Leaves from the Diary of an Army Surgeon; or, Incidents of the Field Camp, and Hospital Life* (New York: John Bradburn, 1863), 300.
22. *Medical and Surgical History* (Jonathan Letterman), 96 ("A great deal") and 99 ("large amounts").
23. Quoted in L. C. Duncan, *The Medical Department of the United States Army in the Civil War* (Washington, DC, n.p., 1912–1914; reprinted by Olde Soldier Books, Inc.. Gaithersburg, MD, n.d). 146.
24. Quoted in Maxwell, *Lincoln's Fifth Wheel*, 173.
25. Censer, ed., *Papers of Frederick Law Olmsted*, 422.
26. C. J. Stillé, *History of the United States Sanitary Commission* (Philadelphia: J. B. Lippincott, 1866), 266.
27. Censer, ed., *Papers of Frederick Law Olmsted*, 423.
28. J. Letterman, *Medical Recollections of the Army of the Potomac* (New York: D. Appleton, 1866), 56 ("Before the adoption") and 60 ("of every case").
29. J. H. Brinton, *Personal Memoirs of John H. Brinton, Major and Surgeon U.S.V., 1861–1865* (New York: Neale Publishing, 1914), 91.
30. *Medical and Surgical History* (Jonathan Letterman), 100.
31. C. C. Buel and R. U. Johnson, eds., *Battles and Leaders of the Civil War*, vol. 3, *Retreat from Gettysburg* (New York: A. S. Barnes, 1888), 79.
32. Quoted in *Medical and Surgical History* (Jonathan Letterman), 100.
33. Ibid., 101.
34. *War of the Rebellion*, ser. 1, vol. 21 (report of J. H. Hobart Ward), 368.
35. Ibid. (report of John C. Caldwell), 233.
36. Buel and Johnson, eds., *Battles and Leaders*, 113.
37. Quoted in Duncan, *Medical Department of the United States Army*, 191.
38. *Medical and Surgical History* (Jonathan Letterman), 102.
39. G. T. Stevens, *Three Years in the Sixth Corps* (Albany, NY: S. R. Gray, 1866), 172.
40. *War of the Rebellion*, ser. 1, vol. 21 (report of Daniel E. Sickles), 381.
41. *Medical and Surgical History* (Jonathan Letterman), 102.
42. Buel and Johnson, eds., *Battles and Leaders*, 138.
43. Quoted in G. W. Jones, "The Medical History of the Fredericksburg Campaign: Course and Significance," *Journal of the History of Medicine and the Allied Sciences* 18 (1963): 252.
44. *Medical and Surgical History* (Jonathan Letterman), 103.
45. Quoted in P. Mathless, *Voices of the Civil War, Fredericksburg* (New York: Time-Life Books, 1997), 146.
46. *Medical and Surgical History* (Jonathan Letterman), 104.
47. Quoted in B. I. Wiley, *The Life of Billy Yank, the Common Soldier of the Union* (Indianapolis, IN: Bobbs-Merrill, 1951), 83.
48. S. D. Gross, *A System of Surgery: Pathological, Diagnostic, Therapeutic, and Operative* (Philadelphia: Blanchard & Lea, 1859), vol. 1, 165.

49. *Medical and Surgical History*, appendix to vol. 1, pt. 1 (report of Charles C. Lee), 130.

50. S. Smith, *Hand-book of Surgical Operations* (New York: Baillière Brothers, 1862), 260.

51. W. Davis, *Camp-fire Chats of the Civil War* (Chicago: A. B. Gehman, 1886), 197.

52. P. Fatout, *Letters of a Civil War Surgeon* (West Lafayette, IN: Purdue University Press, 1996), 63.

53. Brinton, *Personal Memoirs of John H. Brinton*, 222.

54. Letterman, *Medical Recollections*, 90.

55. Stillé, *History of the United States Sanitary Commission*, 371.

56. *War of the Rebellion*, ser. 1, vol. 21 (letter of Thomas F. Perley), 958 ("I do not believe") and 959 ("the principal medical").

57. J. S. Woolsey, *Hospital Days* (New York: Van Nostrand, 1870), 158.

58. *Medical and Surgical History*, appendix to vol. 1, pt. 1 (report of De Witt C. Peters), 133.

59. *War of the Rebellion* (Thomas F. Perley), 958.

60. *Medical and Surgical History* (Jonathan Letterman), 104.

61. J. R. Brumgardt, *Civil War Nurse: The Diary and Letters of Hannah Ropes* (Knoxville: University of Tennessee Press, 1980), 114 ("Today we are"), 107 ("terribly sick house"), 114 ("I dare say"), 117 ("We are not going"), 115 ("I had a pleasant"), and 112 ("We are cheered").

62. Louisa May Alcott, *Hospital Sketches* (Boston: J. Redpath, 1863), 26 ("My experiences had begun"), 62 ("I tripped over"), 63 ("consisted of beef"), 65 ("order, method, common"), and 66 ("disorder, discomfort, bad").

63. Brumgardt, *Civil War Nurse*, 121.

64. Quoted in ibid., 40.

65. Quoted in B. Z. Jones, *Hospital Sketches by Louisa May Alcott* (Cambridge, MA: Belknap Press of Harvard University, 1960), xl.

66. *Hospital Sketches*, 77 ("Hours began to") and 78 ("At the sight").

67. Brumgardt, *Civil War Nurse*, 123 ("Mother has been") and 129 ("you would hear").

68. C. Glicksberg, *Walt Whitman and the Civil War* (Philadelphia: University of Pennsylvania Press, 1933), 70 ("One of the first") and 74 ("It is the corpse").

69. W. Lowenfels, *Walt Whitman's Civil War* (New York: Alfred A. Knopf, 1960), 88 ("such as hogs"), 89 ("long train of"), 91 ("In general, the"), 92 ("a regular self-appointed"), 92 ("There are tyrants"), 106 ("I am compelled"), 106 ("Mothers full of"), 91 ("careless, rude, capricious"), 87 ("It was a strange"), 97 ("more impudence and"), 87 ("very good"), 87 ("the best"), 97 ("some of the women"), 98 ("known to fight"), 138 ("I go every day"), 138 ("You can have"), 44 ("Surgeons operating, attendants"), 86 ("The government"), and 97 ("that the earnest").

70. *Medical and Surgical History*, vol. 2, pt. 3, 829.

71. Keen, *Addresses and Other Papers*, 431.

72. *Medical and Surgical History*, vol. 2, pt. 3 (Case 659—Private J. C. Coats), 429.

73. Ibid. (Case 1106—Corporal J. Quick), 767.

74. Ibid. (Case 176—Private J. W. Connor), 83.

75. Keen, *Addresses and Other Papers*, 433.

76. *Medical and Surgical History* (Jonathan Letterman), 99.

CHAPTER EIGHT

1. Quoted in B. E. Blustein, *Preserve Your Love for Science: Life of William A. Hammond, American Neurologist* (New York: Cambridge University Press, 1991), 71.
2. C. J. Stillé, *History of the United States Sanitary Commission* (Philadelphia: J. B. Lippincott, 1866), 110.
3. Quoted in B. I. Wiley, *The Life of Billy Yank, the Common Soldier of the Union* (Indianapolis, IN: Bobbs-Merrill, 1952), 130.
4. S. Smith, editorial, "A Remedy for an Evil," *American Medical Times* 4 (1862): 336.
5. E. W. Locke, *Three Years in Camp and Hospital* (Boston: Geo. D. Russell, 1870), 73.
6. J. M. Greiner, J. L. Coryell, and J. R. Smither, eds., *A Surgeon's Civil War: The Letters and Diary of Daniel M. Holt, M.D.* (Kent, OH: Kent State University Press, 1994), 30.
7. Stillé, *History of the United States Sanitary Commission*, 116.
8. Editorial, *North American Journal of Homeopathy* II (1862): 168.
9. Quoted in Blustein, *Preserve Your Love for Science*, 81.
10. J. H. Brinton, *Personal Memoirs of John H. Brinton, Major and Surgeon U.S.V., 1861–1865* (New York: Neale, 1914), 181.
11. J. H. Brinton, "Closing Exercises of the Session 1895–96, Army Medical School," *Journal of the American Medical Association* 26 (1896): 601.
12. *The War of the Rebellion: A Compilation of the Official Records of the Union and Confederate Armies* (Washington, DC: Government Printing Office, 1880–1901), ser. 3, vol. 2, 752.
13. S. Smith, editorial, "A Military Medical School," *American Medical Times* 5 (1862): 10.
14. Brinton, *Personal Memoirs of John H. Brinton*, 258 ("I had fitted"), 174 ("the dreadful"), and 259 ("They will go").
15. S. Smith, editorial, "Medical and Surgical History of the Rebellion," *American Medical Times* 4 (1862): 359.
16. W. A. Hammond, *A Treatise on Hygiene with Special Reference to the Military Service* (Philadelphia: J. B. Lippincott, 1863), vii.
17. Book review, "W. A. Hammond's *A Treatise on Hygiene, with Special Reference to the Military Service*," *American Journal of the Medical Sciences* 46 (1863): 432.
18. T. T. Ellis, *Leaves from the Diary of an Army Surgeon; or, Incidents of Field Camp, and Hospital Life* (New York: John Bradburn, 1863), 300.
19. Quoted in W. Lowenfels, *Walt Whitman's Civil War* (New York: Alfred A. Knopf, 1960), 107.
20. B. F. Palmer, *The Palmer Arm and Leg: Correspondence with the Surgeon-General, U.S.A., and the Chief of Bureau of Medicine and Surgery, U.S.N., with Letters of Eminent Surgeons and a Communication from B. Frank Palmer to the Board of Surgeons, Convened to Decide on the Best Patent Artificial Limbs to Be Adopted for Use by the Army and Navy of the United States* (Philadelphia: C. Sherman & Son, 1862), 9.

21. S. Smith, "Analysis of Four Hundred and Thirty-nine Recorded Amputations in the Contiguity of the Lower Extremity," in F. H. Hamilton, ed., *Surgical Memoirs of the War of the Rebellion, Collected and Published by the United States Sanitary Commission* (New York: Hurd & Houghton, 1871), vol. 2, 9.

22. P. S. Wales, *Mechanical Therapeutics: A Practical Treatise on Surgical Apparatus, Appliances, and Elementary Operations* (Philadelphia: Henry C. Lea, 1867), 249.

23. C. A. Lee, "Report of the Committee on Medical Literature," *Transactions of the American Medical Association*, 14 (1863): 98.

24. Quoted in M. Fishbein, *A History of the American Medical Association, 1847–1947* (Philadelphia, W. B. Saunders, 1947), 67.

25. V. Y. Bowditch, *Life and Correspondence of Henry Ingersoll Bowditch* (Boston: Houghton, Mifflin & Company, 1902), vol. 2, 11.

26. Editorial, "Need of an Ambulance System," *Boston Medical and Surgical Journal* 69 (1863): 244.

27. Bowditch, *Life and Correspondence of Henry Ingersoll Bowditch*, 17.

28. J. H. Baxter, *Statistics, Medical and Anthropological, of the Provost-Marshal-General's Bureau* (Washington, DC: Government Printing Office, 1875), vol. 1, 323 ("I have examined"), 261 ("In my opinion"), 217 ("Our professional decisions"), 239 ("surgeons of the enrollment"), 459 ("The boards of inspection"), 343 ("I decided to accept"), 161 ("busiest or most eminent"), 281 ("Too many incompetent"), and 189 ("Under the most favorable").

29. P. Josyph, ed., *The Wounded River: The Civil War Letters of John Vance Lauderdale, M.D.* (East Lansing: Michigan State University Press, 1993), 163.

30. F. H. Hamilton, "Hygiene," *New York Journal of Medicine* 7 (1859): 61.

31. S. Smith, editorial, "The Physician as Citizen," *American Medical Times*, 3 (1861): 8.

32. S. Smith, *The City That Was* (New York: Frank Allaben, 1911), 36.

33. S. Smith, editorial, "Health Laws," *American Medical Times* 1 (1860), 64.

34. S. Smith, editorial, "Sanitary Inspection in the Army," *American Medical Times* 5 (1862): 94.

35. S. Smith, *Doctor in Medicine: And Other Papers on Professional Subjects* (New York: William Wood, 1872), 192.

36. Smith, *The City That Was*, 81 ("In certain populous"), 144 ("New York City is"), and 158 ("declared, officially and").

37. Stillé, *History of the Sanitary Commission*, 247.

38. Quoted in G. M. Fredrickson, *The Inner Civil War: Northern Intellectuals and the Crisis of the Union* (New York: Harper & Row, 1965), III.

39. J. Letterman, *Medical Recollections of the Army of the Potomac* (New York: D. Appleton, 1866), 155.

40. Quoted in Stillé, *History of the Sanitary Commission*, 377 ("Thank God, here") and 381 ("It was a grand").

41. Quoted in J. T. Censer, ed., *The Papers of Frederick Law Olmsted*, vol. 4, *Defending the Union* (Baltimore: Johns Hopkins University Press, 1986), 655.

42. M. A. Livermore, *My Story of the War: A Woman's Narrative of Four Years Personal Experience as a Nurse in the Union Army* (Hartford, CT: A. D. Worthington, 1887), 418 ("banners flying, drums"), 420 ("John Brown's body"), and 427 ("transferred for the nonce").

43. Censer, ed., *Papers of Frederick Law Olmsted*, 668 ("I think that"), 663 ("I believe the Commission"), 646 ("Our men never"), and 647 ("Its moral effect").

44. A. Nevins and M. H. Thomas, eds., *The Diary of George Templeton Strong*, vol. 3, *The Civil War, 1860–1865* (New York: Macmillan, 1952), 350.

CHAPTER NINE

1. Quoted in J. T. Censer, ed., *The Papers of Frederick Law Olmsted*, vol. 4, *Defending the Union* (Baltimore: Johns Hopkins University Press, 1986), 502.

2. Quoted in W. Q. Maxwell, *Lincoln's Fifth Wheel: The Political History of the United States Sanitary Commission* (New York: Longmans, Green & Co., 1956), 237.

3. L. C. Duncan, "The Days Gone By—The Strange Case of Surgeon General Hammond," *Military Surgeon*, 64 (1929): 103.

4. A. Nevins and M. H. Thomas, eds., *The Diary of George Templeton Strong*, vol. 3, *The Civil War 1860–1865* (New York: Macmillan, 1952), 314.

5. W. A. Hammond, *A Treatise on Hygiene with Special Reference to the Military Service* (Philadelphia: J. B. Lippincott, 1863), vii.

6. J. King, editorial, "Calomel with the Regulars," *Eclectic Medical Journal* 22 (1863): 434.

7. S. Smith, editorial, "Calomel and Tartar Emetic in the Army," *American Medical Times* 6 (1863): 297.

8. Quoted in *The Medical and Surgical History of the War of the Rebellion* (Washington, DC: Government Printing Office, 1870–1888), vol. 1, pt. 2, 720.

9. Anon., editorial, "The Surgeon-General in a New Order," *Lancet* (Cincinnati) 6 (1863): 557 ("Dr. Hammond has") and 559 ("official organ").

10. Editorial, "A Friendly Greeting to Our Readers," *Cincinnati Medical Observer*, 2 (1857), 34.

11. S. D. Gross, *Autobiography of Samuel D. Gross, M.D.* (Philadelphia: George Barrie, 1887), vol. 1, 55.

12. Quoted in S. Smith, editorial, "Progress of the Medical Bureau," *American Medical Times* 7 (1863): 138.

13. Nevins and Thomas, eds., *Diary of George Templeton Strong*, 353.

14. Quoted in S. Smith, editorial, "The Surgeon-General and the Profession," *American Medical Times* 8 (1864): 117.

15. Duncan, "The Days Gone By," 109.

16. C. J. Stillé, *History of the United States Sanitary Commission* (Philadelphia: J. B. Lippincott, 1866), 136.

17. S. Smith, editorial, "Position of the Surgeon-General," *American Medical Times* 8 (1864): 9.

18. Nevins and Thomas, eds., *Diary of George Templeton Strong*, 394.

19. Duncan, "The Days Gone By," 252.

20. Nevins and Thomas, eds., *Diary of George Templeton Strong*, 489.

21. J. H. Brinton, *Personal Memoirs of John H. Brinton, Major and Surgeon U.S.V., 1861–1865* (New York: Neale, 1914), 342.

22. Stillé, *History of the United States Sanitary Commission*, 136.

23. Quoted in Maxwell, *Lincoln's Fifth Wheel*, 244.

24. Duncan, "The Days Gone By," 257.

25. S. Smith, editorial, "Case of Surgeon General Hammond," *American Medical Times* 9 (1864): 118.

26. *New York Times*, August 22, 1864.

27. Anon., "Statement of the Late Surgeon-General of the United States," *Boston Medical and Surgical Journal* 71 (1864): 360.

28. Stillé, *History of the United States Sanitary Commission*, 137.

29. *The Congressional Globe: The Official Proceedings of Congress* (Washington, DC: John C. Rives, 1862), 466.

30. *Medical and Surgical History*, vol. 1, pt. 3, 943.

31. *The War of the Rebellion: A Compilation of the Official Records of the Union and Confederate Armies* (Washington, DC: Government Printing Office, 1880–1901), ser. 3, vol. 3 (report of E. D. Townsend), 944.

32. Quoted in G. W. Adams, *Doctors in Blue* (New York: Henry Schuman, 1952), 180.

33. F. Tiffany, *Life of Dorothea Lynde Dix* (Boston: Houghton Mifflin, 1890), 339.

34. Brinton, *Personal Memoirs of John H. Brinton*, 308.

35. Quoted in Maxwell, *Lincoln's Fifth Wheel*, 311.

36. *Medical and Surgical History*, appendix to vol. 1, pt. 1 (report of Thomas A. McParlin), 151.

37. Quoted in ibid., 153.

38. J. S. C. Abbott, *The History of the Civil War in America* (New York: Ledyard Bill, 1865), vol. 2, 494.

39. Anon., "Scenes at Fredericksburg," *Harper's Weekly*, June 11, 1864, 379.

40. *Medical and Surgical History* (Thomas A. McParlin), 157.

41. Anon., "Scenes at Fredericksburg," 379.

42. Quoted in A. H. Guernsey and H. W. Alden, eds., *Harper's Pictorial History of the Great Rebellion* (New York: Harper & Brothers, 1866), 630.

43. *Medical and Surgical History* (Thomas A. McParlin), 161.

44. Ibid., 167.

45. Anon., "Scenes at Fredericksburg," 379.

46. *Medical and Surgical History*, appendix to vol. 1, pt. 1 (report of George E. Cooper), 301.

47. Ibid. (Thomas A. McParlin), 166.

48. Anon., *Memorial of Edward B. Dalton, M.D.* (New York: n.p., 1872), 37.

49. *War of the Rebellion*, ser. 1, vol. 47, pt. 1 (report of W. T. Sherman), 191.

50. *Medical and Surgical History* (Thomas A. McParlin), 206.

51. Ibid., vol. 2, pt. 1, xxxi.

52. S. W. Mitchell, "Some Personal Recollections of the Civil War," *Transactions of the Studies of the College of Physicians of Philadelphia* 27 (1905): 93.

53. *Medical and Surgical History*, vol. 2, pt. 1, xxix.

BIBLIOGRAPHY

BOOKS

Abbott, John S. *The History of the Civil War in America.* 2 vols. New York: Ledyard Bill, 1863 and 1865.

Adams, George. *Doctors in Blue: The Medical History of the Union Army in the Civil War.* New York: Henry Schuman, 1952.

Anderson, Edward C. *A Texas Surgeon.* Tuscaloosa, AL: Confederate Publishing, 1957.

Andrews, Edmund. *Complete Record of the Surgery of the Battles Fought Near Vicksburg, December 27, 28, 29, and 30, 1862.* Chicago: George H. Fergus, 1863.

Andrews, Edmund, and John M. Woodworth. *The Primary Surgery of General Sherman's Campaigns.* Chicago: George H. Fergus, 1866.

Ashburn, Percy. *A History of the Medical Department of the US. Army.* Boston: Houghton Mifflin, 1929.

Atkinson, William B. *The Physicians and Surgeons of the United States.* Philadelphia: Charles Robson, 1878.

Austin, J. *The Woolsey Sisters of New York.* Philadelphia: American Philosophical Society, 1917.

Baker, Nina Brown. *Cyclone in Calico: The Story of Mary Ann Bickerdyke.* Boston: Little, Brown, 1952.

Barnes, Joseph K., ed. *The Medical and Surgical History of the War of the Rebellion, 1861–1865.* 6 vols. Washington, DC: Government Printing Office, 1870–1888.

Bartholow, Roberts. *A Manual of Instructions for Enlisting and Discharging Soldiers, with Special Reference to the Medical Examination of Recruits, and the Detection of Disqualifying and Feigned Diseases.* Philadelphia: J. B. Lippincott, 1863.

Barton, George. *Angels of the Battlefield: A History of the Labors of the Catholic Sisterhoods in the Late Civil War.* Philadelphia: Catholic Art Publishing, 1897.

Baruch, Simon. *Reminiscences of a Confederate Surgeon.* New York: privately printed, 1915.

Baxter, J. H., ed. *Statistics, Medical and Anthropological, of the Provost-Marshal-General's Bureau.* 2 vols. Washington, DC: Government Printing Office, 1875.

Beers, Fannie A. *Memories: A Record of Personal Experience and Adventure During Four Years of War.* Philadelphia: J. B. Lippincott, 1889.

Beller, Susan P. *Medical Practices in the Civil War.* Cincinnati: Betterway Books, 1992.

Bengtson, Bradley P., and Julian E. Kuz. *Photographic Atlas of Civil War Injuries.* Grand Rapids, MI: Medical Staff Press, 1996.

Berlin, Jean V., ed., *A Confederate Nurse: The Diary of Ada W. Bacot, 1860–1863.* Columbia: University of South Carolina Press, 1994.

Bigelow, Henry J. *Surgical Anaesthesia, Addresses and Other Papers.* Boston: Little, Brown, 1900.

Billings, John D. *Hardtack and Coffee, or The Unwritten Story of Army Life.* Boston: George M. Smith, 1887.

Blanton, Wyndham B. *Medicine in Virginia in the Nineteenth Century.* Richmond, VA: Garrett & Massie, 1933.

Blustein, Bonnie E. *Preserve Your Love for Science: Life of William A. Hammond, American Neurologist.* New York: Cambridge University Press, 1991.

Bollet, Alfred J. *Civil War Medicine, Challenges and Triumphs.* Tucson, AZ: Galen, 2002.

Bowditch, Henry I. *A Brief Plea for an Ambulance System for the Army of the United States.* Boston: Ticknor & Fields, 1863.

Bowditch, Vincent Y., ed. *Life and Correspondence of Henry Ingersoll Bowditch.* 2 vols. Boston: Houghton Mifflin, 1902.

Boyden, Anna L. *Echoes from Hospital: A Record of Mrs. Rebecca R. Pomroy's Experience in War-Times.* Boston: D. Lothrop, 1884.

Breeden, James O. *Joseph Jones, M.D.: Scientist of the Old South.* Lexington: University Press of Kentucky, 1975.

Brieger, Gert H. *Medical America in the Nineteenth Century.* Baltimore: Johns Hopkins University Press, 1972.

Briggs, Walter D. *Charles Edward Briggs: Civil War Surgeon in a Colored Regiment.* Berkeley: University of California Press, 1960.

Brinton, John H. *Personal Memoirs of John H. Brinton, Major and Surgeon U.S.V., 1861–1865.* New York: Neale, 1914.

Brockett, Linus P. *The Camp, the Battlefield and the Hospital; or, Lights and Shadows of the Great Rebellion.* Philadelphia: National Publishing, 1866.

Brockett, Linus P., and Mary C. Vaughan. *Women's Work in the Civil War: A Record of Heroism, Patriotism, and Patience.* Philadelphia: Zeigler, McCurdy, 1867.

Brooks, Stewart M. *Civil War Medicine.* Springfield, IL: Charles C. Thomas, 1966.

Brown, Harvey E. *The Medical Department of the United States Army from 1775 to 1873.* Washington, DC: Surgeon General's Office, 1873.

Brown, Thomas J. *Dorothea Dix, New England Reformer.* Cambridge, MA: Harvard University Press, 1998.

Brumgardt, John R., ed. *Civil War Nurse: The Diary and Letters of Hannah Ropes.* Knoxville: University of Tennessee Press, 1980.

Bryant, William S., ed. *Henry Bryant, M.D., 1820–1867.* New York: privately printed, 1952.

Bucklin, Sophronia E. *In Hospital and Camp: A Woman's Record of Thrilling Incidents Among the Wounded in the Late War.* Philadelphia: John E. Potter, 1869.

Buel, C. C., and R. U. Johnson, eds. *Battles and Leaders of the Civil War.* Vol. 1, *From Sumter to Shiloh.* Vol. 2, *North to Antietam.* Vol. 3, *Retreat from Gettysburg.* Vol. 4, *The Way to Appomattox.* New York: A. S. Barnes, 1888.

Burbank, Morris J., ed. *To My Beloved Absent Companion: Letters of a Civil War Surgeon to His Wife at Home.* Cullman, AL: S. Morris, 1996.

Burr, Anna R. *Weir Mitchell: His Life and Letters.* New York: Duffield, 1929.

Catton, Bruce. *Mr. Lincoln's Army, Glory Road,* and *A Stillness at Appomattox.* Garden City, NY: Doubleday, 1951, 1952, and 1953.

Censer, Jane T., ed. *The Papers of Frederick Law Olmsted.* Vol. 4, *Defending the Union: The Civil War and the U.S. Sanitary Commission.* Baltimore: Johns Hopkins University Press, 1986.

Chase, Julia A. *Mary A. Bickerdyke, "Mother."* Lawrence, KS: Journal Publishing, 1896.

Chisolm, John J. *A Manual of Military Surgery, for the Use of Surgeons in the Confederate Army.* Richmond, VA: West & Johnston, 1861.

Citizens' Association. *A Typical American; or, Incidents in the Life of Dr. John Swinburne of Albany, the Eminent Patriot, Surgeon, and Philanthropist.* Albany, NY: Citizen Office, 1888.

Clarke, Edward H. *A Century of American Medicine, 1776–1876.* Philadelphia: Henry C. Lea, 1876.

Cleave, E. *Biographical Cyclopedia of Homoeopathic Physicians and Surgeons.* Philadelphia: Galaxy, 1873.

Clements, Bennett A. *Memoir of Jonathan Letterman, M.D.* New York: G. P. Putnam's Sons, 1883.

Coco, Gregory A. *A Vast Sea of Misery: A History and Guide to the Union and Confederate Field Hospitals at Gettysburg, July 1–November 20, 1863.* Gettysburg, PA: Thomas Publications, 1988.

———. *A Strange and Blighted Land; Gettysburg: The Aftermath of a Battle.* Gettysburg, PA: Thomas Publications, 1995.

Cook, William H. *A Treatise on the Principles and Practice of Physio-Medical Surgery.* Cincinnati: Moore, Wilstach & Keys, 1858.

Culpepper, Marilyn M. *Trials and Triumphs: Women of the American Civil War.* East Lansing: Michigan State University Press, 1991.

Cumming, Kate. *A Journal of Hospital Life in the Confederate Army of Tennessee.* New Orleans: John P. Morgan, 1866.

Cunningham, Horace H. *Doctors in Gray: The Confederate Medical Service.* Baton Rouge: Louisiana State University Press, 1958.

———. *Field Medical Services at the Battles of Manassas (Bull Run).* Athens: University of Georgia Press, 1968.

Dammann, Gordon. *Pictorial Encyclopedia of Civil War Medical Instruments and Equipment.* 3 vols. Missoula, MT: Pictorial Histories, 1983, 1988, and 1998.

Daniel, F. E. *Recollections of a Rebel Surgeon (and Other Sketches); or, In the Doctor's Sappy Days.* Austin, TX: Von Boeckmann, Schutze, 1899.

Dannett, Sylvia G., and Rosamond H. Burkart. *Confederate Surgeon, Aristides Monteiro*. New York: Dodd & Mead, 1969.

Davis, Nathan S. *History of Medical Education and Institutions in the United States*. Chicago: S. C. Griggs, 1851.

Davis, William C. *Battle at Bull Run*. Garden City, NY: Doubleday, 1977.

Dean, Eric T. *Shook over Hell: Post-Traumatic Stress, Vietnam, and the Civil War*. Cambridge, MA: Harvard University Press, 1997.

DeLeeuw, A. *Civil War Nurse, Ann Bickerdyke*. New York: Messner, 1973.

Denney, Robert E. *Civil War Medicine: Care & Comfort of the Wounded*. New York: Sterling, 1994.

Derbyshire, Robert C. *Medical Licensure and Discipline in the United States*. Baltimore: Johns Hopkins University Press, 1969.

Dixon, Edward H. *Scenes in the Practice of a New York Surgeon*. New York: De Witt & Davenport, 1855.

Douglas, J. H., and C. W. Brink. *Reports on the Operations of the Inspectors and Relief Agents of the Sanitary Commission After the Battle of Fredericksburg, December 13, 1862*. New York: W. C. Bryant, 1863.

Duffy, John. *The Healers: A History of American Medicine*. Urbana: University of Illinois Press, 1979.

Duncan, Louis. *The Medical Department of the United States Army in the Civil War*. Washington, DC: privately printed, 1912–1914; reprinted by Olde Soldier Books, Gaithersburg, MD, n.d.

Earnest, Ernest. *S. Weir Mitchell: Novelist and Physician*. Philadelphia: University of Pennsylvania Press, 1950.

Edmonds, S. Emma. *Nurse and Spy in the Union Army*. Hartford, CT: W. S. Williams, 1865.

Edmonson, James M. *American Surgical Instruments: An Illustrated History of Their Manufacture and a Directory of Instrument Makers to 1900*. San Francisco: Norman, 1997.

Ellis, Thomas T. *Leaves from the Diary of an Army Surgeon; or, Incidents of Field Camp, and Hospital Life*. New York: John Bradburn, 1863.

Epler, Percy H. *The Life of Clara Barton*. New York: Macmillan, 1926.

Evans, Bruce A. *A Primer of Civil War Medicine, Non Surgical Medical Practice During the Civil War Years*. Knoxville, TN: Bohemian Brigade Bookshop, 1998.

Fatout, Paul, ed. *Letters of a Civil War Surgeon*. West Lafayette, IN: Purdue University Press, 1991.

Fishbein, Morris. *A History of the American Medical Association, 1847 to 1947*. Philadelphia: W. B. Saunders, 1947.

Flexner, James T. *Doctors on Horseback: Pioneers of American Medicine*. New York: Viking, 1937.

Flint, Auston, ed. *Contributions Relating to the Causation and Prevention of Disease, and to Camp Diseases*. New York: Hurd & Houghton, 1867.

Foote, Shelby. *The Civil War: A Narrative*. Vol. 1, *Fort Sumter to Perryville*. Vol. 2, *Fredericksburg to Meridian*. Vol. 3, *Red River to Appomattox*. New York: Random House, 1958, 1963, and 1974.

Forbes, Hildegarde B., ed. *Correspondence of Dr. Charles H. Wheelwright, Surgeon of the United States Navy*. Boston: privately printed, 1958.

Forman, Jacob G. *The Western Sanitary Commission.* St. Louis: R. P. Studley, 1864.

Formento, F. *Notes and Observations on Army Surgery.* New Orleans: L. E. Marchand, 1863.

Fox, William. *Regimental Losses in the American Civil War, 1861–1865.* Albany, NY: Albany Publishing, 1889.

Francis, Samuel W. *Biographical Sketches of Distinguished Living New York Surgeons.* New York: John Bradburn, 1866.

Francis, Valentine M. *A Thesis on Hospital Hygiene.* New York: J. R. Trow, 1859.

Frederickson, George M. *The Inner Civil War: Northern Intellectuals and the Crisis of the Union.* New York: Harper & Row, 1968.

Freeman, Douglas S. *Lee's Lieutenants: A Study in Command.* Vol. 1, *Manassas to Malvern Hill.* Vol. 2, *Cedar Mountain to Chancellorsville.* Vol. 3, *Gettysburg to Appomattox.* New York: Charles Scribner's Sons, 1942, 1943, and 1944.

Freemon, Frank R. *Microbes and Minie Balls: An Annotated Bibliography of Civil War Medicine.* Madison, NJ: Fairleigh Dickinson University Press, 1993.

———. *Gangrene and Glory: Medical Care During the American Civil War.* Madison, NJ: Fairleigh Dickinson University Press, 1998.

Gaillard, Edwin S. *The Medical and Surgical Lessons of the Late War.* Louisville, KY: Louisville Journal Job Print, 1868.

Gallman, J. Matthew. *The North Fights the Civil War: The Home Front.* Chicago: Ivan R. Dee, 1994.

Garrison, Fielding H. *An Introduction to the History of Medicine.* Philadelphia: W. B. Saunders, 1913.

———. *John Shaw Billings, A Memoir.* New York: G. P. Putnam's Sons, 1915.

———. *Notes on the History of Military Medicine.* Washington, DC: Government Printing Office, 1922.

Gerrish, Theodore. *Army Life, A Private's Reminiscences of the Civil War.* Portland, ME: Hoyt, Fogg & Donham, 1882.

Gevitz, Norman, ed. *Other Healers: Unorthodox Medicine in America.* Baltimore: Johns Hopkins University Press, 1988.

Gillett, Mary C. *The Army Medical Department, 1818–1865.* Washington, DC: Center of Military History, 1987.

Glicksberg, Charles I., ed. *Walt Whitman and the Civil War.* Philadelphia: University of Pennsylvania Press, 1933.

Goldsmith, M. *A Report on Hospital Gangrene, Erysipelas and Pyaemia, as Observed in the Departments of the Ohio and the Cumberland, with Cases Appended.* Louisville, KY: Bradley & Gilbert, 1863.

Gorham, George C. *Life and Public Services of Edwin M. Stanton.* 2 vols. Boston: Houghton Mifflin, 1899.

Grace, William. *The Army Surgeon's Manual, for the Use of Medical Officers, Cadets, Chaplains, and Hospital Stewards.* New York: Baillière Brothers, 1864.

Greenbie, Marjorie B. *Lincoln's Daughters of Mercy.* New York: G. P. Putnam's Sons, 1944.

Greenleaf, Charles R. *A Manual for the Medical Officers of the United States Army.* Philadelphia: J. B. Lippincott, 1864.

Greiner, James M., Janet L. Coryell, and James R. Smither, eds. *A Surgeon's Civil War: The Letters and Diary of Daniel M. Holt, M.D.* Kent, OH: Kent State University Press, 1994.

Gross, Samuel D. *A System of Surgery: Pathological, Diagnostic, Therapeutic, and Operative.* 2 vols. Philadelphia: Blanchard & Lea, 1859.

———. *A Manual of Military Surgery; or, Hints on the Emergencies of Field Camp and Hospital Practice.* Philadelphia: J. B. Lippincott, 1861.

———. *Lives of Eminent American Physicians and Surgeons of the Nineteenth Century.* Philadelphia: Lindsay & Blakiston, 1861.

———. *Autobiography of Samuel D. Gross.* 2 vols. Philadelphia: George Barrie, 1887.

Guernsey, H., and H. W. Alden, eds. *Harper's Pictorial History of the Great Rebellion.* New York: Harper & Brothers, 1866.

Haller, John S. *American Medicine in Transition, 1840–1910.* Urbana: University of Illinois Press, 1981.

———. *Farmcarts to Fords: A History of the Military Ambulance, 1790–1925.* Carbondale: Southern Illinois University Press, 1992.

Hamilton, Frank H. *A Practical Treatise on Fractures and Dislocations.* Philadelphia: Blanchard & Lea, 1860.

———. *A Practical Treatise on Military Surgery.* New York: Baillière Brothers, 1861.

———. *A Treatise on Military Surgery and Hygiene.* New York: Baillière Brothers, 1865.

———, ed. *Surgical Memoirs of the War of the Rebellion: Collected and Published by the United States Sanitary Commission.* 2 vols. New York: Hurd & Houghton, 1870 and 1871.

———. *The Principles and Practice of Surgery.* New York: William Wood, 1872.

———. *Health Aphorisms, and an Essay on the Struggle for Life Against Civilization, Luxury, and Aestheticism.* New York: Bermingham, 1882.

Hammond, William A. *A Treatise on Hygiene with Special Reference to the Military Service.* Philadelphia: J. B. Lippincott, 1863.

———. *Military Medical and Surgical Essays, Prepared for the United States Sanitary Commission.* Philadelphia: J. B. Lippincott, 1864.

———. *A Statement of the Causes Which Led to the Dismissal of Surgeon-General William A. Hammond from the Army, with a Review of the Evidence Adduced Before the Court.* Washington, DC: privately printed, 1864.

———. *The Official Correspondence Between Surgeon-General William A. Hammond, U.S.A., and the Adjutant-General of the Army, Relative to the Founding of the Army Museum and the Inauguration of the Medical and Surgical History of the War.* New York: D. Appleton, 1883.

Hecht, Lydia P., ed. *Echoes: From the Letters of a Civil War Surgeon.* Houston: Bayou Publishing, 1996.

Helmuth, William T. *Surgery and Its Adaptation to Homoeopathic Practice.* Philadelphia: Moss & Brother, 1855.

Hill, Benjamin L., and James G. Hunt. *The Homoeopathic Practice of Surgery, Together with Operative Surgery.* Cleveland: J. B. Cobb, 1855.

Hodges, Richard M. *A Narrative of Events Connected with the Introduction of Sulphuric Ether into Surgical Use.* Boston: Little, Brown, 1891.

Holland, Mary G. *Our Army Nurses*. Boston: B. Wilkins, 1895.

Holmes, Oliver W. *Currents and Counter-Currents in Medical Science*. Boston: Ticknor & Fields, 1861.

Holstein, Anna M. *Three Years in Field Hospitals of the Army of the Potomac*. Philadelphia: J. B. Lippincott, 1867.

Houck, Peter W., ed. *Confederate Surgeon: The Personal Recollections of E. A. Craighill*. Lynchburg, VA: H. E. Howard, 1989.

Houck, Peter W. *A Prototype of a Confederate Hospital Center in Lynchburg, Virginia*. Lynchburg, VA: Warwick House, 1986.

Humphreys, Charles A. *Field, Camp, Hospital and Prison in the Civil War, 1863–1865*. Boston: George H. Ellis, 1918.

Hyde, Solon. *A Captive of War*. New York: McClure, Phillips, 1900.

Ingersoll, L. D. *A History of the War Department of the United States*. Washington, DC: Francis B. Mohun, 1880.

James, W. W. Keen. *The Memoirs of William Williams Keen, M.D.* Doylestown, PA: A Keen Book, 1990.

Jaquette, H. S., ed. *South After Gettysburg: Letters of Cornelia Hancock, 1863–1868*. New York: Thomas T. Crowell, 1937.

Johnson, Charles B. *Muskets and Medicine; or, Army Life in the Sixties*. Philadelphia: F. A. Davis, 1917.

Jones, Bessie Z. *Hospital Sketches by Louisa May Alcott*. Cambridge, MA: The Belknap Press of Harvard University, 1960.

Josyph, Peter, ed. *The Wounded River: The Civil War Letters of John Vance Lauderdale, M.D.* East Lansing: Michigan State University Press, 1993.

Kaufman, Martin. *Homeopathy in America: The Rise and Fall of a Medical Heresy*. Baltimore: Johns Hopkins University Press, 1971.

———. *American Medical Education: The Formative Years, 1765–1910*. Westport, CT: Greenwood, 1976.

Keen, William W, and J. William White, eds. *An American Textbook of Surgery*. Philadelphia: W. B. Saunders, 1893.

Keen, William W. *Addresses and Other Papers*. Philadelphia: W. B. Saunders, 1905.

———. *Selected Papers and Addresses*. Philadelphia: J. B. Lippincott, 1922.

Kelly, Howard A., and Walter L. Burrage. *Dictionary of American Medical Biography*. New York: D. Appleton, 1928.

Kernek, Clyde B. *Field Surgeon at Gettysburg*. Indianapolis, IN: Guild Press, 1993.

Kett, Joseph F. *The Formation of the American Medical Profession: The Role of Institutions, 1780–1860*. New Haven, CT: Yale University Press, 1968.

Keyes, Edward L. *Civil War Memories of Lewis A. Stimson, M.D.* New York: Knickerbocker Press, 1918.

King, John H. *Three Hundred Days in a Yankee Prison*. Kennesaw, GA: Continental Book, 1959.

King, William H. *History of Homoeopathy and Its Institutions in America*. 4 vols. New York: Lewis, 1905.

Kuz, Julian E., and Bradley P. Bengtson. *Orthopaedic Injuries of the Civil War*. Kennesaw, GA: Kennesaw Mountain Press, 1996.

Letterman, Jonathan. *Medical Recollections of the Army of the Potomac*. New York: D. Appleton, 1866.

Livermore, Mary A. *My Story of the War: A Woman's Narrative of Four Years of Personal Experience*. Hartford, CT: A. D. Worthington, 1889.

Locke, E. W. *Three Years in Camp and Hospital*. Boston: Geo. D. Russell, 1870.

Lowenfels, Walter, ed. *Walt Whitman's Civil War*. New York: Alfred A. Knopf, 1960.

Lowry Thomas P. *The Story the Soldiers Wouldn't Tell: Sex in the Civil War*. Mechanicsburg, PA: Stackpole, 1994.

Ludmerer, Kenneth M. *Learning to Heal: The Development of American Medical Education*. New York: Basic Books, 1985.

Lusk, William T. *War Letters of William Thompson Lusk, Captain, Assistant Adjutant-General, United States Volunteers, 1861–1863, Afterward M.D., L.L.D.* New York: privately printed, 1911.

Lyle, William W. *Lights and Shadows of Army Life; or, Pen Pictures from the Battlefield, the Camp, and the Hospital*. Cincinnati: R. W. Carroll, 1865.

McGuire, H., and George L. Christian. *The Confederate Cause and Conduct in the War Between the States*. Richmond, VA: L. H. Jenkins, 1907.

McKay, C. E. *Stories of Hospital and Camp*. Philadelphia: Claxton, Remsen & Haffelfinger, 1876.

McMullen, Glenn L., ed. *A Surgeon with Stonewall Jackson: The Civil War Letters of Dr. Harvey Black*. Baltimore: Butternut & Blue, 1995.

McPherson, James M. *The Battle Cry of Freedom: The Civil War Era*. New York: Oxford University Press, 1988.

Macfarlane, Charles. *Reminiscences of an Army Surgeon*. Oswego, NY: Lake City Print Shop, 1921.

Maher, M. *To Bind Up the Wounds: Catholic Sister Nurses in the Civil War*. Westport, CT: Greenwood, 1989.

Marshall, Helen E. *Dorothea Dix: Forgotten Samaritan*. Chapel Hill: University of North Carolina Press, 1937.

Massey, Mary E. *Bonnet Brigades*. New York: Alfred A. Knopf, 1966.

Mathless, Paul, ed. *Fredericksburg*. Alexandria, VA: Time-Life Books, 1997.

Maxwell, William Q. *Lincoln's Fifth Wheel: The Political History of the United States Sanitary Commission*. New York: Longmans & Green, 1956.

Memorial of Edward B. Dalton, M.D. New York: privately printed, 1872.

Miller, Francis T. *The Photographic History of the Civil War, Prisons and Hospitals*. Vol. 7. New York: Review of Reviews, 1911.

Mitchell, S. Weir, George R. Morehouse, and William W Keen. *Gunshot Wounds and Other Injuries of Nerves*. Philadelphia: J. B. Lippincott, 1864.

Monteiro, Aristides. *War Reminiscences by the Surgeon of Mosby's Command*. Richmond, VA: C. N. Williams, 1890.

Moore, Frank. *Women of the War: Their Heroism and Self-Sacrifice*. Hartford, CT: S. S. Scranton, 1867.

Moore, Samuel, ed. *A Manual of Military Surgery, Prepared for the Use of the Confederate States Army*. Richmond, VA: Ayres & Wade, 1863.

Mouat, Malcolm P., ed. *Dr. Henry Palmer, "The Fighting Surgeon," 1827–1895*. Detroit: privately printed, 1977.

Murdock, Eugene C. *One Million Men: The Civil War Draft in the North*. Madison: State Historical Society of Wisconsin, 1971.

Nason, Elias, and Thomas Russell. *The Life and Public Services of Henry Wilson, Late Vice-President of the United States*. Boston: R. B. Russell, 1876.

Nevins, Allan. *The War for the Union.* Vol. 1, *The Improvised War.* Vol. 2, *War Becomes Revolution.* Vol. 3, *The Organized War.* Vol. 4, *The Organized War to Victory.* New York: Scribner's, 1959–1971.

Nevins, Allan, and M. H. Thomas, eds. *The Diary of George Templeton Strong.* 4 vols. New York: Macmillan, 1952.

Newberry, John. S. *The U.S. Sanitary Commission in the Valley of the Mississippi, During the War of the Rebellion, 1861–1866.* Cleveland: Fairbanks & Benedict, 1871.

Newcomb, Mary A. *Four Years of Personal Reminiscences of the War.* Chicago: H. S. Mills, 1893.

Norwood, William F. *Medical Education in the United States Before the Civil War.* Philadelphia: University of Pennsylvania Press, 1944.

Oates, Stephen B. *A Woman of Valor: Clara Barton and the Civil War.* New York: Simon & Schuster, 1994.

Olmsted, Frederick L. *A Journey in the Seaboard Slave States with Remarks on Their Economy.* New York: Dix & Edwards, 1856.

———. *A Journey Through Texas; or, a Saddle-Trip on the Southwestern Frontier with a Statistical Appendix.* New York: Dix & Edwards, 1857.

———. *A Journey in the Back Country.* New York: Mason Brothers, 1860.

———. *The Cotton Kingdom: A Traveler's Observations on Cotton and Slavery in the American Slave States Based upon Three Former Volumes of Journeys and Investigations by the Same Author.* 2 vols. New York: Mason Brothers, 1861.

———. *Hospital Transports: A Memoir of the Embarkation of the Sick and Wounded from the Peninsula of Virginia in the Summer of 1862.* Boston: Ticknor & Fields, 1863.

Ordronaux, John. *Hints on the Preservation of Health in Armies.* New York: D. Appleton, 1861.

———. *Manual of Instructions for Military Surgeons on the Examination of Recruits and Discharge of Soldiers.* New York: D. Van Nostrand, 1863.

Otis, George A. *Histories of Two Hundred and Ninety-Six Surgical Photographs, Prepared at the Army Medical Museum.* Washington, DC: Surgeon General's Office, 1865–1872.

———. *Photographs of Surgical Cases and Specimens: Taken at the Army Medical Museum.* 8 vols. Washington, DC: Surgeon General's Office, 1865–1881.

Packard, Francis R. *History of Medicine in the United States.* 2 vols. New York: P. B. Hoeber, 1931.

Packard, John H. *A Manual of Minor Surgery.* Philadelphia: J. B. Lippincott, 1863.

Patriot Daughters of Lancaster. *Hospital Scenes After the Battle of Gettysburg, July 1863.* Philadelphia: Henry B. Ashmead, 1864.

Patterson, Gerard A. *Debris of Battle: The Wounded of Gettysburg.* Mechanicsburg, PA: Stackpole, 1997.

Peabody, Charles N., ed. *Zab (Brevet Major Zabdiel Boylston Adams, 1829–1902: Physician of Boston and Framingham).* Boston: Francis A. Countway Library, 1984.

Perry, Martha D., ed. *Letters from a Surgeon of the Civil War.* Boston: Little, Brown, 1906.

Petrie, Stewart J., ed. *Letters and Journal of a Civil War Surgeon*. Raleigh, NC: Pentland Press, 1998.

Porcher, Francis P. *Resources of the Southern Fields and Forests, Medical, Economical, and Agricultural; Being Also a Medical Botany of the Confederate States*. Charleston, SC: Evans & Cogswell, 1863.

Potter, Alonzo. *Notes of Hospital Life*. Philadelphia: J. B. Lippincott, 1864.

Potter, William W. *Reminiscences of Field-Hospital Service with the Army of the Potomac*. Buffalo, NY: Buffalo Medical and Surgical Journal, 1889.

Powers, Elvira. *Hospital Pencillings*. Boston: Edward Mitchell, 1866.

Priest, John M., ed. *Turn Them Out to Die Like a Mule: The Civil War Letters of John N, Henry, 49th New York, 1861–1865*. Leesburg, VA: Gauley Mount Press, 1995.

———. *One Surgeon's Private War: Doctor William W. Potter of the 57th New York*. Shippensburg, PA.: White Mane, 1996.

Reed, William H. *Hospital Life in the Army of the Potomac*. Boston: William V. Spencer, 1866.

Regulations for the Army of the Confederate States, 1862. Richmond, VA: J. W. Randolph, 1862.

Reverby, Susan M. *Ordered to Care: The Dilemma of American Nursing, 1850–1945*. New York: Cambridge University Press, 1987.

Revised Regulations for the Army of the United States. Philadelphia: J. G. L. Brown, 1861.

Rockwell, Alphonso D. *Rambling Recollections: An Autobiography*. New York: Paul B. Hoeber, 1920.

Rose, Anne C. *Victorian America and the Civil War*. New York: Cambridge University Press, 1992.

Rosenberg, Charles E. *The Care of Strangers: The Rise of America's Hospital System*. New York: Basic Books, 1987.

Ross, Ishbel. *Angel of the Battlefield: The Life of Clara Barton*. New York: Harper & Brothers, 1956.

Rothstein, William. *American Physicians in the Nineteenth Century*. Baltimore: Johns Hopkins University Press, 1972.

———. *American Medical Schools and the Practice of Medicine: A History*. New York: Oxford University Press, 1987.

Rutkow, Eric. *Harvey Cushing and the Battle of Boston Common: The Surgeon's Role in Military Medical Preparedness*. Unpublished thesis on file with Yale University, 2003.

Rutkow, Ira M. *The History of Surgery in the United States, 1775–1900*. 2 vols. San Francisco: Norman, 1988 and 1992.

———. *Surgery: An Illustrated History*. St. Louis: Mosby, 1993.

———. *American Surgery: An Illustrated History*. Philadelphia: Lippincott-Raven, 1998.

Rutkow, Lainie. *Their Own Civil War: The Struggle by Homeopathic Physicians in the United States Army to Achieve Medical Pluralism, 1861–1865*. Unpublished thesis on file with Yale University, 1999.

Rybczynski, Witold. *A Clearing in the Distance: Frederick Law Olmsted and America in the Nineteenth Century*. New York: Scribner, 1999.

Sandburg, Carl. *Abraham Lincoln: The War Years*. 4 vols. New York: Harcourt Brace, 1939.

Scaife, William F. *Confederate Surgeon*. Atlanta: privately printed, 1985.

Schaadt, Mark J. *Civil War Medicine: An Illustrated History*. Quincy, MA: Cedarwood, 1998.

Schildt, John W. *Hunter Holmes McGuire: Doctor in Gray*. Chewsville, VA: John W. Schildt, 1986.

———. *Antietam Hospitals*. Chewsville, VA: Antietam Publications, 1987.

Schroeder-Lein, Glenna R. *Confederate Hospitals on the Move: Samuel H. Stout and the Army of Tennessee*. Columbia: University of South Carolina Press, 1994.

Schuppert, M. *A Treatise on Gun-Shot Wounds: Written for and Dedicated to the Surgeons of the Confederate States Army*. New Orleans: Bulletin Book & Job Office, 1861.

Shafer, Henry B. *The American Medical Profession, 1783 to 1850*. New York: Columbia University Press, 1936.

Shaw, Maurice F. *Stonewall Jackson's Surgeon, Hunter Holmes McGuire: A Biography*. Lynchburg, VA: H. E. Howard, 1993.

Shryock, Richard. *Medicine and Society in America, 1660–1860*. New York: New York University Press, 1960.

———. *Medicine in America: Historical Essays*. Baltimore: Johns Hopkins University Press, 1966.

Shutes, Milton H. *Lincoln and the Doctors: A Medical Narrative of the Life of Abraham Lincoln*. New York: Pioneer Press, 1933.

Skinner, Henry A. *The Origin of Medical Terms*. Baltimore: William & Wilkins, 1948.

Smith, Adelaide W. *Reminiscences of an Army Nurse During the Civil War*. New York: Greaves, 1911.

Smith, Edward P. *Incidents of the United States Christian Commission*. Philadelphia: J. B. Lippincott, 1869.

Smith, George. *Medicines for the Union Army*. Madison, WI: American Institute of the History of Pharmacy, 1962.

Smith, Henry H. *A Treatise on the Practice of Surgery*. Philadelphia: J. B. Lippincott, 1856.

Smith, Stephen. *Hand-Book of Surgical Operations*. New York: Baillière Brothers, 1862.

———. *Doctor in Medicine: And Other Papers on Professional Subjects*. New York: William Wood, 1872.

———. *Manual of the Principles and Practice of Operative Surgery*. Boston: Houghton & Osgood, 1879.

———. *The City That Was*. New York: Frank Allaben, 1911.

Starr, Paul. *The Social Transformation of American Medicine*. New York: Basic Books, 1982.

Stearns, Amanda A. *The Lady Nurse of Ward E*. New York: Baker & Taylor, 1909.

Steiner, Paul E. *Physician-Generals in the Civil War: A Study in Nineteenth Mid-Century American Medicine*. Springfield, IL: Charles C. Thomas, 1966.

———. *Medical-Military Portraits of Union and Confederate Generals*. Philadelphia: Whitmore, 1968.

———. *Disease in the Civil War: Natural Biological Warfare in 1861–1865*. Springfield, IL: Charles C. Thomas, 1968.

————. *Medical History of a Civil War Regiment: Disease in the Sixty-fifth United States Colored Infantry*. Clayton, MO: Institute of Civil War Studies, 1977.

Sternberg, Martha L. *George Miller Sternberg: A Biography*. Chicago: American Medical Association, 1920.

Stevens, George T. *Three Years in the Sixth Corps*. Albany, NY: S. R. Gray, 1866.

Stevenson, B. F. *Letters from the Army*. Cincinnati: W. E. Dibble, 1884.

Stewart, Miller J. *Moving the Wounded: Litters, Cacolets, and Ambulance Wagons, U.S., 1776–1876*. Fort Collins, CO: Old Army Press, 1979.

Stillé, Charles J. *History of the United States Sanitary Commission*. Philadelphia: J. B. Lippincott, 1866.

Strait, Newton A. *An Alphabetical List of the Battles of the War of the Rebellion . . . and a Roster of All the Regimental Surgeons and Assistant Surgeons in the Late War and Hospital Service*. Washington, DC: G. M. Van Buren, 1883.

Straubing, Harold E., ed. *In Hospital and Camp: The Civil War Through the Eyes of Its Doctors and Nurses*. Harrisburg, PA: Stackpole, 1993.

Taylor, William H. *De Quibus, Discourses and Essays*. Richmond, VA: Bell Book & Stationery, 1908.

Thacher, James. *American Medical Biography*. Boston: Richardson, Lord, Cottons, & Barnard, 1828.

Thomas, Benjamin P., and Harold Hyman. *Stanton: The Life and Times of Lincoln's Secretary of War*. New York: Alfred A. Knopf, 1962.

Tiffany, Francis. *Life of Dorothea Lynde Dix*. Boston: Houghton Mifflin, 1890.

Tobey, James A. *The Medical Department of the Army: Its History, Activities and Organization*. Baltimore: Johns Hopkins University Press, 1927.

Tripler, Charles S., and George C. Blackman. *Hand-Book for the Military Surgeon*. Cincinnati: Robert Clarke, 1861.

Trudeau, Noah A. *Bloody Roads South: The Wilderness to Cold Harbor, May–June 1864*. Boston: Little, Brown, 1989.

United States Sanitary Commission. *The Sanitary Commission of the United States Army: A Succinct Narrative of Its Works and Purposes*. New York: United States Sanitary Commission, 1864.

————. *The Western Sanitary Commission: A Sketch*. St. Louis: R. P. Studley, 1864.

————. *Documents of the US. Sanitary Commission*. 3 vols. New York: United States Sanitary Commission, 1866–1871.

————. *Sanitary Memoirs of the War of the Rebellion*. New York: Hurd & Houghton, 1867.

United States War Department. *The War of the Rebellion: A Compilation of the Official Records of the Union and Confederate Armies*. 127 vols. Washington, DC: Government Printing Office, 1880–1901.

Van Buren, William H. *Contributions to Practical Surgery*. Philadelphia: J. B. Lippincott, 1865.

Wales, Phillip S. *Mechanical Therapeutics: A Practical Treatise on Surgical Apparatus, Appliances, and Elementary Operations*. Philadelphia: Henry C. Lea, 1867.

Ward, Patricia S. *Simon Baruch: Rebel in the Ranks of Medicine, 1846–1921*. Tuscaloosa: University of Alabama Press, 1994.

Warren, Edward. *An Epitome of Practical Surgery, for Field and Hospital*. Richmond, VA: West & Johnston, 1863.

————. *A Doctor's Experiences in Three Continents.* Baltimore: Cushings & Bailey, 1885.

Welch, S. G. *A Confederate Surgeon's Letters to His Wife.* New York: Neale, 1911.

Welsh, Jack D. *Medical Histories of Confederate Generals.* Kent, OH: Kent State University Press, 1995.

————. *Medical Histories of Union Generals.* Kent, OH: Kent State University Press, 1996.

Wheelock, Julia S. *The Boys in White: The Experience of a Hospital Agent in and Around Washington.* New York: Lange & Hillman, 1870.

Whitman, Walt. *The Wound Dresser: A Series of Letters Written from the Hospitals in Washington During the War of the Rebellion.* Boston: Small & Maynard, 1898.

Wilbur, C. Keith. *Civil War Medicine, 1861–1865.* Old Saybrook, CT: Globe Pequot, 1998.

Wiley, Bell I. *The Life of Johnny Reb: The Common Soldier of the Confederacy.* Indianapolis, IN: Bobbs-Merrill, 1943.

————. *The Life of Billy Yank: The Common Soldier of the Union.* Indianapolis, IN: Bobbs-Merrill, 1951.

————, ed. *A Southern Woman's Story: Life in Confederate Richmond by Phoebe Yates Pember.* Jackson, MS: McCowat-Mercer, 1959.

Williams, T. Harry. *Lincoln and His Generals.* New York: Alfred A. Knopf, 1952.

Wilson, Dorothy C. *Stranger and Traveler: The Story of Dorothea Dix, American Reformer.* Boston: Little, Brown, 1975.

Wilson, Sadye T, Nancy T. Fitzgerald, and Richard Warwick, eds. *Letters to Laura: A Confederate Surgeon's Impressions of Four Years of War.* Nashville: Tunstede Press, 1996.

Women's Central Association of Relief. *A Manual of Directions, Prepared for the Use of Nurses in the Army Hospitals, by a Committee of Physicians of the City of New York.* New York: Baker & Godwin, 1861.

Woodhull, Alfred A. *Catalogue of the Surgical Section of the United States Army Museum.* Washington, DC: Government Printing Office, 1866.

Woodward, Joseph J. *The Hospital Steward's Manual.* Philadelphia: J. B. Lippincott, 1862.

————. *Outline of the Chief Camp Diseases of the United States Armies.* Philadelphia: J. B. Lippincott, 1863.

Woolsey, Jane S. *Hospital Days.* New York: Van Nostrand, 1870.

Worley, Ted R., ed. *The Camp, the Bivouac, and the Battle Field by W. L. Gammage, Brigade Surgeon of McNair's Brigade.* Little Rock: Arkansas Southern Press, 1958.

Wormeley, Katherine P. *The United States Sanitary Commission: A Sketch of Its Purposes and Its Work.* Boston: Little, Brown, 1863.

————. *The Other Side of War: With the Army of the Potomac.* Boston: Ticknor, 1889.

ARTICLES

Abrahams, Harold J. "Secession from Northern Medical Schools." *Transactions of the College of Physicians of Philadelphia* 36 (1968): 29–45.

Adams, George W. "Confederate Medicine." *Journal of Southern History* 6 (1940): 151–66.

Anderson, Donald L., and Godfrey T. Anderson. "Nostalgia and Malingering in the Military During the Civil War." *Perspectives in Biology and Medicine* 28 (1984): 156–66.

Berman, Alex. "The Heroic Approach in 19th Century Therapeutics." *Bulletin of the American Society of Hospital Pharmacists* II (1954): 320–27.

Billings, John S. "Medical Reminiscences of the Civil War." *Transactions of the College of Physicians of Philadelphia* 27 (1905): 115–21.

Blaisdell, F. William. "Medical Advances During the Civil War." *Archives of Surgery* 123 (1988): 1045–50.

Blustein, Bonnie E. "To Increase the Efficiency of the Medical Department: A New Approach to U.S. Civil War Medicine." *Civil War History* 33 (1987): 22–41.

Bollet, Alfred J. "Scurvy and Chronic Diarrhea in Civil War Troops: Were They Both Nutritional Deficiency Syndromes?" *Journal of the History of Medicine and the Allied Sciences* 47 (1992): 49–67.

Breeden, James O. "A Medical History of the Later Stages of the Atlanta Campaign." *Journal of Southern History* 35 (1969): 31–59.

———. "The 'Forgotten Man' of the Civil War: The Southern Experience." *Bulletin of the New York Academy of Medicine* 55 (1979): 652–69.

———. "The Winchester Accord: The Confederacy and the Humane Treatment of Captive Medical Officers." *Military Medicine* 18 (1993): 689–92.

Brieger, Gert H. "Therapeutic Conflicts and the American Medical Profession in the 1860's." *Bulletin of the History of Medicine* 41 (1967): 215–22.

Brodman, Estelle, and Elizabeth B. Carrick. "American Military Medicine in the Mid-Nineteenth Century: The Experience of Alexander H. Hoff, M.D." *Bulletin of the History of Medicine* 64 (1990): 63–78.

Bryan, Leon S. "Blood-Letting in American Medicine, 1830–1892." *Bulletin of the History of Medicine* 38 (1964): 516–29.

Bullough, Bonnie, and Vern Bullough. "Nursing and the Civil War." *Nursing Forum* 2 (1963): 12–27.

Casey, James B. "The Ordeal of Adoniram Judson Warner: His Minutes of South Mountain and Antietam." *Civil War History* 38 (1982): 213–36.

Cassedy, James H. "Numbering the North's Medical Events: Humanitarianism and Science in Civil War Statistics." *Bulletin of the History of Medicine* 66 (1992): 210–33.

Cullen, Joseph P. "Chimborazo Hospital." *Civil War Times Illustrated* 19 (1981): 36–42.

Cunningham, Horace H. "The Confederate Medical Officer in the Field." *Bulletin of the New York Academy of Medicine* 34 (1958): 461–88.

Dammann, Gordon E. "Jonathan A. Letterman, Surgeon for the Soldiers." *Caduceus* 10 (1994): 23–34.

Dannett, Sylvia G. "Lincoln's Ladies in White." *New York State Journal of Medicine* 61 (1961): 1944–52.

Davenport, Horace W. "Such Is Military: Dr. George Martin Trowbridge's Letters from Sherman's Army, 1863–1865." *Bulletin of the New York Academy of Medicine* 63 (1987): 844–82.

Dennis, Frederick S. "The Achievements of American Surgery." *Medical Record* 42 (1892): 637–48.

Duncan, Louis C. "Evolution of the Ambulance Corps and Field Hospital." *Military Surgeon* 32 (1913): 221–49.

———. "The Days Gone By—The Strange Case of Surgeon General Hammond." *Military Surgeon* 64 (1929): 98–110, and 252–62.

Eastwood, Bruce S. "Confederate Medical Problems in the Atlanta Campaign." *Georgia Historical Quarterly* 47 (1963): 276–92.

Elsas, Frederick J. "The Journal of Henry L. Dye, Confederate Surgeon." *Surgery* 63 (1968): 352–62.

Figg, Laurann, and Jane Farrell-Beck. "Amputation in the Civil War: Physical and Social Dimensions." *Journal of the History of Medicine and Allied Sciences* 48 (1993): 454–75.

Flannery, Michael A. "Another House Divided: Union Medical Service and Sectarians During the Civil War." *Bulletin of the History of Medicine* 54 (1999) 478–510.

Freemon, Frank R. "Administration of the Medical Department of the Confederate States Army, 1861 to 1865." *Southern Medical Journal* 80 (1987): 630–37.

Friend, H. C. "Abraham Lincoln and the Court-Martial of Surgeon-General William A. Hammond." *Commercial Law Journal* 62 (1957): 71–80.

Garrison, Fielding H. "The History of Bloodletting." *New York Medical Journal* 97 (1913): 500–08.

———. The Statistical Lessons of the Crimean War." *Military Surgeon* 41 (1917): 457–73.

Greisman, Harvey C. "Wound Management and Medical Organization in the Civil War." *Surgical Clinics of North America* 64 (1984): 625–38.

Hall, Courtney R. "Confederate Medicine: Caring for the Confederate Soldier." *Medical Life* 42 (1935): 443–508.

———. The Rise of Professional Surgery in the United States: 1800–1865." *Bulletin of the History of Medicine* 26 (1952): 231–62.

———. "The Lessons of the War Between the States." *International Record of Medicine* 171 (1958): 408–30.

Hanchette, William. "An Illinois Physician and the Civil War Draft, 1864–1865: Letters of Dr. Joshua Nichols Speed." *Journal of the Illinois State Historical Society* 59 (1966): 143–60.

Hanson, Kathleen S. "A Network of Service: Female Nurses in the Civil War." *Caduceus* II (1995): 11–22.

Hart, Albert G. "The Surgeon and the Hospital in the Civil War." *Military Historical Society of Massachusetts Papers* 13 (1913): 229–86.

Hasegawa, Guy R. "Pharmacy in the American Civil War." *American Journal of Health-System Pharmacists* 57 (2000): 475–89.

———. "The Civil War's Medical Cadets: Medical Students Serving the Union." *Journal of the American College of Surgeons* 193 (2001): 81–89.

Hume, Edgar E. "Chimborazo Hospital, Confederate States Army, America's Largest Military Hospital." *Virginia Medical Monthly* 61 (1934): 189–95.

Hutchinson, John F. "Rethinking the Origins of the Red Cross." *Bulletin of the History of Medicine* 63 (1989): 557–78.

Irwin, Bernard. J. "Notes on the Introduction of Tent Field Hospitals in War." *Proceedings of the 4th Annual Meeting of the Association of Military Surgeons* 4 (1894): 108–36.

Jarcho, Saul. "Edwin Stanton and American Medicine." *Bulletin of the History of Medicine* 45 (1971): 153–58.

Jones, Gordon W. "The Medical History of the Fredericksburg Campaign: Course and Significance." *Journal of the History of Medicine and the Allied Sciences* 18 (1963): 241–56.

———. "Wartime Surgery" *Civil War Times Illustrated* 2 (1963): 7–30.

———. "Sanitation in the Civil War." *Civil War Times Illustrated* 5 (1966): 12–18.

Kaufman, Howard H. "Treatment of Head Injuries in the American Civil War." *Journal of Neurosurgery* 78 (1993): 838–45.

Keen, William W. "Surgical Reminiscences of the Civil War." *Transactions of the College of Physicians of Philadelphia* 27 (1905): 95–114.

———. "Military Surgery in 1861 and in 1918." *Annals of the American Academy of Political and Social Science* 80 (1918): 11–22.

Kenney, Edward C. "From the Log of the Red Rover, 1862–1865; A History of the First U.S. Navy Hospital Ship." *Missouri Historical Review* 60 (1965): 31–49.

Key, Jack D. "U.S. Army Medical Department and Civil War Medicine." *Military Medicine* 133 (1968): 181–92.

King, Joseph E. "Shoulder Straps for Aesculapius: The Vicksburg Campaign 1863." *Military Surgeon* 114 (1954): 216–26.

———. "Shoulder Straps for Aesculapius: The Atlanta Campaign." *Military Surgeon* 114 (1954): 296–306.

Kozol, Robert A. "Frank Hastings Hamilton: Medical Educator and Surgeon to President Garfield." *American Journal of Surgery* 151 (1986): 759–60.

Kramer, Howard. "Effect of the Civil War on the Public Health Movement." *The Mississippi Valley Historical Review* 35 (1948): 449–62.

Kuhns, William J. "Blood Transfusion in the Civil War." *Transfusion* 5 (1965): 92–94.

Lamb, D. S. "The Army Medical Museum, Washington, DC" *Military Surgeon* 53 (1923): 89–140.

Lane, Alexander G. "The Winder Hospital, of Richmond, VA." *Southern Practitioner* 26 (1904): 35–41.

Layton, Thomas R. "Stonewall Jackson's Wounds." *Journal of the American College of Surgeon* 183 (1996): 514–24.

McGuire, Stuart. "Hunter Holmes McGuire, M.D., LL.D." *Annals of Medical History* 10 (1938): 1–14.

Middleton, William S. "Turner's Lane Hospital." *Bulletin of the History of Medicine* 40 (1966): 14–42.

Miller, Genevieve. "Social Services in a Civil War Hospital in Baltimore." *Bulletin of the History of Medicine* 17 (1945): 439–59.

Mitchell, S. Weir. "Some Personal Recollections of the Civil War." *Transactions of the College of Physicians of Philadelphia* 27 (1905): 87–94.

———. The Medical Department in the Civil War." *The Journal of the American Medical Association* 62 (1914): 1335–1450.

Murdock, Eugene C. "Pity the Poor Surgeon." *Civil War History* 16 (1970): 18–36.

Nevins, Allan. "The Glorious and the Terrible." *Saturday Review* 44 (1961): 9–11 and 46–48.

Numbers, Ronald L. "The Making of an Eclectic Physician." *Bulletin of the History of Medicine* 47 (1973): 155–66.

Parrish, William E. "The Western Sanitary Commission." *Civil War History* 36 (1990): 17–35.

Peckham, Stephen F. "Recollections of a Hospital Steward During the Civil War." *Journal of American History* 18 (1924): 151–58, 275–82, and 335–41.

Phalen, James M. "The Life of Charles Stuart Tripler." *Military Surgeon* 82 (1938): 459–63.

———. "Surgeon Thomas A. McParlin—Letterman's Successor with the Army of the Potomac." *Military Surgeon* 87 (1940): 68–71.

Pilcher, James E. "The Annals and Achievements of American Surgery" *Journal of the American Medical Association* 14 (1890): 629–36.

———. "Brevet Brigadier General Clement Alexander Finley, Surgeon General of the United States Army, 1861–1862." *Military Surgeon* 15 (1904): 59–66.

———. "Brigadier General William Alexander Hammond, Surgeon General of the United States Army, 1862–1864." *Military Surgeon* 15 (1904): 145–55.

———. "Brevet Major General Joseph K. Barnes, Surgeon General of the United States Army, 1864–1882." *Military Surgeon* 15 (1904): 219–24.

———. "Dr. Samuel Preston Moore, Surgeon General of the Confederate Army" *Military Surgeon* 16 (1905): 210–15.

Purcell, Peter N., and Robert P. Hummel. "Samuel Preston Moore: Surgeon-General of the Confederacy." *American Journal of Surgery* 164 (1992): 361–65.

Randolph, B. M. "The Blood Letting Controversy in the Nineteenth Century" *Annals of Medical History* 7 (1935): 177–82.

Reasoner, M. A. "The Development of the Medical Supply Service." *Military Surgeon* 63 (1928): 1–21.

Redding, Joseph S., and John C. Matthews. "Anesthesia During the American Civil War." *Clinical Anesthesia* 2 (1968): 1–18.

Riley, Harris D. "Medicine in the Confederacy." *Military Medicine* 118 (1956): 53–64 and 144–53.

Rosenberg, Charles. "The Practice of Medicine in New York a Century Ago." *Bulletin of the History of Medicine* 41 (1967): 223–53.

Rutkow, Eric I., and Ira M. Rutkow. "George Crile, Harvey Cushing, and the Ambulance Américaine: Military Medical Preparedness in World War I." *Archives of Surgery* 139 (2004): 678–85.

Rutkow, Ira M. "William Tod Helmuth and Andrew Jackson Howe: Surgical Sectarianism in 19th Century America." *Archives of Surgery* 129 (1994): 662–68.

Rutkow, Lainie W, and Ira M. Rutkow. "Homeopaths, Surgery, and the Civil War: Edward C. Franklin and the Struggle to Achieve Medical Pluralism in the Union Army." *Archives of Surgery* 139 (2004): 785–91.

Ryons, Fred B. "The United States Army Medical Department 1861 to 1865." *Military Surgeon* 79 (1936): 341–56.

Sharpe, William D. "The Confederate States Medical and Surgical Journal: 1864–1865." *Bulletin of the New York Academy of Medicine* 52 (1976): 373–418.

Shrady, George. "American Achievements in Surgery." *The Forum* 17 (1894): 167–78.

Shryock, Richard H. "A Medical Perspective on the Civil War." *American Quarterly* 14 (1962): 161–73.

Souchon, Edmond. "Original Contributions of America to Medical Sciences." *Transactions of the American Surgical Association* 35 (1917): 5–171.

Stark, Richard B. "Plastic Surgery During the Civil War." *Plastic and Reconstructive Surgery* 16 (1955): 103–20.

Stark, Richard B., and Janet C. Stark. "Surgical Care of the Confederate States Army." *Bulletin of the New York Academy of Medicine* 34 (1958): 387–407.

Steiner, Paul E. "Patriotic Gore, Introduction to Civil War Books by Physicians." *Journal of the American Medical Association* 200 (1967): 2–6.

Stimson, Julia C., and Ethel C. Thompson. "Women Nurses with the Union Forces During the Civil War." *Military Surgeon* 62 (1928): 1–17 and 208–30.

Tanner, James. "Experiences of a Wounded Soldier at the Second Battle of Bull Run." *Military Surgeon* 60 (1927): 121–39.

Thompson, D. G. Brinton. "From Chancellorsville to Gettysburg: A Doctor's Diary." *Pennsylvania Magazine of History and Biography* 89 (1965): 292–315.

Thompson, William Y. "The U.S. Sanitary Commission." *Civil War History* 2 (1956): 41–63.

———. "Sanitary Fairs of the Civil War." *Civil War History* 4 (1958): 51–67.

Tinker, Martin B. "America's Contributions to Surgery." *Johns Hopkins Hospital Bulletin* 13 (1902): 209–13.

Todd, Gary L. "An Invalid Corps." *Civil War Times Illustrated* 24 (1985): 10–19.

Tomes, Nancy. "The Private Side of Public Health: Sanitary Science, Domestic Hygiene, and the Germ Theory, 1870–1900." *Bulletin of the History of Medicine* 64 (1990): 509–39.

Warner, John H. "The Nature-Trusting Heresy: American Physicians and the Concept of the Healing Power of Nature in the 1850s and 1860s." *Perspectives in American History* II (1977): 291–324.

Weld, Stanley B. "A Connecticut Surgeon in the Civil War: The Reminiscences of Dr. Nathan Mayer." *Journal of the History of Medicine and the Allied Sciences* 19 (1964): 272–86.

Weld, Stanley B., and David A. Soskis. "The Reminiscences of a Civil War Surgeon, John B. Lewis." *Journal of the History of Medicine and the Allied Sciences* 21 (1966): 47–58.

Whitehouse, Walter M., and Frank Whitehouse. "The Daily Register of Cyrus Bacon, Jr.: Care of the Wounded at the Battle of Gettysburg." *Michigan Academician* 8 (1976): 373–86.

Winans, H. M. "Evolution of the Concept of Fever in the Nineteenth Century." *Annals of Medical History* 7 (1935): 27–35.

Zeidenfelt, Alex. "The Embattled Surgeon-General, William A. Hammond." *Civil War Times Illustrated* 17 (1978): 24–32.

Zellem, Ronald T. "Wounded by Bayonet, Ball, and Bacteria: Medicine and Neurosurgery in the American Civil War." *Neurosurgery* 17 (1985): 850–60.

JOURNALS
American Homeopathic Review
American Journal of the Medical Sciences
American Medical Times
Boston Medical and Surgical Journal
Bulletin of the New York Academy of Medicine
Chicago Medical Journal
Cincinnati Lancet and Observer
Confederate States Medical and Surgical Journal
Eclectic Medical Journal
Medical and Surgical Reporter (Philadelphia)
New Orleans Medical and Surgical Journal
North American Journal of Homeopathy
Ohio Medical and Surgical Journal
Pacific Medical and Surgical Journal
St. Louis Medical and Surgical Journal
Transactions of the American Medical Association

ACKNOWLEDGMENTS

I owe a great debt of gratitude to many individuals. To various members of the Society of Civil War Surgeons; personnel at the National Museum of Civil War Medicine in Frederick, Maryland; the library and research staffs at the New York Academy of Medicine and the College of Physicians of Philadelphia; and the innumerable Civil War medical buffs that I often badgered, I say thank you. In particular, Robin Siegel of CentraState Medical Center in Freehold, New Jersey, must be singled out for her help in obtaining medical books and journal articles from the 1860s. To Susan Disbrow, my office manager, I offer a sincere "you're the best" for making my professional life run as smoothly as it does.

Few history books stand alone, and *Bleeding Blue and Gray* draws both inspiration and direction from a more than fifty-year-old body of writing on Civil War medicine. Starting with the 1950s research of George Adams and Horace Cunningham through the books of Paul Steiner up to contemporary works by Alfred Bollet, Bonnie Blustein, and Frank Freemon, hundreds of authors (as enumerated in the bibliography) should be recognized for bringing this fascinating topic to light.

In 1997, I first spoke with Eric Simonoff. He is a literary agent extraordinaire. Without his gentle coaxing and sage advice this project would never have commenced. To Eadie Klemm, Eric's assistant, thank you for the cheerful voice at the other end of the telephone.

My parents, Bea and Al Rutkow, have always been at my side encouraging my various endeavors. This book stands as a testament to their unwavering support and, hopefully, validates the sacrifices they made to ensure that I received such a wonderful education. To my wife, Beth, and our children, Lainie and Eric, I dedicate this book. Lainie, lawyer and public health advocate, is my private editor within our family. Her light illuminates my writing. Eric, a lawyer-to-be, provides the encouragement and enthusiasm necessary to organize my literary projects. Beth affords me all the love, patience, and support that any husband could possibly ask for. Without her sustenance, my life would not be what it is. Finally, I tip my hat to Dr. Sherwin Nuland. He has served as a mentor by demonstrating that a physician can be both a surgeon and a serious writer.

INDEX

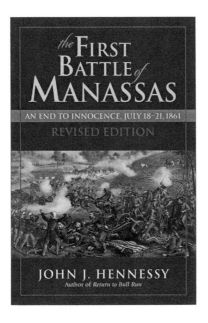